D1692841

Connecting Communities in Archaic Greece

This is a new history of Greece in the seventh and sixth centuries BC written for the twenty-first century. It brings together archaeological data from over 100 years of 'Big Dig' excavation in Greece, employing experimental data analysis techniques from the digital humanities to identify new patterns about Archaic Greece. By modelling trade routes, political alliances, and the formation of personal- and state-networks, this book sheds new light on how exactly the early communities of the Aegean basin were plugged into one another. Returning to the long-debated question of 'what is a polis?', this study also challenges Classical Archaeology more generally: proposing that the discipline has at its fingertips significant datasets that can contribute to substantive historical debate – and that what can be done for the next generation of scholarship is to re-engage with old material in a new way.

MICHAEL LOY is a Leverhulme Early Career Fellow in the Faculty of Classics at the University of Cambridge. Previously he was Assistant Director of the British School at Athens (2019–22). As a field archaeologist, he has over ten years of experience working on projects in Greece, Britain, and Turkey. He is currently co-director of the West Area of Samos Archaeological Project (2021–25).

BRITISH SCHOOL AT ATHENS STUDIES IN GREEK ANTIQUITY

Series editor
Rebecca Sweetman
Director of the British School at Athens

British School at Athens Studies in Greek Antiquity builds on the School's long-standing engagement with the study of ancient Greece from prehistory to Late Antiquity. This series aims to explore a wide range of topics through a variety of approaches attractive to anyone with interests in the ancient Greek world.

Titles in this Series

Byzantium, Venice and the Medieval Adriatic: Spheres of Maritime Power and Influence, c. 700–1453
  Magdalena Skoblar
Human Mobility and Technological Transfer in the Prehistoric Mediterranean
  Evangelia Kiriatzi and Carl Knappett

Connecting Communities in Archaic Greece

Exploring Economic and Political Networks through Data Modelling

MICHAEL LOY

University of Cambridge

Shaftesbury Road, Cambridge CB2 8EA, United Kingdom

One Liberty Plaza, 20th Floor, New York, NY 10006, USA

477 Williamstown Road, Port Melbourne, VIC 3207, Australia

314–321, 3rd Floor, Plot 3, Splendor Forum, Jasola District Centre,
New Delhi – 110025, India

103 Penang Road, #05–06/07, Visioncrest Commercial, Singapore 238467

Cambridge University Press is part of Cambridge University Press & Assessment,
a department of the University of Cambridge.

We share the University's mission to contribute to society through the pursuit of
education, learning and research at the highest international levels of excellence.

www.cambridge.org
Information on this title: www.cambridge.org/9781009343817

DOI: 10.1017/9781009343794

© The British School at Athens 2023

This publication is in copyright. Subject to statutory exception and to the provisions
of relevant collective licensing agreements, no reproduction of any part may take
place without the written permission of Cambridge University Press & Assessment.

First published 2023

A catalogue record for this publication is available from the British Library.

A Cataloging-in-Publication data record for this book is available from the Library of Congress.

ISBN 978-1-009-34381-7 Hardback

Cambridge University Press & Assessment has no responsibility for the persistence
or accuracy of URLs for external or third-party internet websites referred to in this
publication and does not guarantee that any content on such websites is, or will
remain, accurate or appropriate.

Contents

List of Figures   [*page* vi]
List of Tables   [xiii]
Acknowledgements   [xv]
List of Abbreviations   [xvii]

1 Introduction   [1]

2 Economic Networks: The Transport of Heavy Freight   [31]

3 Economic Networks: Commodities and Semi-Luxuries   [88]

4 Entangled Networks: The Transfer of Technical Knowledge   [145]

5 Political Networks: Expressions of Political Affiliation   [189]

6 Political Networks: State Alliance and Amphiktyonies   [247]

7 Conclusions   [280]

Appendices www.cambridge.org/loy
  1 Freestanding Marble Statue Dataset
  2 Ceramics Source Publications and Pottery Count
  3 Coins Dataset
  4 Inscription Dataset

Bibliography   [290]
Index   [326]

Figures

1.1 View of Corinth during the first years of the 'big dig' excavation campaign. BSA SPHS 01/2105.5577, 'Ancient Corinth: Agora excavations'. [*page* 2]

1.2 Illustrative network graphic. Nodes and edges are weighted; the arrows on the edges indicate that edges in this graph have direction. [12]

1.3 Distribution of sites discussed in this book. [21]

2.1 Samian *kouros*, Vathy Archaeological Museum. Photograph by author. [35]

2.2 Fragment of a *kore* (A.4062) from the Archaeological Museum on Delos. Photograph by author. [36]

2.3 Distribution of sites discussed in this chapter, for which marble statues have been found. [41]

2.4 Heights and marble sources of *kouroi* over time. The 'type' of *kouros* is given as is in their source catalogues, without mapping or combination of data classes. The 'negative' date range indicates BC dates, while the height of statues is given in metres. [44]

2.5 Heights and marble sources of *korai* over time. The 'type' of *kore* is given as is in their source catalogues, without mapping or combination of data classes. The 'negative' date range indicates BC dates, while the height of statues is given in metres. [44]

2.6 Heights and marble sources of *kouroi* over time, with data points for unprovenanced marble removed. Other datapoints are described as is in their source catalogues, without mapping or combination of data classes. The 'negative' date range indicates BC dates, while the height of statues is given in metres. [45]

2.7 Heights and marble sources of *kouroi* from the Ptoion sanctuary over time. Datapoints are described as is in their source catalogues, without mapping or combination of data

List of Figures   vii

classes. The 'negative' date range indicates BC dates, while the height of statues is given in metres. [45]

2.8 Heights and marble sources of *korai* from the Athenian Acropolis over time. The type of marble is indicated according to three top-level points of origin based on quarry location: Penteli (i.e. in Attica) or from one of the various Naxian or Parian quarries. [56]

2.9 Heights of *kouroi* from Delos over time. No distinction is made between marbles originating in different places or of different stylistic groups, given that information was unavailable in the source catalogues. [56]

2.10 Heights of marble sculptures over time, from Athens, Delos, and Ptoion, distributed across time from 650 BC to 500 BC. [57]

2.11 Marathi marble quarries from the island of Paros. Photograph by author. [59]

2.12 Raw marble sources available within the Aegean and western Anatolia. Dot colour represents whether marble from this source has certain colour-tinges in its quality. This graphic has been produced from the marble database of Ben Russell, available on the OxRep website, http://oxrep.classics.ox.ac.uk/databases/stone_quarries_database [60]

2.13 Visualisation for the weighted frequency of routes travelled between marble quarry and destination sanctuary site, using PPA modelling. Weight is a term relative to the total quantity of marble transported across the whole of the Archaic period. [75]

2.14 Visualisation for the weighted frequency of routes travelled between marble quarry and destination sanctuary site, using random simulation modelling. Weight is a term relative to the total quantity of marble transported across the whole of the Archaic period. [79]

2.15 Estimate for the number of ships required to transport Aegean marble, with respect to an estimate of how much sculpture survives in the material record. The x axis adjusts the figure given by Snodgrass 1983: 228 for the percentage of marble surviving in the material record, while the y axis shows the effect this has on the overall calculation of ships required to move this marble in the Aegean. [86]

List of Figures

3.1 Distribution of sites discussed in this chapter, for which pottery data is available to a sufficient quality. [93]

3.2 Representative Attic (*skyphos*) and Corinthian (*aryballos*) pottery types of the Archaic period. BSA Museum MUS.A004 and MUS.A351. Photographs by Matt Stirn and copyright British School at Athens. [95]

3.3 Distribution of sites for which Attic pottery is attested across four time periods investigated. Size of site marker is proportional to the amount of pottery found, relative to all other types of pottery. a) 700–650 BC b) 650–600 BC c) 600–550 BC d) 550–500 BC [99]

3.4 Distribution of sites for which Corinthian pottery is attested across four time periods investigated. Size of site marker is proportional to the amount of pottery found, relative to all other types of pottery. a) 700–650 BC b) 650–600 BC c) 600–550 BC d) 550–500 BC [104]

3.5 Distribution of sites for which Ionian pottery is attested across four time periods investigated. Size of site marker is proportional to the amount of pottery found, relative to all other types of pottery. a) 700–650 BC b) 650–600 BC c) 600–550 BC d) 550–500 BC [108]

3.6 Distribution of sites for which Local pottery is attested across four time periods investigated. Size of site marker is proportional to the amount of pottery found, relative to all other types of pottery. a) 700–650 BC b) 650–600 BC c) 600–550 BC d) 550–500 BC [113]

3.7 Results of PCA on ceramic data from sites broadly defined as 'urban' and with respect to ware categorisation. a) 700–650 BC b) 650–600 BC c) 600–550 BC d) 550–500 BC [119]

3.8 Results of PCA on ceramic data from sites broadly defined as 'sanctuary' and with respect to ware categorisation. a) 700–650 BC b) 650–600 BC c) 600–550 BC d) 550–500 BC [121]

3.9 Results of PCA on ceramic data from sites broadly defined as 'urban' and with respect to shape categorisation. a) 700–650 BC b) 650–600 BC c) 600–550 BC d) 550–500 BC [125]

3.10 Results of PCA on ceramic data from sites broadly defined as 'sanctuary' and with respect to shape categorisation. a) 700–650 BC b) 650–600 BC c) 600–550 BC d) 550–500 BC [127]

3.11 Results of PCA on ceramic data from sites broadly defined as 'funerary' and with respect to shape categorisation. a) 600–550 BC b) 550–500 BC   [130]

3.12 Visualisation for the weighted frequency of routes travelled between rough point of ceramic production and place of consumption, using PPA modelling. a) 700–650 BC b) 650–600 BC c) 600–550 BC d) 550–500 BC. Weight is a term relative to the total quantity of ceramic transported across the whole of the Archaic period as investigated in this chapter; the same colour-gradient scale is used as in Chapter 2.   [137]

4.1 Illustrative Archaic period silver coin from Corinth, a) obverse and b) reverse. BSA Museum MUS.C103. Photographs by author.   [150]

4.2 Distribution of sites for which there is evidence of coin minting. a) Pre-600 BC b) 600–580 BC c) 580–560 BC d) 560–540 BC e) 540–520 BC f) 520–500 BC.   [154]

4.3 SNA visualisation of the sites minting coins 600–580 BC. Sites are represented by nodes, and ties are drawn between sites that share a weight standard: a) Nodes are placed according to their approximate geographic location in the Aegean; b) Nodes are distributed randomly in abstract space.   [168]

4.4 SNA visualisation of the sites minting coins 580–560 BC. Sites are represented by nodes, and ties are drawn between sites that share a weight standard: a) Nodes are placed according to their approximate geographic location in the Aegean; b) Nodes are distributed randomly in abstract space.   [169]

4.5 SNA visualisation of the sites minting coins 560–540 BC. Sites are represented by nodes, and ties are drawn between sites that share a weight standard: a) Nodes are placed according to their approximate geographic location in the Aegean; b) Nodes are distributed randomly in abstract space.   [170]

4.6 SNA visualisation of the sites minting coins 540–520 BC. Sites are represented by nodes, and ties are drawn between sites that share a weight standard: a) Nodes are placed according to their approximate geographic location in the Aegean; b) Nodes are distributed randomly in abstract space. This image is available in a larger format online at www.cambridge.org/loy.   [171]

4.7 SNA visualisation of the sites minting coins 520–500 BC. Sites are represented by nodes, and ties are drawn between sites

x   List of Figures

that share a weight standard: a) Nodes are placed according to their approximate geographic location in the Aegean; b) Nodes are distributed randomly in abstract space. This image is available in a larger format online at www.cambridge.org/loy. [174]

4.8   SNA visualisation of the sites producing amphoras 700–650 BC. Sites are represented by nodes, and ties are drawn between sites at which amphoras produced elsewhere are found: a) Nodes are placed according to their approximate geographic location in the Aegean; b) Nodes are distributed randomly in abstract space. [178]

4.9   SNA visualisation of the sites producing amphoras 650–600 BC. Sites are represented by nodes, and ties are drawn between sites at which amphoras produced elsewhere are found: a) Nodes are placed according to their approximate geographic location in the Aegean; b) Nodes are distributed randomly in abstract space. [179]

4.10 SNA visualisation of the sites producing amphoras 600–550 BC. Sites are represented by nodes, and ties are drawn between sites at which amphoras produced elsewhere are found: a) Nodes are placed according to their approximate geographic location in the Aegean; b) Nodes are distributed randomly in abstract space. [180]

4.11 SNA visualisation of the sites producing amphoras 550–500 BC. Sites are represented by nodes, and ties are drawn between sites at which amphoras produced elsewhere are found: a) Nodes are placed according to their approximate geographic location in the Aegean; b) Nodes are distributed randomly in abstract space. [182]

5.1   The 'Nikandre *kore*', indicative of a piece of freestanding sculpture that has been inscribed using an epichoric version of the Greek alphabet. The inscription on the left leg is printed below. Photograph by author. [194]

5.2   Distribution of 'red', 'blue' and 'green' alphabet types after Kirchhoff 1863. [201]

5.3   Distribution of sites discussed in this chapter, for which writing containing the target lettersets for analysis has been found. [204]

5.4   SNA visualisation of the sites clustered according to similar writing styles, 700–650 BC: a) Nodes are distributed randomly in abstract space, clustered under 0.5 modularity parameter; b) Nodes are placed according to their approximate geographic location in the Aegean, clustered under 0.5 modularity parameter; c) Nodes are distributed randomly in abstract space, clustered under 1.0 modularity parameter; d) Nodes are placed according to their approximate geographic location in the Aegean, clustered under 1.0 modularity parameter; e) Nodes are distributed randomly in abstract space, clustered under 1.5 modularity parameter; f) Nodes are placed according to their approximate geographic location in the Aegean, clustered under 1.5 modularity parameter. This image is available in a larger format online at www.cambridge.org/loy. [210]

5.5 SNA visualisation of the sites clustered according to similar writing styles, 650–600 BC: a) Nodes are distributed randomly in abstract space, clustered under 0.5 modularity parameter; b) Nodes are placed according to their approximate geographic location in the Aegean, clustered under 0.5 modularity parameter; c) Nodes are distributed randomly in abstract space, clustered under 1.0 modularity parameter; d) Nodes are placed according to their approximate geographic location in the Aegean, clustered under 1.0 modularity parameter; e) Nodes are distributed randomly in abstract space, clustered under 1.5 modularity parameter; f) Nodes are placed according to their approximate geographic location in the Aegean, clustered under 1.5 modularity parameter. This image is available in a larger format online at www.cambridge.org/loy. [216]

5.6 SNA visualisation of the sites clustered according to similar writing styles, 600–550 BC: a) Nodes are placed according to their approximate geographic location in the Aegean, clustered under 0.5 modularity parameter; b) Nodes are distributed randomly in abstract space, clustered under 1.0 modularity parameter; c) Nodes are placed according to their approximate geographic location in the Aegean, clustered under 1.0 modularity parameter; d) Nodes are distributed randomly in abstract space, clustered under 1.5 modularity parameter; e) Nodes are placed according to their approximate geographic location in the Aegean, clustered under 1.5 modularity parameter. This image is available in a larger format online at www.cambridge.org/loy. [221]

5.7 SNA visualisation of the sites clustered according to similar writing styles, 550–500 BC: a) Nodes are placed according to their approximate geographic location in the Aegean, clustered under 0.5 modularity parameter; b) Nodes are distributed randomly in abstract space, clustered under 1.0 modularity parameter; c) Nodes are placed according to their approximate geographic location in the Aegean, clustered under 1.0 modularity parameter; d) Nodes are distributed randomly in abstract space, clustered under 1.5 modularity parameter; e) Nodes are placed according to their approximate geographic location in the Aegean, clustered under 1.5 modularity parameter. [226]

5.8 Sanctuary of Apollo at Delphi, view from the theatre looking down the mountain. Photograph by author. [231]

5.9 Sites at which writing was found 550–500 BC by context category: a) bin one, small personal objects; b) bin two, dedications; c) bin three, short texts giving information intended to be read (e.g. boundary stones, *stelai*); d) bin four, longer texts for record (e.g. building records); e) bin five, public law codes [238]

5.10 Slabs of the law code, Gortyn. Photograph by author. [243]

6.1 Sanctuary of Poseidon at Kalaureia, as it can be seen today. Most of the standing remains across the site date after the end of the Archaic period. Photograph by author. [253]

6.2 View from Samos across the Mykale strait to the Anatolian mainland, comprising part of the region of Ionia. Photograph by author. [257]

6.3 View from the Sanctuary of Aphaia on Aegina indicating both the distance from the sanctuary to the sea and the steep topography that must be traversed to reach the site from the coast. Photograph by author. [271]

Tables

1.1 Sites discussed in this book, according to the materials available for analysis in each case. [*page* 22]

2.1 Ratio of body part to full whole body (after http://www.exrx.net/Kinesiology/Segments.html) [42]

2.2 Reconstructed height and tonnage of statues from a) Ptoion Sanctuary b) Athenian Acropolis c) Delos. Additional information on date and marble type is included where available. [47]

2.3 Estimate for the total marble tonnage in freestanding statue record a) organised by place of consumption b) organised by place of production. [63]

2.4 Marble source and statue destination pairs. A relative route weight is calculated on the basis of marble tonnage conveyed between each pair as a proportion of the total marble tonnage. Weight is a term relative to the total quantity of marble transported across the whole of the Archaic period. [76]

2.5 Estimated temple stone tonnages for groups of buildings discussed throughout this chapter. a) Archaic period temples b) Fifth century temples. [84]

3.1 Number of discrete pottery units (sherds or vessels) available for study by period for sites discussed in this chapter. [92]

3.2 Proportion (expressed as a percentage) of wares in the total ceramic assemblage from each site a) 700–650 BC b) 650–600 BC c) 600–550 BC d) 550–500 BC. [96]

4.1 Coin hoards dated to the seventh and sixth centuries. Sources are Thompson, Mørkholm and Kraay 1973 (TMK), and numbered editions of *Coin Hoards* (CH 1.3 = *Coin Hoards* 1, entry no. 3, etc.). [149]

4.2 Sites minting coins throughout the sixth century BC, with weight standards used for each. [161]

4.3 Sites for producing amphoras throughout the Archaic period, according to the dataset used in the previous chapter. [177]

5.1 Sites for which writing containing the target lettersets for analysis has been found. [196]

5.2 Number of inscriptions analysed by period. Inscriptions that are dated across two 'periods' (e.g. 600–525 BC) are counted more than once. [200]

5.3 Alphabet groups after Kirchhoff, organised by most frequently occurring shape and approximate sound values. Letter shapes under investigation in this chapter are highlighted. [203]

5.4 Number of inscriptions in period four (550–500 BC) by finds context category. Bin one: small personal objects. Bin two: dedications. Bin three: short texts giving information intended to be read (e.g. boundary stones, *stelai*). Bin four: longer texts for record (e.g. building records). Bin five: public law codes. [237]

A1.1 Dataset of freestanding statues and statue fragments. 'RichterKouroi' is Richter 1942, 'RichterKorai' is Richter 1968, 'MeyerBrueggemann' is Meyer and Brüggemann 2007, 'Karakasi' is Karakasi 2003.

A2.1 Bibliographic list of sources consulted to produce the ceramics dataset used in this chapter.

A2.2 Number of discrete pottery units (sherds or vessels) analysed by ware a) 600–550 BC funerary sites b) 550–500 BC funerary sites c) 700–650 BC sanctuary sites d) 650–600 BC sanctuary sites e) 600–550 BC sanctuary sites f) 550–500 BC sanctuary sites g) 700–650 BC urban sites h) 650–600 BC urban sites i) 600–550 BC urban sites j) 550–500 BC urban sites.

A2.3 Number of discrete pottery units (sherds or vessels) analysed by shape a) 600–550 BC funerary sites b) 550–500 BC funerary sites c) 700–650 BC sanctuary sites d) 650–600 BC sanctuary sites e) 600–550 BC sanctuary sites f) 550–500 BC sanctuary sites g) 700–650 BC urban sites h) 650–600 BC urban sites i) 600–550 BC urban sites j) 550–500 BC urban sites.

A3.1 Dataset of coins. Source reference refers to the *Handbooks of Coins* edited by Oliver Hoover. 6/427 is Volume 6, coin 427 etc.

A4.1 Dataset of inscriptions and lettersets. Abbreviations for inscription sources are given in the 'list of abbreviations'. Numbered inscriptions without a header come from *LSAG*.

Acknowledgements

This book began life as a PhD thesis, completed at Cambridge University and funded jointly by the Arts and Humanities Research Council (AHRC) and Pembroke College, award number AH/L503897/1. Additional funding for travel, conferences, and research was received generously from the Faculty of Classics (Henry Arthur Travel award), the AHRC (Student Development Fund and Research Training Support Grant), and the Deutscher Akademischer Austauschdienst.

Some of the material in Chapter 3 was studied in the Milet-Archiv (at that time housed at the Ruhr-Universität, Bochum), October–December 2017. I am most grateful to Christof Berns and to Sabine Huy for making this resource available to me, and for the welcome they offered me in Germany. Background research for Chapter 6 was conducted in Greece April–September 2018, during which time various sections of the thesis were productively written up at the library of the British School at Athens. I am grateful to all staff (later colleagues!) for facilitating this stay, but most of all I am thankful to Natalia Elvira Astoreca, Alexandra Katevaini, Epameinondas Kazolis, and Christina Koureta for making this a particularly memorable and enjoyable episode in the PhD journey.

Both during its life as a thesis and later as a book, this study has benefited enormously from both formal and informal critique from several friends and colleagues who read at various stages of readiness, offered helpful suggestions, or pointed me in the direction of resources or data. I thank most sincerely Erica Angliker, Zosia Archibald, John Bennet, Kate Caraway, Paul Christesen, Rob Crellin, Enrico Crema, Natalia Elvira Astoreca, Yannis Galanakis, Mahnoor Javed, Daniel Jew, Jannis Kozatsas, Hannah Lee, Naoíse Mac Sweeney, Jana Mokrišová, Alex Mullen, Katie Phillips, Adi Popescu, Ben Russell, Hanneke Salisbury, Reinhard Senff, Anja Slawisch, Pippa Steele, and Katerina Volioti. I thank also Enrico Crema, Scott Vanderbilt, John Wallrodt, and Toby C. Wilkinson for technical advice either for the book specifically or for helping me to develop data skills more generally, and the organisers of the conferences and workshops at which parts of this work were exhibited, especially Myles

Lavan, Catie Steidl, and Marek Verčik. During the more itinerant stages of my PhD I was hosted for short stays by Becky Bennion, Anne Herriot, Ellie Maw, Jessi Schellig and Ludo Pontiggia, and I am also grateful for site tours offered by Andy Bevan and Brenna Hassett, Maria Choleva, Anastasia Christophilopoulou, and Alexandra Katevaini. And I am most grateful for proofreading and editorial advice offered at various stages by John Bennet, Rachael Gregory, Deborah Harlan, Rinna Keefe, Hannah Lee, Tricia Loy, Jana Mokrišová, Catherine Rowley, Sarah Sheard, Jonathan Triffitt and Anastasia Vassiliou. The font used in the inscriptions chapter was drawn by Natalia Elvira Astoreca, and the phenomenal artwork on the front cover was designed by Charlotte Ellery.

Last (but most certainly not least) I owe the largest extension of thanks to my PhD supervisors Robin Osborne and Cyprian Broodbank, who were both so generous with their time and forthcoming with their advice. This project would not have been completed without their enduring support and wisdom – nor without Robin's willingness to offer such extensive and sound advice with lightning-fast e-mail reaction. This book has also benefited greatly from additions and revisions suggested by my PhD examiners, Martin Millett and James Whitley. James, in particular, I thank for all of the kind advice and support that he has offered over the past couple of years – both for this project and for others.

The lion's share of this manuscript was prepared during a rather dark period of lockdown in the Covid-19 pandemic, and it is therefore dedicated to all friends and family who, having been there throughout the PhD, could still be present on a screen when we all needed each other. To those from Yorkshire, Cambridge, Athens and Pylos, those who called from New York, Glasgow, Germany or Italy – too many to name, but each and every one very important to me. To single out just a few: my brothers Andrew and Stephen and parents Peter and Tricia, who all celebrated too many important milestones together over Zoom; John and Debi, who were my 'support bubble' and made sure I stayed well-fed; my 'Greek family' – especially and always Anastasia, but also Eleni and Yannis; Annette, my 'other' Mum, for all our happy times in Athens, Pylos, and adventures further afield; and the late Mark Langham, not only the warmest, most generous, most remarkable and – even in the face of everything that was going on – most deeply joyful of my lockdown pen pals, but also the architect of so many of my (and countless others') happiest memories from Cambridge; I last saw Fr Mark in-person, beaming like a proud parent, on the day of my PhD graduation: *requiescas in pace et resurges in gloria*.

Abbreviations

ABV	Attic Black-Figure Vase-Painters
ADelt	*Archaiologikon Deltion*
AR	Silver coin
AU	Gold coin
CH	*Coin Hoards*
Chr	*Chronika*
CEG	*Carmina Epigraphica Graeca*
CPC	Copenhagen Polis Centre
EL	Electrum coin
EM	Epigraphic Museum inventory number
FD	*Fouilles de Delphes*
FrGrHist	Fragments of Greek History
GIS	Geographic Information System
HN	*Historia Numorum*
IC	*Inscriptiones Creticae*
IG	*Inscriptiones Graecae*
IGCH	*Inventory of Greek Coin Hoards*
LSAG	Local Scripts of Archaic Greece
NAA	Neutron Activation Analysis
OCG	Online Greek Coinage
PCA	Principal Component Analysis
PPA	Proximal Point Analysis
PPI	Peer Polity Interaction
SEG	*Supplementum Epigraphicum Graecum*
SNA	Social Network Analysis
TMK	Thompson, Mørkholm and Kraay 1973
XRF	X-ray fluorescence
Ath. Pol.	*Athenaion Politeia*
fr.	fragment
Il.	*Iliad*
Od.	*Odyssey*

ID numbers that are underlined refer to items listed in the **appendix**

1 | Introduction

At the end of the nineteenth century and upon the founding of the first foreign schools of archaeology in Athens, national teams began long-term investment at archaeological sites that would become the 'household names' of classical archaeology in Greece.[1] The École Française d'Athènes started excavating at Delos (1873) and Delphi (1892), the Deutsches Archäologisches Institute at Olympia (1875), and the American School of Classical Studies at Athens began work at Corinth (1896). These early excavations – characteristically clearing as much ground as possible, revealing monumental architecture, and conducted in pursuit of highly aesthetic objects like fine painted pottery – have been described as 'big dig' archaeology *par excellence* (*cf.* Davies 2009, 12–14): archaeology conducted on an enormous scale, and archaeology generating huge datasets.

This early activity conducted by the foreign schools was in part responsible for establishing a particular 'pattern' for the archaeology of Greece. Although much valuable data now comes from Greek universities and learned societies since established and from the rescue excavations of the Ephorates of Antiquities,[2] it is the research at those 'big dig' sites that have shaped the peculiarity of the discipline's history. That is, there has been long-term excavation at single sites led by single national teams, recovering enormous quantities of objects which are published within quite specific formats established early in a project's history.[3] Corinth (Fig. 1.1) – a site

---

[1] A full history (with bibliography) of archaeological field activity conducted by the British School at Athens is available through the online interactive 'Collection Events' database, prepared by Anastasia Vassiliou, Michael Loy, Deborah Harlan and others, and part funded by the AridanePLUS Horizon 2020 initiative (https://digital.bsa.ac.uk/fieldwork.php).

[2] For English (and French) language summaries of work of this nature, see the *Archaeology in Greece Online* database at chronique.efa.gr

[3] On the phenomenon of there being sites in Greece that are close to one another but under investigation by different Foreign Schools and that, as a result, their teams might not be in regular communication with one another, see Slawisch and Wilkinson 2016 and Koporal 2020. There is also the risk with 'big dig' archaeology of creating 'intellectual silos' (*cf.* Whitley in press), or institutional networks or personal networks (Whitley 2015b, *cf.* Loy 2020a) that become so entrenched and specialised within the cycle of discovery, study and publication on site that their discussion can become echo-chambers.

Figure 1.1 View of Corinth during the first years of the 'big dig' excavation campaign. BSA SPHS 01/2105.5577, 'Ancient Corinth: Agora excavations'

which, like those others listed above, is still currently under investigation over 100 years later – is a good example: after years of continued exploration, the major publication series of the Corinth excavations was established in 1932 as a monograph series ('red books'), produced by the American School of Classical Studies at Athens, with the publication of the *Topography and Architecture* of the site by Harold North Fowler and Richard Stillwell. Although field reports from Corinth continue to appear in the journal *Hesperia* (and elsewhere), the monograph series, now with forty-seven volumes and more in preparation, remains the principal venue for disseminating data from the site. And, with similar long-running monograph series established for publication of material from Delos, Delphi, Olympia – and for many *other* 'big dig' sites established around this time too – one can see that this really is quite a distinct pattern for how a lot of archaeology in Greece gets done.[4]

The format of publication dictates, to a large extent, the sorts of questions that are asked about the excavation material. To stay with Corinth, volumes are generally dedicated to the study of one type of object or material, the work of a scholar who is specialist in the typology and chronology of certain objects. This specialisation ranges from architecture (vol. I.2, Stillwell, Scranton and Freeman 1941), to sculpture (vol. IX.1, Johnson 1931), to small finds (vol. IV.2 on lamps, Broneer 1930; vol. VI on coins, Edwards 1933), to specific styles of pottery (vol. VII.1 on geometric pottery, Weinberg 1943; vol. VII. 4 on red-figure pottery, Herbert 1977; vol. VII.7 on Hellenistic fine wares, James 2018). Monographs provide first and foremost lists of objects organised by their types, described for their shape, appearance, decoration, chronology, place of production; and less space is given to how these objects fit into the longer and broader history of the site in question. When one examines what is done with the data in these sorts of publications, the answer in many cases is that archaeological debate focuses on relatively few contexts, characteristically used to answer chronological questions, or questions that do not move beyond a few excavation contexts.[5] In some senses, this goes back to the roots of classical archaeology in *Altertumswissenschaft*, that a 'science of the object' ought to be produced in the same mould as a 'science of the text', with no fundamental requirement within the early discipline to produce a wider narrative based on archaeology. Moreover, while these extensive studies cover a range of object types, by virtue of the vast amount of data that exists from the long-term investment in a site, in many cases only a sample of the total

---

[4] On the issue of overburden and the accumulation of material far outstripping the rate at which objects can be studied and published, see Snodgrass 1993, Huggett 2012: 539.

[5] *cf.* comments made in a review by Papadopoulos (2001) concerning the nature of archaeological publication: 'Put bluntly, this is a very large book about a lot of very small fragments.' Relatively little work has been done on using these vast datasets to investigate the worlds of ancient Greece more broadly beyond the boundaries of certain objects, contexts, or sites. For Archaic Greece, the furthest that the conversation got was probably in the work of Anthony Snodgrass (esp. 1980) and his 'school' of former PhD students (*cf.* Whitley 2018a), in using (primarily quantitative) archaeological data to answer questions of interest to ancient historians, an 'archaeological historical' approach to material culture.

assemblage of objects discovered in excavation can be published in such a catalogue. In essence, the pattern on national school 'big dig' archaeology dictates that the priority must be to sift through backlogs of primary material, to establish the objects' chronologies and contexts, and to produce catalogues of data, painstakingly studied at the micro-level. But this also raises a broader question: why investigate at a 'big' scale if not to ask 'big' questions?[6]

Large quantities of archaeological data are particularly well-placed for helping us to uncover patterns about the behaviour of individuals and groups over the long term and across large areas. Patterns in the distribution of large quantities of material evidence tell us that people in the past were either acting in similar ways or different ways to one another, and, upon finding evidence for these behaviours, it becomes possible to evaluate the extent to which those patterns are historically meaningful. Particularly useful are the sorts of things that are found commonly at many sites and in high numbers, where the variation between objects is such that by measuring their similarities and differences, patterns in behaviours can also be identified through their distributions. Patterns can tell us about the access that people had to different resources, their production and consumption habits, the desires and motivations that they had to acquire, manipulate and consume different types of objects. Practically, this means that most useful are smaller objects like pottery sherds and coins, but bigger things, like inscribed objects and sculptures, can also be usefully deployed in this way. And, to return to the point of publication, the *desideratum* to have large sets of smaller objects whose difference can be distinguished fairly easily on a macroscopic scale certainly plays to the strength of classical (Greek) archaeology, where a traditional interest in connoisseurship and aesthetic has (explicitly or implicitly) lent the bias in favour of publishing large amounts of these sorts of things (Snodgrass 2007: 13–19; Haggis and Antonaccio 2015: 1–4; Whitley 2018a: 1–3). The discipline is not short of catalogues of pottery, databases of coins, nor inventories of inscriptions. The archaeological data exist in substantial number, and, were the data to be mobilised in such a way, a wide-reaching analysis of their distribution offers significant potential for understanding behaviour in and the shape of the ancient Greek world.

The problems, however, are twofold in bringing together large quantities of material data for broader historical enquiry. First, there is the issue of

---

[6] On the problem of needing the data to ask 'big' questions but on 'big' efforts required to get that data to a workable state, see Bevan 2015 and Green 2020: 430–1.

organising the data in a meaningful way (i.e. of classifying data into useful categories for analysis); and then of finding ways to address inconsistencies between datasets (both in completeness and in quality) so that meaningful patterns can be found.[7] This book will propose that, for the seventh and sixth centuries BC, 'Archaic Greece', there *are* suitable ways to handle this information – and that one can indeed find meaningful patterns about ancient behaviours through looking at 'big data'.

How to Make 'Big Archaeology' Work for 'Big History'

The 'big data' phenomenon, born out of computational developments over recent decades to mine, store and manipulate huge sets of generally *contemporary* data (e.g. demographic data, population statistics, epidemiological trends), has arrived in archaeology over recent years, (Cooper and Green 2015; McCoy 2017) albeit in ways that cannot be simply cut-and-pasted directly from techniques developed in the hard or social sciences. Even if the amount of material that comes out of the ground in an excavation (or across a region of excavations) could truly be classed as 'big data', once one considers the volume of data that is actually published and of the right quality and shape for analysis, the amount of *usable* and readily digestible data is somewhat smaller. So, any attempt to grapple with archaeological data on the scale indicated will never quite be 'big data' in the sense of other disciplines *per se*, but it is certainly 'bigger data' than the sorts of scales with which the humanities usually engage (*cf.* Gattiglia 2015: 114; Green 2020: 432). What *is* useful to borrow from elsewhere are the tools for making data work: techniques for cleaning and classifying data, and techniques for finding meaningful patterns in them.

The first step towards a broader understanding of the seventh and sixth centuries, then, is to identify datasets that are both comprehensive and representative of the material culture of Archaic Greece. The first of these criteria is simpler to handle, as this involves the systematic mining of all data available. The second, however, presents a more complicated challenge, and this is one of the major methodological challenges of a project

---

[7] Recognising that there is now (and there has been for many years) a critical mass of data that exists, many important synthesis projects (many begun in the past decade) have taken up this challenge across all wings of Classical Greek and Roman Archaeology (*Archaeology in Greece Online/ Chronique des Fouilles en Ligne*, AtticPOT, Portable Antiquities Scheme, the EAGLE portal, to name just a few of many). It is completely timely, particularly now with widespread access to suitable computing technology, to think about ways to bring datasets like these together.

like the present study. To ascertain that the data used are indeed representative, one must subject the data gathered to various levels of qualitative and quantitative review.

First, the qualitative review of data. This involves a sampling strategy for mining data only from sources that have been published to a suitable standard. In practical terms, this involves looking at published site reports and excavation volumes that include within them catalogues of material recorded to the required degree of precision. The publication of 'highlight' objects or single pieces (e.g. in the Greek periodical *Archaiologikon Deltion*) might be excluded from the main data mining, as reports of this type typically precede the publication of a much more extensive site catalogue. Such objects are usually published independently for the sole reason of their *exceptional* nature, not because they are in some way representative of the material culture of a given site. Secondary publications might also be excluded, on the basis that any further sorting and selection of material from a base dataset reduces the likelihood that they discuss a full, comprehensive and representative dataset.

Once the material has been selected, the second issue is how messy the dataset is: can all the data that have been gathered be used? The challenge here is that one deals not with completely mute nor even data points. Archaeological data are 'human' or 'social' data in two senses: first, this is information produced within particular social and historical contexts (*cf.* Hodder 1986; Roskams and Whyman 2007), and, second, this is data *discovered, recorded* and *made available* within particular social and historical contexts. How one fits these complex and quite subjective social units into an analysable objective data-framework is not necessarily so simple.[8]

Thinking through how data are recorded goes some way towards illustrating the problem. It is often at the discretion of the field archaeologist to make a judgement on what is worth recording, how extensively, in what way and with what sort of vocabulary.[9] It is not impossible to escape human error at this stage, and invariably some data points will be incorrectly or incompletely recorded. Then the excavator (or, in some cases, someone else who was not involved in the generation of the data) further selects which of

---

[8] For the idea that there can never be a completely 'raw' and 'empirical' archaeological data – or even any sort of data, for that matter – partly because the data creation process is subject to far too many variables that can be conceived or controlled, see Gitelman and Jackson 2013.

[9] Particularly in the case of the pottery of Archaic Greece, this often presents a problem for older publications, where coarseware sherds (particularly small ones) were frequently thrown in favour of more aesthetically appealing finewares.

these 'raw data' need to be published, choosing how that information should be cleaned and presented, which (if not all) categories of information are published, in what sort of format, and employing what sort of language. In a final publication of data (as one does in a bibliographic study such as this) it is sometimes difficult to understand how all of these decisions have been made; but without access to the original material or without extensive restudy one must accept the decisions made with a degree of confidence.

And then there are issues of coverage. Quite simply, not every 'big dig' excavation has been published to the same degree (in discrete number of publications or in the granularity of information available), nor are the 'big digs' distributed evenly across Greece. On chronology, as noted, much detailed and painstaking work has been done on establishing chronological sequences for material from ancient Greece; but the intensity of study is variable between different regions – even *within* a site, different classes of material might have been more intensively studied and disseminated than others – and there still exist questions about how exactly these chronologies might relate to one another in absolute terms. Furthermore, although scientific analysis is becoming more common across the field, many of our existing chronologies are based on typology or style alone (i.e. there is little external contextual information available). Then there is the problem of the intensity of exploration. For classical archaeology, there are far more 'dots on the map' around Athens and Attica for the simple reason that this area has been more extensively explored. Can we really write a truly horizontal history of how the regions of ancient Greece fit together if each of those component parts is a different shape? As becomes clear from this rather brief overview, although over 100 years of 'big dig' excavation within the Aegean has generated substantial publication, the amount of data that is usable for a project like the present study, while still 'big', is not the 'biggest' in any absolute sense.[10]

Using the remaining data, then, will necessarily result in some degree of 'mess' or 'noise', but it does not prevent us from finding patterns within the dataset. It is not an unrecoverable situation of 'rubbish in, rubbish out'. First, the nature of those factors generating 'noise' within a dataset is not patterned. That is, inconsistencies or gaps within datasets are random and, while random errors might mask patterns or make real patterns much

---

[10] There is also naturally a bias towards particular types of sites (e.g. sanctuaries, where there has been much exploration and significant publication) and data which comes from particular national schools that have traditionally prioritised horizontal and empirical publication of individual artefacts (e.g. systematic German publications).

harder to see, this 'noise' is not so systematic across the archaeological record that it will force us to see *false* patterns. The patterns that emerge from analysis, one might reasonably suggest, are real patterns, and 'noise' will only prevent us from seeing other patterns – but nothing more. To account for this random 'noise' in the dataset, one useful strategy is to keep the scale of the analysis as broad as possible, that is, there will always be errors in the datapoints, but if the total number of datapoints analysed is much larger, then each of those random errors in itself becomes less significant in distorting the overall pattern. The questions raised in this book are best answered by looking at the Aegean basin in the very broadest terms: in approaching the target area through a largely survey-based archaeology of regions. The scale of the study region and the timespan investigated is large enough that even though there will undoubtedly be (sometimes undetectable) variations and fluctuations caused by rogue data points or gaps in the dataset, by working at this scale the 'bumpiness' is smoothed over to give, it is hoped, a solid and reliable overall *general* picture for the Aegean.

The second thing that can be done is to think carefully about categorisation in making units drawn from different sources comparable with one another.[11] That is, the researcher must take some subjective judgement in combining classes of information that might be recorded as different in the source publications (e.g. 'cup' vs. '*kotyle*' vs. 'Ionian bird bowl'), aggregating where it makes sense for the particular questions being asked to categorise similar sorts of data together. Some might call this 'mapping' the information, others 'lumping' (*sensu* Snodgrass 1977).[12] Archaeologists necessarily use different language even within a national tradition to describe the same or similar things (e.g. pot, vessel, ceramic, vase):[13] these differences must be

---

[11] Clearly, if one begins a new project or designs a new database then these principles can be adopted from the outset, using tools and workflows to help guide non-specialist users towards good data curation (Powlesland and May 2010; Vlachidis et al. 2010; Wallrodt 2016; Strupler and Wilkinson 2017), following guidelines on creating 'good' and 'clean' datasets (Parthenos et al. 2018). The issue here is how to produce clean data *after* the data have been created and published.

[12] Morris 1987 demonstrated that Snodgrass 1980 had distorted his picture of Archaic Greek society by 'lumping' together categories of child and adult burial data, and he (and many others subsequently) advocated the opposite approach of 'splitting' data down into as many non-equivalent units as possible, necessarily making the size of each data class much smaller.
A secondary aim of this book is to demonstrate that there is still value in 'lumping', and that, while a broad-level analysis might bring to light a different order of patterns than one would in adopting a close and more contextual view of the data, the patterns that are discernible are still useful for helping to write history.

[13] Paradoxically, even though the interest of this book is in lumping together data to assess broad-level patterns, the analysis is also enabled by splitting. In taking an object like the Nikandre *kore*:

smoothed over by adopting some type of common vocabulary (*cf.* Kintigh 2006: 570; Bodard et al. 2011; Cooper and Green 2015: 290; Bodard et al. 2017; Green 2020: 434–5). Data standards, thesauri and lists of fixed vocabulary terms provide the bases against which heterogeneous datasets can be homogenised for collective analysis, and indeed this book makes use of standardised vocabularies against which myriad different terms are mapped for convenience.

But mapping different classes of data to one another is not without its challenges. Further to the fact that the mapping process itself is a subjective process that requires the creative input of a user (*cf.* Roskams and Whyman 2007), clearly in transforming data one cannot generate new information that is not there, and it is only possible to 'map-down' to less specific common classes. The necessary consequence of this is an apparent 'simplification' of some of the data that we are handling: one might be left with lumpy and far-reaching categories like 'urban' vs. 'sanctuary', while losing the nuance of more specific terms like 'filled well', or 'floor deposit'. Requiring a certain level of data specificity would duly shrink the dataset available for analysis, not to mention the possibility that one predetermines the types of conclusions drawn from the data by fixing the categories of things that are being looked for too early. Although data synthesis and data mapping are not without challenges – and ones that can be overcome – the alternative seems even more grave: to simply junk all of the old data. We may all lament the state of old and 'bad' data, but that does not remove the need to engage with it, nor to think through its particular characteristics intelligently and pragmatically. We are required to take each dataset in its own context, to massage data together in a workable format, and to see inconsistencies between datasets not as deficiencies but as challenges to be solved.

This book analyses four sets of things that we have in great number from many sites across all parts of the Aegean: pottery, coins, inscriptions and marble sculpture. As will be discussed, assemblages of these objects taken on a macro-scale variously demonstrate connections with local and non-local sites in both quality and quantity. These sorts of objects all inhabited the same world and are similar enough that they can usefully be put side-by-side with one another; but they are necessarily different enough that analysis of their distribution will put different sorts of behaviours in the spotlight. The spread of material is also fairly even across the Aegean basin, such that most

_{this object is both a freestanding stone statue that can be analysed alongside other sculptures, and yet it can also be analysed quite separately in the context of its inscription. This issue of simultaneous lumping and splitting will be evaluated and discussed in the penultimate chapter.}

parts of the Aegean world (with some necessary adjustment) can be productively discussed. And, on a more practical note, generations of discovery, research and discussion on this material provides us with a dataset that is a suitable size and shape for study.[14]

To summarise: a particular type of archaeology in Greece has generated large swathes of material data that has, to some extent, been underexploited in historical enquiry. The particular types of questions that this 'big data' might answer are about behaviour, about how individuals and groups of individuals – in the Greek world of 700–500 BC – interacted with one another. Although the data are heterogeneous and messy, they are not beyond the point of being usable. Careful selection, cleaning and mapping of datasets will result in useful units of analysis that can be aggregated to reveal patterns of historical interest for further interrogation. The next important step is to propose useful methods for organising and analysing that data.

Material Networks as Evidence for Behaviour

The solution posed in this book is to look at archaeological 'big data' through the lens of Social Network Analysis (SNA), as a way of organising the data and recovering patterns in their distribution. Commonalities in the distribution of certain types of objects in certain places will be read as proxy for similar activities undertaken both by individuals and by collectives of individuals. These patterns will then be used to think through the connections that existed between different groups, and the extent to which these similarities constituted complex networks of interaction.

The production and distribution of objects reflects human agency. In creating or acquiring objects that either resemble or look distinct from one's neighbours, groups or individuals (either consciously or unconsciously) commit to associating themselves with or distancing themselves from nearby settlements. Access to similar or the same resources or technical information might inform the ways in which communities create objects, and mobile craftspeople might bring different styles, methods or techniques for creating objects to new places. However, in all cases the decision to

---

[14] Excluded here are categories of objects that are somewhat 'exceptional' (e.g. faience, jewellery and scarabs: things that were traded between different parts of the Aegean, but which were moved in much lower quantities). Such objects do not show us the normal range of a site's connections; their acquisition was entangled with unusual circumstances beyond the everyday set of networks.

produce or acquire objects of a certain type is always a *conscious* one, and the objects must, therefore, reflect to some degree the people who projected them. The material record is entangled with all these human decisions. In looking across assemblages of things from different places, we can begin to disentangle some of the interactions that created these distributions.

If we are to understand how a whole region like 'Archaic Greece' functioned and how its component parts interacted in a *broad-scale* 'connectivity' (*sensu* Hordon and Purcell 2000: 123–72; Broodbank 2013), we cannot look simply at single objects: the size of the dataset must be adjusted to the level of the questions being asked. In going from mute objects to dynamic processes of interconnection, two things are required: a dataset large enough to identify continuities and discontinuities between sites, without background noise; and formal methodologies for sorting and interpreting data on this scale. The challenge is to find ways of putting these data together systematically and comparing them in a productive way that can allow us to make reliable and robust conclusions about the interactions of the communities that produced them.

The nuts-and-bolts of social network analysis are now so familiar to archaeologists, ancient historians and classicists that it is not necessary to rehearse here yet another explanation for the fundamentals of SNA,[15] but it suffices to say that under this framework real or imagined individuals or collectives are visualised as nodes, and the relations between them as links or edges: the structure of an interconnected network of nodes can therefore be visualised descriptively, or investigated with exploratory statistics, as a formal means of visualising, interpreting and explaining connections between various actors (Fig. 1.2).[16] Crucially, there is no 'one-size-fits-all' network approach (*cf.* Mills 2018), and each adapts techniques and frameworks to the particularities of each dataset under analysis.

Largely thanks to the work of Tom Brughmans (2010 and 2012) and Carl Knappett (2011), *computational* SNA network analysis has now become a serious and significant branch of study within the scholarship of the ancient world,[17] itself much inspired by ongoing 'big data' network analysis

---

[15] A range of approaches have been adopted both in the articles of edited collections (Collar et al. 2015, Brughmans, Collar, and Coward 2016, Leidwanger and Knappett 2018) and individual studies (Constantakopoulou 2007; Knappett, Evans and Rivers 2008; Mol 2013; Iacono 2016; Orengo and Livarda 2016), some tending to more literal uses of SNA, while others adopt this framework as a more general metaphor.

[16] On the development of SNA in sociology, see Hanneman and Riddle 2005 *cf.* Barnes and Harary 1983, Wasserman and Faust 1994, and Freeman 2004.

[17] See Brughmans 2014 for a quantitative overview of computational network studies, and their exponential increase in uptake.

12 *Introduction*

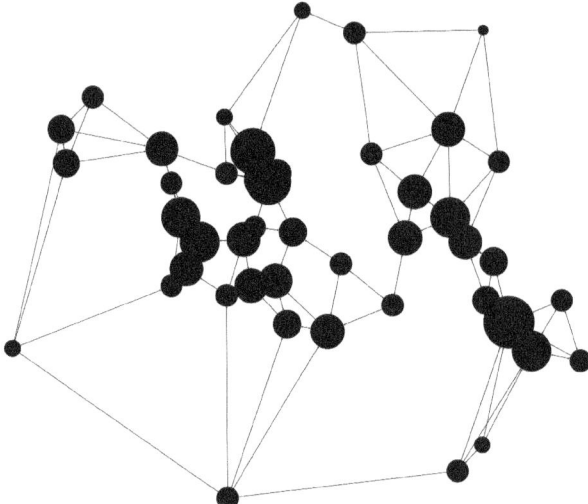

Figure 1.2 Illustrative network graphic. Nodes and edges are weighted; the arrows on the edges indicate that edges in this graph have direction.

conducted in the sciences, in mathematics and on contemporary datasets. The 'computational' aspect of SNA conducted in this way pertains both to the size of the dataset that can be handled in such an analysis, but also to the complexity of the analysis that can be run: literally hundreds or thousands of connections can be drawn in the overall network, and their overall structure and sub-groups analysed in a matter of seconds. Computational tools are used to run descriptive and exploratory statistical tests on these networks to facilitate their interpretation (i.e. to let one see much *quicker* patterns that could be seen otherwise) but also to elucidate patterns that one would not otherwise be able to see. Network analysis helps, therefore: to visualise a large number of relationships simultaneously; to put emphasis on the nature of the relationships between nodes, rather than on the nodes themselves; to explore the overall structure of all combined interactions, and how they might change over time; and to extract and to evaluate the role of individual nodes in a wider system.

A note on the interpretive framework of the network analysis. The network – although useful for putting emphasis on the activities of units interacting with one another – is to some extent an artificial and anachronistic framework, an 'etic' tool into which data might be forced in order to see patterns:[18] to put this another way, network analytical perspectives

---

[18] 'Emic' and 'etic', although terms gleaned from linguistics (Pike 1954), are useful for thinking through the interpretation of the sorts of data discussed here. See Mostowlansky and Rota 2020

encourage us to see data in categories that would not have been meaningful to ancient people. To handle data at the high level such that it is available for this study, a very broad-brush and top-level analysis has been conducted, adopting mapping principles to 'reduce' the complexities of data to more easily manipulated units. This necessarily removes some of the nuance behind each cultural unit examined, with each level of simplification moving us further from any 'emic' possibility to a progressively more 'etic' framework. Somewhat more crucially, in going from material culture to activities, the networks described have had to be necessarily broad-brush too. A 'political network' or an 'economic network' can mean a range of different things, and, unless defined more precisely, stopping simply at such definitions risks being too 'etic' to be useful.

This type of framework – although more common in other parts of World Archaeology – goes against the tide of the more 'emic' approaches undertaken recently within the Ancient History of Archaic and Classical Greece (e.g. Anderson 2018; Blok 2017). Recent studies part of this 'ontological turn' have taken a very useful, cautious and much-needed re-analysis of rather generalising and outdated frameworks and assumptions about the Greek world, providing a challenge to some of the (anachronistic) terms that we use to describe the ancient world – for instance the 'economy'. And, yet, in the face of the success of this sort of scholarship, what is being proposed here almost looks like a backwards step towards processualism, an uncritical 'archaeology by numbers' that prizes manipulation of the data without full contextual discussion of each datapoint.[19] Can such an approach still be defended in the twenty-first century?

The solution is to be completely explicit about what is being modelled, and to move very gently through the interpretative framework. That is, this study will take large sets of material data, and it will use SNA simply as a heuristic for sorting groups of similar materials together according to units of place around the Aegean basin. Those similar materials will be understood to represent the cumulation of a set of similar activities, and it is those similar practices undertaken in the same way at the same places that are understood to represent the historically meaningful building blocks of wider networks. Nothing more and nothing less. Using SNA to

for a summary on the history of interpretation of these terms, particularly their usefulness for archaeology. This binary opposition is perhaps unfair. 'Emic' and 'etic' understandings of a community need not be in opposition with one another, and can be adopted quite successfully in synergy, cf. Berger et al. 1976; Feleppa 1986; and Geertz 1976.

[19] This is perhaps an unfair over-generalisation. Much recent work done by computational archaeologists could be more precisely labelled as the coarsely defined 'processual+', still bringing in substantial bodies of theory but championing above all else method and data.

sort the material record will therefore help to reveal simple units of behaviour, whose similarity or difference can be discussed next to one another. It is from here that our understanding of the dynamics of the Aegean basin in the seventh and sixth centuries will emerge. Ironically, this 'etic' approach demands that one is as equally agnostic about definitions as in an 'emic' approach. That is, words like the 'economy' or 'community' will be used as neutrally as possible, steering us away from the precise and specific definition of each datapoint towards the broad patterns that exist between them in combination. And that is the defence for a more data-led archaeology: that our interest is not in the data themselves but in the *questions* and *problems* that are raised by their patterning.

Having established the interpretative framework, the next step is to establish those 'basic units', those collectives of individuals, located in the same places.

The Community, and Communities of Activity

To analyse a network in which nodes represent places at which certain activities take place, a neutral vocabulary is required that presupposes nothing about a group's composition nor about its behaviours.[20] What is proposed here is that the notion of the 'community' is one that is both appropriately unspecific yet descriptive enough, although subject to a history of debate on its own definition.

The particularly useful thing about adopting a community-focused framework is that the community is an idea that has been conceptualised far less as a physical thing than in the case of the *polis* or state. With the exception of geographers and urban theorists in the mid-twentieth century who theorised the community as something environmentally defined that bounded together groups of people who did similar things or had similar practices owing to the fact that they were located proximate to one another,[21] the important thing for theorists in identifying communities

---

[20] The PhD thesis on which this book is based used the 'state' as the basic indicator of activity taken at a specific place. But the 'state' is weighed down by much more interpretive baggage than the 'community', as a term first adopted within a neo-evolutionary progressive framework (Service 1962). Even though scholarship has now moved on and the 'state' has been theorised in myriad different ways (Boardman 1980; Osborne 1985; Haldon 1993; Yoffee 2005), this is still a problematic term to use in Aegean studies, principally because many of the models developed by the Michigan School have focused on non-familiar case studies from Mesoamerica (*cf.* Whitley 2015b) and have received less critical analysis within Mediterranean scholarship.

[21] The discussion here is necessarily brief, but a full literature review is given by Mac Sweeney 2011: 13–15.

has been that the *activities* of its members are mutually similar enough that this is some form of meaningful collective. Catie Steidl (2020) has recently laid out a useful framework that illustrates how the behaviour of individuals – with one another, with their landscape and with material culture (*cf.* Bourdieu 1977; Van Dommelen, Gerritsen, and Knapp 2005; DeMarrais 2011) – creates a community, either consciously or unconsciously (*cf.* Houston et al. 2003; *contra* DeMarrais 2016):[22] communities share practices of maintaining their built environment; practices of religion and ritual; and they have a shared social experience. Steidl's case studies from western Anatolia help to illustrate this framework, wherein she indicates that individuals at Ephesos formed a community of shared practice, using the same pottery vessels for stewing meats and for feasting: by using the same types of objects to process the same sorts of foods, the individuals who prepared these foods clearly have some shared experience and outlook of their immediate environment, and this similarity can be called, as neutrally as possible, a 'community' of individuals (*cf.* Whittle 2005; Harris 2014). Quite clearly this is a very specific example from a particular place, but the framework can be scaled up to much larger units, with the crucial notion being that communities are units that are defined by the actions taken by the people within them – they are by no means static entities.

The framework of the community is also particularly useful in this study for two additional reasons. First, as suggested, the community does not have to be bounded to a specific geographic place, nor does it operate at a fixed scale. Quite obviously, in sharing practice with other individuals, one does necessarily need to inhabit the same physical space (*cf.* Anderson 1983; Cohen 1985; Canuto and Yaeger 2000; *contra* Knapp 2003 on the importance of *both* shared geographic space *and* experience). The diaspora of Greek citizens living internationally – as an example – can certainly be understood as a community, even though many of its members have not met one another. It is their shared heritage – a shared understanding of spaces, a common iconography or language – that gives its members a particular and shared outlook on the world, making these individuals part of a community. And in an increasingly globalised, international and digitally connected world, it makes quite logical sense to us that one can share experiences, thoughts and practices with non-proximate individuals, and in doing so one can be considered to be a 'community' with those

---

[22] Naoíse Mac Sweeney 2011 arrives at a similar definition of community but suggests that collective ideologies must be more consciously maintained. The present discussion tends more towards Steidl's idea, that a group can be a collective, loosely defined and based on their similarities even if they do not actively identify themselves with one another in that way.

others, whether that be groups of just a few individuals or groups that include millions of members.

For the Archaic Greek world in which we are dealing with settlements and collectives of different sizes and complexities, not to mention with groups of Greeks who are 'on the move' (*sensu* Antonaccio 2007), the more flexible the definition of their collectives, the better. It is well recognised that Greeks might identify themselves simultaneously with different communities (*cf.* Taylor and Vlassopoulos 2015), and just as, for example, one could reasonably be a member of the deme of Thorikos and a citizen of Athens at the same time, it is clear that the size and scale of these units were flexible and non-overlapping.[23] And so the 'community' here is a catch-all for a commonality of belonging, identity or practice, created through the conscious or unconscious shared beliefs and practices of its members – where membership of one community does not exclude one from membership of another.

A second reason that this is a useful model is that it is a framework defined by the practices of its individuals, one which puts emphasis on the *positive* actions of individuals as a group rather than on the things to which they are *negatively* opposed. Communities have also been variously defined by scholars on the basis that an 'us' and 'them' dichotomy helps to define a collective spirit more strongly (e.g. Cohen 2002). Particularly prevalent within the definition of Greek ethnicity is this notion of having an 'other' (see Chapter 5). While some form of opposition can contribute to making a communal identity *stronger*, it might not be the most effective way of *creating* a sense of community among smaller or more isolated groups: small mountain or island village sites, particularly prevalent throughout Greece, might not have regular contact with other outside groups to create significant antagonism, and that should not negate the idea that these small groups can form and harbour strong communal feelings with one another. Practice, activity and experience shared among any number of individuals create collective groups – whatever sort of groups those are, however big, and operating at whatever scale.

This framework is useful for the current study. The notion of the 'community' will thus be employed as a fairly neutral term that operates across different scales, crossing both physical and unbounded space, and informed by the dynamic activities of its constituent members. The aim remains to make sense of the 'big data', and the 'community' is just as much

---

[23] The general orthodoxy that Greeks belonged first and foremost to 'communities of cult' (*sensu* Morgan 2003, *cf.* Anderson 2018) will be addressed in the conclusion, Chapter 7.

a tool for achieving that aim: the patterns in the 'big data' do not simply require a panoply of separate communities, they demand that those communities are in some sense a network. It is unhelpful to use sets of arbitrary criteria (e.g. population sizes) to try and designate some communities as anything like a state or a non-state; it is acknowledged that in the diverse world of Archaic Greece there were communities of various sizes and scales that exercised different political and economic structures, and yet they might be seen as somewhat roughly equivalent autonomous political units. The community, therefore, is a unit of collective activity, whose actions have a mutual impact upon the activity of the group. Clearly, it is the *actions* of a community that more importantly define it, and the main interest of this book is not on definitions *per se*, but on investigating what these groups did and what they did with each other. The term 'community' will be used almost somewhat interchangeably with 'political community', 'economic community' or 'political-economic community', depending on the sorts of activities that are being presently described.

Another methodological note: 'community' is a flexible unit, and while in many cases this will refer to quite large collectives, in others the focus is on a smaller group of individuals *who represent* the wider community. In the interest of maintaining a fairly neutral vocabulary that does not presuppose the nature of these basic units of analysis, the term 'peers' will be used or (to borrow from the language of those who have investigated these phenomena for Archaic Greece) 'elite peers'. The use of this term is not to presuppose ideas of class, status, aristocracy or wealth,[24] but to adopt a framework similar to that of Alain Duplouy (2006), in which 'eliteness' was not something one was born with in the world of Archaic Greece, but rather something that one attained; 'eliteness' was not a permanent state and it could be lost. Essentially, the world of Archaic Greece was one with very little (if any) inherent class, but individuals were constantly striving to achieve this level of 'eliteness' in everything they did. Moreover, certain activities could be performed by individuals to generate status, through public recognition; by acting in this way individuals did things that were recognised in the community as 'elite', and through this *performance* they increased the likelihood that they would be viewed by others as themselves 'elite'. In this model, the consumption of material culture and quest for

---

[24] Van Wees and Fisher (2015) and Duplouy (2002 and 2005) explain that this view was the result of two misconstructed beliefs: first, that ancient 'elites' were analogues to feudal lords of the European medieval period; and second, that many scholars took their picture of a hereditary elite straight from the pages of Homer and projected it towards the Archaic period.

social recognition were entangled – an idea that will be key to the forthcoming analysis in this book.

To reiterate, then: SNA will be used throughout this book to organise the plethora of archaeological 'big data' from the Aegean of the seventh and sixth centuries BC, as a way of identifying patterns in the distributions of objects across sites: marble, pottery, coins and inscribed objects. These patterns will be used to think about behaviour where 'communities' are the basic unit of analysis, and where those communities – or elite peers representing those communities – are the abstract nodes in a series of networks connecting across the worlds of Archaic Greece.

Chronological Boundaries

The 'Archaic period' analysed in this book begins in 700 BC and ends in 500 BC.[25] These seemingly 'fixed points' are somewhat arbitrary – as are any dates that classical archaeologists assign to material culture on the basis of style. On the one hand, while there do actually exist certain synchronisms for the Classical Aegean that can help to assign genuine fixed points to horizons of material culture styles (e.g. the sacking of Miletos or the Athenian Acropolis),[26] on the other hand, a few fixed points at the end of the sixth century are not necessarily helpful to the questions asked in this book: this book examines *long-term change* and shifts in economic and political activity over time rather than *specific calendrical events*. And, therefore, changes in style that we heuristically but imprecisely assign to chronological periods are perfectly acceptable for this analysis. For example, it is relatively unimportant whether a pot that our catalogue tells us was painted 'in the second half of the sixth century BC' was actually painted in the 540s or the 520s – or even the

---

[25] For various (equally arbitrary) definitions for the start and end points of the Archaic period, see Davies 2009. The most frequently cited date range for this period is 776–480 BC, based on two historical events: respectively, the first Olympic games, and the second Persian invasion of Greece.

[26] One might wonder why the analysis does not go as far as 480 BC to take in the exceptional quantity of material yielded from Persian destruction layers. The issue here is context. As has been outlined above, this book is interested in thinking through objects in motion: material culture as part of dynamic processes in the formation and co-ordination of networks. Objects found within Persian destruction contexts are not objects in transaction and, paradoxically, even though their archaeological context might be more helpful in this case for providing firm dating, such objects are considered contextually less useful here. Scale is another issue, that the range 500–480 BC would yield so much material that it is both beyond the scope of the present study to synthesise, and (providing an opposite problem to include the eighth century), its inclusion could weight modelling to such an extent that it would mask more subtle patterns from the start of the seventh century, from which there is less data.

490s. What matters is that this pot shows clear and measurable change from something that was painted at the start of the seventh century BC.

How then does a broad-range and imprecise chronological framework of time slices help? First, it helps to mask some of the 'edge effect' that might arise in analysing data either side: there is a much smaller quantity of material available for study from the eighth century as opposed to the seventh or sixth, and extending the same models for analysis into the eighth century would create problems for data comparability. That is not to say that the results of the analysis conducted will be taken in isolation, and qualitatively at least the story that emerges from the formal network analysis for the seventh and sixth centuries will be put next to the narrative of the eighth century. It is a question of balance: the 'Archaic period' as it is analysed here pertains to the seventh and sixth centuries BC, centuries which provide reasonably comparable amounts of data such that modelling these two centuries together can produce more evenly discernible results.

The second reason for adopting this framework is to do with style. The dataset for this book is material culture, and analysis relies on categories defined in previous studies, building on the legacy of art history's treatment of these data. The timeframe for analysis must map, therefore, onto the stylistic categories as defined in previous scholarship. The year 700 BC marks a good point of departure, marking the end of the Late Geometric period (in Attica, Ionia and in the Cyclades, at least). This also provides an interesting start point from which regional pottery styles begin to take on a character even more distinct than in the Geometric period, such that they can be distinguished from one another relatively simply in macroscopic terms (e.g. one can quite readily distinguish visually Orientalizing from Wild Goat from Proto-attic): and these relative distance measures of similarity and difference are required for the modelling proposed above. Contextual find information is rarely considered, and style is the place to start in looking for temporal information. Furthermore, a century-based approach is sensible stylistically when it comes to dealing not only with pottery, but also with the other main material datasets that feature in this book: coins and inscriptions. Both datasets are subject to long histories of stylistic analysis, often related to categories that consider centuries (e.g. 'seventh century BC', 'end of sixth century BC') or parts of centuries (e.g. 'last quarter sixth century', 'first half seventh century').[27] It makes sense, therefore, to follow where possible similar chronologies to the source data,

---

[27] It is useful to consider briefly what these date ranges represent. A date-range estimate is essentially a 'probability' value: for an inscription as 625–550 BC, we might decide that within this range there is a certain likelihood that the 'actual' date of the inscription is somewhere near

and to work within the same limits of reference.[28] As a result, for both reasons of data quantity and of previous stylistic analysis on the target data, 700 BC–500 BC is taken as the main chronological framework here.

The final point to make here is on chronological subdivisions. Data will be analysed in this book under a four-part division based on half-centuries: 700–650 BC, 650–600 BC, 600–550 BC and 550–500 BC. These 'time slices' are broad enough to account for the variation in precision and accuracy of the dating assigned to each object in previous studies, while also being narrow enough that change can be detected between each group. It is also important in this context to deal with time slices of equal duration.

Geographical Boundaries

The scope of this study is limited to communities located in, around and principally facing into the Aegean Sea. The main areas for analysis include the coasts of the Saronic Gulf, the Cycladic islands, the Dodecanese, and the region of Aegean Turkey known as 'Ionia', in addition to parts of northern Greece and Crete. Within these broadly defined areas of interest, sites for analysis are selected on the basis of data available in each area (Fig. 1.3, Table 1.1). But in general there is a particular emphasis in this book on *coastal* sites of the Aegean. Studies of Mediterranean 'connectivity' and networking from the last twenty years have placed particular emphasis on the geographical factors that enable connectedness, and, above all, that the sea affords a medium of mobility. One of the aims of this study, therefore, is to assess the extent to which these models are appropriate for the particular historic setting of the Archaic period. This is not to make the *a priori* assumption that maritime transport and seascape mobility were responsible for the intensification of interaction in Archaic Greece, but it acknowledges that the role of the sea in enabling connectivity needs to be considered.

the middle of this estimate (e.g. 590 BC), or that it is just as likely to be somewhere near the 'edges' of this (e.g. 610 BC or 555 BC). Essentially, the question in treating date ranges as probability distributions is in deciding what those probability distributions ought to look like. Is there an equal probability that the date of the inscription could fall anywhere within the range 625–550 BC (a uniform distribution), or is there a most likely value in the middle of this range, and dates towards the edges of this boundary are more unlikely (a normal distribution)? This book understands that a uniform distribution can suitably represent a range of dates, as there is no good reason to think the dataset requires otherwise (*cf.* Sinn 1980), and that 'Early', 'mid' and 'late' dates given within a century were also distributed across a fifty-year range (e.g. early sixth century = 600–550 BC; mid-sixth century = 575–525 BC; late sixth century = 550–500 BC).

[28] See further discussion below on data mapping, that categories can be reduced but that they cannot be made more precise.

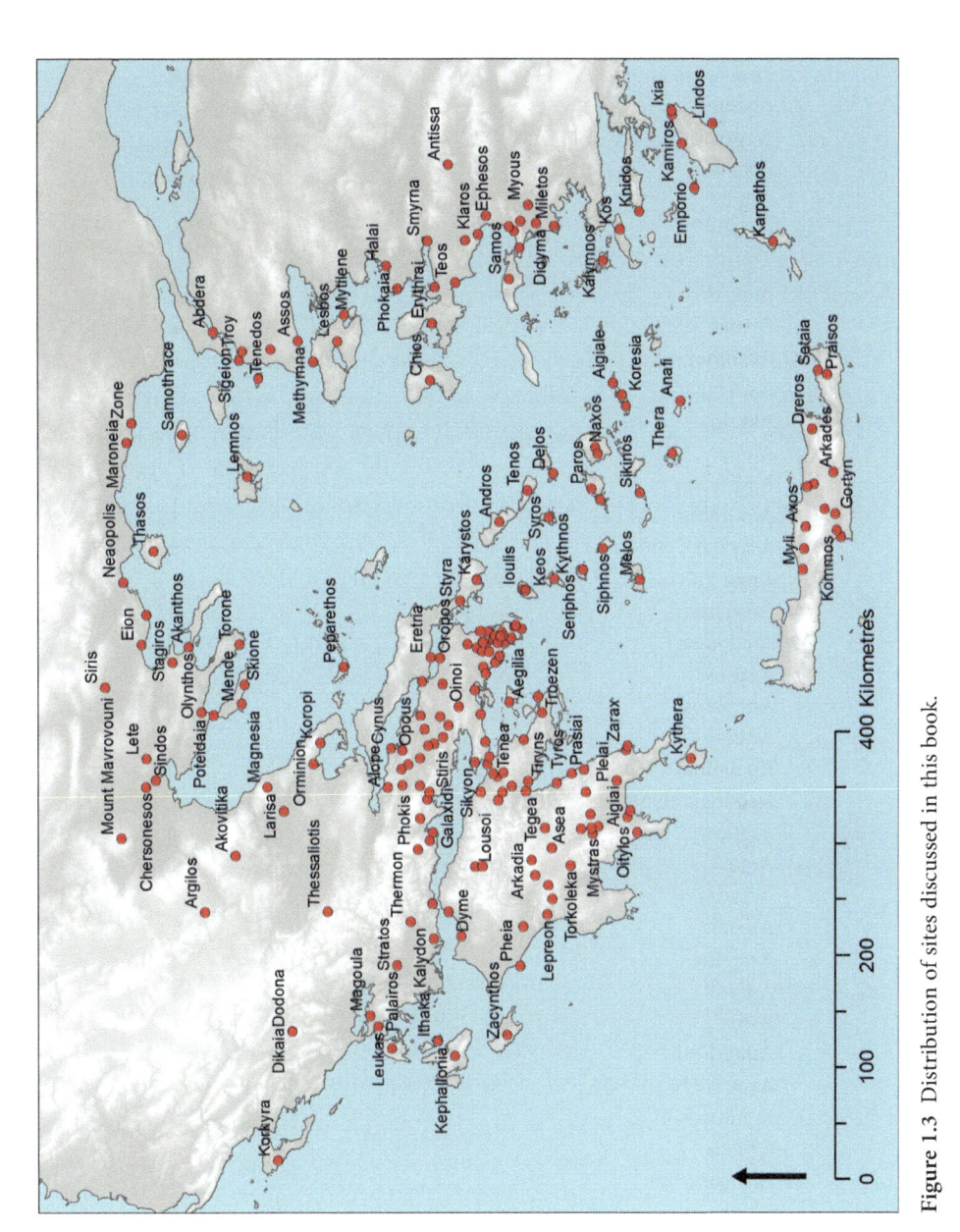

Figure 1.3 Distribution of sites discussed in this book.

Table 1.1 *Sites discussed in this book, according to the materials available for analysis in each case.*

Site	Marble	Pottery	Coins	Lettersets
Abai				x
Abdera			x	
Abydos				x
Achaea				x
Aegilia				x
Aegina	x	x	x	x
Aigiai	x			
Aigiale				x
Aixone				x
Akanthos			x	
Akovitika				x
Akraifia		x	x	
Alope				x
Ambryssos				x
Amorgos	x			x
Amyklai				x
Anafi	x			x
Anagyrous				x
Anavyssos	x			
Andros	x		x	
Antiparos	x			
Antissa				x
Apollonia				x
Apollonis Hyperteleatae				x
Argilos			x	
Argos				x
Arkades				x
Arkadia				x
Arkesine				x
Asea				x
Assos				x
Athens	x	x	x	x
Axos				x
Brauron				x
Chalkis			x	x
Chersonesos			x	x
Chios	x		x	x
Chrysapha	x			
Corinth		x	x	x
Cynus				x

Table 1.1 (cont.)

Site	Marble	Pottery	Coins	Lettersets
Delos	x	x	x	x
Delphi	x		x	x
Dichova				x
Didyma	x			x
Dikaia			x	
Dodona				x
Dreros				x
Dyme				x
Eion			x	
Elateia				x
Eleusis	x			x
Eleutherna				x
Eltynia				x
Emporio				x
Ephesos	x		x	x
Epidauros	x			x
Erchia				x
Eretria	x		x	x
Erythrai	x			x
Eutresis	x			
Galaxidi				x
Gargettos				x
Gortyn				x
Gortyna	x			
Halai				x
Halai Araphenides				x
Haliartos			x	
Halikarnassos	x			
Hyperteleaton				x
Ialysos			x	x
Ikarion				x
Ioulis			x	
Isthmia	x			x
Ithaka				x
Ixia				x
Kalapodi		x		x
Kalaureia		x		
Kalavryta				x
Kalydon				x
Kalymnos	x			x
Kamiros	x		x	x
Karpathos			x	

Table 1.1 (*cont.*)

Site	Marble	Pottery	Coins	Lettersets
Karthaia			x	
Karystos			x	
Karystos				x
Keos	x			x
Kephale				x
Kephallonia				x
Keratea	x			
Klaros	x			x
Klazomenai	x	x	x	x
Kleonai			x	
Knidos	x		x	
Knossos		x		x
Kolophon				x
Kommos		x		
Koresia			x	
Korkyra	x		x	x
Koropi				x
Kos			x	x
Kosmas				x
Krommyon				x
Kythera				x
Kythnos			x	
Larisa				x
Laurion	x			
Lemnos				x
Leontinoi	x			
Lepreon	x			
Lesbos			x	x
Lete			x	x
Leukas				x
Limnai				x
Lindos	x	x	x	x
Lousoi				x
Magnesia			x	x
Magoula				x
Markopoulo	x			
Maroneia			x	
Megara	x			x
Melie				x
Melos	x		x	x
Melpeia				x

Table 1.1 (*cont.*)

Site	Marble	Pottery	Coins	Lettersets
Mende			x	
Mesogaia	x			
Methana				x
Methymna				x
Miletos	x	x	x	x
Mount Mavrovouni				x
Mycalessus			x	
Mycenae				x
Mykale				x
Myli				x
Myous				x
Myrrhinous	x			x
Mystras				x
Mytilene		x	x	x
Naupaktos				x
Naxos	x		x	x
Neandria				x
Neaopolis			x	x
Nemea				x
New Phaleron	x			
Oinoi				x
Oitylos				x
Olympia	x	x		x
Olynthos		x	x	
Opous				x
Orchomenos	x		x	x
Orminion				x
Oropos				x
Paiania				x
Palairos				x
Paros	x		x	x
Penteskouphia				x
Peparethos			x	
Perachora		x		x
Phaistos				x
Pheia	x			
Phigaleia	x			
Phleious			x	x
Phokaia			x	
Phokikon				x
Phokis			x	

Table 1.1 (cont.)

Site	Marble	Pottery	Coins	Lettersets
Pleiai				x
Poteidaia			x	
Praisos				x
Prasiai				x
Priene				x
Prospalta				x
Ptoan sanctuary	x			x
Rhizenia				x
Samos	x	x	x	x
Samothrace	x	x		x
Sangri				x
Selinous				x
Sellasia				x
Seriphos			x	
Setaia				x
Sigeion				x
Sikinos				x
Sikyon				x
Sindos		x		
Siphnos	x		x	
Siris				x
Skione				x
Smyrna		x	x	x
Sounion	x	x		x
Sparta				x
Sphettos				x
Stagiros			x	
Stiris				x
Stratos				x
Styra				x
Syros				x
Tanagra	x		x	x
Tegea		x		x
Tenea	x			
Tenedos			x	
Tenos			x	x
Teos			x	x
Thasos	x	x	x	x
Thebes			x	x
Thera	x		x	x
Thermon				x

Table 1.1 (cont.)

Site	Marble	Pottery	Coins	Lettersets
Thespiai				x
Thessaliotis				x
Thorikos		x		x
Thrace	x			
Tiryns				x
Torkoleka	x			
Torone		x		
Triteia				x
Troezen				x
Troy				x
Tyros				x
Vlachomandra				x
Volomandra	x			
Vourva	x			
Zacynthos				x
Zarax				x
Zone		x		

It is also important to note areas that are *not* included within this book. Quite clearly the 'Greek world' at this time was much more than just the Aegean, taking in the Greek settlements of the Black Sea region in the northwest, Magna Graecia, Sicily, and all the way to Massalia in the west, North Africa (including major sites at Libya at Naukratis), not to mention Cyprus, often considered alongside other 'Greek' territories but far out of reach of the immediate Aegean zone.[29] And what about those communities in contact with the edges of the Aegean – particularly to the north – which, although not using the 'Greek' language, would still cut across all sorts of economic and cultural networks that were being exercised elsewhere: social networks do not map directly onto barriers of language nor of geography. The answer, quite simply, is that the unit of analysis must stop somewhere, and that there will always be opportunity to think about what effect there might have been for linking a little further beyond the edges.[30]

---

[29] See Archibald 2017 on going 'beyond Greek archaeology', *cf.* Foxhall 2017.

[30] It is not new to suggest that the Greek world at this time was part of a wider world system (Sherratt and Sherratt 1993), and the network approach is a useful one for reminding us that the 'end' of a network is not necessarily the 'end' of any sort of cultural or geographical unit – that there could always be some other network right on the side pulling or pushing on the Aegean network.

Undoubtedly new patterns might be uncovered and other patterns might fall into much sharper focus once the geographic remit is extended, and perhaps a similar study that goes beyond the Aegean to a Mediterranean-level analysis of the 'Greek world' is a project to be undertaken elsewhere: but, as it stands, this book already contains over 30,000 individual units for analysis and the boundary has to be drawn somewhere.

So for this book, at least, the main focus is on the *internal* dynamics and formation of networks *within* the Aegean region. 'Archaic Greece' will be used as a shorthand for 'the Archaic Aegean' and, while acknowledging that the Greek-speaking world was much larger with its settlements abroad and subject to a much broader set of contacts at this time, the Aegean remains here the focus.

Scope and Structure of this Book

The purpose of this book is to run some experiments on the myriad of archaeological data available from the world of Archaic Greece and to see whether the patterns that emerge are in any way meaningful or historically interesting. This will integrate new archaeological data into the debate on the structure of Archaic Greece, specifically with a view to exploring how political and economic interrelations contributed to processes of community-level interaction between 700 and 500 BC. Undoubtedly there will be some misfires in the experiments run owing to the quality of data available and gaps in the dataset, but this will also allow for critical reflection on the current state of data availability.

Although this book is about using methodologies that are new for this period of study, it is written in a way to be accessible and broadly appealing to ancient historians and classical archaeologists more generally. Supporting data and models for reproducing the analysis conducted are hosted elsewhere for a more specialist audience, but the focus here is opening up the possibility of new historical narratives to a broader audience in a way that does not isolate the non-specialist.

This book is framed around four separate case studies, brought together in the final section for more general discussion. All four case studies, though, are interested with the broader issue of what an analysis of big data can tell us about the 'big issues' that have been of concern to historians of early Greece, and can be most easily expressed in two key research questions:

- How formally organised were the political communities of early Greece, and what role within these communities was played by elite peers?
- To what extent can methods of modern economics appropriately be used to analyse the ancient economy?

Chapter 2 looks at the transport of raw marble in the production of freestanding sculptures. The first part of the chapter estimates the rate at which *kouroi* and *korai* statues were produced in the sixth century, and in the second half of the chapter various types of maritime shipping routes are reconstructed. The focus of this case study is on economic networks, and on the extent to which economic activity was entangled with the embedded social activities of elite peers.

Chapter 3 takes this idea of maritime shipping routes further by bringing ceramics into the discussion. Here the interrelation of 'luxury' and 'commodity' shipping is considered, considering both the ceramic dataset quite separately, and putting it directly alongside the marble dataset. Discussion follows on the extent to which parts of the Aegean world might have targeted certain products at certain times, making way for discussion of an early market-based economy.

The networks discussed in Chapter 4 are considered 'entangled' in that they relate to both issues of political affiliation and issues of economics. The first coinage is analysed in relation to the network of shared weight standards that spread across the Aegean and, following discussion on the extent to which the data give evidence for consumption and/or production, coinage is put alongside the distribution of certain types of transport amphorae to elucidate the shape and chronology of some economic networks even more clearly.

Chapter 5 considers the inscriptional record, and, specifically, the use of different forms of the early Greek alphabet. By looking at the co-existence of various lettersets in different parts of the Aegean, this chapter considers how consciously Greeks chose to associate themselves with or distance themselves from each other; and it explores ways in which writing was used to advertise personal and communal identities. This chapter also asks a broader question about data modelling, and about the extent to which certain patterns can be encouraged or masked depending on the models used.

The previous discussions are set in a wider historical framework in Chapter 6. Alliances, leagues and *amphiktyonies* attested in textual and historical sources are discussed side-by-side with the patterns of the previous four chapters. Both a 'top-down' and a 'bottom-up' approach are considered, working both from networks that the historical record tells us ought to exist, and, by contrast, beginning with the material data and evaluating the patterns that emerge. This chapter also considers the extent to which communication and knowledge were pre-requisites in the formation of other types of networks.

2 | Economic Networks
The Transport of Heavy Freight

The four case studies in this book divide into two groups. This chapter and the next are concerned with physical objects that move around the Aegean; Chapters 4 and 5 are concerned with ways of conceptualising the world (metaphysical objects, if you will) that are unevenly shared across the Aegean. Each chapter will first lay out the patterning of distribution revealed by the relevant 'big data' and will then consider what behaviour might best account for that distribution pattern.

Setting the Scene: Overseas Exchange in the Early Iron Age

That things were consumed in places away from where they originated was not new for the Archaic period. But from the Early Iron Age there is no possibility of investigating patterns of consumption through big data since the quantity of data available is exiguous. To get an impression of Early Iron Age consumption we must resort to case studies. But exceptional data is exceptionally significant, and two examples from the Early Iron Age of imported goods and imported materials allow certain deductions. First, a bronze amphora found in one of the Toumba-Lefkandi grave shafts (Catling 1993). Excavations of the Protogeometric building at Toumba (Lefkandi) were conducted by the British School at Athens between 1981 and 1983 (Popham, Calligas and Sackett 1993), during which two grave shafts were found beneath the Toumba building dating to c. 950 BC (Popham 1993: 101) – a discovery familiar to classical archaeologists. One grave to the north contained a horse burial, and one adjacent to the south contained the bones of a female and a bronze amphora with the ashes of another individual (Catling 1993). Based on comparisons with five similar vessels of which four come from post-Mycenaean burial contexts on Cyprus (Catling 1993: 86–92), the excavators at Lefkandi thought it highly likely that the amphora was an import from Cyprus. Indeed, the uniqueness of this object on Euboea strongly suggests that it was not locally made. The mechanism of its arrival at Lefkandi and in the grave shaft is not immediately relevant to the issue of imports. Was this owned in life by the deceased? Had the deceased travelled personally to Cyprus? Had the amphora come straight to Lefkandi, or did it pass through intermediate hands *en route*?: the mere presence of this object some 900 km away from its place of production is enough to tell us that, on occasion at least, objects did travel.

Second, one might look at the gold earrings of the c. 850 BC 'rich Athenian lady' grave of the Athenian Areopagus. In 1967 a trench-and-hole type grave was discovered here at the west end of the 'South Road' just near the southern boundary of the Agora (Smithson 1968). Dated to c. 850 BC and similar in form to contemporary burials found at the Kerameikos and at Eleusis, this familiar grave has been nicknamed the 'tomb of a rich Athenian lady', based on the outstanding quantity and quality of grave goods found interred. Among significant quantities of fine pottery were ivory stamp seals, faience, glass beads and gold jewellery. And although the gold earrings of the Areopagus burial were likely manufactured locally (*cf.* Smithson 1968: 111–12), the gold in its raw and unprocessed form was most certainly imported (*cf.* Healey 1978: 45–7). Again, the details of the mechanism by which this gold arrived in Athens is not of immediate concern: the presence alone of imported gold suggests that the individual or community assemblage this grave had privileged access to restricted and specific exchange networks. Moreover, the *quantity* of gold suggests that access to these networks was not fleeting but more developed. Whatever their means of travel, things were being consumed far away from the place of origin.

These two cases make rather limited requirements as to the scale and organisation of exchange in the tenth and ninth centuries. Both objects were relatively small portable things: there was no need for specialist carrying equipment or labour-intensive loading/unloading processes in getting things from A to B. In fact, such exchanges might actually be best organised by individuals – not communities – based to a large extent on exploiting personal social networks of personal contacts (*cf.* Morris 1986; Shepherd 2000; van Wees 2002; von Reden 2003: 18–37). Since the amphora and the earrings as imports comprise only a small part of assemblages which contained far more 'local' than imported goods,[1] they give no reason to suppose that the supply of imported materials was abundant at either Lefkandi or at Athens. Thus the importing of objects was plausibly both low-intensity and rather *ad hoc*.[2] On this evidence, and based on both

---

[1] A fuller discussion on the entanglement between the use of imported goods as a marker of conspicuous consumption and the aspiration for social recognition will follow.

[2] I refer here to the exchange of these highly regarded 'luxury' goods, like the bronze or gold previously mentioned. There is a growing body of evidence that by the eighth century at least

frequency and quantity, it is questionable whether such sporadic activity constitutes an 'economy' of imported goods.[3]

These particular cases also suggest some reasons motivating exchange in the Early Iron Age. The individuals of both graves discussed were evidently somewhat distinct members of their respective communities (e.g. Smithson 1968: 83; Calligas 1988; Mazarakis Ainian 1997; Papadopoulos and Smithson 2017). In Lefkandi, the burial space beneath the Toumba building was reserved for two individuals, while others in the community were buried in cemetery plots east of Toumba; in Athens the sheer quantity and quality of goods interred in that particular grave suggests aspiration for social recognition, signalling to others access to far-reaching and specialised networks. These were clearly exclusive burial spaces, and the physical differentiation of the grave might have mirrored a social distinction that these individuals received in life (*cf.* Parker Pearson 1999: 74-5). What is important for the notion of exchange is that the material culture of both graves contributed to marking out even *further* the exclusivity of its owners. The presence of these objects, given the *absence* of similar objects elsewhere at Lefkandi and Athens at this time, suggests that the owners had *access* to materials and resources from Cyprus and elsewhere that others in the community did not. The bronze amphora and the gold earrings were physical representations of their owners' (direct or indirect) involvement in exclusive exchange networks. They were a visual reminder to those in the community – and to the owners themselves – that they were a little bit different from others.

These two examples suggest that in the Early Iron Age the consumption of objects manufactured elsewhere could be entangled with games of status acquisition, for the simple reason that certain objects were not easily accessible to all strata of society. That would imply that the flow of those goods around the Aegean was highly restricted, involving only relatively small and portable goods moved around on quite a small scale and with low levels of systematisation to exchange. It is useful to compare this pattern with those that will be encountered in the Archaic period: even though some of those notions of *why* people sought to acquire things persist, the scale and extent of that sort of consumption steps up to a different order of magnitude.

---

there was quite wide circulation of utilitarian pottery 'exchanged' beyond the immediately local (Murray 2017; Knodell 2021); *cf.* with the discussion in the Chapter 3.

[3] Here and throughout the 'economy' is not understood to be an organised system in any sort of modernist sense but is a shorthand for 'economic activity', that is, people with various motivations producing, acquiring and consuming things in both small and large quantities and with varying levels of frequency and repetition to process.

Shifting Gears in the Archaic Period

In contrast to the Early Iron Age of the Aegean, the seventh and sixth centuries saw larger *quantities* of things and *physically larger* things being moved around: things like stone, metal ores and timber. Of these, the one substance we can track archaeologically is stone. Stone had already been used as a building material in the Early Iron Age: architectural remains from Eretria (Konstantinou 1952, 1955), Helike (Kolia and Gadolou 2007, 2011), Perachora (Dunbabin 1940: 27–34) and Tiryns (Frickenhaus 1912) offer just a few eighth-century examples of buildings made from stone.[4] The stones used were generally local (predominantly limestone), both rough cut and lightly shaped. In temple architecture, at least, a common blueprint was to construct a stone foundation and to monumentalise the rest of the structure with other materials such as wood (Mazarakis Ainian 1997). Owing both to this minimal use of stone within the building itself and to the fairly small size of the buildings constructed, the overall quantity of stone used for Early Iron Age buildings was understandably low. In the Archaic period, however, the situation was changing. Buildings were larger in the seventh and sixth century than in the eighth century, necessarily requiring greater quantities of raw stone. What is more, although there had already been in the eighth century and at the start of the seventh century a tradition of producing freestanding figurines in ivory, wood, terracotta and bronze (Stuart Jones 1895: 1–29; Akurgal 1968; Meiggs 1982; Donohue 1988; Boardman 2006: 1–12), the Archaic period saw the widespread creation of freestanding *stone* sculptures.[5] Clearly, this combination demanded a greater quantity of resources: some of this need was met through local supply, while a not insignificant proportion was imported non-local stone. This chapter investigates the latter, and how the 'bulk' import of material across the Aegean changed in the seventh and sixth centuries.

A good index to *measure* this sort of scaling up is via the statue dataset. The dataset is larger, more geographically spread and, since less episodic, allows one to observe greater change over time than looking simply at temples. Thus it provides a decent road in thinking about how scale and distribution changed over the course of two centuries. Over 600 stone statues are well documented from the Archaic period – with new fragments

---

[4] The use of stone was not exclusively for architecture, and there are many examples of stone-lined or stone-built graves from the same period, e.g. *ADelt* 68 (2013), *Chr.*, 440–4, *ADelt* 66 (2011), *Chr.*, 147, https://chronique.efa.gr/?kroute=report&id=1827

[5] There was in the early years some regional preference as to the stone used. See Palagia 2006, xiii for examples of dark limestone (Crete) and grey marble (Spartan) sculpture.

discovered every year. These are distributed not only across the Aegean basin but also throughout the wider Mediterranean. Of the freestanding limestone and marble statues of human figures sculpted in the Archaic period, there are two main types: the nude male *kouros* (Fig. 2.1) and the draped female *kore* (Fig. 2.2). *Kouroi* were frontal-facing figures, with an even distribution of weight across the body, but typically with one foot placed in front of the other. These figures were avowedly Greek but

Figure 2.1 Samian *kouros*, Vathy Archaeological Museum. Photograph by author.

Figure 2.2 Fragment of a *kore* (A.4062) from the Archaeological Museum on Delos. Photograph by author.

seemingly based on an Egyptian style of sculpture (Carpenter 1960: 3–20; Cook 1967; Boardman 2006: 12–8), where Greek artists copied directly from statues either in Egypt or from prototype *kouroi* produced in Ionia (Kaplan 2003; *contra* Carter and Steinberg 2010). It is possible that the presence of Greek mercenaries overseas in Ionia and Egypt played a key role in transporting these artistic ideas to Greece. *Kouroi* statues appear both in sanctuaries – leading some scholars to believe that a number of the sculptures were connected with the god Apollo, either as direct representations of the god or of 'heroic' youths dedicated in his honour (Deonna 1909; Steiner 2001; *contra* Stewart 1986; *cf.* Spivey 2013: 12–49) – and, particularly in Attica, as grave markers. The *korai*, by contrast, are thought to have been based on the Cretan prototype of Daedalic statues (Guralnick 1981; Boardman 2006: 24). *Korai* are typically much smaller than *kouroi*: they are also front-facing and they exhibit a balanced posture, but their defining feature is that they wear either a peplos or a chiton. A large number of *korai* were dedicated on the Athenian Acropolis, and these statues in particular constitute a large part of the overall corpus of surviving female statue figures.

As was the case for the Early Iron Age, the consumption of non-functional objects like these can be linked to some extent to a need to mark oneself out as different, and to demonstrate that one could consume an object that few people had access to. It is certainly not surprising to suggest that statues could be made and deployed to create social recognition (*cf.* Renfrew 1986): dedicating expensive objects (Duplouy 2006: 151–84), positioned prominently in public spaces (such as sanctuaries) where many individuals could see, guaranteed at least local renown. Freestanding statues could well have been part of a strategy of consumption. As we shall see, the time and labour required to produce a statue was such that these objects were 'luxury' products not widely available to all. The prestige of such objects might be further enhanced when produced in relatively rarer stones or by relatively more renowned artists. By having access to such resources and products, the individuals who put up statues could mark themselves out from the rest of the community.[6] Further, it would have been possible to link these freestanding statues back to the individuals seeking social validation (a necessary step in conspicuous consumption) as many of these statues had inscribed bases with the name of the purchaser or dedicator.

Key here is the notion of 'conspicuous consumption'. As a term coined in the late nineteenth century by economist Thorstein Veblen in his seminal work *The Theory of the Leisure Class* (Veblen 1899),[7] 'conspicuous consumption' describes the process of *consciously* investing one's wealth (or resources,

---

[6] There is a distinction of course between an individual being perceived (passively) as distinct from the community because they have access to a certain object and an individual using their access to material culture to project and (actively) construct such an image.

[7] For subsequent reinterpretation of the 'conspicuous consumption' paradigm, see Coelho and McClure 1993, Bernheim 1995, Pesendorfer 1995, Bagwell and Bernheim 1996 and Corneo and Jeanne 1997. This model has been subject to critique by Campbell 1995 and Trigg 2001.

or labour-hours) into obtaining a product that has been designed (at least in part) to serve as a *symbol for wealth or status*. *Kouros* and *kore* statues dedicated as votives within sanctuary spaces certainly fit this definition. They were designed to be seen – large in size, polychromatic, bearing on their bases the name of the dedicator or artist – and they were placed in prominent positions in sanctuaries. The most obvious examples are the *kouroi* from Sounion (MARB 2–5), which would have been placed at the east end of the Temple of Poseidon on the Sounion promontory, looking out towards the sea as a beacon to be seen by those approaching towards the sanctuary (*cf.* Loy forthcoming). Those *kouroi* placed as grave markers fulfilled a similar performative function: during the seventh and sixth century, a vast majority of the graves that have been discovered were simple pits or cists, in many cases unmarked (e.g. and most selectively: ADelt 63 (2008), Chr., 835; ADelt 64 (2009), Chr., 419–22, ADelt 68 (2013), Chr., 73–4), such that the few examples we have of *kouros* grave markers must have been meant to be seen. And it was this desire to be seen – to create something larger, something more elaborate, something more *luxurious* – that drove the escalation of the freestanding statue production network.

In juxtaposing the Early Iron Age and the Archaic period like this, even in a rather coarse and uneven way, elements of similarity and difference are in evidence. In the case of the seventh and sixth century, however, the process of marking oneself out as different was 'stepped up', both in terms of the size of the objects that were being consumed for communicating status but equally in the number of things that were being consumed in all parts of the Aegean. This 'exchange' is clearly a socially motivated activity, but the extent to which it intersected with other factors – and indeed the extent to which this 'exchange' was regular or systematised – remains to be explored.

The Economy, an Economy, or a Cultural Economy?

Although scholars have studied this set of objects in various ways, Greek statues have not generally been used to think about issues of economy.[8] The primary study conducted on this set of objects has been one of cataloguing and classification. One of the earliest attempts at constructing a catalogue for the *kouroi* was by Waldemar Deonna (1909), and for the *korai* the first catalogue collected together the statues found during the excavation of the

---

[8] This is in contrast to statues of the Roman world, which have attracted the interest of economic historians for the issue of replication (i.e. of objects mass-produced for widespread distribution). Bowman and Wilson 2009, Russell 2013.

Athenian Acropolis and was compiled by Ernst Langlotz (Schrader, Langlotz, and Schuchhardt 1939: 3–184). Gisela and Irma Richter expanded on these works by assembling catalogues and chronologies that took into account more recent discoveries for both the *kouroi* and the *korai* (Richter 1942, Richter 1968).[9] In doing so they split the corpus into various stylistic 'regional' workshops and argued that styles of sculpture could be attributed to various sets of artists from different parts of the Aegean. These catalogues still constitute the most complete and most frequently cited works in the field, but, nevertheless, separate site- and regional-based collections have since been published (e.g. Tuchelt 1970; Freyer-Schauenburg 1974). Furthermore, new pieces of monumental marble statues have now been found, and they are included in subsequently published catalogues (Rolley 1994; Meyer and Brüggemann 2007). More recent scholarship on the freestanding sculpture of Archaic Greece has focused, for the large part, on three main areas: describing the stylistic changes and variations between *kouroi* over time and between different regions of the Greek world (Woodford 1986: 38–56; Spivey 1997: 133; Sturgeon 2006; Neer 2012: 153; Spivey 2013: 17–83); using the sculptures to explore the wider social history of the people who made, dedicated and interacted with them (Schneider 1975; von Steuben 1980; Martini 1990; Osborne 1998: 75–85; Hochscheid 2015); and interpreting the 'inner' or 'poetic' meaning of the sculptures and the identity of the figures represented by the *kouroi* and *korai* (Harrison 1988; Ridgeway 1990; Stewart 1990: 124; Osborne 1994: 90–1; Hurwit 1999: 126). Essentially, these objects have been used for forming chronologies and for general art history; they have not necessarily provided units of analysis for studies of the ancient economy.

Anthony Snodgrass is one of the few who have used this dataset in a different way. In a paper of 1983, Snodgrass discussed the shipping of 'heavy' goods in the Archaic period, the sort of large-scale transport that was referred to above. He focused on two types of materials and two products in particular (metal ores and marble stone statues), both things that other sources tell us were transported overseas around the Aegean during the Archaic period. Essentially, he used ballpark figures to estimate *the order of magnitude* for which these two products were traded, relying on very rough figures extrapolated from surviving known material data.[10] Specifically, the estimate that Snodgrass reached was in the region of 270 tons of marble (or 350 average-sized '*kouros* units' weighing some three quarters of a ton each)

---

[9] Both volumes were updated with subsequent editions as more material came to light, with the most recent on the *kouroi* being published in 1970 and for the *korai* in 1988.

[10] He also had a wider agenda in demonstrating the usefulness of archaeological data in answering historical questions, a similar line taken throughout this book.

in circulation throughout the Aegean on an annual basis, not taking into account the marble also required for the production of stone temples. That average figure was derived from an estimate of the representative dataset of *kouroi* printed in the publication of Richter, based on Richter's data for the sanctuary of Apollo at Ptoion versus the number of statue fragments that had been found at the site up until the 1980s. Although roughly defined, this ballpark figure did permit Snodgrass to think through the problem of mass transport to a certain order of magnitude, indicating that, as expected, both marble and metal ores constituted very significant investments in the overall picture of 'trade' in the Archaic Greek world. Snodgrass' figures will be discussed further, and they will be evaluated in light of the present analysis.

There are two obvious ways to advance Snodgrass' work with regard to the shape of the Archaic period economy and its intersection with social and cultural processes. First, where Snodgrass used round figures to estimate the scale of the economy, this chapter aggregates individual datapoints from across various sources. The chances are that this will not deliver a wildly different ballpark estimate, but it will at least help to clarify with the weight of some data the extent of Archaic period economic activity. Second, Snodgrass' discussion was largely theoretical, treating points of product origin and delivery rather generally. This chapter aims to go further by evaluating the possibility of certain shipping routes and their impact on parts of the Aegean basin, employing some network analytical techniques. Not only does a spatial dimension allow one to test the economic model further, it also helps to bring an amorphous concept like 'economic system' into a more specific reality.

Marble Statues as Products

In using the freestanding sculpture dataset to think about the scale and extent of ancient trade, 305 *kouroi* statues (10 whole sculptures, 295 fragments) are analysed here, and 174 *korai* statues (14 whole sculptures, 160 fragments) (Table **A1.1**).[11] As for distribution of consumption, the majority of *kouroi* and *korai* whose marble has been identified as Parian or 'island' has been found in the southern Aegean basin (Fig. 2.3, *cf.* Table 1.1): principally in

---

[11] Sufficient synthesis has been done on Archaic marble sculpture that the data for this study are drawn from only a few published catalogues. For the *kouroi* Richter's third edition publication has been used (i.e. the most up-to-date version of the most widely used catalogue for *kouros* studies, 1970), and this has been supplemented with *kouroi* discovered after the publication of Richter and listed by Marion Meyer and Nora Brüggemann (2007). For the *korai* the data are drawn from the recent work of Katerina Karakasi (2003), which, likewise, builds on an early collection of Richter (1968).

Figure 2.3 Distribution of sites discussed in this chapter, for which marble statues have been found.

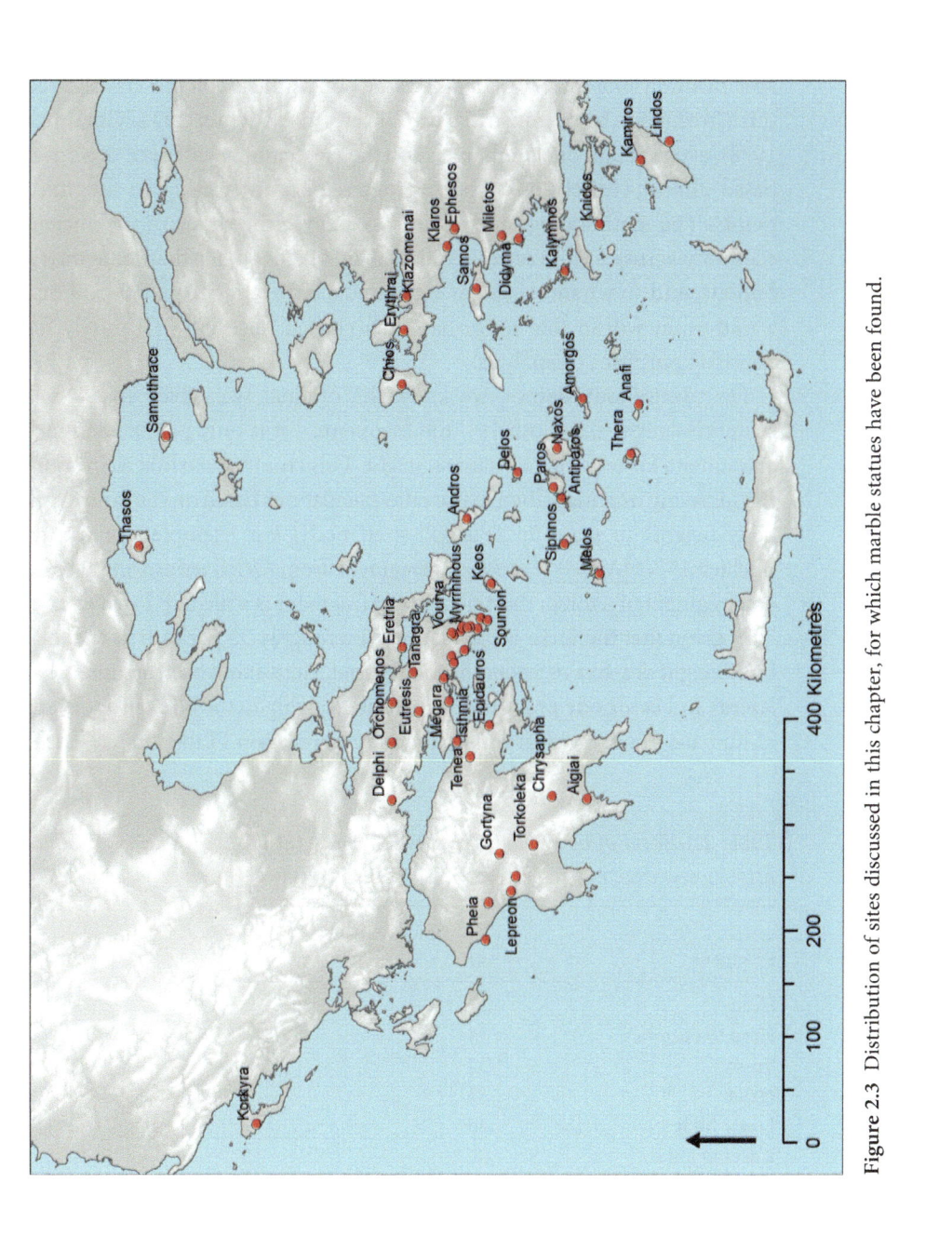

Attica, but with a not insignificant number in central and western Greece, the Aegean islands, and in Ionia.

The sculptures studied in this chapter are dated between 635–500 BC. Sculptures are generally dated to a range of ten years, or to the year specifically: a long history of detailed study on statue typologies has allowed this chronology to be constructed (Caskey 1924, Richter 1934, Guralnick 1978), even though one might question the epistemological merit of a series based almost entirely on stylistic progression and relating to few fixed points. The methodology used below to analyse the shape of the ancient economy across a time series requires single dates rather than date distributions, and so where study has suggested a date range (e.g. 560–550 BC) a mid-point within this range has been chosen (e.g. 555 BC) purely for heuristic purposes of analysis.

For twenty-four statues, we know the original size, given that whole sculptures survive. For others – the fragments – it is only possible to make an estimate for the original statue's height. This requires one first to measure the surviving fragment, then to use ratio calculations based on the limb to full body heights to scale up to a full-sized body. For example, concerning 'Richter 17' (MARB 14), a *kouros* fragment from Delos measuring 0.85 m as a fragment of a torso, the height of the fragment is scaled up by a factor of 2.86, given that the torso is calculated to be roughly 35 per cent of the total body height of a *kouros* under the model used. Here, it has been assumed that *kouros* and *kore* body proportions correlate roughly to the body proportions of humans as observed in a contemporary population (Table 2.1).[12] This is

Table 2.1 *Ratio of body part to full whole body (after http://www.exrx.net/Kinesiology/Segments.html).*

Fragment	Percentage of whole body size
Head	17
Head to pectorals	24
Torso	35
Hand	7
Lower body	46
Knees to ankle	30
Foot and lower leg	21

---

[12] The source for anatomical reference used is http://www.exrx.net/Kinesiology/Segments.html, accessed 15 December 2021.

clearly a simplification, as sculptures of different stylistic groups are known to have had different body proportions (Richter 1934: 16–25); however, the differences are not so significant that setting them aside places the results of this study into a wildly different ballpark.

Type of marble is a more difficult variable to control in a purely bibliographic study. In distinguishing marble origin, the source data as recorded combine both categories of place ('Naxian', 'Pentelic') with categories of physical description such as colour ('blue', 'whitish grey'). These two categories are not mutually exclusive, and for some statues a marker of place was given based on the physical description of the marble as macroscopically observed (Attanasio 2003): brilliant white marble with crystalline inclusions is more likely to have come from Paros, and so the categories 'white' and 'Parian' are somewhat related to one another (even if 'Parian marble' is rather too broad as a category). As discussed in Chapter 1, the best thing to do in making sense of heterogeneous datasets like these is to combine down (or re-code) to a 'common denominator' type of categorisation. But when that cannot be done reliably or with any sort of accuracy (as would be the case here when one cannot conduct a whole re-analysis of the dataset), one option is to leave the data categories as they are and omit any classes that fall outside the main parameters of analysis. That is what has been done here: minimal cleaning has taken place, and categories of both place and colour will appear on the same plot.

The reconstructed height of each known *kouros* (Fig. 2.4) or *kore* (Fig. 2.5) is plotted here alongside the heights of the surviving statues against both time and against marble provenance. This allows us to solicit some basic patterns for the sculpture dataset that we can test further.

The *kouroi* are generally up to 2 m tall, but certainly before 550 BC there is a not insignificant number of larger statues; furthermore, the general trend is towards smaller statues over time. Evidence of colossal statues (>8 m) dedicated on Naxos and Delos is provided by fragments (e.g. feet) which are scaled up to a full body height (Boardman 1978: 23; Rolley 1994: 165–7; Kokkorou-Alevras 1995: 37–130). Clustering of data points suggests that the main fashion for producing and dedicating statues was around 550 BC, but one must be cautious that arbitrary dating in the catalogues to the mid-sixth century may produce a false pattern.

If we filter out the 'noise' created by the statues of undetermined marble (Fig. 2.6), we observe that there is a rough trend towards the use of Naxian marble in the first half of the sixth century, and towards Parian marble in the second (*cf.* Pedley 1976: 38–40; Kokkorou-Alevras 2010; Sturgeon 2006: 43–7); most of these statues are larger-than-life sized, at 2–4 m in height.

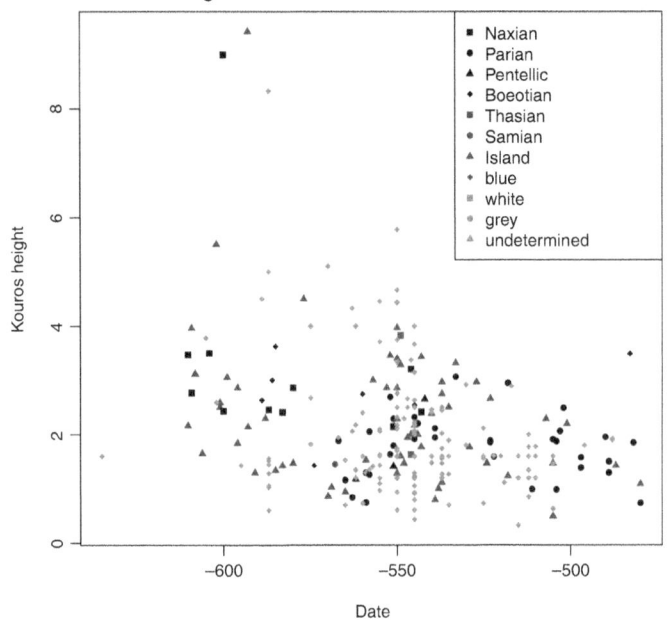

Figure 2.4 Heights and marble sources of *kouroi* over time. The 'type' of *kouros* is given as is in their source catalogues, without mapping or combination of data classes. The 'negative' date range indicates BC dates, while the height of statues is given in metres.

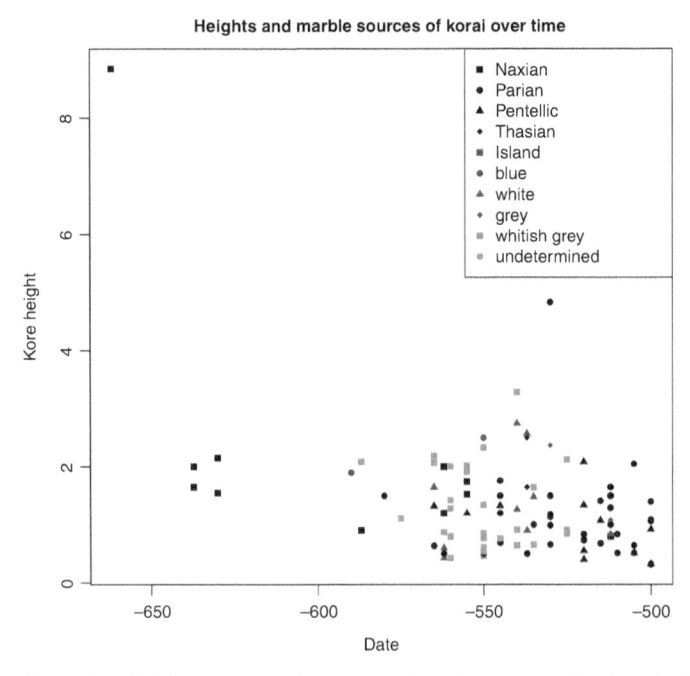

Figure 2.5 Heights and marble sources of *korai* over time. The 'type' of *kore* is given as is in their source catalogues, without mapping or combination of data classes. The 'negative' date range indicates BC dates, while the height of statues is given in metres.

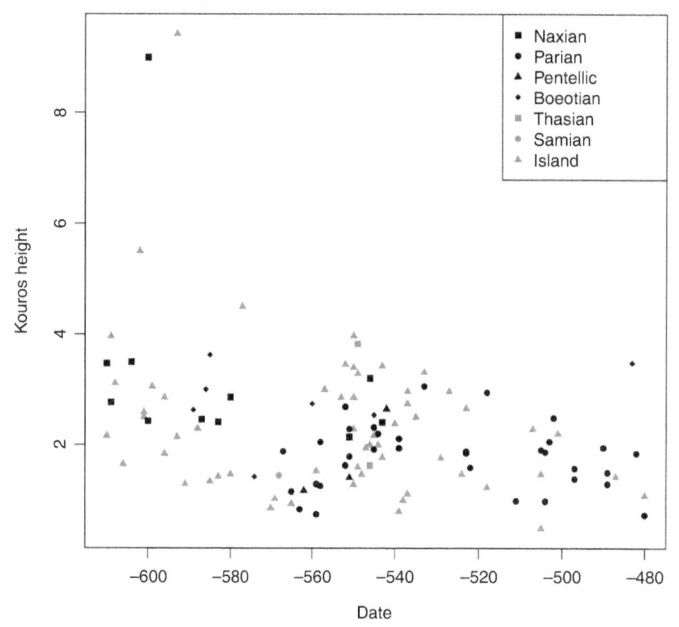

Figure 2.6 Heights and marble sources of *kouroi* over time, with data points for unprovenanced marble removed. Other datapoints are described as is in their source catalogues, without mapping or combination of data classes. The 'negative' date range indicates BC dates, while the height of statues is given in metres.

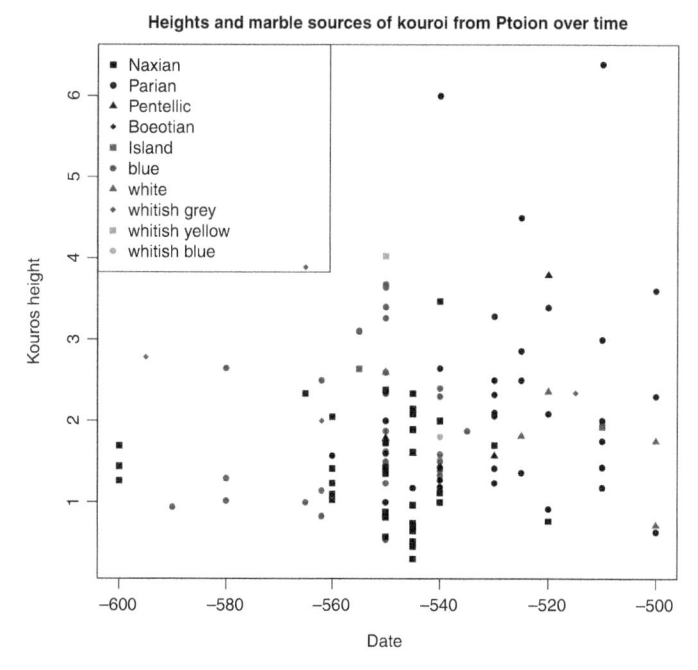

Figure 2.7 Heights and marble sources of *kouroi* from the Ptoion sanctuary over time. Datapoints are described as is in their source catalogues, without mapping or combination of data classes. The 'negative' date range indicates BC dates, while the height of statues is given in metres.

All other varieties of marble are represented in low numbers. There is some mild preference for Boeotian marble in the first part of the century, and for Pentelic around 550 BC. Of the little Thasian sculpture plotted here, datapoints are likewise around the 550 BC mark. There is no significant evidence for a correlation between the type of marble used and the height of the statue sculpted.

The distribution of *korai* heights, by contrast, exhibits a different pattern. These statues are, overall, smaller than their male counterparts, and they remain at around the 1.6 m or less mark throughout the Archaic period. We do not have evidence of colossal female statues in the same way that we do for male figures. In terms of their raw material, though, there is similar patterning between the *korai* and the *kouroi*, in that Naxian marble is the most commonly used marble throughout the first half of the sixth century, and it is gradually replaced by Parian by 500 BC. The end of the sixth century also had many *korai* sculpted from Pentelic marble, and these *korai* are, for the most part, the statues of the Athenian Acropolis.

These patterns are all rather broad-brush and generalising, but they can be broken down further by site to distinguish any site- or regional-level variations. There are insufficient data to analyse the trend for all parts of the Greek world, but we can look in detail at three sites from which extensive data have been well published: the Ptoion sanctuary in Boeotia (7 whole sculptures, 143 fragments, Ducat 1971, Table 2.2a); the Athenian Acropolis (*korai* only;[13] 6 whole sculptures, 43 fragments, Karakasi 2003, Table 2.2b); and the sanctuary of Apollo on Delos (2 whole sculptures, 29 fragments, Richter 1934; Meyer and Brüggemann 2007; Table 2.2c). The *kouroi* from Delos date back to the mid-seventh century and give a wide chronological spread of datapoints, even though the marble provenance for statues at this site is so uncertain that we cannot say anything about the distribution of marble types. For both Ptoion and the Acropolis, statues were made from a range of Naxian, Parian, Pentelic and other marble sources, and they date, respectively, across the whole of the sixth century, and from the mid-sixth to early-fifth centuries BC. The data from each sanctuary have been visualised site-by-site in the same way as above (Ptoion Fig. 2.7, Athens Fig. 2.8, Delos Fig. 2.9), and also plotted all together on the same graph (Fig. 2.10).

Marble sculptures were erected at Ptoion from the beginning of the sixth century onwards. In his study of this set of objects from Ptoion, Jean Ducat gave both a date and a suggested marble provenance for the stone of the

---

[13] It is only *korai* that are analysed as a group here so that the dataset is large enough to see meaningful patterns. The smaller number of *kouroi* and *kouros*-like figures (e.g. the Blond Boy head) are not included in the Athenian Acropolis case study.

Table 2.2 *Reconstructed height and tonnage of statues from a) Ptoion Sanctuary b) Athenian Acropolis c) Delos. Additional information on date and marble type is included where available.*

Table 2.2a

ID	Name	Date (BC)	Marble	Reconstructed height (m)	Reconstructed tonnage (tonnes)
MARB PTOION 1	Thebes 714	600–590	White	2.3	1.55
MARB PTOION 2	Thebes (no number)	590	Blue	3.6	2.43
MARB PTOION 3	Thebes 713	580	Blue	3.39	2.29
MARB PTOION 4	Thebes (no number)	early C6	Naxian	3.79	2.56
MARB PTOION 5	Athens MN 70	580	Local	0.91	0.62
MARB PTOION 6	Athens MN	580	Local	2.36	1.59
MARB PTOION 7	Athens MN 15	580	Blue	2.06	1.39
MARB PTOION 8	Thebes 716	580	Blue	2.1	1.42
MARB PTOION 9	Thebes (no number)	570–560	White	1.7	1.15
MARB PTOION 10	Thebes (no number)	570–560	Blue	3.89	2.63
MARB PTOION 11	Thebes (no number)	560	White	0.83	0.56
MARB PTOION 12	Thebes 1	560–550	Local	2	1.35
MARB PTOION 13	Thebes (no number)	560–550	Blue	2.5	1.69
MARB PTOION 14	Thebes (no number)	560–550	Blue	2.32	1.57
MARB PTOION 15	Thebes (no number)	575–550	Blue	2.3	1.55
MARB PTOION 16	Thebes 732	575–550	Blue	1.5	1.01
MARB PTOION 17	Thebes (no number)	575–550	Blue	1.33	0.9
MARB PTOION 18	Thebes (no number)	575–550	White	1.27	0.86
MARB PTOION 19	Thebes 773 + 712	550	Yellow	2.65	1.79
MARB PTOION 20	Thebes (no number)	550	Local	1.59	1.07
MARB PTOION 21	Athens MN	550	Local	2.4	1.62
MARB PTOION 22	Thebes 747	550	Blue	1.81	1.22
MARB PTOION 23	Thebes (no number)	560	Naxian	1.39	0.94
MARB PTOION 24	Thebes (no number)	540	Blue	1.43	0.96

Table 2.2a (*cont.*)

ID	Name	Date (BC)	Marble	Reconstructed height (m)	Reconstructed tonnage (tonnes)
MARB PTOION 25	Thebes (no number)	540	Blue	1.19	0.8
MARB PTOION 26	Thebes 711	550	Blue	1	0.68
MARB PTOION 27	Thebes 651	550	Blue	6	4.05
MARB PTOION 28	Thebes 2	550	Blue	2	1.35
MARB PTOION 29	Thebes (no number)	550	Blue	1.12	0.75
MARB PTOION 30	Thebes (no number)	550	Pentellic	1	0.68
MARB PTOION 31	Thebes (no number)	550	Blue	3.47	2.34
MARB PTOION 32	Thebes (no number)	550	Parian	4.03	2.72
MARB PTOION 33	Thebes 715	540	Blue	2.56	1.73
MARB PTOION 34	Thebes (no number)	540	Parian	2.19	1.48
MARB PTOION 35	Thebes (no number)	540	Parian	1.63	1.1
MARB PTOION 36	Thebes (no number)	540	Blue	3.68	2.48
MARB PTOION 37	Thebes (no number)	540	Blue	3.26	2.2
MARB PTOION 38	Thebes (no number)	550	Naxian	2.6	1.76
MARB PTOION 39	Thebes 758	550	Naxian	3.64	2.46
MARB PTOION 40	Athens MN	550	Blue	1.79	1.21
MARB PTOION 41	Thebes 731 + 734	550	Blue	3.4	2.3
MARB PTOION 42	Thebes (no number)	550	Blue	1	0.68
MARB PTOION 43	Thebes (no number)	550	White	0.81	0.55
MARB PTOION 44	Thebes (no number)	550	Blue	2.38	1.61
MARB PTOION 45	Thebes (no number)	550	Parian	3.67	2.48
MARB PTOION 46	Thebes (no number)	550	Parian	2.33	1.58
MARB PTOION 47	Thebes 742	550	Parian	0.54	0.36
MARB PTOION 48	Athens MN 3059	550	Parian	2.6	1.76

Table 2.2a (*cont.*)

ID	Name	Date (BC)	Marble	Reconstructed height (m)	Reconstructed tonnage (tonnes)
MARB PTOION 49	Athens MN	560–540	Blue	1.5	1.01
MARB PTOION 50	Thebes (no number)	540	Blue	1.6	1.08
MARB PTOION 51	Thebes (no number)	540–530	Blue	1	0.68
MARB PTOION 52	Thebes (no number)	540	Blue	2	1.35
MARB PTOION 53	Thebes (no number)	540–520	Parian	2.36	1.59
MARB PTOION 54	Thebes 727	560–520	Blue	0.88	0.59
MARB PTOION 55	Thebes (no number)	530	Parian	0.82	0.56
MARB PTOION 56	Athens MN	600	Naxian	1.73	1.17
MARB PTOION 57	Thebes (no number)	600	Naxian	1.43	0.96
MARB PTOION 58	Thebes (no number)	550	Naxian	0.57	0.39
MARB PTOION 59	Athens MN 19	560–550	Island	1.24	0.83
MARB PTOION 60	Thebes (no number)	570–550	Parian	1.35	0.91
MARB PTOION 61	Thebes (no number)	550–540	Pentellic	0.88	0.6
MARB PTOION 62	Thebes (no number)	530	Parian	1.07	0.72
MARB PTOION 63	Thebes (no number)	520	Parian	1.24	0.83
MARB PTOION 64	Thebes 720	540–500	Parian	2.05	1.38
MARB PTOION 65	Thebes 15	540	Parian	1.1	0.74
MARB PTOION 66	Thebes (no number)	540	Parian	1.41	0.95
MARB PTOION 67	Athens MN 17	520–510	White	1.29	0.87
MARB PTOION 68	Athens MN 586	530–520	Parian	0.75	0.5
MARB PTOION 69	Athens MN 3453	520	Pentellic	1.04	0.7
MARB PTOION 70	Thebes 633 + 633a	500	Parian	1.02	0.69
MARB PTOION 71	Thebes 634	500	Parian	2.65	1.79
MARB PTOION 72	Thebes 14	570–550	Naxian	0.94	0.64
MARB PTOION 73	Athens MN 3452	540	Parian	1.26	0.85

Table 2.2a (*cont.*)

ID	Name	Date (BC)	Marble	Reconstructed height (m)	Reconstructed tonnage (tonnes)
MARB PTOION 74	Athens MN 16	540–520	Pentellic	1.44	0.97
MARB PTOION 75	Thebes (no number)	540–520	Parian	0.63	0.42
MARB PTOION 76	Athens MN 10	550	Naxian	1.75	1.18
MARB PTOION 77	Thebes (no number)	550	Naxian	0.71	0.48
MARB PTOION 78	Athens MN 2325	560	Naxian	2	1.35
MARB PTOION 79	Thebes (no number)	560	Naxian	6.39	4.31
MARB PTOION 80	Thebes (no number)	560	Naxian	1.75	1.18
MARB PTOION 81	Thebes (no number)	570–560	Naxian	1.93	1.3
MARB PTOION 82	Thebes (no number)	550	Naxian	1.43	0.96
MARB PTOION 83	Thebes (no number)	550	Naxian	1.18	0.8
MARB PTOION 84	Athens MN	550	Blue	3	2.03
MARB PTOION 85	Athens MN 11	550–540	Naxian	2.34	1.58
MARB PTOION 86	Thebes 3	550–540	Local	1.36	0.92
MARB PTOION 87	Thebes (no number)	550–540	Parian	2.86	1.93
MARB PTOION 88	Thebes (no number)	550	Naxian	2.5	1.69
MARB PTOION 89	Thebes (no number)	550	Naxian	1.81	1.22
MARB PTOION 90	Thebes 6	550–540	Naxian	4.5	3.04
MARB PTOION 91	Thebes 717	550–540	Naxian	2.08	1.41
MARB PTOION 92	Thebes 733	540	Parian	0.76	0.52
MARB PTOION 93	Athens MN	540–500	Naxian	1.24	0.83
MARB PTOION 94	Athens MN 69	540	Naxian	1.57	1.06
MARB PTOION 95	Thebes 5	540	Naxian	1.41	0.95
MARB PTOION 96	Thebes (no number)	540	Naxian	3.29	2.22
MARB PTOION 97	Thebes (no number)	540	Naxian	1.88	1.27
MARB PTOION 98	Thebes (no number)	550–540	Naxian	1.6	1.08

Table 2.2a (*cont.*)

ID	Name	Date (BC)	Marble	Reconstructed height (m)	Reconstructed tonnage (tonnes)
MARB PTOION 99	Thebes (no number)	550–540	Naxian	2.33	1.58
MARB PTOION 100	Thebes 757	550–540	Naxian	0.77	0.52
MARB PTOION 101	Thebes (no number)	550–540	Naxian	1.18	0.79
MARB PTOION 102	Thebes (no number)	550–540	Naxian	0.69	0.46
MARB PTOION 103	Thebes (no number)	550–540	Naxian	2.08	1.41
MARB PTOION 104	Thebes (no number)	550–540	Naxian	0.3	0.2
MARB PTOION 105	Thebes (no number)	550–540	Naxian	0.45	0.3
MARB PTOION 106	Thebes 759	550–540	Naxian	0.68	0.46
MARB PTOION 107	Thebes 753	550–540	Naxian	0.51	0.35
MARB PTOION 108	Thebes 4	530	Naxian	2.14	1.45
MARB PTOION 109	Thebes 799	530	Local	1.89	1.28
MARB PTOION 110	Thebes 746	530	Local	0.74	0.5
MARB PTOION 111	Thebes 754	530	Local	0.65	0.44
MARB PTOION 112	Athens MN 3451	530	Parian	1.62	1.09
MARB PTOION 113	Thebes (no number)	530	Parian	0.96	0.65
MARB PTOION 114	Thebes 737	530–520	Parian	1.53	1.03
MARB PTOION 115	Thebes (no number)		Parian	1.88	1.27
MARB PTOION 116	Athens MN 12	520	Parian	1.6	1.08
MARB PTOION 117	Athens MN 12A	530–520	White	3.1	2.09
MARB PTOION 118	Thebes (no number)	530–520	Parian	3.11	2.1
MARB PTOION 119	Thebes (no number)	520	White	2.64	1.78
MARB PTOION 120	Thebes 730	540–520	Parian	1.57	1.06
MARB PTOION 121	Athens MN 20	520–500	Parian	1.03	0.7
MARB PTOION 122	Thebes 739	520–500	Parian	3.89	2.63
MARB PTOION 123	Thebes (no number)	520–500	Parian	1	0.68
MARB PTOION 124	Thebes (no number)	520–500	Island	2.33	1.58
MARB PTOION 125	Thebes 736	520–500	Parian	1.14	0.77

Table 2.2a (*cont.*)

ID	Name	Date (BC)	Marble	Reconstructed height (m)	Reconstructed tonnage (tonnes)
MARB PTOION 126	Thebes (no number)	520–500	Parian	0.83	0.56
MARB PTOION 127	Thebes (no number)	520–500	Parian	2.5	1.69
MARB PTOION 128	Thebes 845	500–480	Parian	2	1.35
MARB PTOION 129	Athens MN	500–480	White	2.79	1.88
MARB PTOION 130	Athens MN	500–480	White	1.69	1.14
MARB PTOION 131	Thebes (no number)		Pentellic	1.12	0.75
MARB PTOION 132	Thebes (no number)		Parian	0.75	0.51
MARB PTOION 133	Thebes (no number)		Parian	0.82	0.55
MARB PTOION 134	Thebes (no number)		Parian	1.11	0.75
MARB PTOION 135	Thebes (no number)		Parian	1.29	0.87
MARB PTOION 136	Thebes (no number)		Blue	1.15	0.77
MARB PTOION 137	Thebes (no number)		Parian	0.83	0.56
MARB PTOION 138	Thebes (no number)		Parian	0.83	0.56
MARB PTOION 139	Thebes (no number)		Parian	0.71	0.48
MARB PTOION 140	Thebes (no number)		White	1.71	1.16
MARB PTOION 141	Thebes (no number)		Parian	0.93	0.63
MARB PTOION 142	Thebes (no number)		Parian	0.8	0.54
MARB PTOION 143	Thebes (no number)		Naxian	0.5	0.34
MARB PTOION 144	Thebes (no number)		Parian	0.61	0.41
MARB PTOION 145	Thebes (no number)		Pentellic	0.73	0.49
MARB PTOION 146	Thebes (no number)		Parian	0.77	0.52

Table 2.2a (*cont.*)

ID	Name	Date (BC)	Marble	Reconstructed height (m)	Reconstructed tonnage (tonnes)
MARB PTOION 147	Thebes (no number)		Island	0.55	0.37
MARB PTOION 148	Thebes (no number)		Naxian	1.04	0.7
MARB PTOION 149	Thebes (no number)		Parian	0.94	0.63
MARB PTOION 150	Thebes 740, 748		White	0.66	0.45

Table 2.2b

ID	Name	Date (BC)	Marble	Reconstructed height (m)	Reconstructed tonnage (tonnes)
MARB ATHENS 1	Akr.1360	510–500	Parian	2.05	1.38
MARB ATHENS 2	Akr.1361	530	Parian	0.66	0.44
MARB ATHENS 3	Akr.269/163/164	550–540	Attic	1.33	0.9
MARB ATHENS 4	Akr.3511	510–500		0.54	0.37
MARB ATHENS 5	Akr.582	570–560	Pentellic	1.33	0.89
MARB ATHENS 6	Akr.584	510–500	Parian	0.51	0.35
MARB ATHENS 7	Akr.585	540–530	Island	0.76	0.51
MARB ATHENS 8	Akr.589	570–560	Parian	0.64	0.43
MARB ATHENS 9	Akr.593	560–550	Attic	1.2	0.81
MARB ATHENS 10	Akr.594	500	Island	1.74	1.18
MARB ATHENS 11	Akr.595	500	Parian	1.4	0.95
MARB ATHENS 12	Akr.598	520	Island	0.69	0.46
MARB ATHENS 13	Akr.602	530	Island	0.94	0.64
MARB ATHENS 14	Akr.603	510–500	Island	1.11	0.75
MARB ATHENS 15	Akr.611	520	Parian	0.74	0.5
MARB ATHENS 16	Akr.612	520	Attic	0.4	0.27
MARB ATHENS 17	Akr.613	510–500	Island	1.17	0.79
MARB ATHENS 18	Akr.619	560–550	Naxian	1.75	1.18
MARB ATHENS 19	Akr.614	530–520		0.53	0.36
MARB ATHENS 20	Akr.626	540–530	Parian	1	0.68
MARB ATHENS 21	Akr.636	510	Parian	0.51	0.35
MARB ATHENS 22	Akr.639	520	Attic	0.55	0.37
MARB ATHENS 23	Akr.643/307	510	Parian	0.84	0.56
MARB ATHENS 24	Akr.645	520	Parian	0.84	0.56

Table 2.2b (cont.)

ID	Name	Date (BC)	Marble	Reconstructed height (m)	Reconstructed tonnage (tonnes)
MARB ATHENS 25	Akr.652	520	Parian	0.73	0.49
MARB ATHENS 26	Akr.654	550–540	Parian	0.69	0.46
MARB ATHENS 27	Akr.656	550–540	Island	0.31	0.21
MARB ATHENS 28	Akr.659	520–510	Parian	1.41	0.95
MARB ATHENS 29	Akr.662	500	Parian	1.06	0.71
MARB ATHENS 30	Akr.666	520–510	Island	0.38	0.26
MARB ATHENS 31	Akr.667	500	Pentellic	0.32	0.22
MARB ATHENS 32	Akr.668	500	Parian	0.32	0.21
MARB ATHENS 33	Akr.669	530	Parian	2	1.35
MARB ATHENS 34	Akr.670	520	Pentellic	1.34	0.91
MARB ATHENS 35	Akr.671	520	Pentellic	2.08	1.41
MARB ATHENS 36	Akr.672	525	Island	1.02	0.69
MARB ATHENS 37	Akr.673	520–510	Pentellic	1.07	0.72
MARB ATHENS 38	Akr.674	500	Parian	1.08	0.73
MARB ATHENS 39	Akr.675	510–500	Parian	0.64	0.43
MARB ATHENS 40	Akr.677	560–550	Naxian	1.53	1.03
MARB ATHENS 41	Akr.678	530	Parian	1.13	0.77
MARB ATHENS 42	Akr.679	530	Parian	1.18	0.8
MARB ATHENS 43	Akr.680	530–520	Island	1.34	0.91
MARB ATHENS 44	Akr.681	525	Island	2.01	1.36
MARB ATHENS 45	Akr.682	525	Island	1.82	1.23
MARB ATHENS 46	Akr.683	510		2.33	1.57
MARB ATHENS 47	Akr.696/493	500	Pentellic	0.92	0.62
MARB ATHENS 48	Akr.660	530	Parian	1.4	0.95
MARB ATHENS 49	Akr.681	525	Island	1.65	1.11

Table 2.2c

ID	Name	Date (BC)	Reconstructed height (m)	Reconstructed tonnage (tonnes)
MARB DELOS 1	Delos A333	600	2.43	1.64
MARB DELOS 2	Delos 4045	580	1.47	0.99
MARB DELOS 3	Delos A4051	550	2.17	1.47
MARB DELOS 4	Delos A4083	550	3.43	2.31
MARB DELOS 5	Delos A4048	550	2.86	1.93
MARB DELOS 6	Delos A1742	550	3.46	2.33
MARB DELOS 7	Delos A4047	530	2.66	1.79
MARB DELOS 8	Delos A1741	530	2.96	2
MARB DELOS 9	Delos A4084	500	1.43	0.96
MARB DELOS 10	Nikandre	630	1.75	1.18
MARB DELOS 11	Delos A4064	510	2.69	1.81

Table 2.2c (cont.)

ID	Name	Date (BC)	Reconstructed height (m)	Reconstructed tonnage (tonnes)
MARB DELOS 12	Delos A4067	510	1.02	0.69
MARB DELOS 13	Delos A4063	510	1.07	0.72
MARB DELOS 14	Delos 4089	545	1.43	0.97
MARB DELOS 15	Delos 4327	545	1.6	1.08
MARB DELOS 16	Delos 2464	635	1.6	1.08
MARB DELOS 17	Delos 3990	537	2.02	1.36
MARB DELOS 18	Delos 4112	562	2.06	1.39
MARB DELOS 19	Delos 4294	547	2.07	1.39
MARB DELOS 20	Delos 4114	567	2.18	1.47
MARB DELOS 21	Delos 4296	547	2.66	1.79
MARB DELOS 22	Delos	510	0.94	0.64
MARB DELOS 23	Delos 4113	520	1.71	1.15
MARB DELOS 24	Delos	530	1.74	1.18
MARB DELOS 25	Delos	540	2.11	1.43
MARB DELOS 26	Delos	550	2.18	1.47
MARB DELOS 27	Delos	560	2.76	1.86
MARB DELOS 28	Delos	570	3.33	2.25
MARB DELOS 29	Delos	580	4.67	3.15
MARB DELOS 30	Delos	590	5.78	3.9
MARB DELOS 31	Delos	600	3.75	2.53

sculptures used, such that it is possible to analyse the changes over time of the heights of the sculptures dedicated, and the marbles from which they were carved. Most of the *kouroi* from this sanctuary date from the mid-sixth century (560–530 BC) and are 3 m or less in height. The largest Ptoion *kouroi* (4–6 m), although few, are, in fact, all from the end of the century (in contrast to the pattern elsewhere where over life-size kouroi are early). There is some evidence, however, for changing trends in the marbles used at this site over time. Most of the *kouroi* dedicated at the start of the sixth century are made from blue marble, which was probably sourced locally and could be transported over short distances by land transport. In the middle of the century most of the marble used was Naxian. Overall, though, there was a great variety in source material used throughout this period. By the end of the sixth century, the marble of choice at Ptoion was Parian. There is perhaps some weak correlation between the type of marble used and the height of the figure carved, as the largest *kouroi* are made from Parian marble (and the number of *kouroi* of height 3–4 m is significantly higher in Parian than Naxian marble), while the Naxian marbles are used

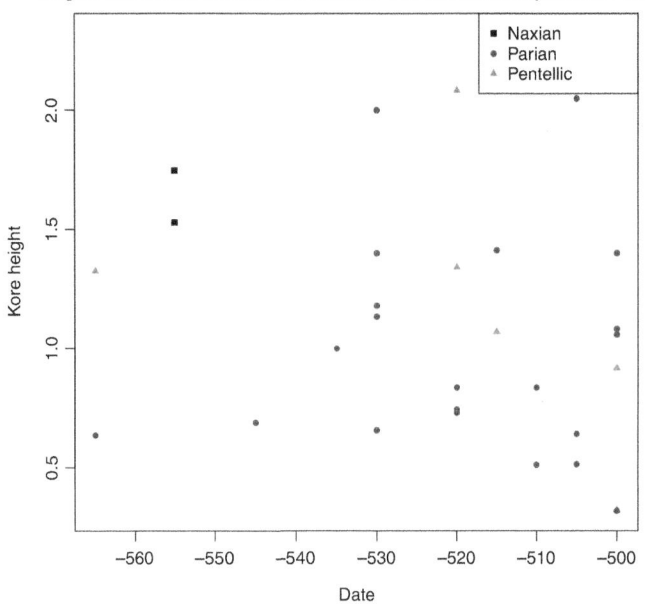

Figure 2.8 Heights and marble sources of *korai* from the Athenian Acropolis over time. The type of marble is indicated according to three top-level points of origin based on quarry location: Penteli (i.e. in Attica) or from one of the various Naxian or Parian quarries.

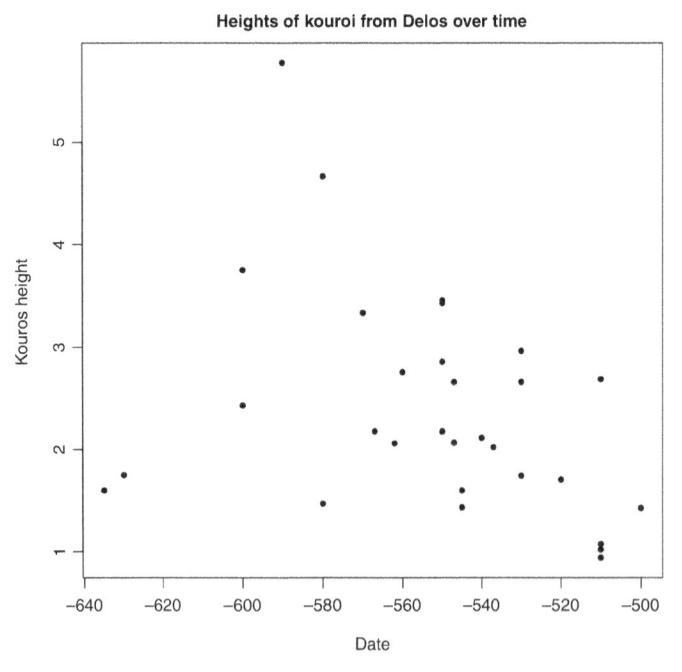

Figure 2.9 Heights of *kouroi* from Delos over time. No distinction is made between marbles originating in different places or of different stylistic groups, given that information was unavailable in the source catalogues.

Marble Statues as Products 57

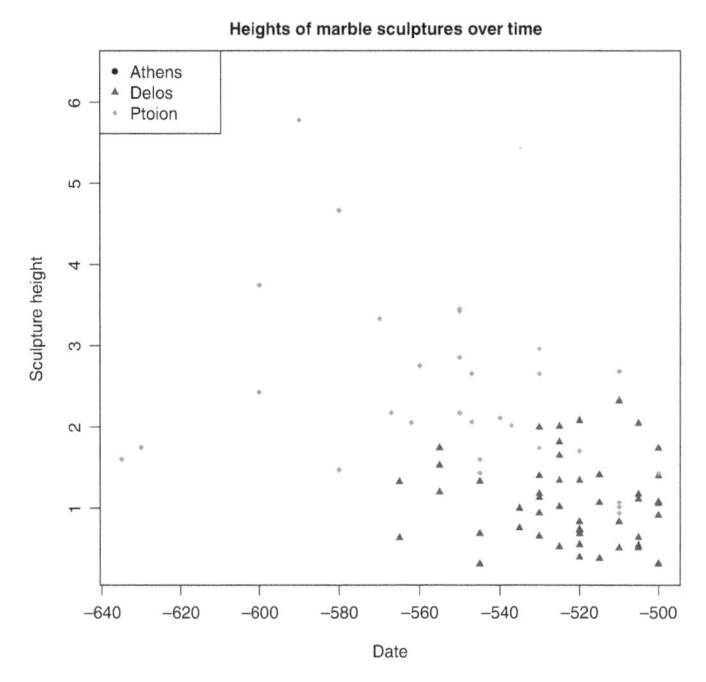

Figure 2.10 Heights of marble sculptures over time, from Athens, Delos, and Ptoion, distributed across time from 650 BC to 500 BC.

for shorter *kouroi*, including the less than life-size 'miniatures' of less than 1 m.

There are fewer datapoints available for Athens and for Delos, but there are still enough to discern both patterning and variation with regard to size and chronology. The main production period for the *korai* dedicated at Athens was between 530–500 BC for sculptures made principally from Parian marble and generally in the range of 0.5–1.5 m. There is no discernible connection between the type of marble (or its localness), and the size or date of the *korai*. In general, this dataset demonstrates that there was a short-term impetus to dedicate *korai*, and that the raw marble used to meet this demand was sourced from the islands. At Delos, by contrast, there is evidence of a changing preference for statues of different heights over time. Throughout the sixth century, sculptors produced smaller statues, and after the mid-sixth century there is no evidence for monumental freestanding sculpture: indeed, between 540–500 the range of statue heights is quite consistently narrow at 1–3 m. In terms of demand, 590–530 BC represents the greatest activity at the site for dedicating sculptures, and both earlier and later than these dates there is less evidence for freestanding sculpture. The resolution of the data is such that we cannot discuss the various source quarries for the Delian statues.

In putting these data side-by-side, three general patterns emerge. First, the size of sculptures became progressively smaller over time; second, there was in parallel an increase in the discrete number of statues constructed towards the end of the sixth century;[14] third, there was a preference later in the sixth century for Parian over Naxian marble. And although it is insufficient to offer monocausal or deterministic views that account for all of these changes, it *is* worth noting that these three patterns together support the narrative offered above that material-status entanglements experienced some 'ramping up' throughout the sixth century BC.

This narrative does not negate issues of quality, however. One might even be inclined to assume, based on the present data, that there was a general trend in the latter part of the sixth century to use in place of Naxian marble a more 'luxurious' Parian marble.[15] Certainly during later periods of antiquity, Parian marble was recognised as the best sort of marble one could get for freestanding marble statues (Pliny 36.4–6). Perhaps, then, even in the Archaic period, Parian marble had already attained this reputation, considering that statues made from this material were consumed all over the Greek and Mediterranean world, from Magna Graecia in the west (Richter 171, MARB 125), to Anatolia in the east (Richter 165, MARB 119); and from the Thasos in the north (Richter 14), to Cyrene in the south (Richter 168, MARB 122). If communities had to find new ways to deploy material culture in competing for status, they might choose to focus their efforts on these more highly regarded materials. It is not completely impossible that quality was on the agenda of those commissioning statues, and so it is possible that consideration was given not only to the action of creating and erecting a statue, but also to the appearance and quality of the product created. My discussion will return to this point in considering the role of the artist, but for now it seems sufficient to suggest that the pattern of the dataset is consistent with an acceleration in aspirational elites' competition for social status over time.

---

[14] Or, at least, there is a greater number of statues that *survive* to us from the end of the century than from the beginning.

[15] This could quite easily be a pattern of supply rather than a pattern of demand, discussed more fully below.

Marble Statues as Heavy Freight

Having established the pattern of the general marble statue distribution, the more crucial thing now is to situate that dataset within a production process from point of origin to point of consumption.

Both archaeological and historical evidence inform us of the process by which marble was mined and transported. Clearly, the first step was to identify a suitable marble quarry (Fig. 2.11). Modern geological maps indicate that the Aegean has an abundant supply of raw marble (Fig. 2.12), many stones of which are tinged with veins of different colours (Lepsius 2012 [1890], *contra* Renfrew and Peacey 1968; Lazzarini 2004).[16] Not every one of these marble sources was mined or was even known in antiquity (*cf.* Russell 2013: 68ff.; Kokkorou-Alevras et al. 2014; Russell 2017), and the marble quarries most familiar to the historian of Archaic

Figure 2.11 Marathi marble quarries from the island of Paros. Photograph by author.

---

[16] For intra-island varieties of marble, see Germann et al. 1988

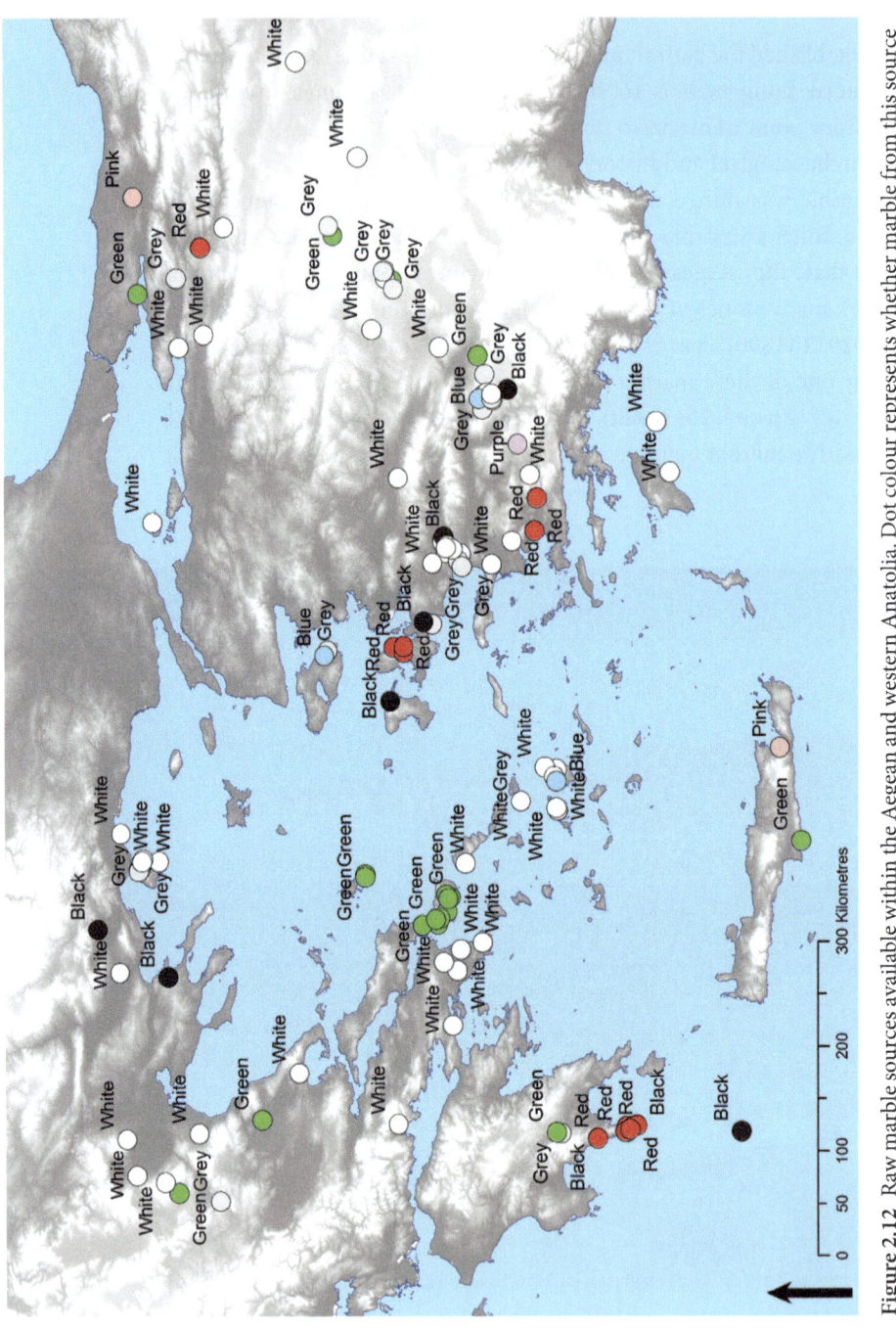

Figure 2.12 Raw marble sources available within the Aegean and western Anatolia. Dot colour represents whether marble from this source has certain colour-tinges in its quality. This graphic has been produced from the marble database of Ben Russell, available on the OxRep website, http://oxrep.classics.ox.ac.uk/databases/stone_quarries_database

and Classical Greece are at Mt Penteli in Attica, and on the islands of Naxos, Paros and Thasos. Even on the same island the quality of the marble could differ (Herz 2010) and be exploited in varying intensities throughout antiquity as fashions and availability changed. Recent evidence from Paros suggests that the mass mining of marble as a raw product began even before the middle of the seventh century BC (Schilardi 2010a).

The process of carving marble is known to us from a variety of sources.[17] The physical layout of caves provides a 'footprint' for the area quarried, suggesting that while the most efficient method of obtaining marble was an opencast technique, vertical strata were frequently dug into hill slopes or caves to 'test' the stone for its quality before bringing out as much opencast as possible and then moving into underground methods (Korres 1995: 78–83; Korres 2010; Schilardi 2010a,). Tool marks found on stones within the caves provide further information on the *chaîne opératoire* of shaping and dressing marble blocks *in situ* (Korres 1995: 76–7, Korres 2010), while the existence of various 'unfinished' pieces suggests that not just crude blocks but statues were roughed out in their most basic shape in quarries (Boardman 1978: 23; Rolley 1994: 165–7; Kokkorou-Alevras 1995: 37–130; Schilardi 2010b). Modern comparisons help to make more tangible certain parts of the process: work continued at the Marathi quarries of Paros by the Belgians in the nineteenth century demonstrated how, through the construction of 'test corridors' the best marbles in the area could be identified (Kordellas 1884).[18] Between locating a suitable source of marble, testing the area, exposing marble veins, and then selecting, sawing roughly, refining the sawing, polishing and shaping, it is evident that a vast amount of work was invested in a marble block before it even left the quarry.

The next step was to move marble blocks from the point of origin to the point of consumption. As has been noted above, many of the marbles commonly used in the Archaic period came from islands but were consumed elsewhere; and so it was necessary to get stone down to the coast for overseas transport. From the quarry, it was required either to roll on rollers (*cf.* Rankov 2013) or to hoist onto a cart and transport via road (Korres 1995: 100–4). Many of these roads are known only fragmentarily or have received only very general descriptions in (non-contemporary) text (Pausanias 1.32, 1.39; see a summary of the evidence in Korres and Tomlinson 2002 on the *Sphettia Hodos* in Attica). But the very fact that

---

[17] For a recent, thorough and convincing suggestion on the *chaîne opératoire* of marble statue production, see Phillips 2021: 322–4.
[18] *cf.* discussion of labour at quarry sites in Russell and Wootton 2015; Russell 2017.

marble was transported long distances is enough to justify assuming that such infrastructure was in place – even if we do not have full knowledge of it. Marble blocks would have required either cranes or similar for lifting, a technology which, although originally thought to have been developed in Greece only in the late sixth century (Roebuck 1955b: 156; Coulton 1975: 271; Rhodes 1987: 550ff.), more recent research has suggested were in use (in a rudimentary form) from the middle of the seventh century (Hemans 2015: 45–9; Pierattini 2019).

The order of magnitude for this production process can be reconstructed, to some extent. This reconstruction is critical for advancing the general narrative to the idea of an 'economy'. And to engage with this issue, it is necessary to work from the heights of statues reconstructed above to the tonnage of the marble blocks from which they were produced. As discussed, scholars are generally agreed that both *kouroi* and *korai* were carved in the round (Guralnick 1978, 1981; Robins 1994; Carter and Steinberg 2010),[19] and formed from single cuboid blocks of stone worked continually from all sides by the sculptor. Therefore, to reconstruct the size of the original marble block from a full-height surviving statue is relatively straightforward (particularly if a plinth survives): one measures the area of the statue base block and multiplies up by the full height of the statue.[20] To reduce error in these calculations – that is, to allow for the fact that a slightly larger block of marble might be used to sculpt a slightly smaller statue, or to compensate for the fact that these are fairly simplistic calculations which, although in a correct ballpark of accuracy, are by no means precise – parametric calculations can be used: buffering input values, computing each calculation 1,000 times from the sampled values, and taking a median average (Table 2.3a–b).

Running the calculation described across the whole *kouros* and *kore* dataset (and using the height values for statues reconstructed earlier in this chapter), one arrives at a value for the total volume of raw marble required to sculpt all the surviving *kouros* and *kore* statues. For each statue there is a distribution of output datapoints (the result of the parametric calculations), but taking the median values suggests that there was a total of at least 334m^3 marble mined for the purposes of statue production in the Archaic period. Multiplying this by the standard density of marble (2.7 metric

---

[19] For a later testament that artists in previous times used the Egyptian canon in sculpting, see Diodorus Siculus 1.98 on the story of Telekles and Theodoros.
[20] The plinth and the main sculpture were often carved from two separate pieces of marble; but this calculation, nevertheless, gives a good ballpark estimate for the height (and therefore volume and weight) of the sculptural block, by using the base block.

Table 2.3 *Estimate for the total marble tonnage in freestanding statue record a) organised by place of consumption b) organised by place of production.*

Table 2.3a

Site	Estimate for marble tonnage in freestanding statue record
Aegina	9.96
Aigiai	1.97
Akarnania	3.86
Amorgos	2.09
Anafi	1.26
Anatolia	2.38
Anavyssos	1.31
Andros	3.53
Antiparos	1.08
Athens	104.95
Attica	9.16
Boeotia	0.96
Chios	9.63
Chrysapha	0.59
Delos	71.58
Delphi	21.52
Didyma	48.85
Eleusis	4.59
Ephesos	3.25
Epidauros	1.35
Eretria	2.57
Erythrai	5.04
Euboea	3.72
Eutresis	2.35
Gortyna	1.25
Halikarnassos	0.95
Islands	0.56
Isthmia	6.4
Kalymnos	0.87
Kamiros	9.5
Keos	1.69
Keratea	4.39
Klaros	10.06

Table 2.3a (cont.)

Site	Estimate for marble tonnage in freestanding statue record
Klazomenai	2.31
Knidos	1.05
Korkyra	2.36
Laurion	1.02
Lepreon	0.71
Lindos	1.29
Markopoulo	0.58
Megara	3.01
Melos	2.27
Merenda	1.19
Mesogeia	5.03
Miletos	16.68
Myrrhinous	1.28
Naxos	269.93
New Phaleron	0.88
Olympia	0.3
Orchomenos	1.49
Paros	49.01
Pheia	1.08
Phigaleia	2.02
Ptoion Sanctuary	28.47
Rhodes	7.97
Samos	92.92
Samothrace	1.23
Sardes	2.7
Siphnos	0.81
Sounion	16.71
Tanagra	0.41
Tenea	1.1
Thasos	12.61
Thera	13.39
Thrace	2.4
Torkoleka	1.08
Trikorgon	0.91
Volomandra	1.21
Vourva	1.82

Table 2.3b

Marble type	Estimate for marble tonnage in freestanding statue record
Boeotian	12.09
Chian	1.01
Grey	32.68
Island	118.78
Naxian	48.39
Orchomenos	2.45
Parian	86.12
Pentellic	13.61
Samian	0.98
Thasian	6.49
Unknown	579.63
White	12.28

tonnes per cubic metre) renders a value of 902 tonnes of raw marble required to sculpt the surviving statues.

These calculations are based on data for the whole Archaic period, but it is important to know what this meant for the ancient economy year-by-year. Snodgrass (1983: 228) estimated that the surviving sculpture record has within it only about 1 per cent of the total sculpture that was once made in the Archaic period. As there is no serious reason to suggest that this figure is within the wrong order of magnitude, it provides a ballpark against which other calculations can be scaled. If the tonnage figure calculated above corresponds to 1 per cent of the original sculptures that were once carved, we might estimate that something like 90,000 tonnes of marble was quarried for the purposes of freestanding sculpture throughout the whole period 650–500 BC.[21] Distributed across 150 years of activity, this would suggest that around 600 tonnes of marble were quarried *per annum* for sculpture alone.

How does this figure compare to the ballpark figure proposed by Anthony Snodgrass? Crucially, this is over 200 per cent greater than Snodgrass' estimate. His figure for annual exploitation of raw marble was 270 imperial tons, roughly equivalent to 245 metric tonnes. However, one must also remember that an average figure like this simplifies the situation

---

[21] Note that there is very little use of marble in freestanding sculpture before 650 BC, so calculations are made for an average output across the most productive 150 years of the Archaic period.

dramatically. Uncertainties of all sorts – environmental and weather related, regional demands and preferences, availability of workforce – would necessarily mean that some areas of the Aegean would variously exploit more or less marble at certain times throughout the Archaic period: but it is still a useful thought-experiment to have this measure of scale in mind.

Having moved marble to the coast and loaded it onto a boat,[22] the next step was to take the cargo overseas. The fifty oared *pentekonter* was, according to literary testimony, the most likely ship for undertaking such a journey (Herodotos I 163.1–2; *cf.* Casson 1995: 63; Gabrielsen 2010: 25). According to Thucydides (I 13), the first *pentekonter* was constructed by the Corinthians for the Samians around the start of the seventh century, and so the chronology is about right for the beginning of marble shipping in the mid-seventh century. Nor should we be concerned that the *pentekonter* is known in later periods of Greek history as a warship. It is likely that the distinction between warship and merchant ship did not exist until the late sixth century (Wallinga 1993: 39; Van de Moortel and Langdon 2017: 383–4), and that an oared longship would be used to carry freight. On the one hand a longship would be less efficient than a specifically built roundship (Hesiod *Works and Days*: 618–93) and there would be need for internal scaffolding and careful packing to most safely and efficiently load the marble product; but on the other hand, what the *pentekonter* had as an advantage over a merchant ship was manoeuvrability, particularly useful if one encounters *en route* pirates or other unfriendly actors (*cf.* Thucydides 1 4ff.; Osborne 1987: 34ff.; Halstead and Jones 1989; Morton 2001: 176–7).

Archaeological evidence suggests that the dimensions of the ship were in the region of 26 m x 2.2 m x 1.2 m, on the basis of the *Schifffundament* found by the German excavators on Samos (Walter and Vierneisel 1959). No shipwrecks of *pentekonters* loaded with cargo have been found for the Archaic period, and so any calculation of the carrying capacity of these ships must be made on a comparative basis. The closest parallel on which we might draw is the Pabuç Burnu shipwreck with its 10–12 m hull, found in the east part of the Aegean off the coast of Halikarnassos and dated by its

---

[22] This is another step whose details are relatively obscure, but a process which must necessarily have taken place. (Coulton 1974: 17; Hochscheid 2015: 139–41). A series of more than 250 channels around the coastline of Paros were at one time thought to have been used in the mooring of boats for the loading of marble; but recent geomorphological research (in particular regarding the rise in sea-level) now most likely points to an agricultural use of the channels (see various articles in Katsanopoulou 2021).

cargo to the sixth century (Greene, Lawall and Polzer 2008). Although not a *pentekonter* (whose hull was more likely 22–6 m), this ship was, at the time it sank, carrying cargo comprising 200 *amphoras* from various eastern Aegean workshops and other smaller fineware pottery.[23] Indeed, this load tells us two things about the shipment of cargo in the Archaic period: that *amphoras* took up most of the space within a shipment; and that cargoes were mixed (*cf.* Ikeguchi 2004). If a ship such as this with a hull half the length could carry 200 *amphoras*, on the principle of scaling up we might expect that the *pentekonter* could carry 400 *amphoras*, and that if a full *amphora* had a mean weight of 30 kg then the carrying capacity of the whole ship was around 12 tonnes (*cf.* estimates made by Coates 1989 and Hadjidaki 1996a).

This is not to say that when shipping marble each *pentekonter* was loaded with 12 tonnes of stone. In fact, it is completely reasonable to suggest that marble would only ever have comprised a small load of a total shipment – perhaps one *kouros* unit at the very most. Apart from any other reason, the density of marble is an issue. Twelve tonnes of marble would be the equivalent of just under 4.5m^3 of raw stone, and unless this stone were cut up into much smaller blocks (i.e. rendering it useless for sculpting monumental statues) this cargo would only occupy a small part of the ship's floorspace. Surely traders would have wanted to use as much of the available area of ships as possible for loading (mixed) cargoes, and a cargo comprising solely marble blocks would therefore 'waste' much of the available shipping space. 'Mixed' cargoes make more economic sense, as small portable things like *amphoras* could be traded *en route* when ships made their various stopovers (Demosthenes 35.10–4; *cf.* Osborne 1996b). It is possible, therefore, that no more than about a quarter of a *pentekonter*'s total shipment would have been marble, with each ship carrying at a maximum three tonnes of stone. This is not a completely arbitrary guess. There is no evidence for a mass production of marble statues, and in fact it seems rather more likely that these things were made to order. There is little reason to believe that more than one statue at a time would be loaded on to a ship; and one might estimate that the 'standard' quantity of marble on mixed cargoes was around the average weight of a single *kouros* or *kore* unit, which falls around the 3 tonne mark. Dividing the total estimate marble tonnage by the estimate for shipping capacity, it follows that of all ships circulating the Aegean, 200 or so

---

[23] Hadjidaki 1996b discusses the varying carrying capacity of ships in the later fifth century, which increased significantly between the start and end of the century. The Phragou shipwreck of the early fifth century could carry 1,500 *amphoras*, while the Alonnesos shipwreck of the late fifth century has an estimated carrying capacity of 4,000 *amphoras*.

per year were also partially engaged with the transport of heavy marble. This is a huge number of ships suggestive of a hyper-mobile Aegean zone; but before returning more fully to the issue of scale, it is necessary to continue in the narrative of the shipping process.

Within the Aegean, ships stayed relatively close to the coastline (*cf.* Horden and Purcell 2000: 123–72, 342–4; Morton 2001: 143ff.). This made good use of over 1,550 harbours and less formal anchorages within the Basin.[24] Sailing in this way allowed ships to move quickly towards shelter if the weather suddenly changed (Schumacher 1993; Mylonopoulos 2006; Papageorgiou 2008; Kowalzig 2018), and it also kept one away from the open waters where pirates tended to sail. There were also risks associated with coastal sailing (rocky shoals and headland winds for one, something that both artists and poets reflected on in the frequency of shipwreck imagery, Hesiod *Works and Days*: 621, 625, 634, and 665–6 and Semonides 1) but ships that regularly sailed these routes would surely have become more familiar with the danger spots and known better how to handle them.[25] The dangers of sailing close to the shore must have outweighed the weather- and pirate-related dangers of sailing further from the land, and it was a balance of risks: if the marble that was being shipped was indeed a 'luxury' cargo (and given that, as shown above, there was a significant time investment in preparing marble blocks, making them 'expensive' products in terms of labour-hours), it was important to sail in a way to avoid risking any ill befalling the load.

Therefore, it seems likely that ships sailed between anchorage nodes, avoiding open seas. This is consistent with the few literary accounts of sea voyages that survive to us from antiquity. The *Periplus* of Ps.-Scylax dated to the fourth century BC (but perhaps referring back to routes first taken in the sixth century, Shipley 2002: 6–8) describes, in part, routes to take between the west and east parts of the Aegean (*Periplus* 48, 58). The author advises taking short trips and 'hopping' between the islands, along the north coasts of Kythnos, Syros, Mykonos, Ikaria and Samos, or taking a route along the north coast of Crete. Although writing four centuries later, Strabo advises taking a similar route (*Geography* 10.5), going via Kythnos and Syros, and again in the second century AD the otherwise

---

[24] Few harbours dating securely to use within the Archaic period have been found; see Blackman et al. 2013 on Abdera (270–6), Corcyra (319–34), the Zea Harbour at Piraeus (420–88) and Thasos (542–54). Mooring at any beach or shore would have been possible, *cf.* Rankov 2013: 102–7.

[25] Knowledge, planning and expertise as part of risk management strategies will be discussed further.

anonymous *Stadiasmus Maris Magni* advises travelling in short hops via Melos, Kimolos, Ios and Amorgos (273–83). In these later centuries the shipping technology would have been more developed, but the dangers from unpredictable weather systems would have remained. It is interesting, therefore, to note that the strategy of taking short trips between anchorages *persisted*, presumably as one of the most effective means of mitigating the risks of sailing.

It should also be noted that these voyages likely took a great deal of time. As a benchmark for Aegean sailing times in the middle of the Classical period, the reconstruction ship built on the design of the Kyrenia shipwreck (Cariolou 1997) took eighty hours over twenty-five days to move from Athens to Rhodes, unable to travel on all consecutive days owing to weather conditions (Katzev 1990). Although some journeys between marble source and destination were shorter than the Athens to Rhodes route (e.g. more simply between Paros and Athens), the shipping technology of the Archaic period, as discussed, was more primitive, and the volume of text extant noting the dangers of sailing would certainly suggest that these little ships were subject to the elements and other risks such that they had to take as many if not more stops (i.e. journeys in the Archaic period would take as long if not longer than in the Classical period). Quite possibly, it would take weeks or even a month to move stone from point of origin to point of consumption – longer if the marble was destined to go outside the Aegean.

Once the marble arrived at its point of consumption, work would be completed by sculptors. The aesthetics and materiality of the statues were entangled with the nature of the economic network. This shows up clearly in the use of imported stones when local stones were available. If sanctuaries such as those on Thasos and at Ptoion imported large quantities of non-local marble, even though they had large reserves of local stone nearby, there must have been something about these 'foreign' marbles that made them preferable. Were stones imported because they made the statue product look in some way different to local products? Different marbles from around the Aegean were certainly tinted with veins of different colours, but there is no compelling case that it was down to colour alone that different stones might be imported (*cf.* Russell 2013: 12–16). In the first instance, apart from the bluish streaks in the Boeotian marble and the slight yellow tint in Parian stone, all marbles quarried in the Archaic period were similar enough as brilliant white or whitish-grey stone that selection on the basis of colour seems implausible. More crucially, though, these sculptures would have been painted polychrome, and the colour of the base marble would have in any case not been seen. A more likely alternative is that the selection process had something to do with the quality of the marble. The differing grain size of marbles from various parts of the Aegean renders the stone harder or softer (Attanasio 2003), and the stones would have responded variously to different tools. Nevertheless, material quality alone seems to be a fairly weak reason on its own for understanding why so many marbles were moved overseas at this time.

This rather lengthy exposition of the marble statue process from quarry to sanctuary brings to our attention two key points. The first is that this *chaîne opératoire* of taking marble from its quarry to its destination was complex and would have required large workforces and a degree of forward-planning. This was a multi-step sequence where one part depended quite heavily on another, a system that constituted economic activity that brought together a network of different people and linked together different corners of the Aegean basin. Numbers suggest that this economic activity operated at quite a large and broad scale, so great that we might readily refer to this sort of activity as an *economy* of marble statues. But even though scale and numbers have been discussed here, in order to settle on the notion (or not) of an economy it is necessary to think also more explicitly about geography.

The second key point is that if we are satisfied with referring to this sort of activity as economic activity, there is compelling evidence that the marble economy was a socially embedded economy. The desires and aspirations of a few elite peers drove the process of statue creation and shipment. Although not a *completely* systematised economy, the deployment of marble statues involved more than just a few examples here and there: numbers indicate that this was a large enough process to talk of a network that brought together the desires of elites with craftspeople, artists and those in charge of shipping. Driven by that drive for status and competition, all these economic processes can be regarded as motivated through socio-cultural activity, the makings of an embedded economy – and one that was operating at a fairly large scale.

Modelling Heavy Freight Sea Journeys

Going beyond a simple narrative, it is possible to visualise and to model conjectured shipping routes between these points if one assumes certain things about how marble was shipped.[26] Ships sailed short distances between formally designated harbours or informal anchorages, making

---

[26] The following adapts and extends a discussion printed in Loy 2021.

several stops to break up long journeys, to offload and to pick up cargo, or to shelter from adverse weather conditions. If we want to take a macro-view of shipping routes, we might, then, want to establish this as a 'rule' by which we expect ships to travel: ships went the most direct route from point of marble source to point of *kouros* or *kore* consumption via stops at the nearest anchorages, always staying as close as possible to coastlines.

This sort of movement through a network of anchorages and their neighbours can be represented generally by a Proximal Point Analysis (PPA). PPA is a model that has received substantial recent attention from scholars of Greek antiquity (Davis 1982; Broodbank 2000; Knappett, Evans and Rivers 2008) and is now widely understood. It is a system that models a navigable space as a network of nodes connected to their neighbours, and through which the distance travelled between a start and end point is via a series of nearest neighbour nodes (*cf.* Evans, Rivers and Knappett 2012: 6–8; Loy 2019: 378–80). As with all models, there are limitations and simplifications, but if we want to explore a '*general* rule' as discussed, a *general* model is a good place to start.

Modelling maritime navigation in this way makes a number of assumptions. First, there is the assumption that ships always took the most direct routes from source to destination once they were loaded with marble cargo. Even if cargo was mixed and some other commodities were destined for alternative destinations, PPA assumes that the shipping of marble to its final destination took priority over this other cargo. Second, it is also taken for granted that ships always navigated to the nearest anchorages. Both weather-related and pirate-related factors make this unlikely; however, at the most zoomed-out 'macro view' of the Aegean, one might choose to smooth over these occasional divergences. Third, there is an assumption that these routes between the sites of statue production and statue consumption would be 'fixed' and subject somewhat more to the rules of a macro-system than to the agency of sailors and traders. Although it is possible that certain routes could become 'familiar' if they were travelled more frequently by a greater number of sailors, paths were not fixed, and individuals could choose, or be forced, to deviate from the 'usual' path for any number of cultural, economic, political or social reasons.

Most crucial is the assumption that all parts of the Aegean were as physically accessible as one another. This is particularly an issue concerning passage between the Cyclades and western Greece: unless one goes the 'long-way' around the coast of the Peloponnese, it is necessary to cross the small land-bridge between the Saronic and Corinthian Gulfs. Clearly, this would then necessitate moving the load (or the ship) from the Saronic Gulf up the *isthmus*. If this was a difficult procedure that took a long time, PPA might not be the most suitable model to use: much more effort would have been required to move marble between nodes on either side of the isthmus than between, for example, two other nodes in the middle of the Aegean Sea where one might more simply (and quickly) sail.

This is *not* an issue, however, if we accept that there was infrastructure in place in the sixth century to make the journey between the Cyclades and western Greece an efficient and easily navigable one. Various scholars have suggested that the Corinthian *diolkos* could have fulfilled such a role, being the paved roadway six kilometres in length connecting the Saronic Gulf to the Corinthian Gulf. Excavated between 1956–1959 (Verdelis 1958, 1959, 1966a, 1966b), the *diolkos* joined the two gulfs in three main sections of large limestone blocks, and it could have been used as a platform over which to convey marble units. Moreover, the chronology seems to fit: the presence of masons' marks on the *diolkos* stones resembling archaic period letter shapes suggests that the road was first constructed in the late seventh or early sixth century BC (Werner 1997: 103–5), that is, around the same time as the mass export of marble statues across the Aegean basin. Furthermore, it is not just a matter of chronology but also of practicality: grooves cut in to the limestone blocks of the *diolkos* could indicate that wheeled carts were intended to go up this road – those carrying heavy loads such as *kouroi* and *korai* (Cook 1979; MacDonald 1986). It is possible, then, that the paved roadway was regularly used to move some of this freight between the Saronic and Corinthian Gulf. If one accepts the possibility of moving freight in this way at this time, PPA does not need to be altogether abandoned: there were means of navigating here with relatively low labour costs or time investments, in other words, a route over the *isthmus* of Corinth was still as *efficient* a route for moving around the Aegean as going from harbour to harbour.

Bearing the above limitations and abstractions in mind, PPA is a suitable means for visualising some of the possible route networks between places of marble production and consumption. It effectively models a scenario in which heavy freight was carried by a rowed ship from points of production to points of consumption, taking the most direct coastal route via a series of intermediary stops at various anchorages. In the following discussion a PPA was used. It was built as a network model in Gephi with anchorages around the Aegean visualised as nodes and where each node was tied to its three nearest neighbours. Anchorages are used for the base unit of analysis here rather than formal harbours, as our knowledge of ancient harbours is undoubtedly incomplete.

'Source' and 'target' nodes were chosen to represent the places of marble statue production and consumption for the same set of statues discussed. Secure provenance information was not available for some objects, and so the dataset was reduced to 207 sculptures. Statues whose provenance has been recorded in the source catalogues as 'island marble' have been analysed where 50 per cent of these datapoints (randomly chosen) have been reclassified as Naxian marble, and 50 per cent as Parian.

Using nearest neighbour analysis in the network model, a 'suggested' route was calculated as the most direct route between source and target nodes for each marble sculpture. These route lines were then collated and weighted in terms of the relative quantities of marble which were transported along each route (i.e. the tonnage of marble taken from one specific quarry to another specific sanctuary as a proportion of all the marble which would have been moved around the Aegean).

Before analysing the results of the PPA modelling, a note first on the nature of the graphs generated. It is most productive to concentrate not on the individual lines themselves but on the general corridors that cut across the Aegean. Route lines are somewhat reductive (Wilkinson 2014: 96–9; Wilkinson and Slawisch in press), and they cannot represent the human-agency and decision-making involved that determined the *actual* routes that people took when going on these journeys. Routes are never purely environmentally determined, but shaped by social, cultural, economic, political and even *climatic* and *weather* factors (*cf.* Medas 2005; Whitewright 2011; Beresford 2013; Leidwanger 2013; Simmons 2014). Even if two ships with very similar cargoes set off at the same time from the same point of origin (e.g. Paros) destined for the same end point (e.g. Athens) we cannot assume that they would have followed largely similar routes. It is much better to see the accumulation of lines as *corridors of probability* along which ships in trade were *more likely* to travel (*cf.* Bell, Wilson and Wickham, 2013; Bicho, Cascalheira and Gonçalves, 2017), if they were going *directly* between two points.[27] Moreover, these corridors might in fact be *route fragments*, only sections of much longer journeys taken across the Aegean, and ones that just happen to be the most

---

[27] Our confidence in these corridors of probability can be related back to the data. The more marble we observe that must have gone between two sites, the more certain we can be that there were routes used that connected these two places. The images generated are based on the empirical data, and so if *a greater number* of route lines appear *with greater weight*, then we might have greater confidence in assuming this part of the Aegean had a corridor that was actually used.

archaeologically visible sections of the journey, documented by robust and ubiquitous pottery.[28]

Does this notion map onto an historical reality? It was certainly the case that, as has been discussed, owing to both the length of time required for sailing long distances and the unpredictability of the weather, there would have been a necessity for many stops along the way. At these stopover points, objects could be traded and exchanged (Herodotus 4.196) even at places that only constituted informal or unofficial trading posts (Demetriou 2011, 2012). Ships and anchorages were presumably well equipped with infrastructure for loading and unloading cargo (Coulton 1974: 17), such that making intermediary stops would not affect the efficiency of a much longer journey.[29] Many of these stops would have been random and circumstantial, and they cannot be encapsulated so easily by the environmentally deterministic route lines drawn.

Bearing such limitations in mind, a visualisation for the modelled transportation network of marble shipment has therefore been produced (Fig. 2.13, Table 2.4), which enables a few comments to be offered on the connectedness of various parts of the Aegean. One can identify here four main corridors of movement for the shipment of marble, all of which originate in the Cyclades. In order of increasing intensity of activity, these routes ran via the Dodecanese, through the Ikarian Sea, along the Euboean straits, and into the Saronic Gulf. What all four corridors have in common, is that they indicate the most efficient route for sailing from the main marble quarries on Naxos and Paros to points of *kouros* consumption involve getting out of the Cyclades as quickly as possible.

This model suggests that, although these are the main *corridors* of movement, the actual shipping lane out of the Cyclades depends on whether one originates in Naxos or Paros. High volumes of Naxian marble were imported east, particularly to Samos and Rhodes – and indeed more Naxian marble was used in the freestanding sculpture of the eastern Aegean than stone from any other source. By contrast, Paros exported marble to a greater number of

---

[28] For route fragments that cut through the Aegean *en route* to and from Al Mina with supporting ceramic evidence, see Forsyth 2021: 511.

[29] It is important to consider here the evidence that shipwrecks provide for cabotage. Of the few but increasing number of shipwrecks identified for the Archaic period, the cargoes were mainly mixed, both in terms of the diversity of material types (pottery loaded alongside metals, textiles stone) and of the provenance of these materials. For the recently discovered Fournoi shipwrecks, for instance (Campbell and Koutsouflakis 2021: 281–4), three of the shipwrecks found originating in the Archaic period (13, 37, 39) have cargoes of mixed amphora types, including ceramics from Ionia (Samian, Klazomenian, Lesbian and Milesian type amphoras) and also from the north Aegean. The mixing of cargoes suggests that ships could have been making various stops along their way to sell on their wares and pick up new goods.

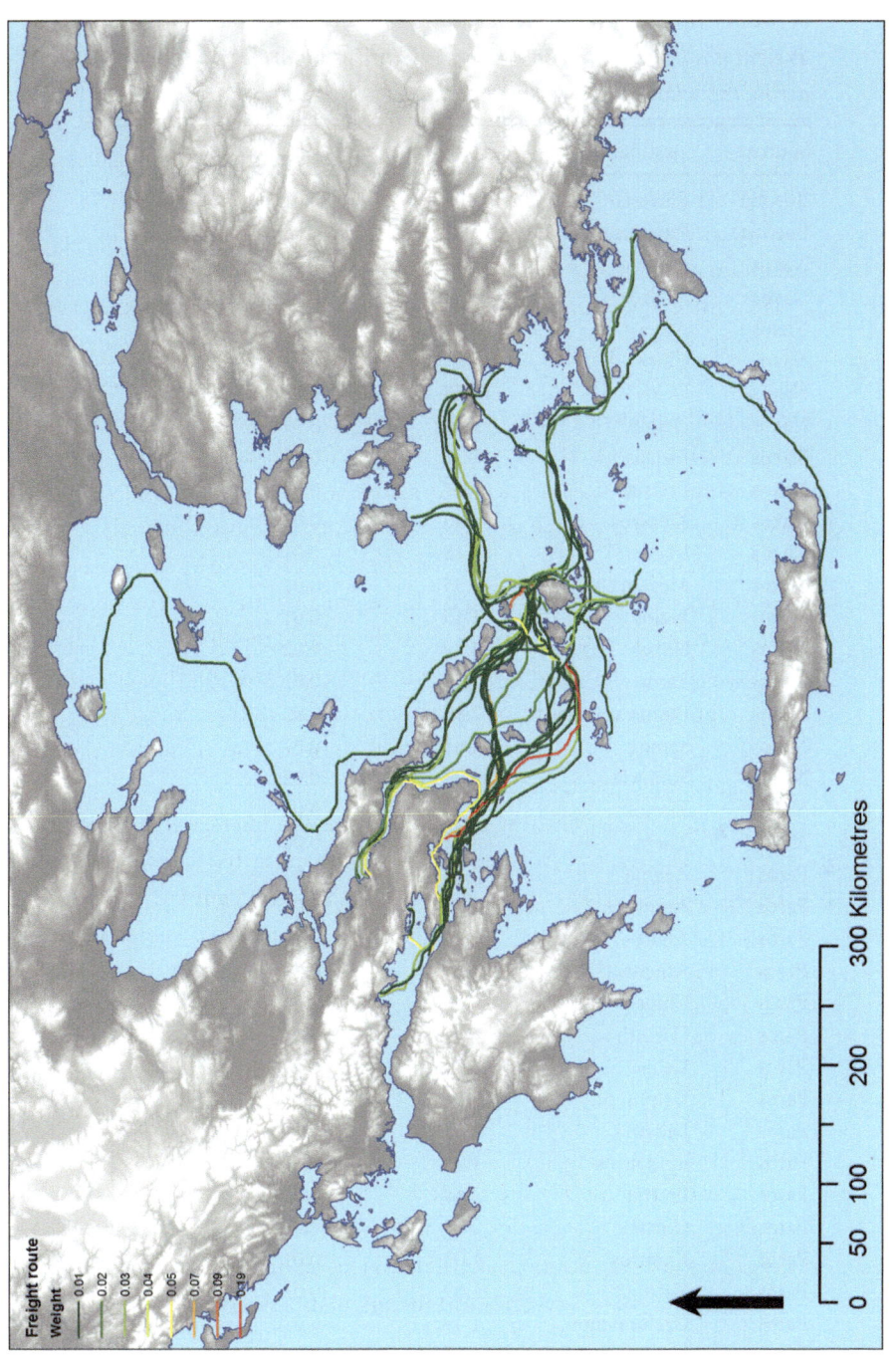

Figure 2.13 Visualisation for the weighted frequency of routes travelled between marble quarry and destination sanctuary site, using PPA modelling. Weight is a term relative to the total quantity of marble transported across the whole of the Archaic period.

Table 2.4 *Marble source and statue destination pairs. A relative route weight is calculated on the basis of marble tonnage conveyed between each pair as a proportion of the total marble tonnage. Weight is a term relative to the total quantity of marble transported across the whole of the Archaic period.*

Source	Destination	Total tonnage	Route weight
Boeotia	Eutresis	2.35	0.01
Boeotia	Ptoion sanctuary	11.22	0.05
Naxos	Aegina	1.96	0.01
Naxos	Andros	0.54	0.01
Naxos	Athens	16.05	0.07
Naxos	Chios	2.8	0.01
Naxos	Delos	19.68	0.09
Naxos	Delphi	1.458	0.01
Naxos	Eleusis	1.31	0.01
Naxos	Eretria	2.54	0.01
Naxos	Kamiros	4.46	0.02
Naxos	Klaros	1.18	0.01
Naxos	Megara	1.35	0.01
Naxos	Melos	1.45	0.01
Naxos	Naxos	3.79	0.02
Naxos	Paros	1.08	0.01
Naxos	Ptoion sanctuary	7.86	0.03
Naxos	Samos	14.83	0.07
Naxos	Sounion	4.87	0.02
Naxos	Thasos	2.36	0.01
Naxos	Thera	4.53	0.02
Paros	Aegina	2.22	0.01
Paros	Amorgos	0.54	0.01
Paros	Anafi	1.26	0.01
Paros	Athens	43.68	0.19
Paros	Chios	1.69	0.01
Paros	Corinth	1.1	0.01
Paros	Delos	10.41	0.05
Paros	Delphi	6.16	0.03
Paros	Didyma	1.61	0.01
Paros	Epidauros	1.35	0.01
Paros	Eretria	2.68	0.01
Paros	Gortyn	1.25	0.01
Paros	Kamiros	1.03	0.01
Paros	Keos	1.69	0.01
Paros	Orchomenos	1.49	0.01
Paros	Paros	9.07	0.04
Paros	Ptoion sanctuary	5.18	0.02

Table 2.4 (cont.)

Source	Destination	Total tonnage	Route weight
Paros	Samos	2.03	0.01
Paros	Sounion	2.8	0.01
Paros	Thera	6.14	0.03
Pentelic	Athens	8.26	0.04
Pentelic	Ptoion sanctuary	0.95	0.01
Samos	Samos	0.98	0.01
Thasos	Thasos	6.49	0.03

sites in Ionia and on the Dodecanese, but the weighted route lines indicate that this was in lower quantity than the exports of Naxos. The clients of both Naxos and Paros who consumed the most marble sculpture were Athens and Delos, but while Parian marble was the main material of choice for the former, it was Naxian marble that was more frequently exported to the latter. To the north of the Cyclades, routes along the straits of Euboea served marble being shipped to central Greece, and analysis indicates that ships originating from Naxos might have gone this way. Furthermore, the main traffic away from both islands (both in terms of distinct number of routes but also in the total weight of marble shipped) went through the Saronic Gulf, both to sites in this area, but also *through* the gulf *en route* to sites along the Corinthian Gulf. The graph produced suggests that, of the shipments from the Cyclades that came through the Gulf, those of Parian origin were more frequent. Indeed, Parian marble used at Olympia would presumably have been shipped along this route. In terms of overall quantity, Naxos made shipments of a much lower quantity to a greater number of parts of the Aegean. Paros, by contrast, shipped higher volumes of marble to fewer destinations: in particular, the most frequently used route for the export of marble connected Paros and Athens.

While this is a set of routes generated somewhat at the touch of a button – and for this reason we might not wish to place too much immediate interpretative weight on them – there are three key reasons why one might choose to see these as historically interesting route corridors. First, these east-west corridors resemble routes described in the travel literature (Ps.-Scylax, Strabo and the author of the *Stadiasmus Maris Magni*). The fact that modelling the material evidence can recreate a pattern described elsewhere is certainly encouraging, lending interpretative weight to each of these datasets. Second, the locations of the major known harbours from the Cycladic islands follow the conjectured routes. This is not a circular point. The fact that a model based on the location of *anchorages* brings one to places where communities chose to build up *harbours* suggests that travelling between anchorage nodes was effective.

Third, even a random simulation model generates the same four corridors as those discussed (see Fig. 2.14). It was discussed earlier that ships carrying marble for statue production would not necessarily (nor perhaps ever) go straight from place of source to destination. These ships were also carrying other cargo that they might want to unload or trade *en route*, or the ships might variously be forced to adapt their routes based on unpredictable weather patterns. To model this scenario, a second model was built that differed from the discussed PPA in two ways. First, it looked at *all* statues in the art historical record and has randomly assigned a place of production for those where provenance information is not securely known. Second, while the *start and end points* of a route are fixed, routes are drawn by moving to random adjacent nodes (as opposed to going straight towards the final destination through intermediate nodes). Based on these results – and although *additional* route corridors are created along the north coast of Euboea, along the coast of Ionia, and a branch both north and south at a point between Tinos and Andros – the four main route corridors identified are still generated. The concept of the route corridor will be interrogated further in Chapter 3; but for now it is sufficient to say that modelling can suggest the shape of some routes taken in transporting raw marble blocks from point of origin to point of consumption.

So in both scale and in geography, the production of just one type of product linked together a network of considerable size, comprising people, places, and processes. The numbers and the extent of this network is great enough and sustained enough throughout the Archaic period that we are not just talking about one-off events, but of an economy that kept different corners of the Aegean connected to one another to a substantial degree over many generations.

Marble as Heavy Freight in Context

This chapter began by suggesting that between the Early Iron Age and the Archaic period there was a significant shifting of gears in people consuming things that were produced non-locally. We have attempted to illustrate this phenomenon with regard to one particular material, marble, which was used to produce one particular type of product, freestanding statues. Both

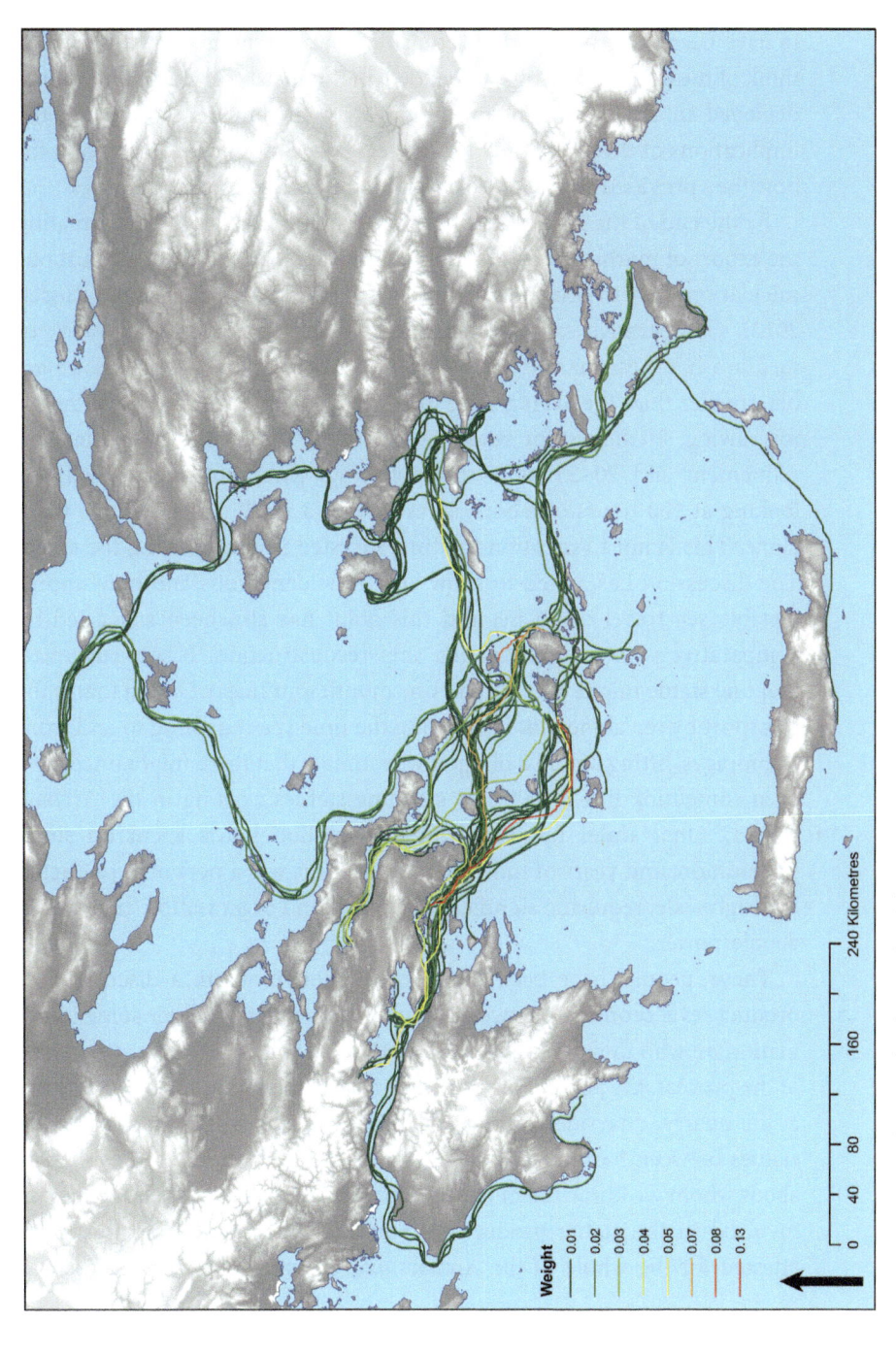

Figure 2.14 Visualisation for the weighted frequency of routes travelled between marble quarry and destination sanctuary site, using random simulation modelling. Weight is a term relative to the total quantity of marble transported across the whole of the Archaic period.

scale and geography were extensive enough that we can be satisfied in referring to this system as an 'economy', and the creation of statues appears to have been motivated by the acquisition of elite status so that we might think of the economic being 'embedded' in the social (or 'real' capital being deployed to achieve 'symbolic' capital). Now it remains to consider the implications of this case study for the scale of economic networks, and for how they provided means to connect communities more broadly.

By the end of the sixth century BC the economic network co-ordinating the export of marble for statue production was vast. But how vast? Labour calculations help to situate us within the correct area (*cf.* Barker and Russell 2012). Comparative estimates suggest that the processing of a block of medium-hardness marble measuring $1m^3$ (i.e. roughly 2.7 tonnes of marble, smaller than the average size of a *kouros*) would require 25–30 hours for sawing, 10 hours for rough work, 17–27 hours for more detailed refinement and 20–25 hours for polishing. One could quite easily be looking at 100 hours of labour invested into a small statue for this work alone. This is not to mention the time invested in transporting the stone. The discussion has aimed to show both how dangerous and how unpredictable sea travel could be, and this point has also been suggested by comparative work of the Kyrenia ship reconstruction. It was suggested that one statue might take around one month to transport – and that is for transport by sea alone, not to mention the time spent hauling to and from anchorages, lifting and installing. If we estimate that there might once have been something like 50,000 free standing statues existing in the Archaic period,[30] that scales up to around five million hours spent on stone preparation, and years of time spent at sea. This was a network conducted at a high scale, requiring significant planning and organisation, labour and people-power.

These 'people' have been kept largely anonymous in a discussion of product-level economic networks, but it is possible to recover some information on who they were. A network of people was required at every stage of the process: the person 'ordering' the statue, the sculptor, those working at the quarry, quayside workers, the rowers or sailors, those transporting statues between harbour and sanctuary. It is those commissioning statues about whom we know the most, and yet, ironically, they were least directly involved in the statue production. For the sculptors, 76 signatures are attested for the whole of the Archaic *and* Classical periods (Hochscheid

---

[30] The average tonnage of statues under study here is 1.68 tonnes. This average/the total estimated tonnage for the Archaic period at 90,000 tonnes = 53,553. This figure is also significantly more than Snodgrass' own ballpark estimate of 20,000 statues.

2015: 487–91), identifying seven places of origin. The rest of the work force, sadly, are largely anonymous, even if we can make some crude estimate about how many they were: around five million hours of work divided by 150 years of the Archaic periods gives over 30,000 hours a year. One might speculate that this is a workforce of fifteen individuals engaged continuously in the process, or (perhaps more likely) the more intensive seasonal use of one or two quarries at a time on Naxos and Paros. It has been postulated that slaves comprised many of the workers (Schilardi 2010a), but unfortunately, apart from talking about them in sheer numbers and labour-hours as above, there is little other contextual information on their identity. Furthermore, one must assume that there was communication throughout this network, somewhat essential to holding the whole production process together. Freestanding sculptures were not mass-produced but made to order: this necessitated communication between the artists and the dedicator, and mediators co-ordinating every stage of the process. Knowledge, planning and organisation are the somewhat invisible attributes of these networks, even if they are the cornerstones on which the whole system rests: this is a point which will be developed in more detail in Chapter 6.

One must also then consider the role of the artist in this story of the materiality of marble (*cf.* Boardman 1978: 19). We know based on inscriptional evidence that at least the commissioner of a marble statue and the sculptor might be from two different cities. Thus, Archermos of Chios is known to us through inscriptional evidence as the sculptor of an island-marble *kore* statue dedicated in Athens at the end of the sixth century BC (EM 6241). Either Archermos travelled to Naxos or Paros to work on the sculpture, and/or to Athens to do the more detailed work, or the stone block was moved to a workshop on Chios (the latter perhaps less likely). On this basis, therefore, it is entirely possible that the sculptor travelled to the marble's source and destination sites, roughing out and refining the sculpture at each stage (Boardman 1978: 23; Rolley 1994: 165–7; Kokkorou-Alevras 1995: 37–130; Schilardi 2010b), in other words, sculptors did not necessarily always work locally (*cf.* Hochsheid 2015). Further to this point, one observes in the art historical record that certain artistic styles of *kouros* and *kore* (i.e. those that were created by a certain group of artists) map quite closely to certain types of marble sourced in different places: as a select example, those *kouroi* designated by Richter as coming from the 'Sounion group' are generally made of 'island' (or, where more specific, Parian) marbles. Is it fair to assume that artists had a *preference* for working with certain types of marbles – perhaps because they were used to the materiality of this particular stone (different grain sizes, workability, appearance)? This would go some way towards explaining why there was so much movement of marble overseas in the Archaic period even when there were more locally available supplies of stone: one was ordering not a particular *stone*, but a particular *artist who preferred to work with a stone from elsewhere*. For instance, if someone on Thasos wanted to commission an artist of a particular *kouros* school to sculpt a statue, but if that artist preferred working with the marble of Naxos because of its material quality (e.g. Richter 14, MARB 11), then the person dedicating would have no choice but to import the marble of Naxos and reject the local and materially different hard marble. Something similar was happening in the fourth century at least, and epigraphic evidence on the construction of the temple of Asklepios at Epidauros indicates that stone-cutters each worked with their own preferred marbles imported from all over the Aegean.[31] The circulation of resources and the resultant mobilisation of labour is understood, therefore, not only as influenced by the desires of the aspirational elite to advertise themselves, but also by the preferences of the artists for the working properties of particular stones.

Given that this provided just one explanation for why stone was being quarried between 700 and 500 BC, we must also consider how the quantity of marble quarried for freestanding statues fits into the overall stone trade in the Archaic period. Even though the building of marble temples is a later phenomenon associated with the Classical and Hellenistic periods (and most stone temples of the Archaic period were constructed from *poros* limestone covered in stucco), we must also look at the *comparandum* (albeit an exceptional example) of the Siphnian Treasury from Delphi, dated to the mid-sixth century. This 'small' building measures around $250m^3$,[32] and, if we assume that something like 75 per cent of this volume will be constituted by 'empty' space *in antis* and in the interior of the treasury, one would require just over $180m^3$ of marble to produce this building alone, weighing some 486 tonnes – equivalent to over three quarters of the marble required for the entire annual output of the Aegean in terms of its freestanding sculpture. Clearly, the shipping of marble for the construction of buildings was of a completely different order, and it reminds us that the economic networks co-ordinated for the production of freestanding sculpture are only part of the story.

---

[31] See Prignitz 2014 for an integrated discussion of the archaeological and inscriptional evidence.
[32] Poulson 1973: 38 and 43 gives the height and width of the treasury as 8.9 m and 6.3 m. No estimate is made for the height but, given that he puts the height of the caryatids at 1.75 m, a total original height for the whole temple as 4.5 m is not unreasonable.

We should also situate this figure alongside the phenomenon of building temples from other types of stone. The size of the Siphnian Treasury has already been discussed (i.e. the case of the first stone temple from the Aegean). Temples built from non-marble stones in the sixth century were much bigger than their predecessors and they necessarily required much more stone (Table 2.5a).[33] Even 'smaller' temples such as the Hekatompedon at Athens and the Old Parthenon (Dörpfeld 1886; *cf.* Dinsmoor 1947) required almost ten times as many cubed metres of stone than temples of the eighth century, while monumental temples at Corinth (Stillwell 1932), Delphi (Courby 1927) and Samos (Gruben 2014) were of a completely different order of magnitude. Much of the requisite building material for these temples was sourced locally, that is, the labour-effort value associated with stone transport would be much lower than the case of overseas marble previously discussed; but in the Classical period, while the size of temples stayed similar to that of the most monumental buildings of the Archaic period (Table 2.5b), certainly some of the architectural sculpture and revetments would be fashioned out of marble, increasing the amount of stone that would be brought from overseas. And yet, this is all just a drop in the ocean compared to the amount of building material that would be moved around the Aegean in the Roman period. Not only was there a much higher demand for marble in various structural and commemorative contexts (Russell 2013: 8–36), but the capacity of Roman ships at around 300 tonnes (rising to around 600 tonnes by the end of the empire, Wilson 2009: 227) would have been sufficient to carry all of the marble required for a year's worth of freestanding sculpture in the Archaic period in a single load. Of course, the demands and infrastructures of all these periods are in no sense necessarily comparable, but two points of historical context should be noted about the marble network discussed. First, its operation represented a major step-up from the scale of stone mining and export in the Early Iron Age; second, this network was of significant size and scale for its day but is still a rather small network in the *longue durée* of the history of the Aegean.

In terms of the Archaic period and the Archaic period alone, one might go as far to say that transporting such quantities of stone around the Aegean Sea required the region to be a hypermobile zone. It has been suggested that 100 ships were used on an annual basis for the transport of freestanding (humanoid) sculpture alone, and the case has also been made for a not insignificant exploitation of non-marble stone resources in the

---

[33] Here, 0.5 is used as the reconstructed height: temple width ratio, consistent with the ratio of more securely known Classical period temples at Bassai, Olympia and Sounion. The maximum reconstructed height has been capped at 15 m.

Table 2.5 *Estimated temple stone tonnages for groups of buildings discussed throughout this chapter. a) Archaic period temples b) Fifth century temples.*

Table 2.5a

Site	Temple length (m)	Temple width (m)	Tonnage estimate
Athens – Hekatompedon	21	14.56	1669.45
Athens – Old Parthenon	34.7	13.45	2353.99
Corinth	53.8	21.5	8675.25
Delphi	60.3	23.8	10763.55
Isthmia	40	14	2940.00
Samos	40	25	7500.00

Table 2.5b

Site	Temple length (m)	Temple width (m)	Tonnage estimate
Aphaia	28.8	13.7	1972.80
Bassai	38.3	14.5	3054.43
Olympia – Temple of Zeus	64	27.7	18348.48
Sounion	31	13.5	2280.83

rest of the Archaic period. And this is before even taking account of the fact that there were significant quantities of *other* heavy products being shipped around the Aegean (*cf.* Burford 1960). Snodgrass drew attention to metal ores (Snodgrass 1983: 229–31). He was not so interested in quantifying amounts of metal ore transported in the same manner that he did for marble blocks (nor indeed *can* this be done in such a straightforward way), but he was more interested in discussing at what stage in a metal ore's life it would have been transported by ship (i.e. shipment most likely took place before smelting, and products made at the furnace would not have much further to travel to their final destination). Timber, too, was shipped in bulk during the Archaic period, with different types of wood required for smelting, shipbuilding, construction of public and private buildings, and also for the production of cork, pitch, tar, dyes and oils (Hughes and Thirgood 1982; Meiggs 1982: 118–23, 188ff.; Veal 2017: 325). And of course this is not to mention foodstuffs such as grain, oil and wine, which will be discussed further in Chapter 3. All these products constituted similar if not more significant networks compared to the marble network; but their datasets – relating to perishable objects – are intangible and their networks much more obscure to reconstruct. The marble statue network was quite clearly just one of many systems that was important to the overall shape of economic activity in the Archaic period, and the size and scale of those networks can be inferred to be, in comparison with the present dataset, quite substantial.

As an addendum to this discussion of scale, however, one must also consider how fragile the story really is: at what point does adjusting the assumptions change the results significantly? By changing the parameters used in the model for marble tonnage versus ships required, we can estimate how the number of ships would change if we adjusted our estimate of what proportion of sculpture survives (Fig. 2.15). If we think we have 2 per cent or more of the original freestanding sculpture currently surviving in the material record, the total estimate of ships required to transport marble drops to around 50 *per annum*. This illustrates with robust data the rather obvious point that if we assume that the amount of sculpture surviving to us in the material record constitutes a substantial quantity of that which once existed in the ancient world, we see that the scale and intensity of the marble trade might actually be much smaller than suggested. By contrast, if we estimate that 0.5 per cent or less of the original sculpture survives, then the number of ships needed for the transport of marble increases enormously. The crucial point here is that a lot depends on how representative we think our dataset is – and this is, in some senses, the most subjective part of the whole study and the hardest value to tie down. Predictably, if we assume that there once existed many marble statues, then we must also conclude that the infrastructure required to ship all of these statues was significant; but this case study has demonstrated how sensitive those interpretations are, and where the limits of this story might lie.

Beyond Economic Networks of Luxury

In concluding this chapter, it is useful to return to where the discussion began. Greeks marked themselves out as different to the rest of the community by consuming in one place things that were either produced or sourced from elsewhere. The rate at which goods were imported for this sort of conspicuous consumption increased significantly across the seventh and sixth centuries. As a socially embedded processes, the fashion for

Estimate of number of ships per annum required for transport of marble given % of statues represented in material record

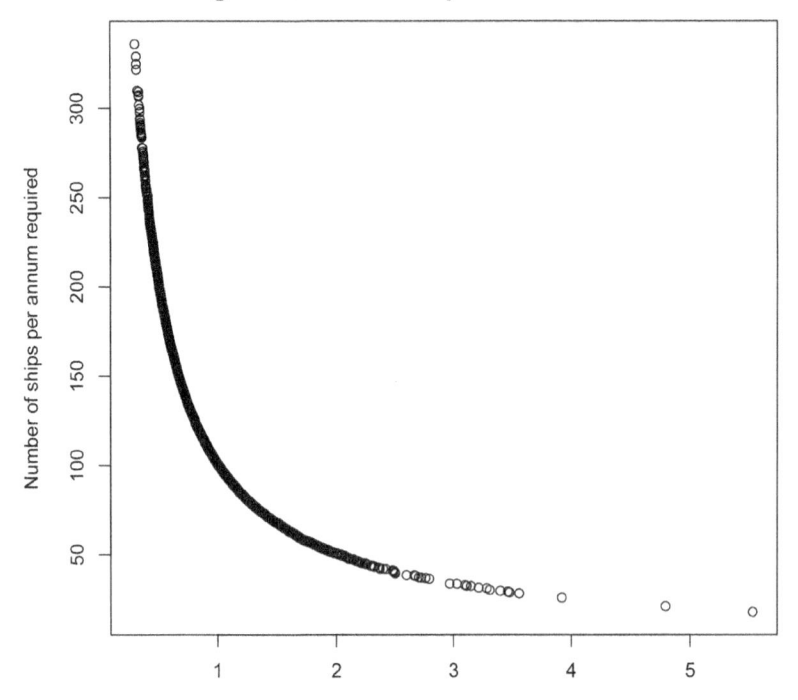

[Scatter plot: x-axis "Statues in the material record as a percentage of all those that once existed" ranging 1 to 5; y-axis "Number of ships per annum required" ranging 50 to 300. Curve shows steep decay from ~300+ at low percentages to ~25 at higher percentages.]

Figure 2.15 Estimate for the number of ships required to transport Aegean marble, with respect to an estimate of how much sculpture survives in the material record. The x axis adjusts the figure given by Snodgrass 1983: 228 for the percentage of marble surviving in the material record, while the y axis shows the effect this has on the overall calculation of ships required to move this marble in the Aegean.

dedicating marble statues increased as the desire for and need to compete for social status also increased, and indeed this chapter has suggested that the network created for moving statues from point of production to point of consumption was great in its scale and extent. Not only were large quantities of stone sourced from all around the Aegean as required to meet the needs of those dedicating statues, but a great number of ships were also needed to transport this marble. The journeys taken by these ships were likely planned to reduce the risk to the precious cargo, and it is possible to plot on a map some of these possible routes by applying a rules-based logic.

Discussion of this network has so far been largely descriptive. However, contextual analysis has suggested that the bulk movement of stone across the Aegean was just one of various heavy freight networks that developed in the Archaic period. Chapter 2 puts the shipment of marble statues in the context of one of these other economic transport networks, aiming to explain how the process for shipping marble relied on and was entangled with the network of shipping other products. This will go some way towards considering *how* and *why* the rate of overseas exchange could suddenly be cranked up in the seventh and sixth century – the levels of organisation, planning and knowledge that, though largely invisible in the material record, were essential to sustaining these networks. But the main point of departure so far is that there is significant evidence (both in terms of quantity and geographic reach) that economic activity of the Archaic period associated with the dedication of marble statues was socially embedded and was aligned towards the acquisition of status by elite peers.

3 | Economic Networks

Commodities and Semi-Luxuries

Having established in Chapter 2 that in the seventh and sixth centuries BC things were being transported around and beyond the Aegean, both in increasing numbers and in a variety of different objects and materials, it is productive here to take a step back and consider once again *why* people want different things.

The discussion so far on marble statues has noted the importance of a *conspicuous* consumption – but what of the *consumption* itself? The evidence of the poets tells us that based both on their quality and their point of origin much smaller and transportable goods were thought of as luxurious: Alkman (fr. 1.67–8) and Sappho (fr. 39) on fine Lydian textiles and garments coloured with rare and exotic purple dyes; Arkhilochos (fr. 2) on Ismarian wine; and Hesiod (589–92) on Byblian wine and the fine cheeses and meats that go with it. Lin Foxhall (2005) has helpfully classified items like textiles and wines, along with other products such as fine scented oils or perfumes and intricate jewellery such as fibulae, as 'semi-luxuries'. Furthermore, she has argued that: 'things, especially foreign things, which convey meanings to and on the consumer and his or her social circle ... become an integral part of the individual and/or group consuming them, constituent elements of their social and political identity.' (2005: 234). Quite clearly, and as already seen in the case of the Early Iron Age, things smaller than marble statues could be considered luxurious because these particular products were not readily available by local means. They do not strictly fall within Veblen's definition of conspicuous consumption, however, in that their manufacture was not *primarily* aligned with status building, and so their status as 'semi-luxuries' is somewhat appropriate for things that could otherwise be eaten, drunk or worn.

As noted above, in the Archaic period people were in general consuming in greater number other sorts of things, not just products considered luxurious (or semi-luxurious). The most clear indicator of this archaeologically is the large and steadily growing record of transport amphoras, attesting to the volume of products that must have been moved across and through the Aegean basin (Grakov 1935, Walbank 1969: 20, Will 1977, Grace 1979, Garlan 1983: 27; Brashinskiï 1984: 15; Garlan 1988: 3–8;

Monachov 1999: 5; for a summary of the most recent data from the past decade, see Lawall and Tzochev 2020). Although we cannot identify in most instances precisely what would have been carried in these transport *amphoras*, dry products like grain, olives and wheat are most likely. Indeed, that there was large-scale transport of grain, olives and wheat around the Aegean by the start of the Classical period is well attested (Ps.-Xenophon, *Ath. Pol.* 2.2–3, Thucydides 6.20.4, Isocrates 17.57; see e.g. Gabrielsen 2015, 2017), with the understanding generally held that growth in exchange took place right down to the Archaic period (Bresson 2008; Ober 2010; *cf.* Pratt 2021: 254–7), largely in response to a rapidly increasing population size (see above, particularly Hansen 2006, and more specifically here Garnsey 1988: 113–17). Most simply: there is a range of evidence for the Archaic period that goods like these were in transit – goods that were not 'luxury' but might be considered either 'semi-luxury' or 'commodity'.

Of course, the distinction between what we consider to be a 'commodity' and what is a 'luxury' is completely arbitrary. These are two value-laden and socially constructed terms that not only mean very different things to each of us today, but, in addition, our understanding of luxury now is very different to an ancient idea of luxury – and even an 'ancient idea of luxury' is a far too generalising and problematic term (Berry 1994; Grewe and Hofmeester 2016: 1–4; Osborne 2021). The definition of luxury is situational, and, moreover, given that these are not terms that can be used in the absolute, one might consider a spectrum for conceptualising where a particular object lies between being a 'luxury' or a 'commodity' (Foxhall's notion of a 'semi-luxury' already leans towards this interpretation).

Two key dimensions to this spectrum would be availability and cultural bias (Waines 2003: 571–3; Mansvelt, Breheny and Hay 2016; Riello 2016; Pratt 2021: 9–21). Something more readily available in the local area to a particular community, might not have been considered a 'luxury' to that group. The availability of knowledge (or lack thereof) on how to process that raw material can transform such an object from a commodity to a luxury: if there were no craftspeople locally available, or if one could see that becoming a master of a particular craft required skill, time, dedication and resource unavailable to all in the community, then the action of crafting a raw material makes an object take on a more luxurious state (Wallerstein 1974: 131–2; Featherstone 2014, *contra* Schneider 1977; Cherrier and Murray 2002). Furthermore, if social, economic or political status become entangled with the production or consumption of certain objects (as was the case for the marble statues, as discussed), then an object might once again become recognised within a community as a luxury. Essentially, owing to the particular values held by a given community (on which there is further discussion in Chapter 4) and owing to the prevalence or scarcity of certain types of objects within a community or through its close networks, objects can variously take on the role of relatively more 'luxury' or 'commodity'.

Naturally, these are very coarse categorisations: but as heuristics, they are useful labels for saying that different levels of things were being produced and consumed in the Aegean of the seventh and sixth centuries and, more crucially, that different classes of objects were circulating and being transported. Bearing these provisos in mind, these distinctions between 'luxury' and 'commodity' will be used in this chapter in only the most general way as tools to explore the extent to which networks involved in the shipments of all different sorts of products were entangled.

Measuring the Distribution of Commodities

The distribution of ceramics is one of the best but most complicated set of indicators for trade activity of perishable goods. There is no need to rehearse here some of those complications, not least that pots equal neither people, nor the products contained within them: consumption patterns do not necessarily mirror import patterns; provenance and consumption might tell us about the start and end of a traded object's life, but say nothing about its part in a longer *chaîne opératoire* of trade; object use, reuse and nature of deposition widen the interpretative gap between consumption and trade import patterns; and the life of an object post-antiquity further muddies the water, since the quantity of objects obtained, studied and published, or accessible in databases, might not be representative of 'real' ancient patterns.

Nevertheless, and as has already been noted, the ceramic dataset of the seventh and sixth centuries BC has the advantage of having been the subject of much study by art historians for the past 150 years, at least, creating a very large, well-understood and published dataset. These studies have provided for the Archaic period a very good reference set of data for two variables crucial to unpicking economic networks: date and regional type. And while on the one hand the resolution that art historians have used to describe these categories in the past – e.g. the workshops and places of production – may not be as *precisely* defined as one might be able to obtain through scientific methods, they are, for the most part and particularly for fineware ceramics where the lion's share of classical archaeological scholarship has looked, broadly *accurate*. It is easy to distinguish macroscopically, for instance, sherds from Corinthian workshops and sherds from Attic workshops: imprecise categories, but ones which we feel we can define quite reliably. There is, however, variation between regions as to how well studied local sequences are known, and we might have far more confidence in identifying something in macroscopic terms as 'Attic' than 'Cycladic'. Coarsewares, by contrast, have received less attention, except for in the substantial sub-field of *amphora* studies. Much recent study (predominantly within German, Russian and Turkish scholarship) has improved our knowledge of these objects through typological analysis (Dupont 1983, 1986; Mommsen, Hertel and Mountjoy 2001; Monachov 2003; Mommsen et al. 2006; Sezgin 2012; Monachov and Kuznetsova 2017: 59–63), and this allows us to look at the provenance of these ceramics with a greater degree of precision. But in general, ceramics, owing to the way in which we can quite neatly classify their point of origin and rough date of manufacture, are a useful dataset for identifying patterns at this sort of zoomed-out, big-picture scale.

Data for this study are drawn from excavation catalogues and archives where, upon analysis of the pottery, it seems reasonably likely that the material published is representative of what was originally dug from a site, and where information on ware, shape and date are offered (Table **A2.1**). Unquantified data and 'highlight' pieces published separately have not been included for analysis because they skew the sample. The database contains both individual sherds and whole vessels, but when the data are analysed these raw counts are converted to the proportion of ceramic material per each individual site.[1]

Thirty-two sites from the area facing inward to the Aegean Basin fit the criteria given for analysis, drawn from fifty publications and from the Miletos Archive, formerly at Bochum, now at Hamburg (Fig. 3.1, Table 3.1). This yields a database of 25,735 vessels. The sample of sites is not perfectly even across the Aegean: there is a concentration of high-quality data available from the Saronic Gulf and from the coast of Ionia but, by contrast, the Cyclades are quite poorly represented (by Delos only), as are the Dodecanese (by Rhodes only) and, given its size, Crete also (datapoints only available from Knossos and Kommos). The North Aegean is better represented in the sixth century, even though the number of sites with data appropriate for this analysis is somewhat less in the seventh century.

---

[1] This does, of course, assume a uniform fragmentation behaviour across a site – an assumption which has had to be made in order to facilitate this study.

Table 3.1 *Number of discrete pottery units (sherds or vessels) available for study by period for sites discussed in this chapter.*

Site	700–650 BC	650–600 BC	600–550 BC	550–500 BC
Akraifia	0	0	793	264
Aphaia	341	338	171	326
Athens	123	155	440	93
Chios	408	422	697	147
Corinth	35	358	1098	804
Delos	132	844	135	83
Eleutherna	0	11	0	0
Kalapodi	4	37	69	88
Kalaureia	0	0	77	41
Kalydon	0	0	0	71
Klazomenai	0	1	116	346
Knossos	174	162	0	30
Kolonna	7	59	84	74
Kommos	43	89	20	16
Lindos	246	196	17	1248
Miletos	6	7	4701	4040
Olynthos	3	15	97	179
Perachora	122	951	746	366
Samos	237	179	37	10
Samothrace	0	0	15	42
Sindos	0	0	20	52
Smyrna	5	34	122	43
Sounion	9	53	0	0
Tanagra	0	0	614	124
Tegea	0	2	24	29
Thasos	18	51	141	195
Thorikos	10	92	144	214
Torone	1	6	21	27
Vroulia	106	100	0	0
Zone	0	10	35	147

Consideration must be given to data mapping. As discussed in Chapter 1, when using data drawn from so many different sources each with their own reference systems and object type/period vocabularies, common categories for analysis must be used that accurately convey the data. At the same time, one must work at the level of the most common denominator – the coarsest data available – otherwise one can give the false impression that some data as presented here in a secondary analysis are more precise than they were first published in their primary analysis. For chronology, even though some

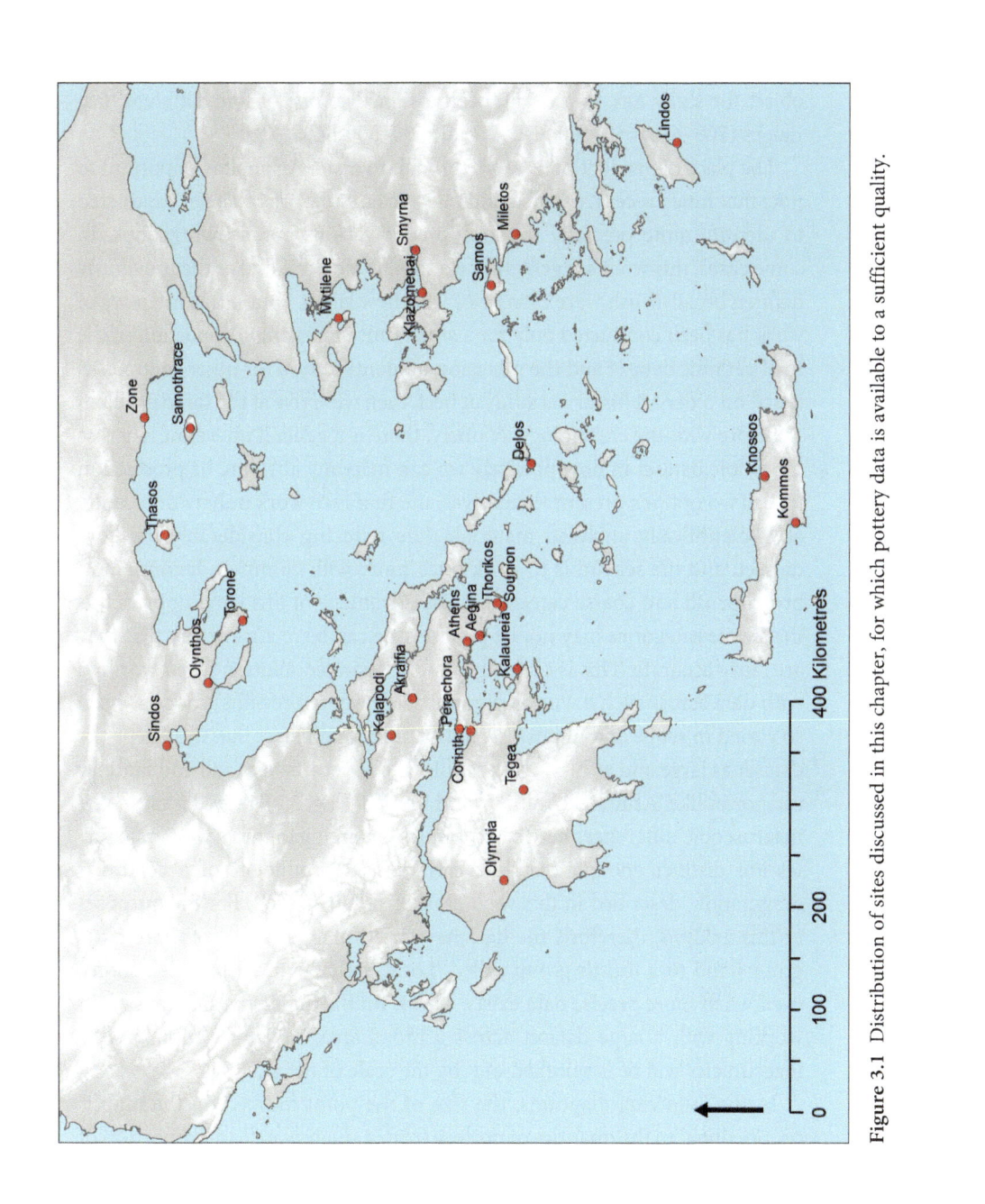

Figure 3.1 Distribution of sites discussed in this chapter, for which pottery data is available to a sufficient quality.

workshops and potters' hands of the Archaic period can be identified to a precision of five–ten years, other ceramics can be dated at best only to the half-century. The solution is to map data in all cases to cover this lowest level of resolution, that is, to work in fifty-year time slices and assign pieces which have been dated much more precisely to these much broader categories. Each object for study has, as a result, been assigned to one of four different date ranges (700–650, 650–600, 600–550, or 550–500 BC).

The place of production is more difficult to distil. Again, it is important to note that much recent, detailed and often scientific work has been conducted to identify quite precisely the locations of various pottery workshops. In some cases, this work suggests that we should replace some of the previously defined broad-brush ware categories with new labels.[2] But if this intensity of work has been conducted only for a small (but increasing) proportion of the total ceramic dataset and the precision of identification for other ceramics is based on older art historical study at best, then we arrive at the same problem as before with the chronology. Namely, there is a general unevenness across the whole dataset in how precisely we can map any attribute or production type. Two options present themselves: the first is to work only with recently and scientifically analysed material, thus reducing considerably the core dataset; and the second is to work once more with common denominator, broad-brush and coarse categories. The advantage of this latter approach is that while categories may not be precise, one can be relatively sure that they are fairly accurate. This is certainly a more desirable solution when working with data across such a wide geographic area where previous work has been so varied in scope and intensity – not to mention the fact that this keeps the dataset as large and as broad as possible. If one resorts to broad and familiar categories like 'Attic', 'Corinthian' and 'Ionian' (Fig. 3.2), then it is clear that macroscopic differences between ceramics belonging to these 'ware' categories are distinct enough that one can be fairly confident of a ceramic's designation, described in this way (*cf.* Sherratt 2000: 6–7). For the purposes of this analysis, therefore, the data have been mapped to these more basic groups and to a fourth group called 'Local' (relative to each site's region), even when more precise data exists. This is on the understanding that when working with a large dataset across a broad area, any small anomalies or inaccuracies will be 'smoothed out' by the scale of the analysis.

In the following diagrams, the size of the point marked on the map is proportional to the quantity of pottery from a single ware as a proportion of

---

[2] See, e.g. Villing and Mommsen 2017 on recategorising a number of 'Rhodian' vessels from the British Museum collection as 'Koan', *cf.* Kerschner 2017.

Figure 3.2 Representative Attic (*skyphos*) and Corinthian (*aryballos*) pottery types of the Archaic period. BSA Museum MUS.A004 and MUS.A351. Photographs by Matt Stirn and copyright British School at Athens.

all of the ceramics found at the sites investigated within a given period. If the map point for Athens indicates that 80 per cent of the total assemblage in the period 700–650 BC comprises Attic pottery, for instance, then quite clearly the size of the datapoint for Athens in the remaining three categories will be no greater in combination than 20 per cent. The data are presented per half century (700–650 BC; 650–600 BC; 600–550 BC; 550–500 BC), according to each of the four ware categories defined above (Table 3.2). Site labels are given on each of these maps only when there is data available for a site in a given period.

Table 3.2 *Proportion (expressed as a percentage) of wares in the total ceramic assemblage from each site a) 700–650 BC b) 650–600 BC c) 600–550 BC d) 550–500 BC.*

Table 3.2a

Site	Attic proportion (%)	Corinthian proportion (%)	Ionian proportion (%)	Local proportion (%)
Aegina	0	90	10	0
Athens	92	7	2	0
Corinth	0	100	0	0
Delos	0	44	0	56
Kalapodi	0	100	0	0
Knossos	1	8	1	91
Kommos	2	23	16	58
Lindos	1	22	9	68
Olympia	0	100	0	0
Perachora	1	96	0	3
Samos	0	0	100	0
Smyrna	0	40	60	0
Sounion	0	100	0	0
Thasos	0	0	100	0
Thorikos	50	50	0	0
Torone	0	100	0	0
Vroulia	3	8	0	89

Table 3.2b

Site	Attic proportion (%)	Corinthian proportion (%)	Ionian proportion (%)	Local proportion (%)
Aegina	0	79	21	0
Athens	89	5	5	1
Corinth	0	100	0	0
Delos	13	57	6	25
Kalapodi	0	100	0	0
Knossos	0	5	4	91
Kommos	7	17	33	44
Lindos	0	30	11	59
Olympia	0	87	0	13
Perachora	0	98	2	0
Samos	16	5	79	0
Smyrna	0	47	53	0
Sounion	0	100	0	0

Table 3.2b (*cont.*)

Site	Attic proportion (%)	Corinthian proportion (%)	Ionian proportion (%)	Local proportion (%)
Tegea	0	0	0	100
Thasos	0	2	43	55
Thorikos	10	90	0	0
Torone	0	33	67	0
Vroulia	2	5	0	45
Zone	50	0	50	0

Table 3.2c

Site	Attic proportion (%)	Corinthian proportion (%)	Ionian proportion (%)	Local proportion (%)
Aegina	71	0	29	0
Akraifia	2	48	0	50
Athens	95	2	2	0
Corinth	0	100	0	0
Delos	11	53	14	21
Kalapodi	0	100	0	0
Kalaureia	13	86	1	0
Klazomenai	2	0	98	0
Kommos	12	29	0	59
Lindos	0	67	33	0
Miletos	6	6	89	0
Olympia	4	67	0	29
Olynthos	5	41	51	3
Perachora	9	89	2	0
Samos	9	0	91	0
Samothrace	7	0	13	80
Sindos	33	39	17	11
Smyrna	5	14	81	0
Sounion	5	95	0	0
Tegea	0	12	0	88
Thasos	6	8	40	46
Thorikos	14	86	0	0
Torone	0	10	48	43
Zone	23	51	26	0

Table 3.2d

Site	Attic proportion (%)	Corinthian proportion (%)	Ionian proportion (%)	Local proportion (%)
Aegina	76	0	24	0
Akraifia	20	32	0	48
Athens	94	1	2	3
Corinth	2	98	0	0
Delos	0	69	10	20
Kalapodi	0	100	0	0
Kalaureia	32	66	2	0
Klazomenai	7	0	93	0
Knossos	13	0	0	87
Kommos	0	0	0	100
Lindos	0	0	100	0
Olympia	43	8	0	49
Olynthos	74	3	0	23
Perachora	22	72	1	5
Samos	8	0	92	0
Samothrace	38	0	21	40
Sindos	38	30	0	32
Smyrna	20	10	70	0
Sounion	49	51	0	0
Tegea	0	3	0	97
Thasos	59	1	4	35
Thorikos	17	83	0	0
Torone	93	7	0	0
Zone	73	0	27	0

Attic pottery (Fig. 3.3a–d) is found almost exclusively within the Saronic Gulf at the start of the seventh century (i.e. at Athens and Sounion, 700–650 BC, Fig. 3.3a), although in small amounts on Rhodes and on Crete, and by the end of the century (650–600 BC, Fig. 3.3b) is also found on Delos and Samos. There are also significant quantities of Attic pottery from this period found at Zone in the north Aegean. In the sixth century there is some amount of Attic pottery found at all sites for which data is recorded, both in period three (600–550 BC, Fig. 3.3c) and in period four (550–500 BC, Fig. 3.3d). In period three (600–500 BC) the large dot on the site of Athens indicates, predictably, that most of the Attic pottery attested within the record was found at Athens, and also nearby at Thorikos. The Attic

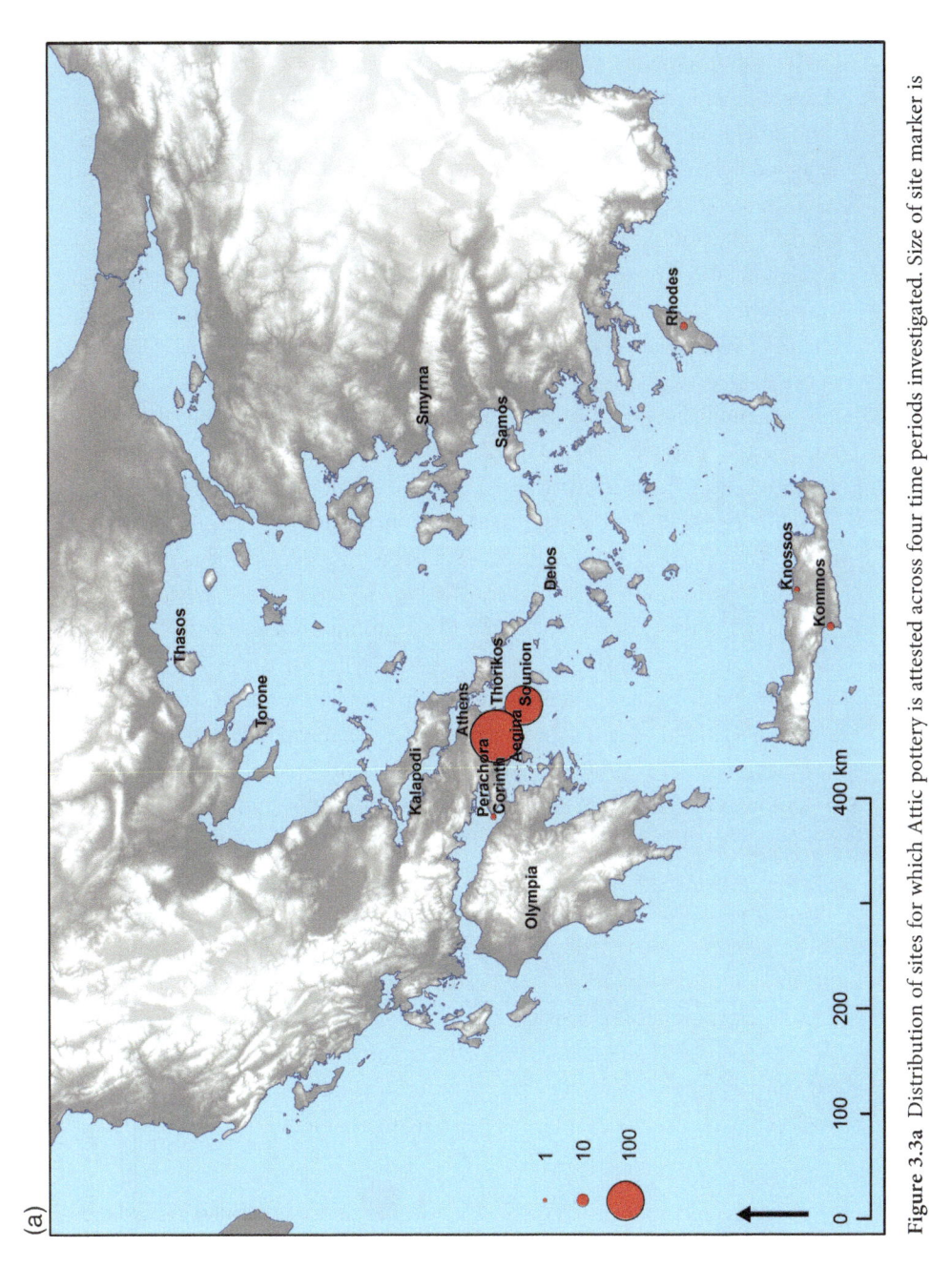

Figure 3.3a Distribution of sites for which Attic pottery is attested across four time periods investigated. Size of site marker is proportional to the amount of pottery found, relative to all other types of pottery. 700–650 BC

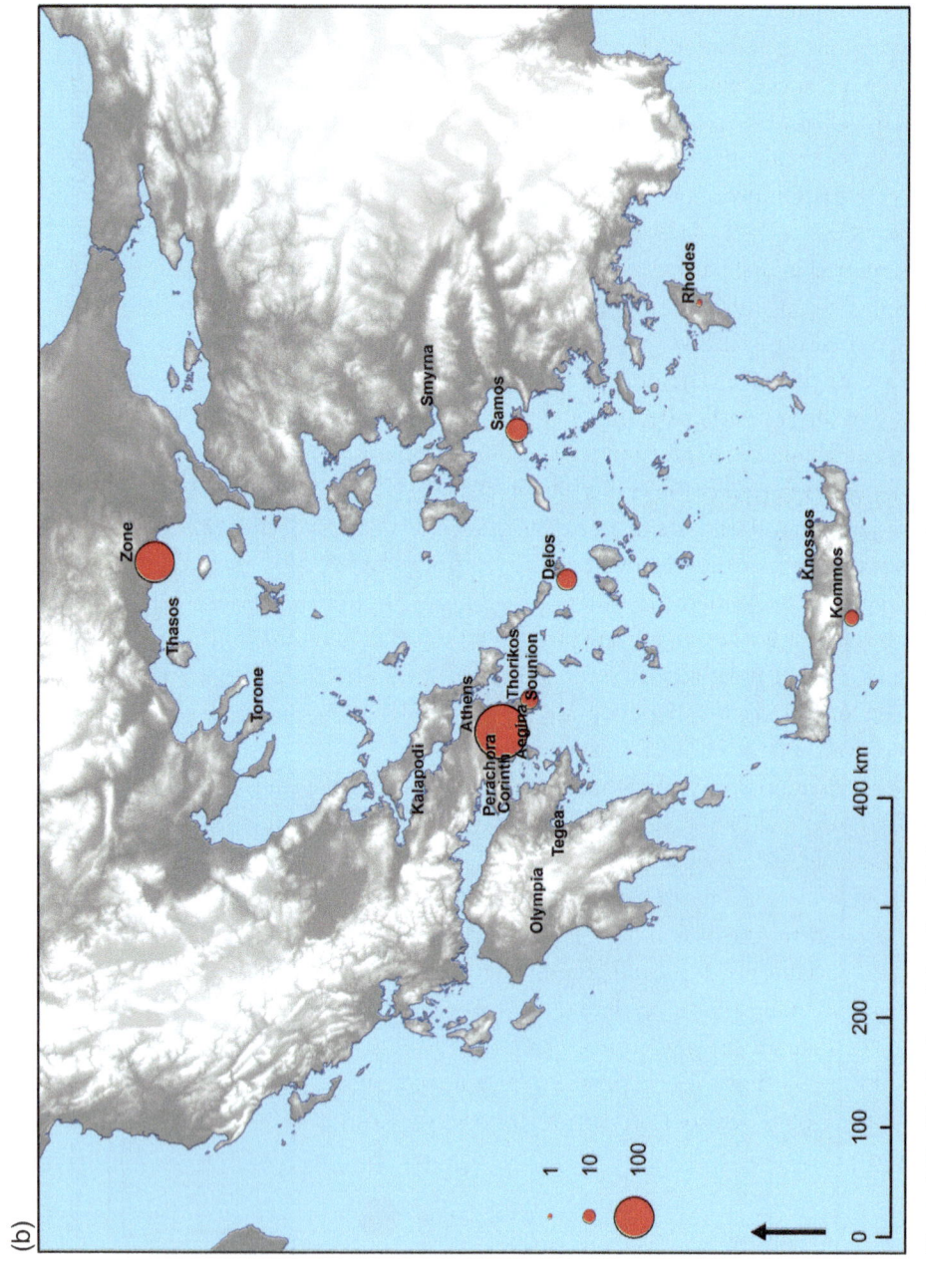

Figure 3.3b Distribution of sites for which Attic pottery is attested across four time periods investigated. Size of site marker is proportional to the amount of pottery found, relative to all other types of pottery. 650–600 BC

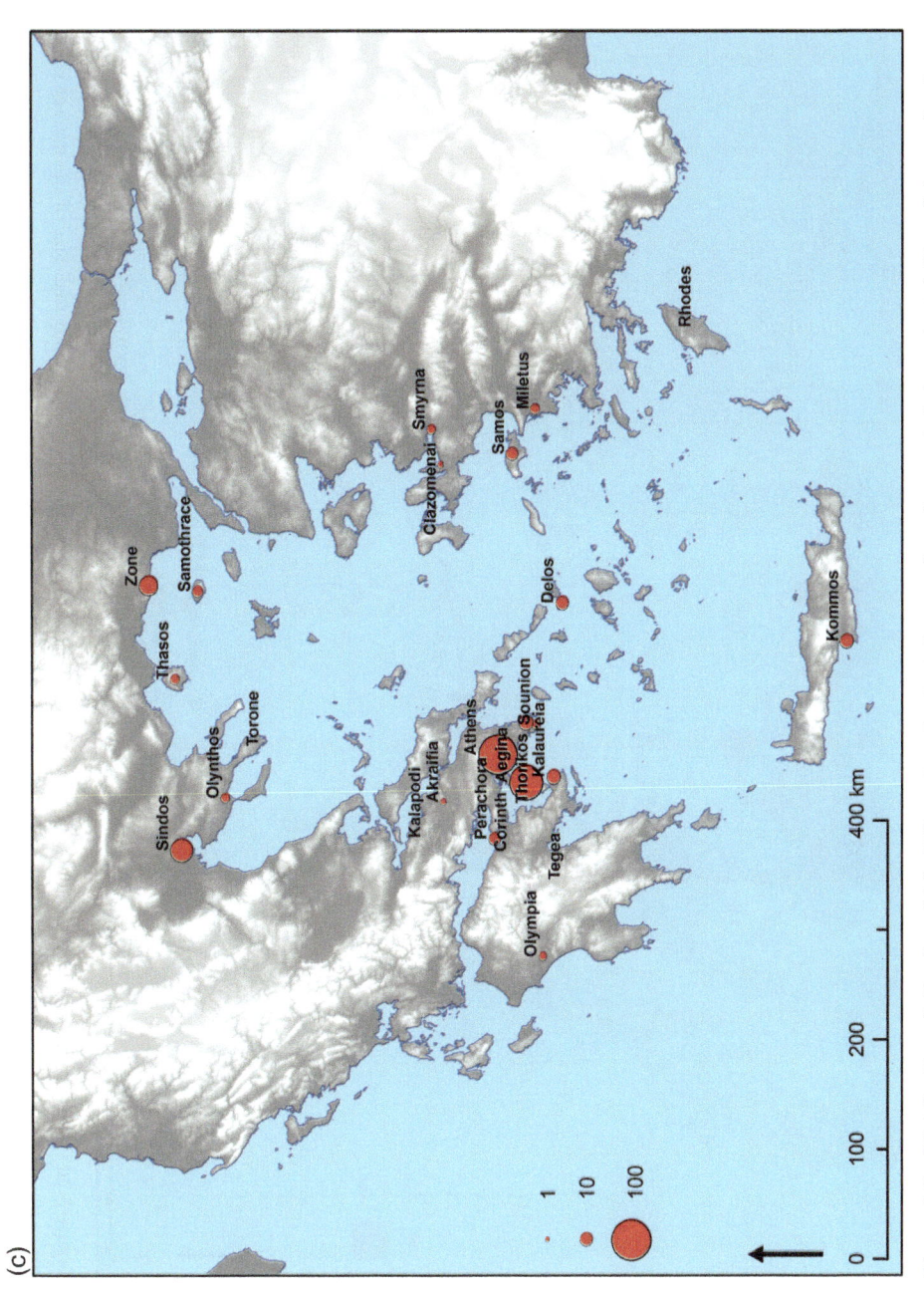

Figure 3.3c Distribution of sites for which Attic pottery is attested across four time periods investigated. Size of site marker is proportional to the amount of pottery found, relative to all other types of pottery. 600–550 BC.

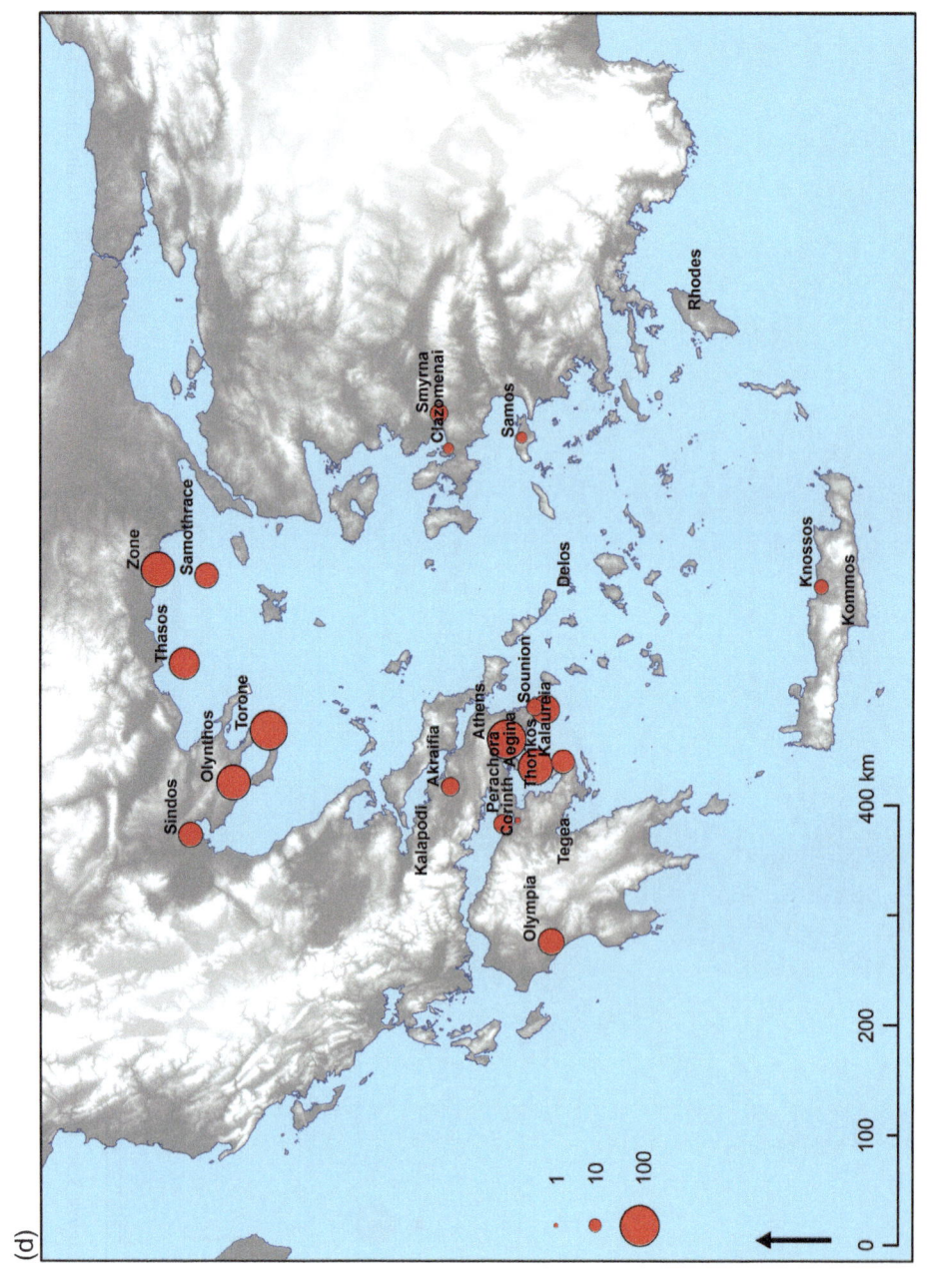

Figure 3.3d Distribution of sites for which Attic pottery is attested across four time periods investigated. Size of site marker is proportional to the amount of pottery found, relative to all other types of pottery. 550–500 BC.

networks also push not insignificantly into the north Aegean, although a smaller point on Zone indicates that other wares were also making their way into the region, more so than in the previous century, at least. The distribution is much the same in period four (550–500 BC, Fig. 3.3d), albeit with a more pronounced presence in the Peloponnese, at Olympia. The main difference here is in quantity, as almost all datapoints illustrated are larger than in the previous half century, making visually patent the significance of Attic as a pottery network that had established itself in the Aegean by this time.

The quantities of Corinthian pottery in the assemblages investigated increases significantly in the sixth century, as Corinthian pottery (Fig. 3.4a–d), by contrast, spread more quickly throughout the Aegean. Already at the start of the seventh century (700–650 BC, Fig. 3.4a) there were ceramics of this ware at all sites of the Saronic Gulf investigated, as well as on Delos, Thasos and Rhodes, and at Kommos and Smyrna. The number of sites at which Corinthian pottery was found in this half-century period is greater than the number of sites at which Attic pottery was found, and indeed this ware penetrates further into the Peloponnese than Attic was at this date. At the end of the seventh century (650–600 BC, Fig. 3.4b) Corinthian pottery was found in greater quantities at all these places, in addition to some pottery at Samos. This appears to indicate the development of the Corinthian pottery network as a major export project already by the end of the seventh century. The quantities of Corinthian pottery increased significantly once again in the sixth century. For period three (600–550 BC, Fig. 3.4c), pottery is found across all parts of the Aegean, albeit in relatively low quantities in Ionia. Corinthian pottery is found in greater proportion of the total assemblage at Delos and on Rhodes than Attic pottery in the same period. Finally, for the end of the sixth century (550–500 BC, Fig. 3.4d), while there is an increase in the proportion of Corinthian pottery in the assemblages at sites around the Saronic Gulf, there is a decrease elsewhere as opposed to in the previous period. This is a *proportional* change, not a reduction in the absolute number of ceramics – it merely indicates that, as the Attic network seemed to extend much further across the Aegean at the end of the sixth century, at the same time the Corinthian network did not change at the same pace.

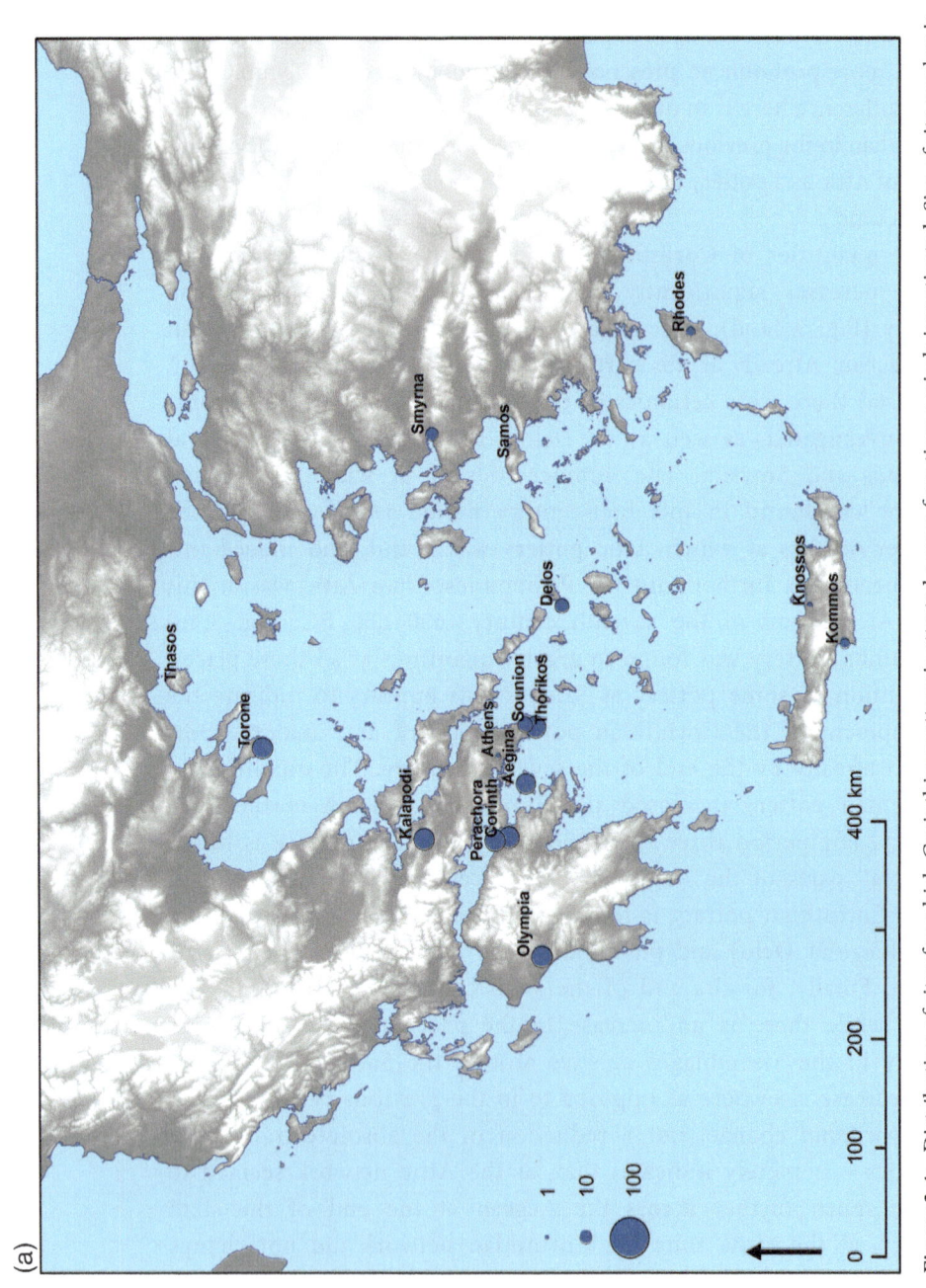

Figure 3.4a Distribution of sites for which Corinthian pottery is attested across four time periods investigated. Size of site marker is proportional to the amount of pottery found, relative to all other types of pottery. 700–650 BC

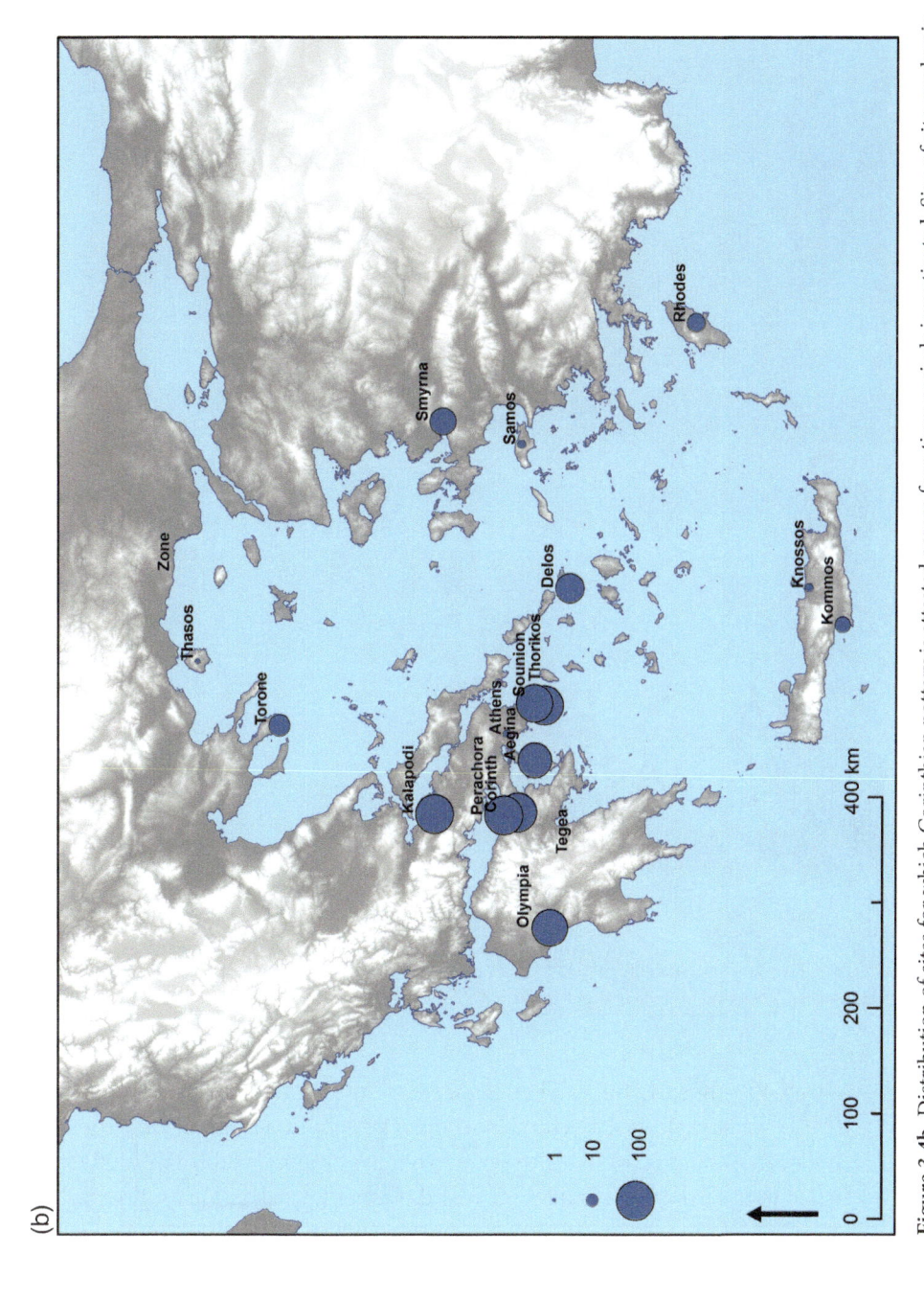

Figure 3.4b Distribution of sites for which Corinthian pottery is attested across four time periods investigated. Size of site marker is proportional to the amount of pottery found, relative to all other types of pottery. 650–600 BC.

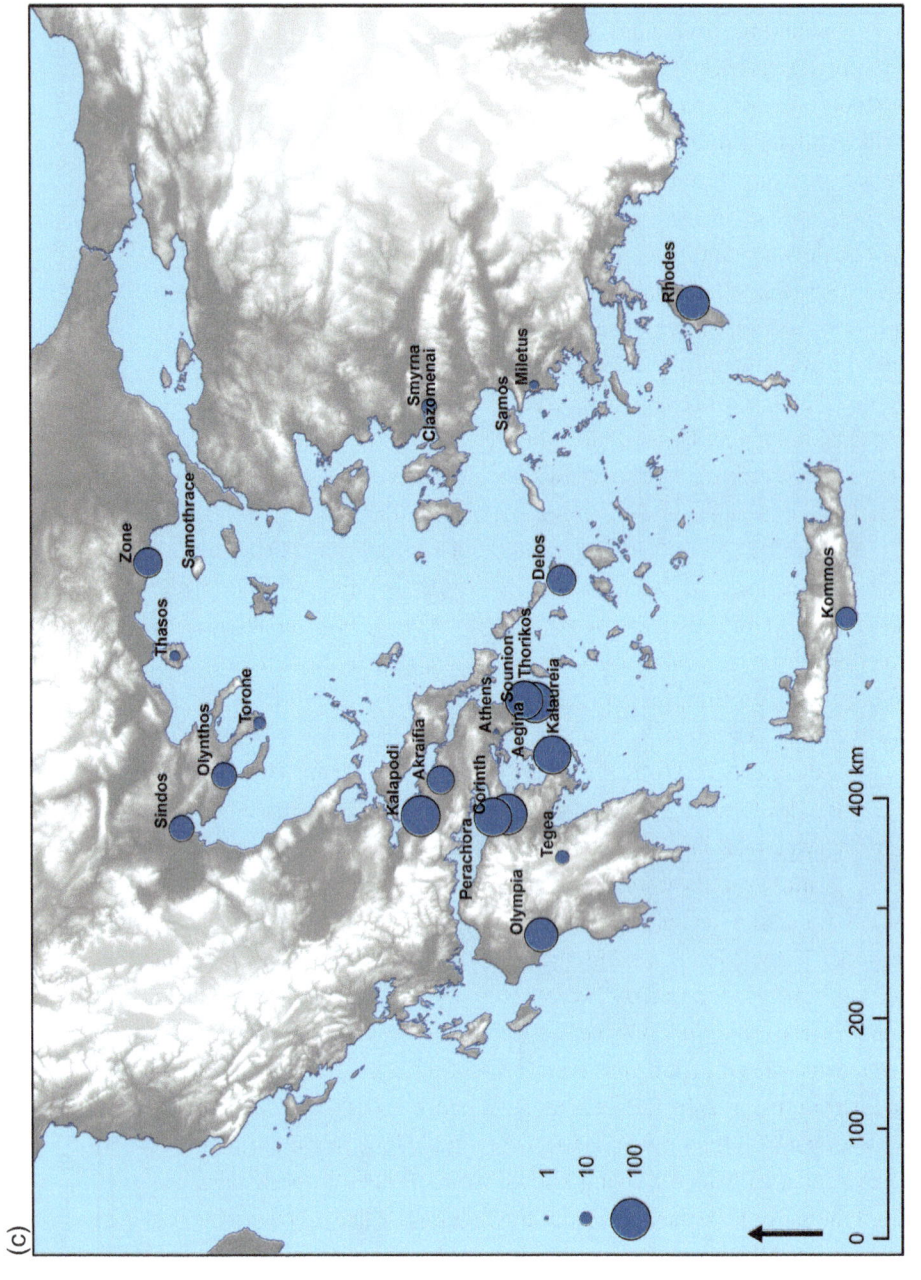

Figure 3.4c Distribution of sites for which Corinthian pottery is attested across four time periods investigated. Size of site marker is proportional to the amount of pottery found, relative to all other types of pottery. 600–550 BC.

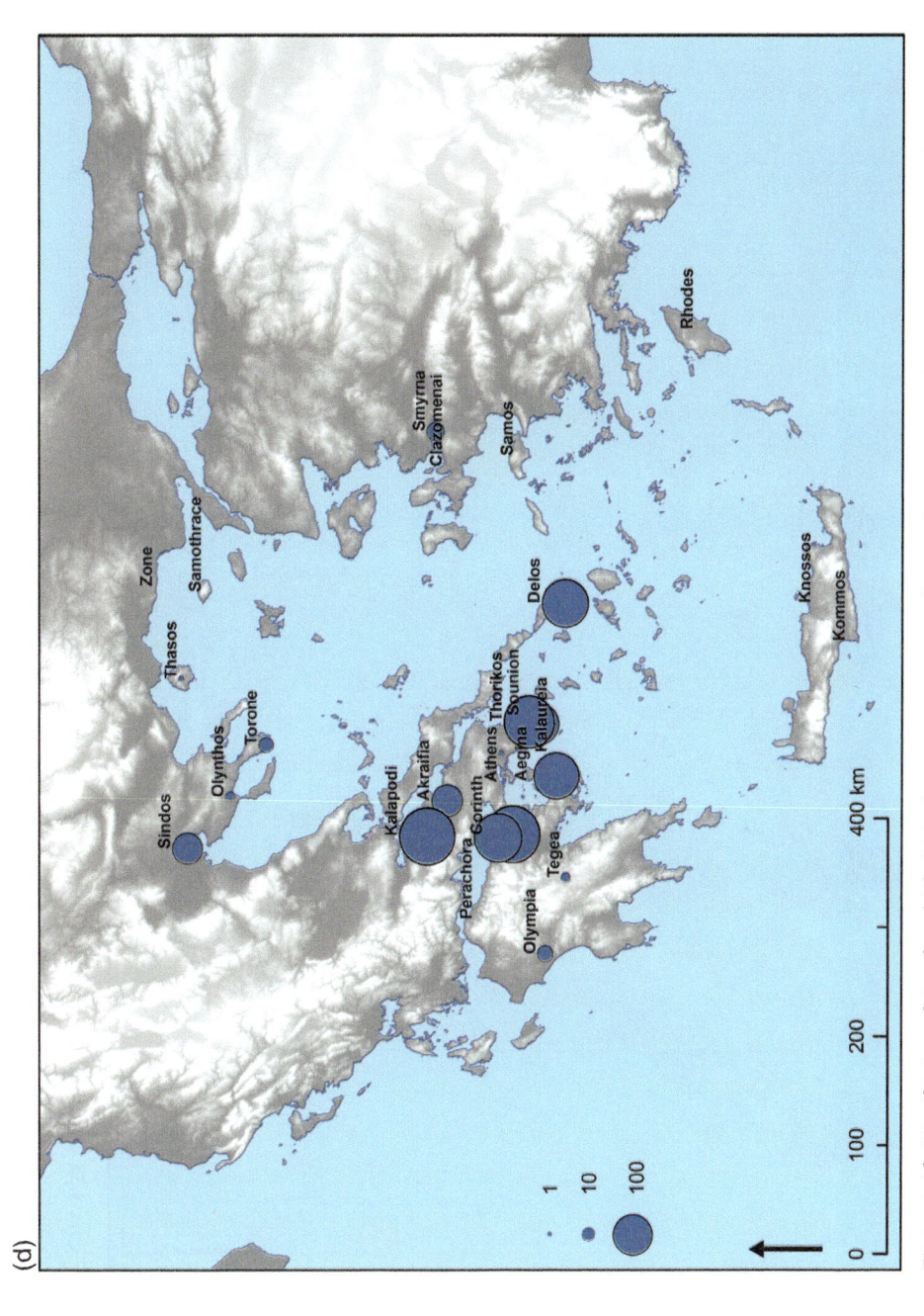

Figure 3.4d Distribution of sites for which Corinthian pottery is attested across four time periods investigated. Size of site marker is proportional to the amount of pottery found, relative to all other types of pottery. 550–500 BC.

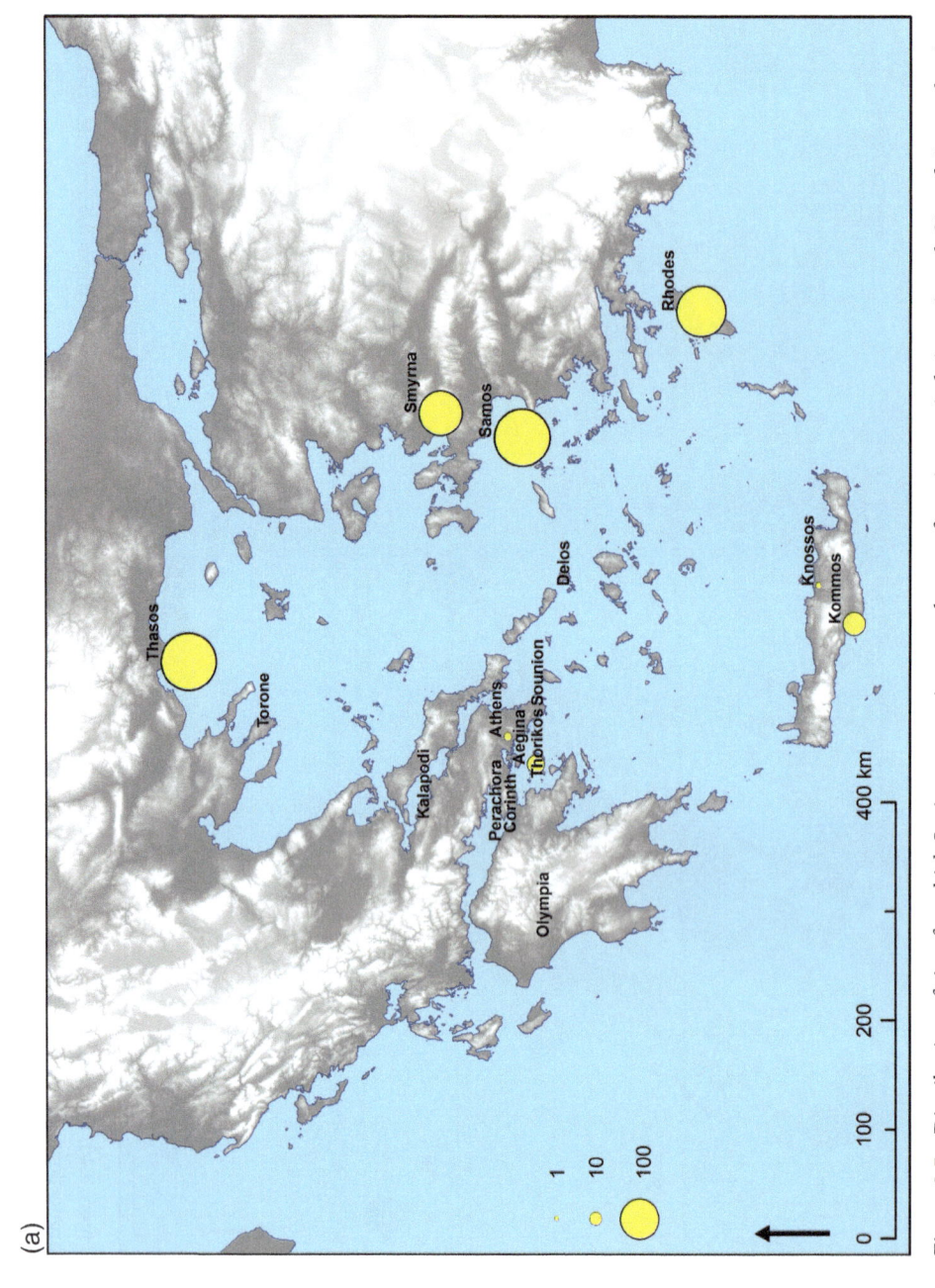

Figure 3.5a Distribution of sites for which Ionian pottery is attested across four time periods investigated. Size of site marker is proportional to the amount of pottery found, relative to all other types of pottery. 700–650 BC

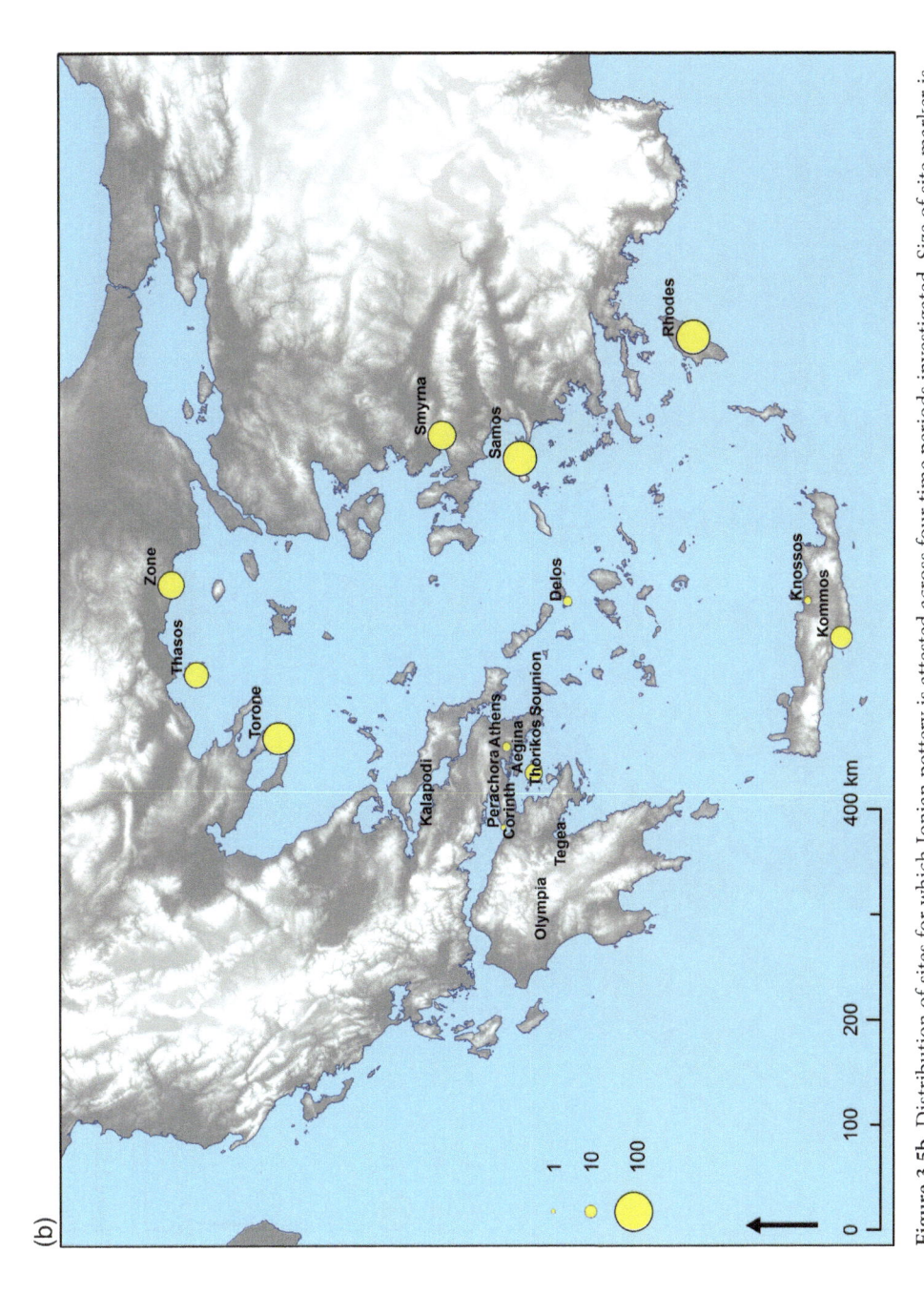

Figure 3.5b Distribution of sites for which Ionian pottery is attested across four time periods investigated. Size of site marker is proportional to the amount of pottery found, relative to all other types of pottery. 650–600 BC.

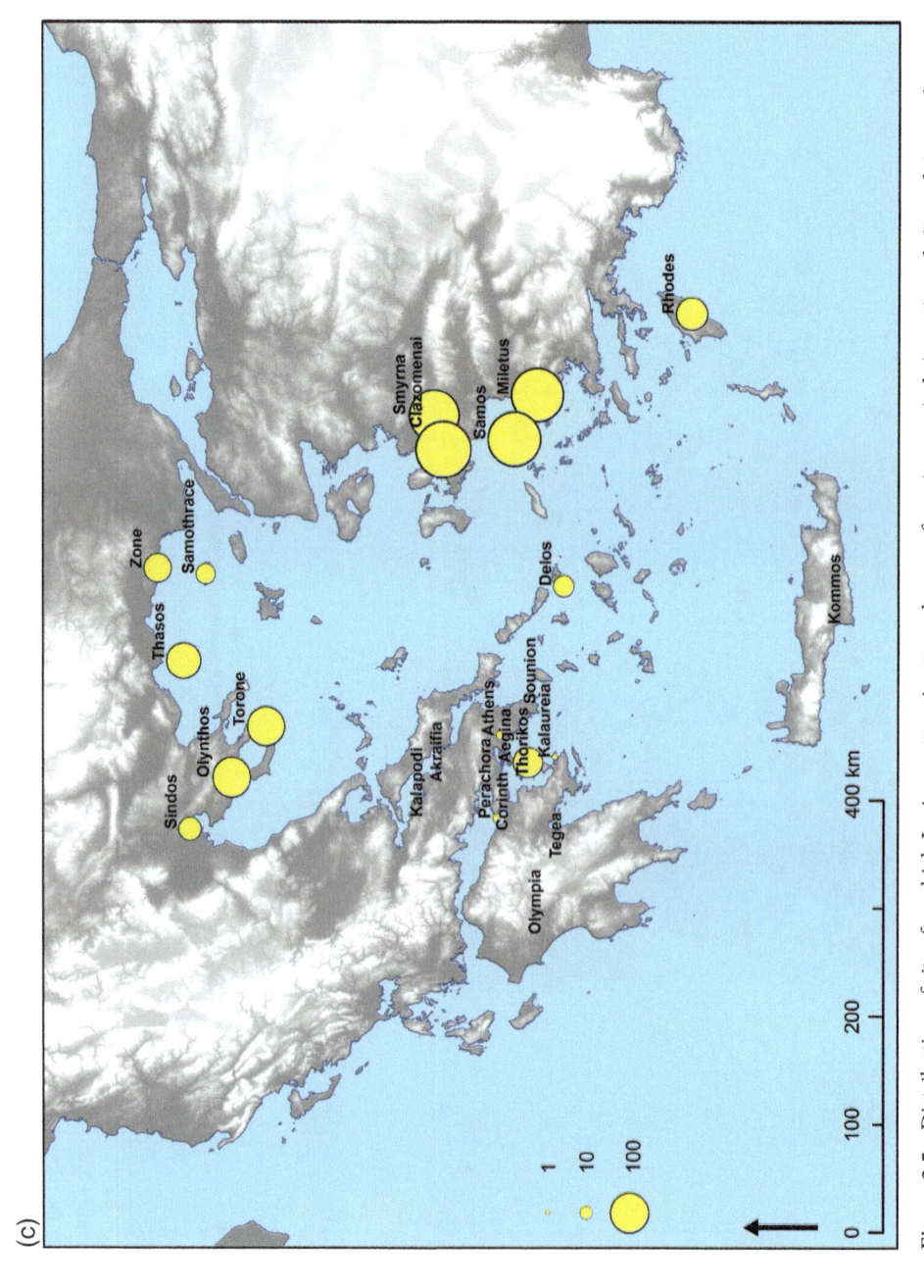

Figure 3.5c Distribution of sites for which Ionian pottery is attested across four time periods investigated. Size of site marker is proportional to the amount of pottery found, relative to all other types of pottery. 600–550 BC.

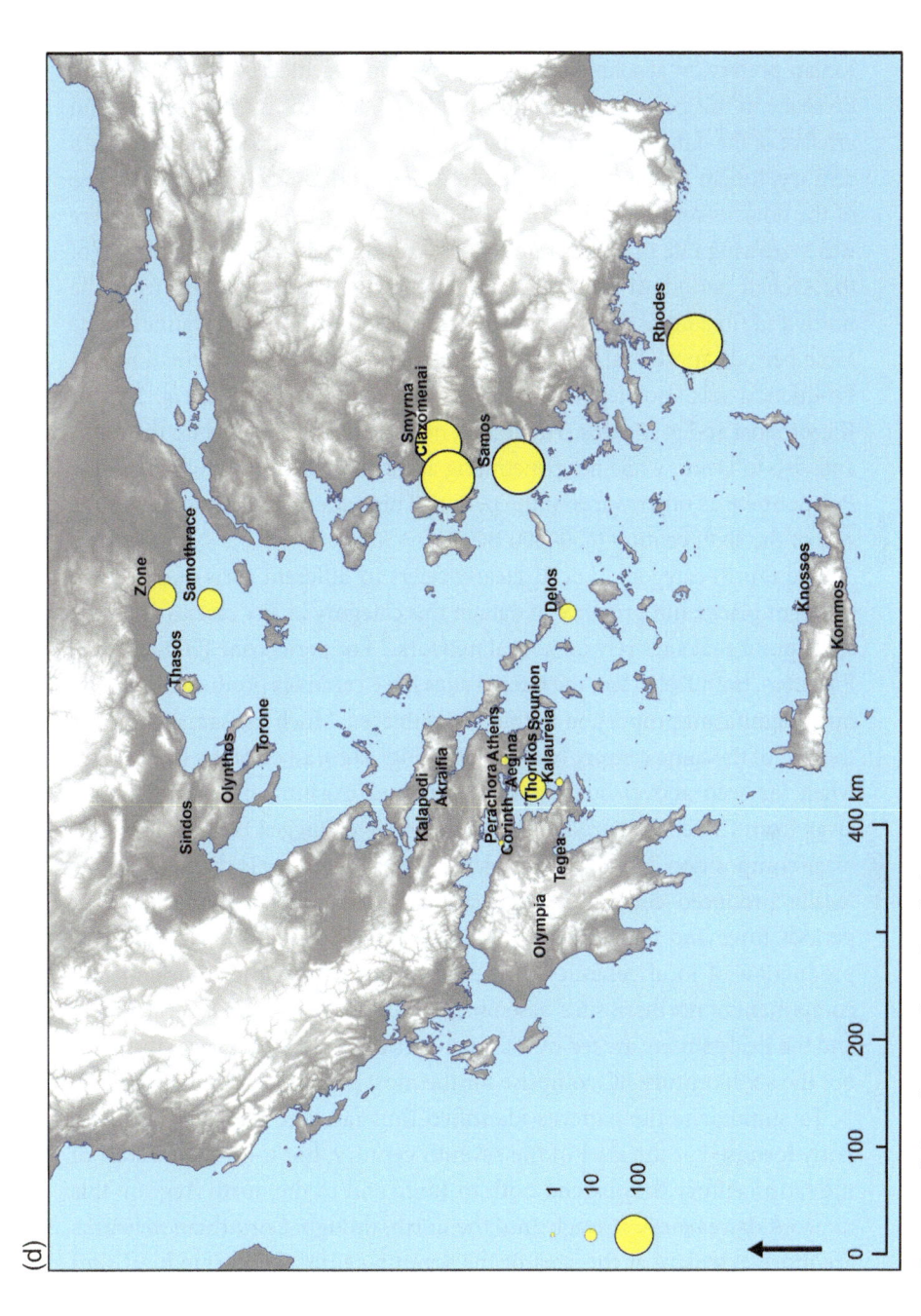

Figure 3.5d Distribution of sites for which Ionian pottery is attested across four time periods investigated. Size of site marker is proportional to the amount of pottery found, relative to all other types of pottery. 550–500 BC.

Understandably, Ionian pottery (Fig. 3.5a–d) is found in high proportions in Ionia from the start of the seventh century (Fig. 3.5a). Although there is also a significant proportion within the total assemblage of Thasos registered as Ionian pottery, in absolute terms it is in fact only eighteen vessels; an Ionian presence in this period must not be overstated, and this is to some extent an artefact of the data being handled here proportionally. Already in the seventh century, Ionian networks connected to Athens and to Kommos, and the size of the dots at Samos and Smyrna (650–600 BC, Fig. 3.5b) indicate that there was a growing rate of production for local ceramics already by the middle of the Archaic period. At the same time, the network was also pushing up to the north and (in contrast to the pattern for Attic and Corinthian ceramics in the same period), more Ionian pottery seemed to be reaching Crete than before. Production was also stepped up in period three (600–550 BC, Fig. 3.5c) at Klazomenai and at Miletos. The Ionian network drove further into the north and also to Delos, while not penetrating as far in the Saronic Gulf nor in the Peloponnese as other wares of the period. This pattern is consistent with the end of the sixth century (550–500 BC, Fig. 3.5d).

The fourth category, 'Local', clearly refers to different sorts of objects in different places, but presence of data in this category in any case conveys the same point that sites rely on a local network.[3] For period one (700–650 BC, Fig. 3.6a), both Delos and the Cretan sites have ceramics produced locally in not insignificant proportion in their assemblages. Much the same is true for the end of the same century (650–600 BC, Fig. 3.6b), albeit at the Cretan sites when (as seen above) quantities of Attic and Corinthian networks move away from Crete, local production seems to have plugged the gap in assemblage composition. Notably also Tegea in the Peloponnese is characterised by locally produced ceramics (from various Peloponnesian workshops). In periods three and four (600–550 BC, Fig. 3.6c; 550–500 BC, Fig. 3.6d) the production of local ceramics in the north contributes a not insignificant component of northern sites' assemblages, while both sites in central Greece and the Peloponnese are fed by local networks. Cretan assemblages throughout the sixth century BC comprise for the most part locally produced wares.

To summarise the patterns identified thus far. The Attic networks are fairly localised at the start of the seventh century, but towards the start of the sixth century they extend both to Ionia and to the north Aegean: this network drives more strongly into the north, though. Corinthian networks are more extensive at the start of the seventh century, covering local sites

---

[3] 'Attic' pottery found at Athens, 'Corinthian' pottery found at Corinth, and 'Ionian' pottery found at the Ionian sites are excluded from this category.

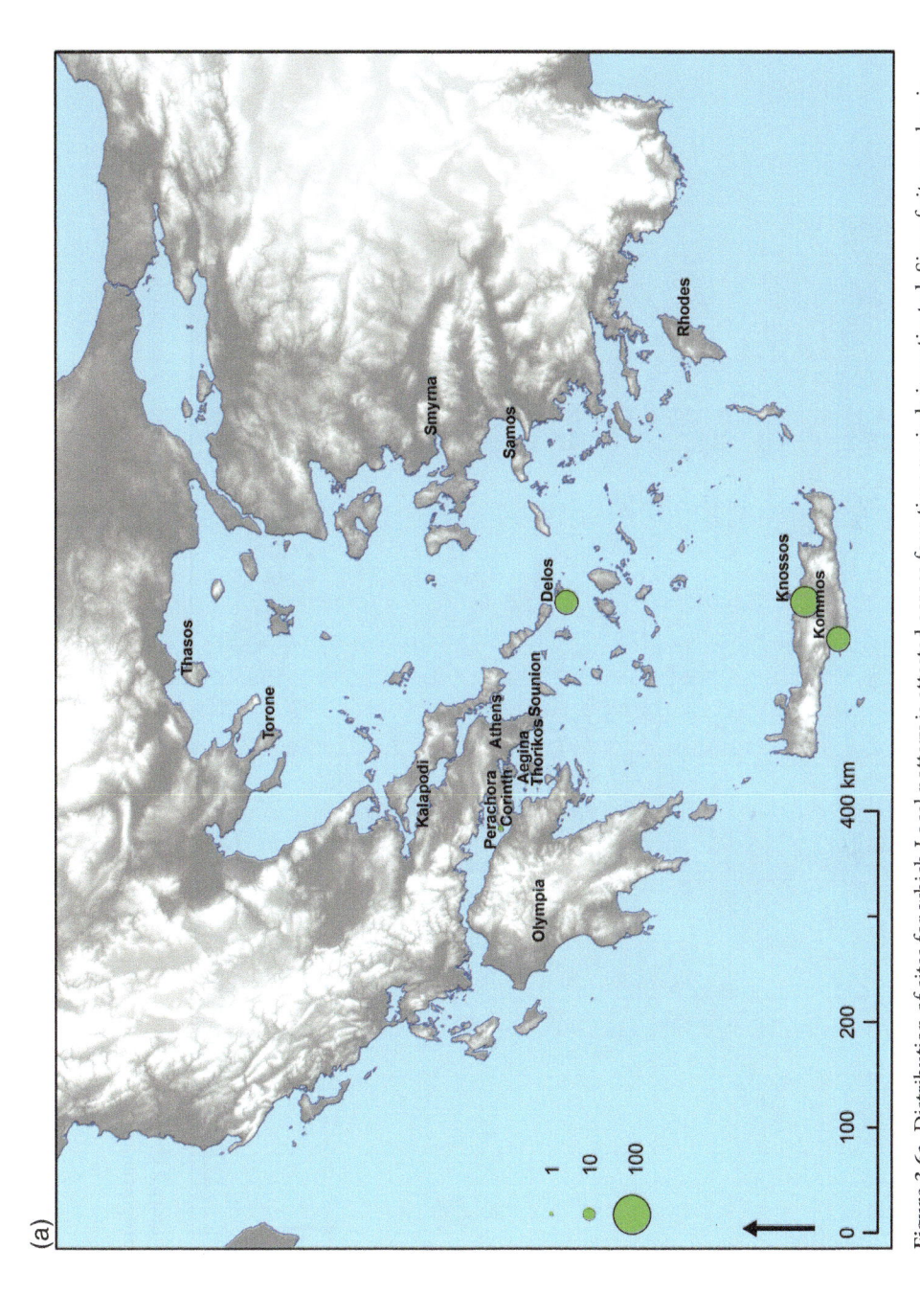

Figure 3.6a Distribution of sites for which Local pottery is attested across four time periods investigated. Size of site marker is proportional to the amount of pottery found, relative to all other types of pottery. 700–650 BC

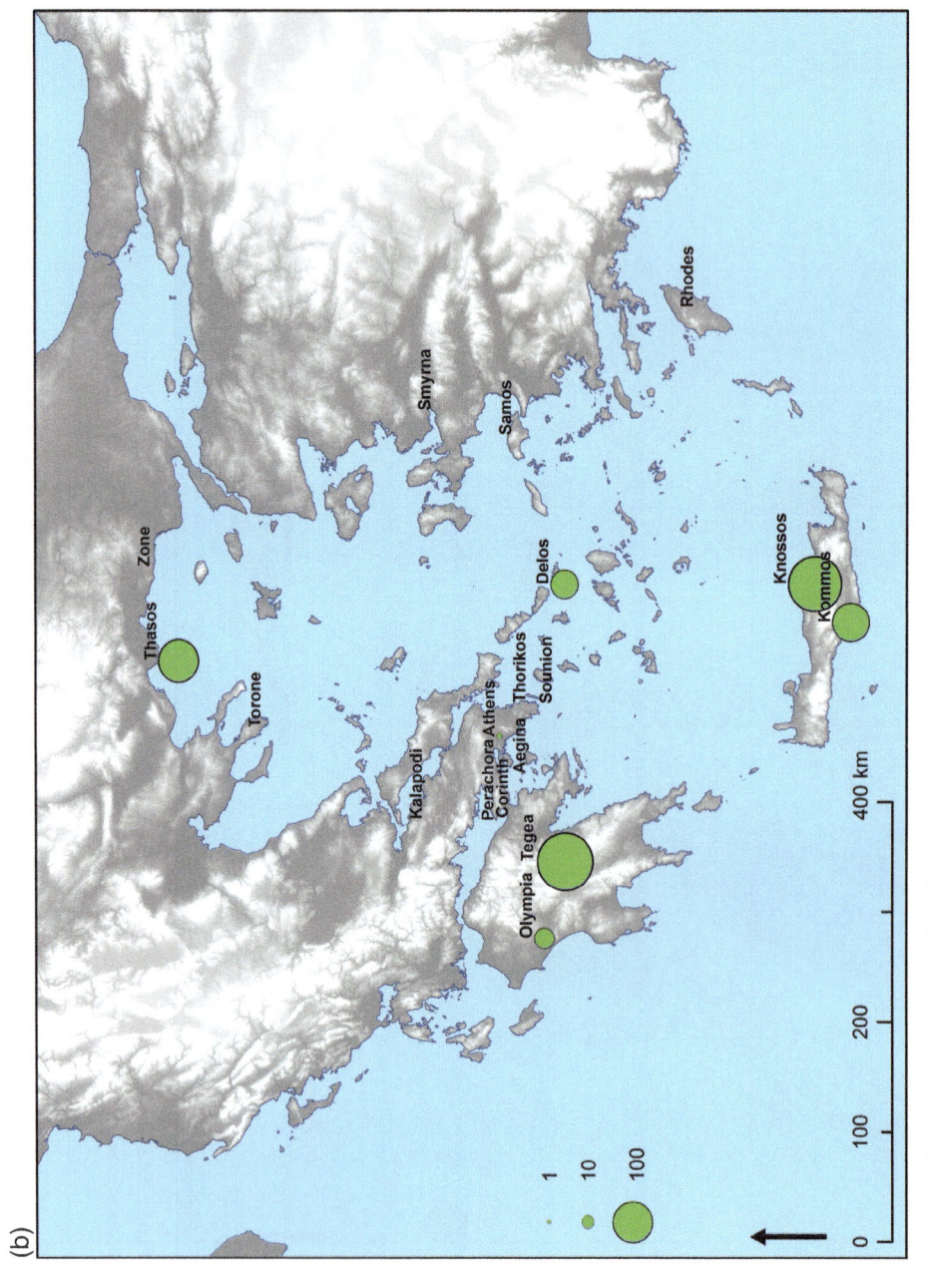

Figure 3.6b Distribution of sites for which Local pottery is attested across four time periods investigated. Size of site marker is proportional to the amount of pottery found, relative to all other types of pottery. 650–600 BC.

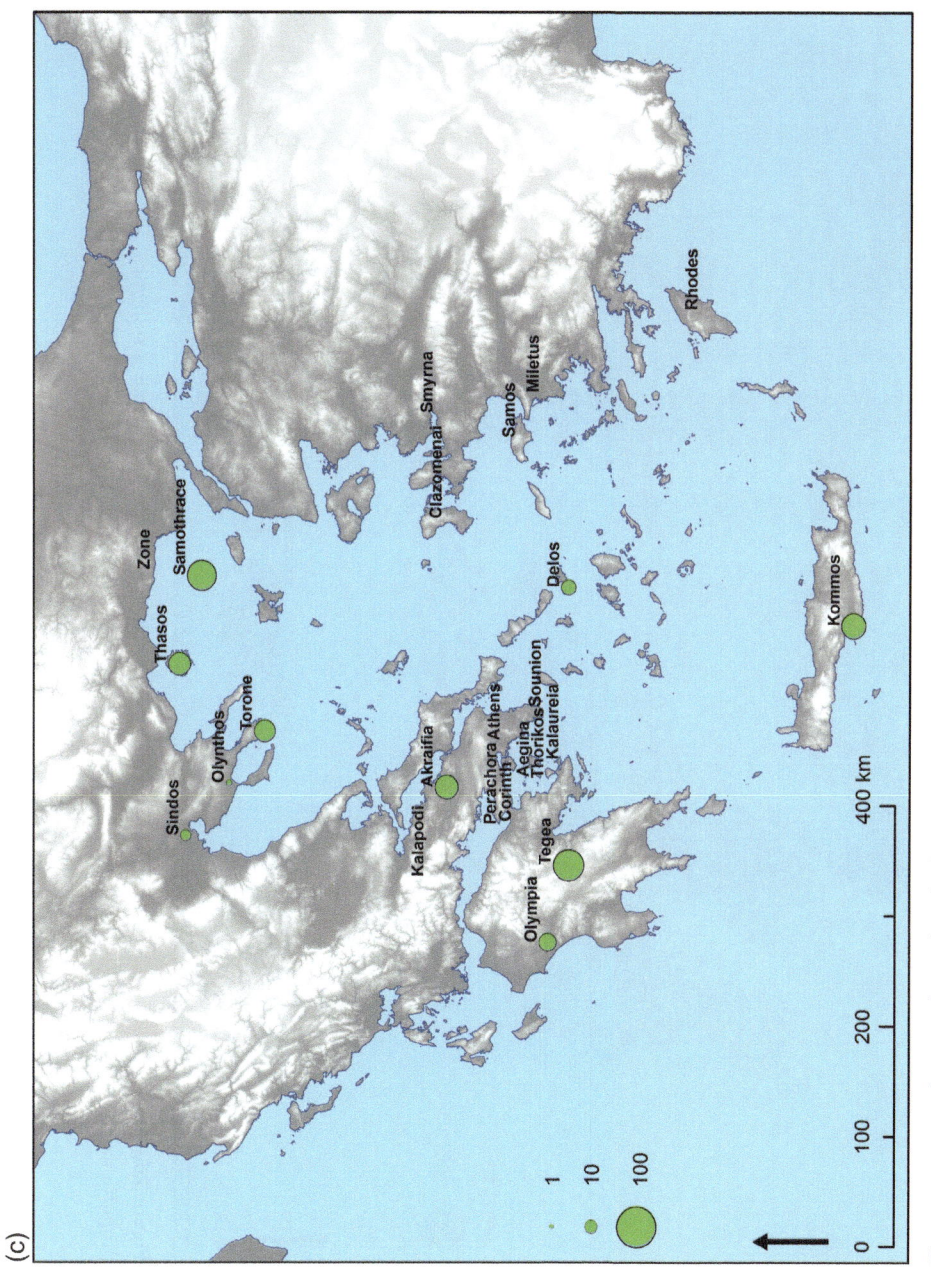

Figure 3.6c Distribution of sites for which Local pottery is attested across four time periods investigated. Size of site marker is proportional to the amount of pottery found, relative to all other types of pottery. 600–550 BC.

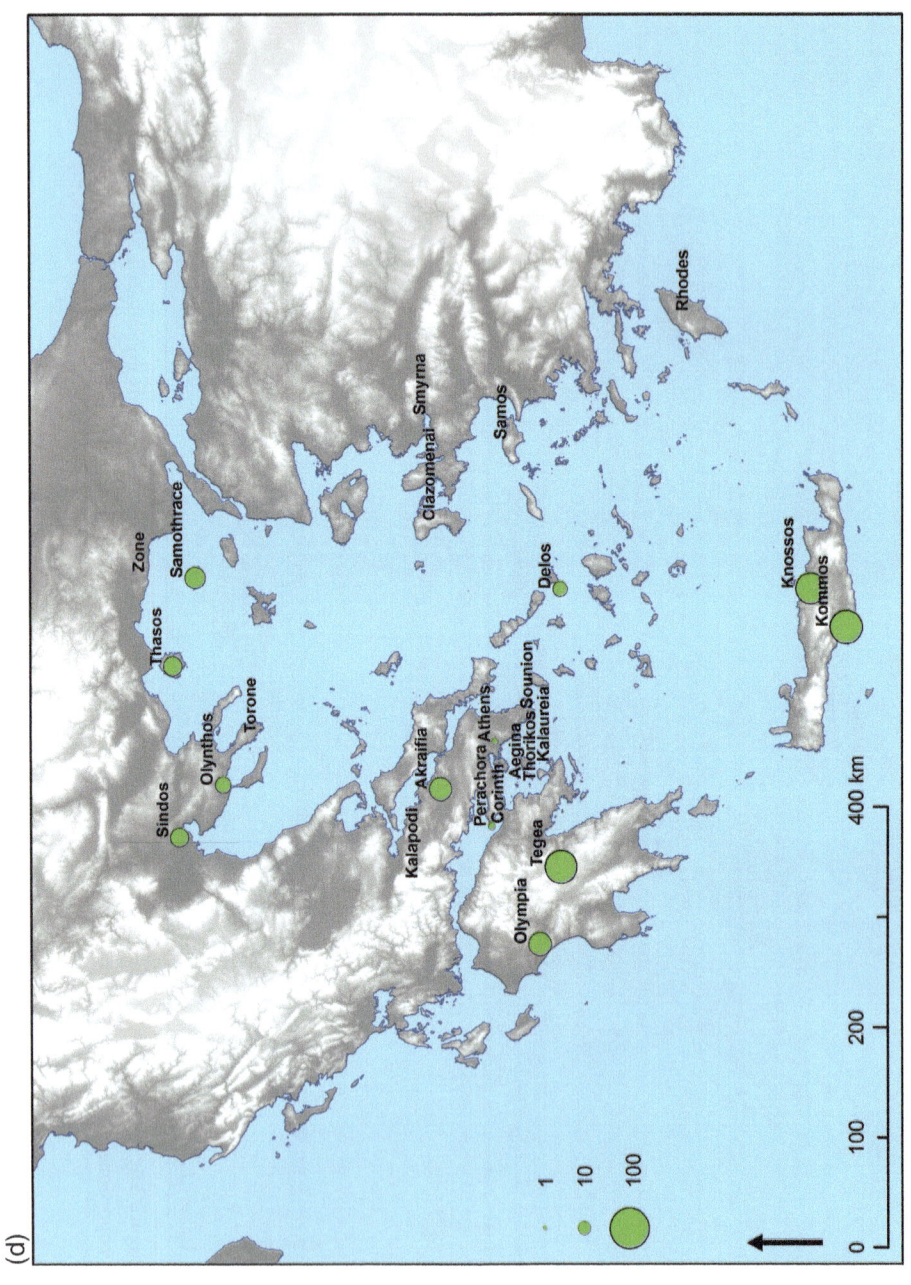

Figure 3.6d Distribution of sites for which Local pottery is attested across four time periods investigated. Size of site marker is proportional to the amount of pottery found, relative to all other types of pottery. 550–500 BC.

but already having a reach into the north, into Ionia and towards Crete. They expand more quickly than Attic networks but by the end of the sixth century they are focused more locally in the Aegean, and they have less extension in the north. The Ionian networks have more limited reach beyond the local, but they do make their way to the Saronic Gulf by the end of the seventh century. Ionian networks also have reach into the north and into the islands. Finally, it has been observed that the sites of Crete, the Peloponnese and central Greece all rely to a greater extent on their local networks, with very little fluctuation in the pattern over the course of the Archaic period. All in all, while these distribution maps are useful for thinking about the spread of various pottery types and systems of exchange, they are less useful for identifying exceptional sites and nuances of the pottery networks. For this, a different set of models is required.

Indeed, it is useful here to think here about different attributes of the pottery at the same time. What we have done is essentially a one-dimensional analysis: 'is Corinthian pottery found at this site? If yes -> it is in the group; if no -> it is not in the group'. More interesting in constructing networks of complex and layered socio-cultural interactions, though, is to adjust those variables, that is, to ask how groups of sites change if we redefine how similar or different sites must be before we place them within the same group. Is Corinthian pottery found at both of these sites *and* in similar quantities *and* is Attic pottery also found *and* is Corinthian pottery a much more common product to find at this site than Attic? To do so requires multivariate modelling, and clustering based on the simultaneous assessment of a number of different variables.

Multivariate statistics are used here to sort the data into significant groups, and as a set of techniques that analyse distance between multiple variables simultaneously (e.g. ware, shape, place of origin; Hodson 1969 and Baxter 1994). This allows one to see the relative similarity or difference between a set of sites based on the various attributes of their ceramic assemblage. The technique used in this chapter is a Principal Component Analysis (PCA), an exploratory data technique used to visualise co-variance. All PCAs were calculated in this section using the R package *cabootcrs*.[4] In the following analysis, roughly defined 'funerary', 'sanctuary' and 'urban' sites were analysed separately for each of the four time periods discussed (700–650 BC, 650–600 BC, 600–550 BC, 550–500 BC) (Table **A2.2**). In the first analysis, distance between sites was measured on the basis of the ceramic wares found in relative proportions of each site. On the output graphs, the location of sites and ware names is arbitrary, but

---

[4] Code written by Ringrose 2013, hosted on CRAN at https://CRAN.R-project.org/package=cabootcrs, accessed 15 December 2021.

the proximity of sites to one another indicates their similarity in terms of ware composition (e.g. if Athens is plotted close to Attic but far from Corinthian, we know that the proportion of the first type of ware within the total assemblage from Athens is relatively high compared to the latter), while their proximity of sites to ware labels indicates that there was a greater proportion of ceramics from this site belonging to that ware category. Data were buffered via a bootstrapping function that resamples core data through a set number of iterations.[5] Resampling takes account, therefore, of some of the uncertainty inherent in the dataset, and this provides a range of output values based on each computation. These results are visualised not as single datapoints, but as 'haloes', within which datapoints considered the 'most likely' are located given the nature of quantitative uncertainties.

The following figures illustrate the results of the PCA for each of the successive four periods analysed, and the results have been split between sites identified as 'urban' (Fig. 3.7a–d) and 'sanctuary' (Fig. 3.8a–d). The location of each ware point within the graph is arbitrary, but the position at which site points are plotted is always relative to the proportion of each ware within the total ceramic assemblage at that site. The halo around each site plot represents the adjustment for the bootstrap, and given the quality of the source data the site point could actually be plotted anywhere within this region. Sites are coloured according to geography, in order to make the patterning between region and ware type even more patent.

In period one (700–650 BC, Fig. 3.7a and Fig. 3.8a), and as already observed above, a large number of sites in the Aegean consume potteries that are locally produced. This is truer for urban sites than for sanctuary sites. Of the urban sites, though, the assemblages are most mixed at Miletos, Torone and Vroulia: while the first two have a fairly even mix of Ionian and Attic pottery, Vroulia is different for its inclusion of more Corinthian pottery. In the sanctuary ware plot, however, there are more sites plotted adjacent to multiple ware nodes, indicating that assemblages are generally more mixed in terms of wares. This is the case for Delos, Kommos and Lindos while there is a great deal of similarity in the composition of the assemblages at Corinth, Kolonna and Sounion. Aphaia on Aegina and the Temple of Athena at Emborio on Chios show the greatest degree of 'specialisation', respectively consuming predominantly Corinthian and Ionian ceramics.

---

[5] The general principle (as outlined in Ringrose 1992: 618) is to 'assess the statistical stability of the scatterplots, that is to determine if small differences in the data matrix can produce (relatively) large differences in the plot(s), and so to assess whether differences in the positions of points on the plots are "significant" or not.' A more specific introduction to bootstrapping with regard to Correspondence Analysis is given in Lockyear 2013.

(a)

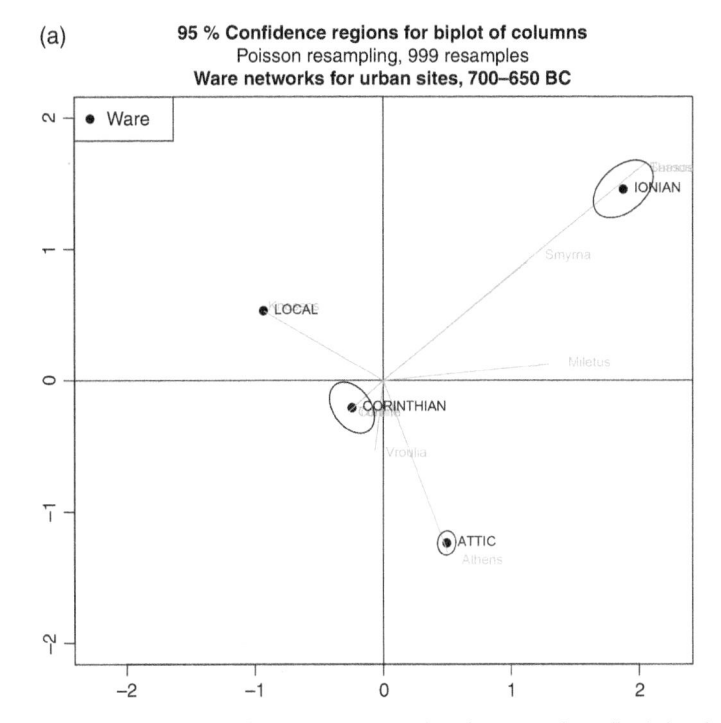

95 % Confidence regions for biplot of columns
Poisson resampling, 999 resamples
Ware networks for urban sites, 700–650 BC

Figure 3.7a Results of PCA on ceramic data from sites broadly defined as 'urban' and with respect to ware categorisation. 700–650 BC

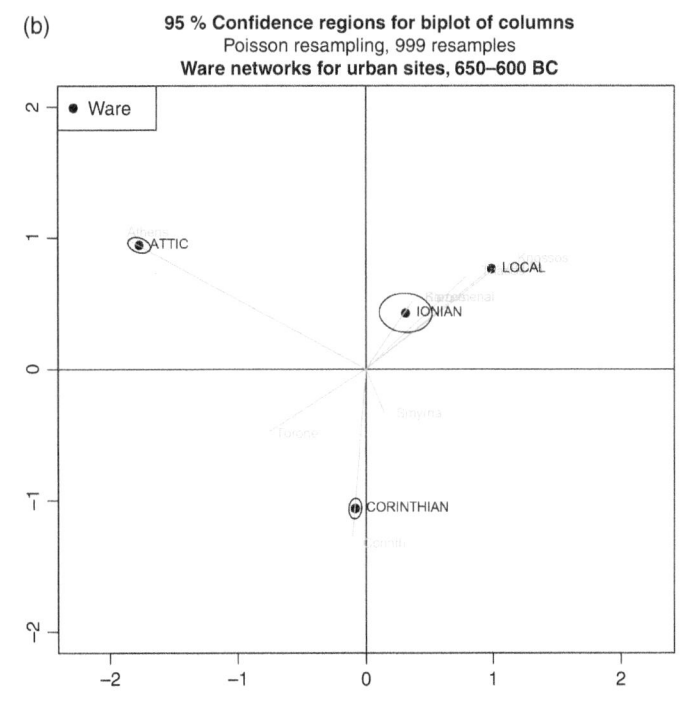

(b)

95 % Confidence regions for biplot of columns
Poisson resampling, 999 resamples
Ware networks for urban sites, 650–600 BC

Figure 3.7b Results of PCA on ceramic data from sites broadly defined as 'urban' and with respect to ware categorisation. 650–600 BC.

(c)

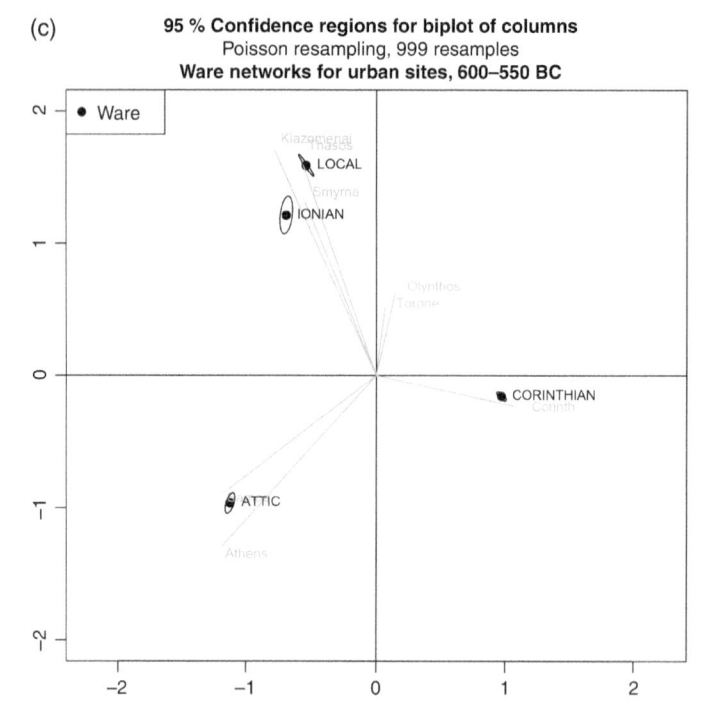

Figure 3.7c Results of PCA on ceramic data from sites broadly defined as 'urban' and with respect to ware categorisation. 600–550 BC.

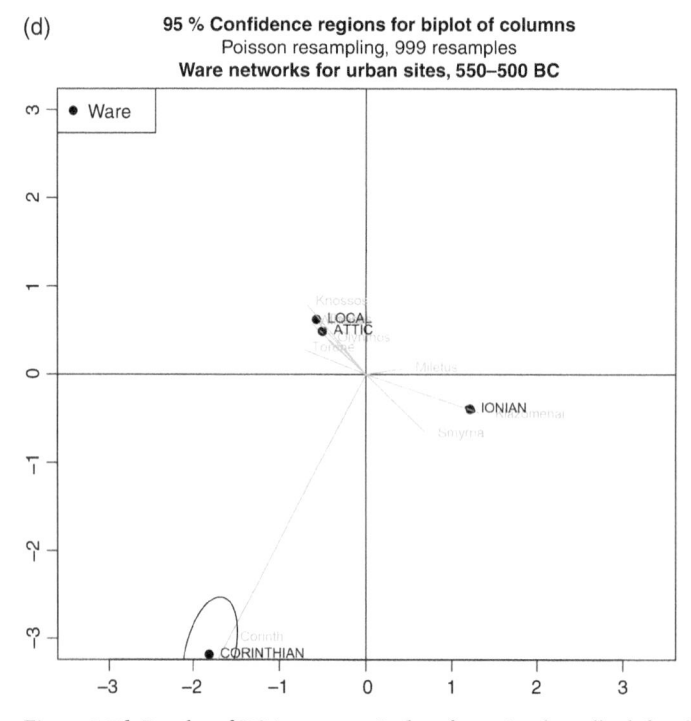

(d)

Figure 3.7d Results of PCA on ceramic data from sites broadly defined as 'urban' and with respect to ware categorisation. 550–500 BC.

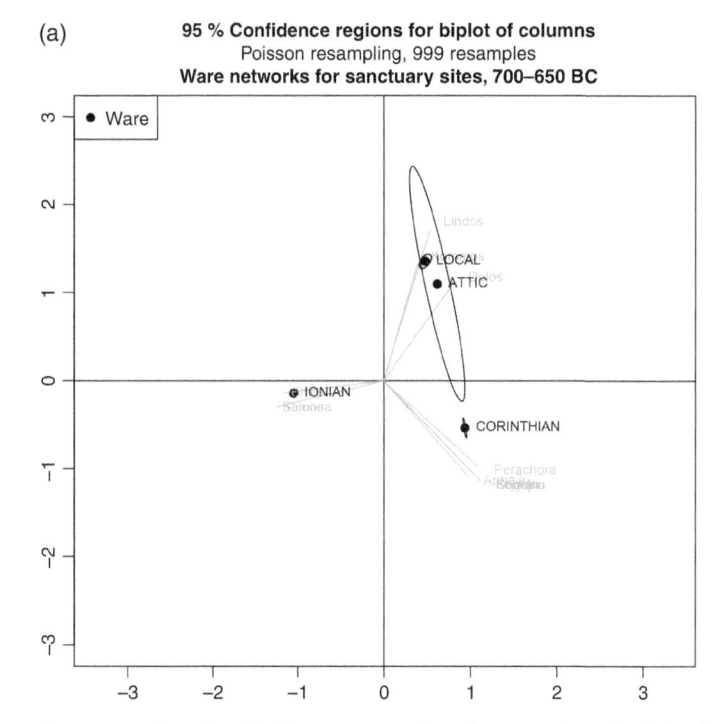

Figure 3.8a Results of PCA on ceramic data from sites broadly defined as 'sanctuary' and with respect to ware categorisation. 700–650 BC

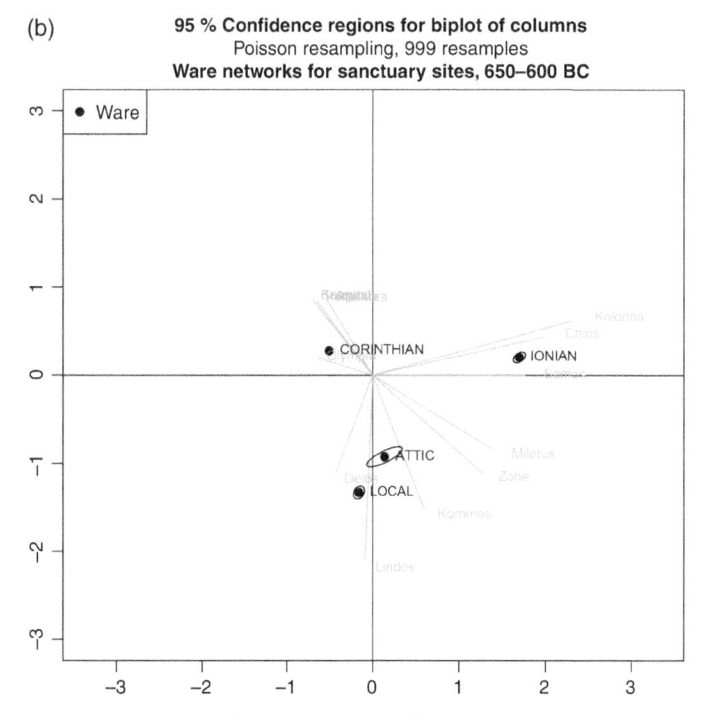

Figure 3.8b Results of PCA on ceramic data from sites broadly defined as 'sanctuary' and with respect to ware categorisation. 650–600 BC.

(c)

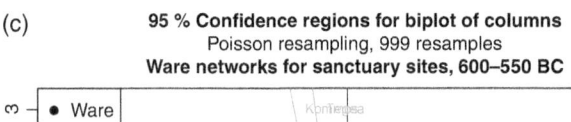

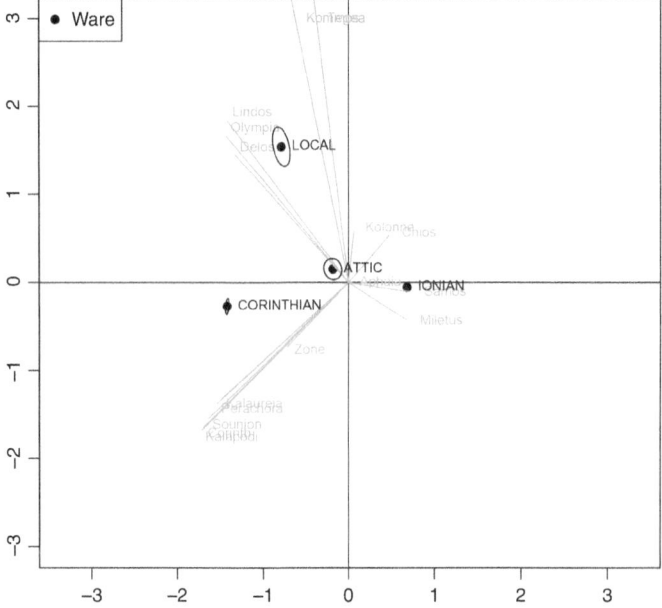

95 % Confidence regions for biplot of columns
Poisson resampling, 999 resamples
Ware networks for sanctuary sites, 600–550 BC

Figure 3.8c Results of PCA on ceramic data from sites broadly defined as 'sanctuary' and with respect to ware categorisation. 600–550 BC.

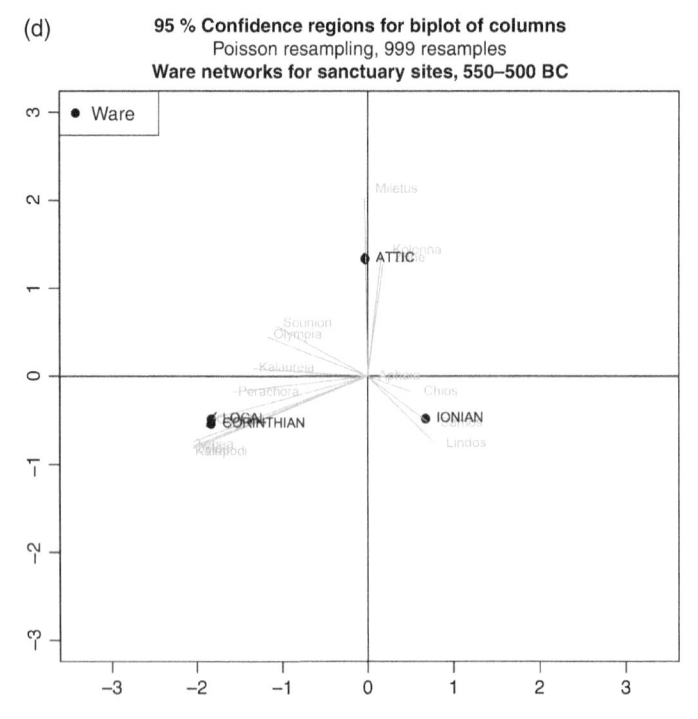

(d)

95 % Confidence regions for biplot of columns
Poisson resampling, 999 resamples
Ware networks for sanctuary sites, 550–500 BC

Figure 3.8d Results of PCA on ceramic data from sites broadly defined as 'sanctuary' and with respect to ware categorisation. 550–500 BC.

In period two (650–600 BC, Fig. 3.7b and Fig. 3.8b), there is a similar pattern in the urban site assemblages to the previous period. Torone still exhibited a rather mixed assemblage (as did Smyrna), but for the other sites, ceramics consumed were predominantly locally made. Again, this is not necessarily the case for sanctuary sites, where the greatest number of sites were consuming ceramics of predominantly mixed wares. This is also not geographically restricted, as there are very similar compositions of the assemblages from Miletos, Kommos and Zone. Kolonna, although not geographically located in Ionia, consumed a large number of Ionian ceramics, and similarly Olympia consumed predominantly Corinthian ceramics.

The patterns for periods three (600–550 BC, Fig. 3.7c and Fig. 3.8c) and four (550–500 BC, Fig. 3.7d and Fig. 3.8d) begin to look both a little different while also revealing a more pronounced version of the patterns identified in the previous century.[6] In the sixth century, there is also sufficient data to look across funerary assemblages. The consuming of ceramics in funerary contexts does not map very neatly onto geography: Samothrace took Ionian ceramics, Akraifia used a combination of Attic and Corinthian ceramics, Sindos and Tanagra combined quite evenly all of these categories, and Corinth consumed by far predominantly local Corinthian ceramics. The pattern for urban sites is consistent with the seventh century in that sites favour locally manufactured ceramics, save for Samos which consumed mainly Attic wares, and Olynthos and Torone that used a mixture of wares. The pattern for sanctuary sites indicates that there is quite a difference in the ware consumption between sites. Some still favoured local consumption (Corinth, Lindos, Miletos, Olympia, Perachora, Samos) while others predominantly consumed wares made elsewhere: Aphaia consumed Ionian wares; Kalapodi and Zone consumed Corinthian wares, and Kolonna consumed a mixture of Ionian and Attic. One noticeable difference between the plots for the urban and sanctuary assemblages is in the relative distance between different ware types. For urban sites, all wares are spaced rather evenly, indicating that (apart from the sites at which there was a high degree of mixed wares evident in the assemblages) these categories are rather distinct: for example, Athens and Corinth did not generally consume one another's potteries. For sanctuary sites, however, ware category labels are plotted much closer to one another, indicating that sites do not generally 'specialise' in the consuming of one

---

[6] This is also probably a product of data quality, as there are more objects available for analysis from the sixth century than the seventh century. Having a larger dataset to analyse helps to smooth out anomalous results that might have been an artefact of the previous period.

ware of pottery alone. Delos consumed *not only* locally produced Cycladic ceramics *but also* similar quantities of Corinthian ceramics; Miletos and Samos consumed *not only* locally produced Ionian ceramics, *but also* similar quantities of Attic wares.

In general, locally produced ceramics supplied the demand of pottery for urban sites; but for sanctuary sites there is less correlation between the geographic position of a site within the region and its consumption of regional potteries. Furthermore, there is less uncertainty in the assemblages of the urban sites, as indicated by the narrower haloes on the PCA output graphs. Kolonna is notable for the predominance of Ionian ceramics in its assemblage from an early date, as are Sounion and Thorikos with regard to Corinthian ceramics. One can also note the presence of Corinthian aryballoi on Rhodes and Delos – although their own locally made ceramics do not circulate far away. Many of these patterns have previously been noted on a case-by-case basis in the commentaries of each assemblage catalogue, but what is new here is that in synthesising these data the pattern is remarkably consistent. Ceramics were produced locally and circulated locally unless there was some specific need to look further afield to different markets, and demand for specific types of vessels was greater in the sixth century than the seventh century.

Similar patterns emerge upon analysing place of consumption vs. shape of ceramic (Table **A2.3**). For period one (700–650 BC, Fig. 3.9a and Fig. 3.10a) sanctuary sites had relatively more aryballoi, *hydriai* and *pyxides*, while urban sites had more mixed assemblages. Ceramics consumed at the sanctuaries of Corinth and Rheneia are the most striking exceptions (favouring amphoras and *hydriai*), while Samos (preference for kraters) and Chios (preference for *oinochoai*) are also notable; urban Knossos also provides an exception, owing to the consumption of aryballoi, *hydrai* and *pyxides*, while Corinth also tends towards the consumption of *pyxides*. Furthermore, although there seems to be some loose relationship between a site and the shapes of pottery consumed, there is very little relationship between a site's geographic region and its assemblage distribution.

There is a similar distribution for period two (650–600 BC, Fig. 3.9b and Fig. 3.10b). Amphoras, hydriai and oinochoai once more make up most of the assemblage at urban sites, particularly at Athens, Samos and Thasos: the plot for other sites is quite centrally clustered, indicating that there is not so much statistically significant distance between site assemblages. At sanctuaries, there begins to be here some distinction in the types of ceramics that different sites consumed. Chios, Corinth, Kolonna, Samos and Zone tended towards the consumption of *kylixes* and kraters, while Aphaia,

(a)

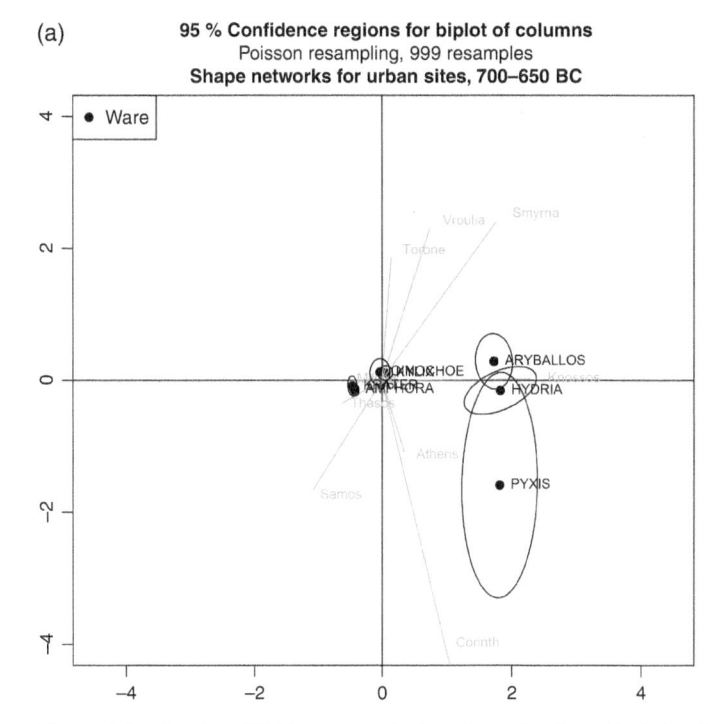

Figure 3.9a Results of PCA on ceramic data from sites broadly defined as 'urban' and with respect to shape categorisation. 700–650 BC

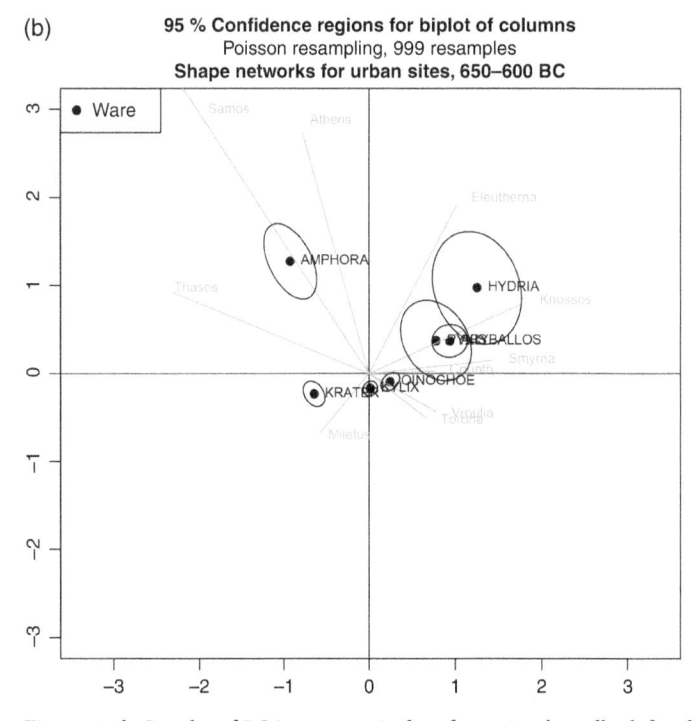

(b)

Figure 3.9b Results of PCA on ceramic data from sites broadly defined as 'urban' and with respect to shape categorisation. 650–600 BC.

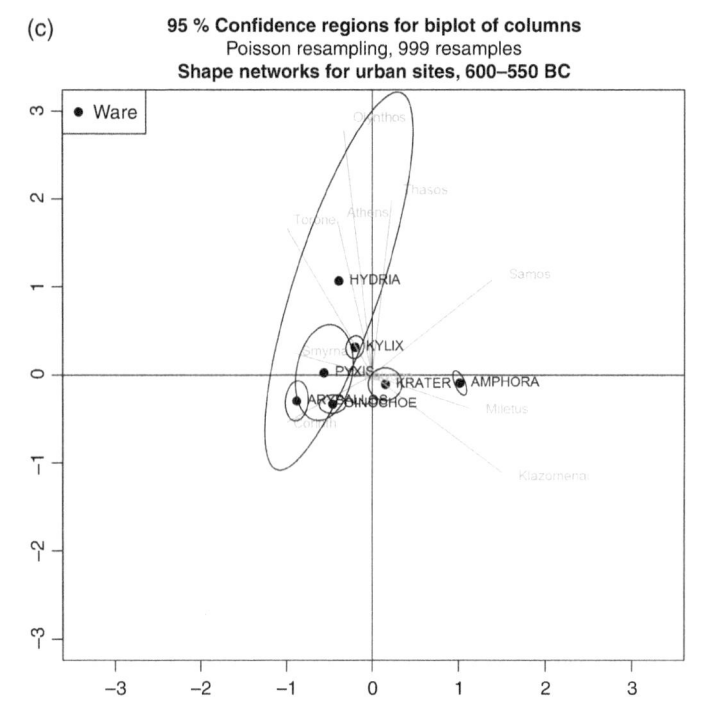

Figure 3.9c Results of PCA on ceramic data from sites broadly defined as 'urban' and with respect to shape categorisation. 600–550 BC.

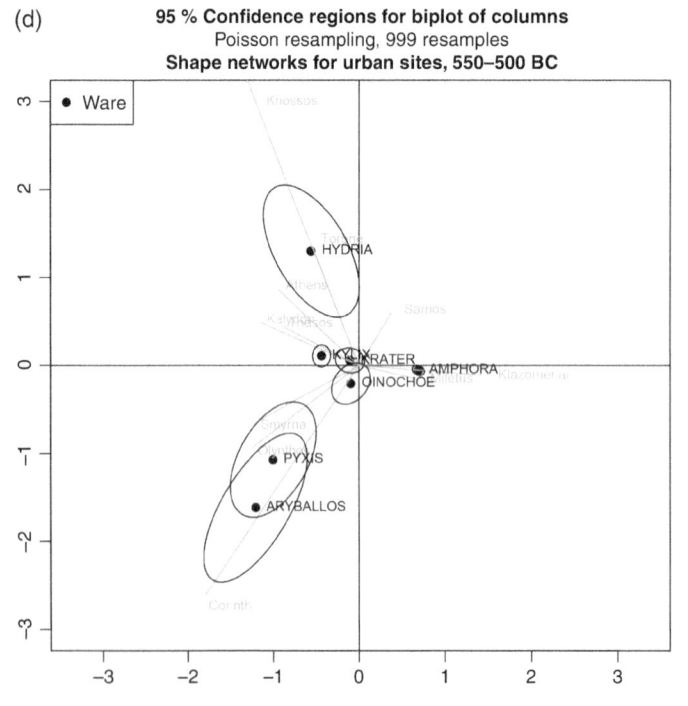

Figure 3.9d Results of PCA on ceramic data from sites broadly defined as 'urban' and with respect to shape categorisation. 550–500 BC.

(a)

95 % Confidence regions for biplot of columns
Poisson resampling, 999 resamples
Shape networks for sanctuary sites, 700–650 BC

Figure 3.10a Results of PCA on ceramic data from sites broadly defined as 'sanctuary' and with respect to shape categorisation. 700–650 BC

(b)

95 % Confidence regions for biplot of columns
Poisson resampling, 999 resamples
Shape networks for sanctuary sites, 650–600 BC

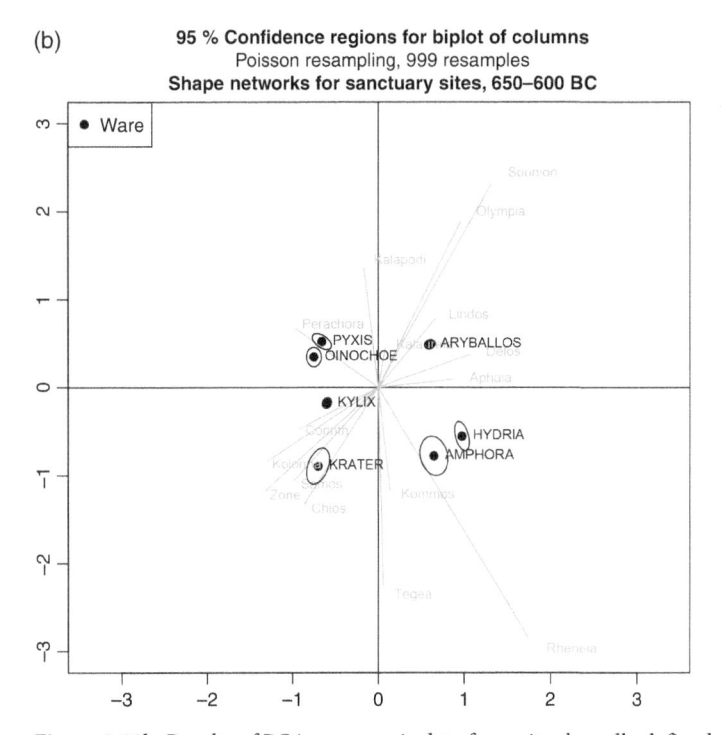

Figure 3.10b Results of PCA on ceramic data from sites broadly defined as 'sanctuary' and with respect to shape categorisation. 650–600 BC.

(c)

95 % Confidence regions for biplot of columns
Poisson resampling, 999 resamples
Shape networks for sanctuary sites, 600–550 BC

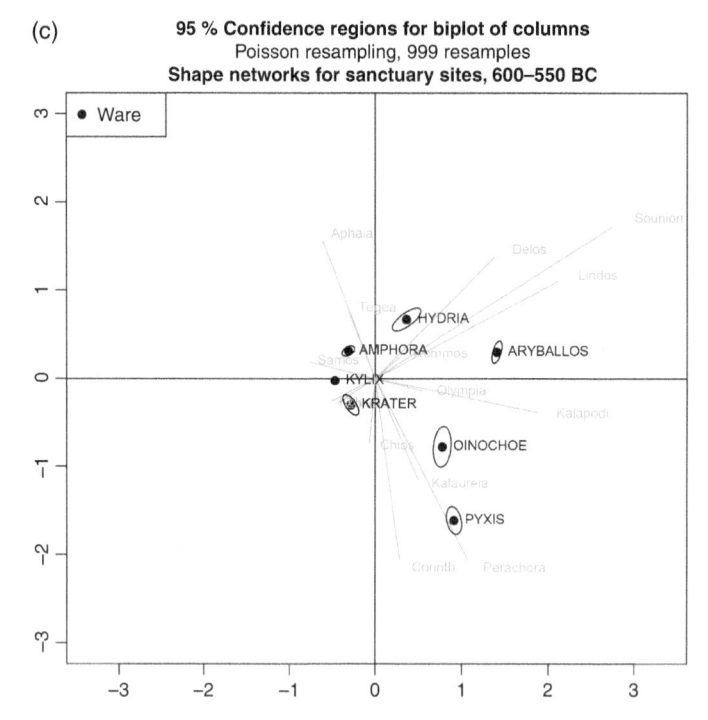

Figure 3.10c Results of PCA on ceramic data from sites broadly defined as 'sanctuary' and with respect to shape categorisation. 600–550 BC.

(d)

95 % Confidence regions for biplot of columns
Poisson resampling, 999 resamples
Shape networks for sanctuary sites, 550–500 BC

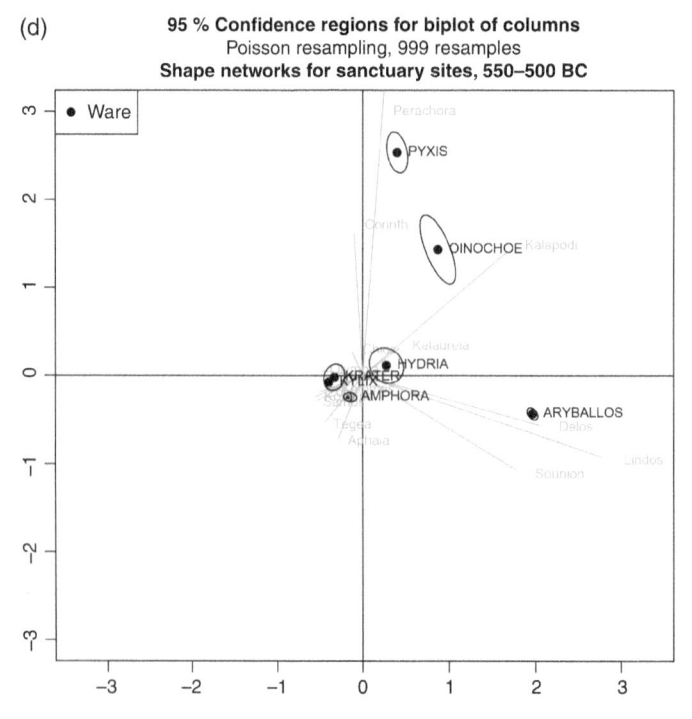

Figure 3.10d Results of PCA on ceramic data from sites broadly defined as 'sanctuary' and with respect to shape categorisation. 550–500 BC.

Delos, Kalaureia, Lindos, Olympia and Sounion tended towards *aryballoi*. In terms of the distribution of the shape labels themselves, the PCA indicates that sites that consume *hydriai* were more likely to also consume amphoras, while those that consume *pyxides* were also likely to consume *oinochoai*.

For period three (600–550 BC), while the urban sites (Fig. 3.9c) in Ionia had assemblages mainly comprising amphoras, Athens, Olynthos, Thasos and Torone had a preference for *hydriai* (the former having a stronger preference), and once again the use of aryballoi and *pyxides* at Corinth is distinct. All other sites consumed a range of shapes, exhibiting little statistically significant distance between the sites. On the PCA graphs there is also close clustering of the shape labels, indicating that there was not so much difference across consumption. At the sanctuaries (Fig. 3.10c) there is a bit more distinction between groups of sites that consumed different sorts of ceramics. Corinth and Perachora preferred *pyxides*; Aphaia, Samos and Tegea, amphoras; and Delos, Lindos and Sounion, *aryballoi*. These sites are not necessarily geographically proximate, but they do, most interestingly, demonstrate similar patterns of consumption. For funerary sites (Fig. 3.11a), Akraifia used *kylixes*, while Corinth, Samothrace and Sindos tended more towards *kraters* and *hydriai*.

Finally, for period four (550–500 BC) the urban sites (Fig. 3.9d) exhibit two patterns. First, there is the clustering of shape types in a way that has already been seen in the previous period. Second, there were distinct usages of *arybal*loi and *pyxides* (Corinth, Olynthos, Smyrna) and *hydriai* (Athens, Knossos, Torone). In general, though, most of the urban sites were consuming a wide range of ceramics, with little preference. Sanctuary sites (Fig. 3.10d), by contrast, show more groups. Delos, Lindos and Sounion had a preference for *aryballoi*, Kalapodi for *oinochoai*, and Corinth and Perachora for *pyxides*. For the other sites, there is more clustering of shapes, although one may distinguish very coarsely a preference at Chios and Kalaureia for *hydriai*, and at Aphaia and Tegea for amphoras. The patterns of shape specialisation for the funerary groups (Fig. 3.11b) is repeated from the previous period.

The main pattern that both emerges and becomes more visible in successive periods is that urban sites consumed a wide range of locally produced ceramics in various shapes, but that different sanctuary sites had preferences for different shapes. This is very clear for sites like Delos, Perachora and Samos, where many *aryballoi, oinochoai* and *pyxides* were consumed, while at other sanctuaries there was a weaker (albeit still present) preference for these shapes and *hydriai* as opposed to amphoras,

(a)

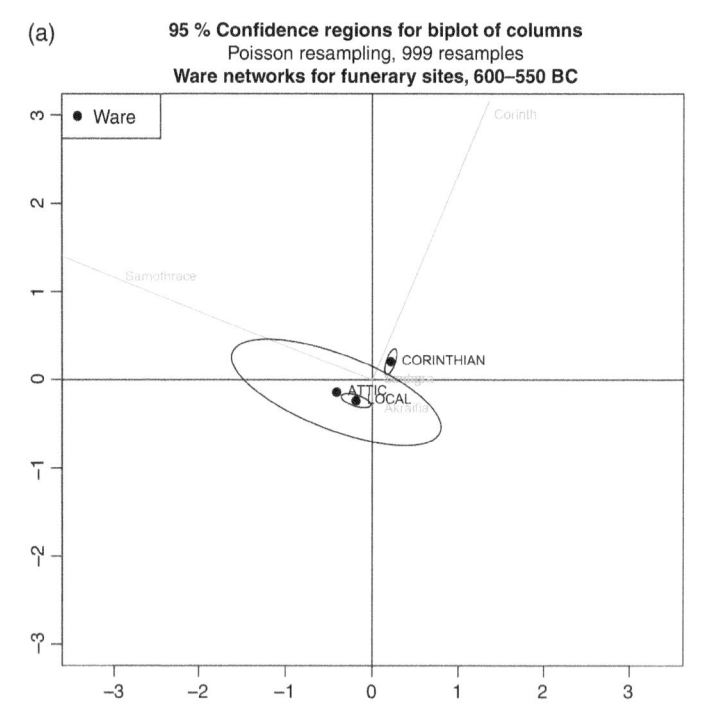

95 % Confidence regions for biplot of columns
Poisson resampling, 999 resamples
Ware networks for funerary sites, 600–550 BC

Figure 3.11a Results of PCA on ceramic data from sites broadly defined as 'funerary' and with respect to shape categorisation. 600–550 BC

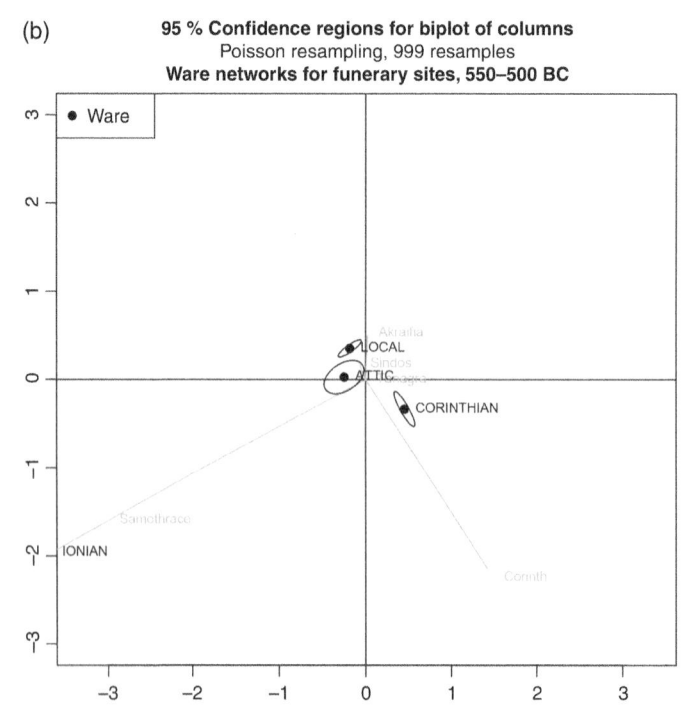

(b)

95 % Confidence regions for biplot of columns
Poisson resampling, 999 resamples
Ware networks for funerary sites, 550–500 BC

Figure 3.11b Results of PCA on ceramic data from sites broadly defined as 'funerary' and with respect to shape categorisation. 550–500 BC.

kraters and kylixes. Clustering of shape labels for urban sites indicates that there was little difference in site preference. For wares, there *was* distinctiveness for the urban sites, and this mainly mapped onto geography: Ionian sites consumed predominantly Ionian ceramics etc. For sanctuary sites, while there was a preference for wares, this does not map so neatly onto geography. One notes, for instance, a predominance in the consumption of Corinthian ceramics on places like Delos, on Rhodes or up in the North Aegean.

Quite clearly, different things are happening at urban and sanctuary sites. On the face of it, urban sites consumed (through a range of pottery shapes) whatever could be produced or obtained locally. But for sanctuary sites, something else was going on. The fact that there was such diversification in both shape and ware indicates that this was not just about consuming whatever was locally available. If it had been, one would expect three things: that the pattern should look the same as the urban sites pattern; that ware and shape patterns would predictably shift at similar rates in similar ways; and that there would be fluctuation between preferences for different shapes over time. This is not the case: for Corinth and Perachora, to take an example, as early as 650–600 BC a preference for consuming (primarily Corinthian) *oinochoai* and *pyxides* develops, and this only becomes more pronounced over subsequent years. This pattern does not seem to waver, and so one is led to believe that there was a particular preference – or perhaps *specialisation*[7] – in the consumption of certain shapes and wares.

If there was a specialisation in the consumption of ceramics, does this mean that there was preference for either shape or ware – or both? More useful than thinking only in terms of category is to think in terms of practice, about what people were doing with those pots.[8] For shape, it is relatively straightforward to think about practice by considering what was usually contained inside these pots, and, by extension, about what sorts of activities those products encouraged. The data indicate that those who participated in cult at Lindos and at Sounion preferred dedicating small quantities of expensive oils, and, therefore, they selected *aryballoi* as the appropriate vessels. These were most probably left at the site as small votive dedications. Those who attended the cult site at Perachora wanted to dedicate quantities of rare and exotic 'foreign' or non-local materials, for

---

[7] See Lewis 2020 on the specialisation of labour and production, much the inverse problem than is discussed here.

[8] Compare the following discussion to Alexandridou 2011: 32–8, who reflects on the entanglement of pottery shape and function in the context of the Athenian symposium, and to Parikh 2020 who compares very different votive assemblages from different (even geographically close) sanctuaries.

which *pyxides* were most appropriate to hold these dedications. And those at Chios, Corinth or Samos might have been involved in ritual feasting that would have demanded use of *kraters*. Evenly crudely, at this level it is possible to start thinking about the different sorts of things that might have been happening at these sites based on the distribution of different *shapes* of ceramics throughout these spaces.

What about the case for ware? If there was a *preference* for consuming some wares over others, one must accept that Greeks selected ceramic products based on aesthetic or physical appearance. This also means that one must accept another contentious point that ceramics themselves were desirable products that one would want to obtain, and that they had some worth to them in addition to the things that they carried (*contra* Gill 1991) – they were not merely 'space fillers' or vessels containing more important products. Others have put forward compelling evidence for the selection of certain wares, decorations or types of images at a site or regional level (Geniere 1991; Osborne 1996b; Giudice 1999; Osborne 2007; Trinkl 2013; Langridge-Noti 2015; Volioti and Smith 2019), but the case is still to be made on whether or not selection on the basis of appearance was ubiquitous across the Aegean.

What is also possible (and of course this option does not exclude visual selection in some cases), is that there was an *entanglement* between shape and ware – that (perhaps more likely) selection of the former necessitated a selection of the latter. Consider, for example, *aryballoi*. This was a shape that was required to fulfil some sort of function at a sanctuary as demanded by cult. Those who wanted to use *aryballoi* were best served by looking to the Corinthian market, as Corinth was the major producer of these goods. Thus it might actually have been the case that the importing of large quantities of Corinthian ceramics was not necessarily a preference for the *Corinthian* market, but for the *types of vessels* that were produced there.[9] Under this sort of model, then, there is indeed a preference for ceramics: but this evidence suggests selection was based on shape and function, with selection of ware being largely the result of this first selection.

---

[9] Some might go one step further and say that one could express some sort of political or cultural affiliation to the major producer of one ware, that is: by using Corinthian ceramics one was particularly aligning themselves to the networks of this state (*cf.* Morgan and Whitelaw 1991). On the basis of the purely practical and economy-driven model discussed, this narrative seems to push the present data a bit too far: one would need to consider many more factors to reach such a conclusion.

And so if cluster analysis does indeed reveal some sort of 'specialisation' or preference for sites consuming certain types of ceramics, we have (at least) three options. First, this could be an entirely random pattern with no historical significance. The 'pattern' as seen in the analysis could have been created by the publication bias of certain site-catalogues for ceramics of given wares and shapes. The other alternatives concede that this is a real pattern: one must untangle, in this case, whether this was (second) a 'push' or (third) a 'pull' pattern. Was there a targeting of certain ceramics by certain consumers (i.e. the sanctuaries wanted to use specific types of pots)? Or was there a targeting of certain ceramics by certain producers (i.e. potters or those co-ordinating supply markets 'pushed' certain types of pottery towards certain sanctuaries)?

We can discount the first alternative with some degree of confidence. As discussed above, there has been a long and detailed study on this dataset over the course of classical archaeology's history, and this is good reason for reflecting that a good (and hopefully representative) range of material from each site has been published. While we might not trust the source publications to represent accurately the true distribution of finewares versus medium wares versus coarsewares, study on the finewares alone has been intensive enough and extensive enough that one might take a leap of faith to believe we have a representative dataset, at least with some ballpark accuracy with relation to roughly defined wares and shapes. Further, the pattern is strong enough and consistent enough across all publications (and periods and regions) that this could not just be an anomaly from one or two sites or their publications. In 'Big Data' approaches such as these, there will undoubtedly be irregularities and anomalous datapoints generated as artefacts of the analysis, but keeping the analysis broad enough at a high enough scale of analysis serves to smooth over the fluctuations and give a good sense of the general pattern over time. Furthermore, and as already noted, there has been some buffering of the raw count data used and all data are presented as proportions of ceramics relative to whole site assemblages to smooth over even further some of these data anomalies. For these reasons, on the balance of things it seems that we *are* dealing with an historical pattern, then, whose significance must be explored further.

Whether we accept option two (a 'push' towards certain consumers) or option three (a 'pull' from producers), both of these options imply that there was a degree of *specialisation* in what sorts of ceramics were being used. And both the geographical and temporal scale at which specialisation seems to have been embedded within the Greek world across different types of sites would suggest that this was not something that came about accidentally or randomly.

Two things (at least) are required for such a system to become embedded across the Greek world: infrastructure and knowledge. Infrastructure has already been considered to a certain degree in Chapter 2, so here the discussion turns to knowledge. If the circulation of goods was targeted to some degree, then either (or both) producers knew what consumers wanted, and/or consumers knew what producers could supply. This is a simple fact of economics: targeting relies on a circulation of knowledge of people's needs (Jones 2014: 106–8). This picture is somewhat contrary to that proposed by Snodgrass almost forty years ago (Snodgrass 1983: 231–2); he argued that 'trade' of the Archaic period was something that took place locally: one simply received what was available nearby. Indeed, this runs contrary to the general orthodoxy within the conversation in ancient Greek economics, where formal markets are seldom of concern. The data presented indicate that this was not the case, and that a significant number of products made their way to places quite far away from the point of manufacture. Snodgrass also argued that trade was an anonymous process, and that the actors involved in a transfer of goods simply did not need to know one another. By contrast, the evidence seems to suggest that actors within the trade network had enough knowledge of one another to know who was looking for what, and how best to get that to them – even if, given the scale and resolution of the present analysis, it is not possible to argue for any sort of *personal* or *direct* relationship between consumers and producers. This notion is certainly not new (Geniere 1991; Osborne 1996b; Giudice 1999; Osborne 2007; Trinkl 2013; Langridge-Noti 2015),[10] but the evidence presented here indicates that this was neither a local nor small-scale process, but one that spread much more widely across the Aegean.

In formal terms, one might call this a system of Comparative Advantage. That is, if some Greeks were specialist in producing commodity x, while others were specialist in producing commodity y, it was quicker, more efficient, and resulted in higher quality products that Greeks would invest their time and resources in producing those products for which they were specialists (i.e. product x), and they would trade these goods in order to acquire other items (i.e. product y).[11] As already noted, Alain Bresson has

---

[10] On things only acquiring specific cultural meaning in use and in circulation, see specific discussion in Gosden and Marshall 1999 and Papadopoulos and Urton 2012: 17, and more generally in Appadurai 1986 and Kopytoff 1986.

[11] The System of Comparative Advantage was first conceived theoretically by David Ricardo (1817), which, albeit framed in terms of *international* trade, proposed that one of the key reasons actors form economic networks is to reduce friction by reducing the time and effort taken to create products that one knows will be made quicker and more effectively elsewhere. The mathematics outlining this principle were derived almost twenty years later by William

previously suggested that the economy of the Greek world was both embedded and had room for a market economy, pointing most probably towards a system of Comparative Advantage (Bresson 2008: 345–7) which, although both more extensive and historically visible in the Classical and Hellenistic periods, had its roots in the Archaic period.[12] On the one hand, certain regions were just better at producing certain products (Bresson 2008: 135–8). This might have been because the climate was better suited to the production of certain products, or because, owing to the size and complexity of urban centres, the capacity for processing certain products was more developed at various places. On the other hand, uncertainty and risk (and especially climate and environmental fluctuations from year to year) had the effect that one might be *required* to look elsewhere to meet a production deficit in tough years (Bresson 2008: 157–74); by the same token, regions might begin to over-produce in certain products if they know that others might turn to them.[13] Furthermore, Bresson argues that by token of geographic location and the shape of shipping routes, some places simply became hubs of production through the amount of traffic that they saw (Bresson 2008: 371–4): the route between the Aegean and Italy or the western parts of the Mediterranean necessarily passed by Athens, and so Athens, knowing that it would have the customers, could scale up its production of pottery until it was a recognised specialist producer.

However these communities, regions or places became comparatively advantaged over one another, the data presented above indicate that progressively throughout the seventh and sixth centuries, networks began to shape themselves around specialist production and consumption – and the thing that held these networks together was knowledge of what was available and where.

The second implication of these results is that if the distribution of ceramics was not totally random, one must also accept that commodity shipping *routes* were not completely random. Products were manufactured in specific places with the intention of delivery to specific places: there may

---

Whewell (1831) and they were properly moved from the realm of theory to empirical data by Donald MacDougall (1951) in comparing the exports (relative to output of worker vs wage-rate) of British and American products. This principle, although familiar in general shape to archaeologists and ancient historians, has only infrequently been cited directly to support ancient evidence (Shennan 1999). See also Samuelson 1953, and Blaug 1999.

[12] The examples cited here move from the ceramic vessels discussed to the products that might be contained within these vessels.

[13] See also Garnsey and Morris 1989; Bissa 2009: 169–77 models the scenario using data and parameters supplied by Osborne, Garnsey, Hansen, Foxhall and others.

have been intermediary stops *en route* and any specific voyage might have just been a 'fragment' of a much larger journey, but on the macro-scale, at least, this indicates there is some merit in exploring shipping routes between places of production and places of consumption.

As discussed, possible routes for the shipping of ceramics from their point of production to their point of consumption have been sketched. Four diagrams have been produced, one for each of the four temporal periods discussed above (700–650 BC, Fig. 3.12a; 650–600 BC, Fig. 3.12b; 600–550 BC, Fig. 3.12c; 550–500 BC, Fig. 3.12d), using the same nearest-neighbour methodology outlined in Chapter 2. Route lines have been weighted and coloured to illustrate the proportion of ceramic material for the relevant period that might have travelled along this route, relative to the total material recorded for that period. For 'production place', the resolution of this data is not precise to the level of the site, and so generalising production points in Attica (near Athens), Corinthia (near Corinth) and Ionia (Çeşme-Karaburun-Urla Peninsula) have been used instead – these points are accurate enough to give an overall picture to the shape of routes internal to the Aegean Sea.

At the start of the seventh century BC, the largest proportion of ceramic shipping took place in the northern half of the Aegean Sea, moving products both up from Attica and Corinthia to Torone, and also from Ionia towards Thasos. There was also significant activity up throughout the Corinthian Gulf. A smaller but not insignificant network linked mainland Greece to Ionia via the island of Delos, while exchanges towards Crete were minimal compared to routes taken elsewhere in the Aegean.

Towards the end of the seventh century BC, the shapes of these route networks were much the same, even if the relative intensity to which they were used was different. The route along the Corinthian Gulf was still one of the most frequented networks of the period, but movement around and across the Saronic Gulf also increased – both in terms of the discrete number of routes that were plotted between sites, but also in terms of the quantities of materials that were transported along each route. Towards the north Aegean, there are a greater number of route lines plotted in this diagram compared to the previous graphic, indicating that there were more connections between places of production and places of consumption – even if the absolute quantity of material taken across any one route was proportionally less than at the start of the century. The networks that connected mainland Greece to Ionia across Delos are of a similar shape and weight than in the previous period, as is the case for Crete.

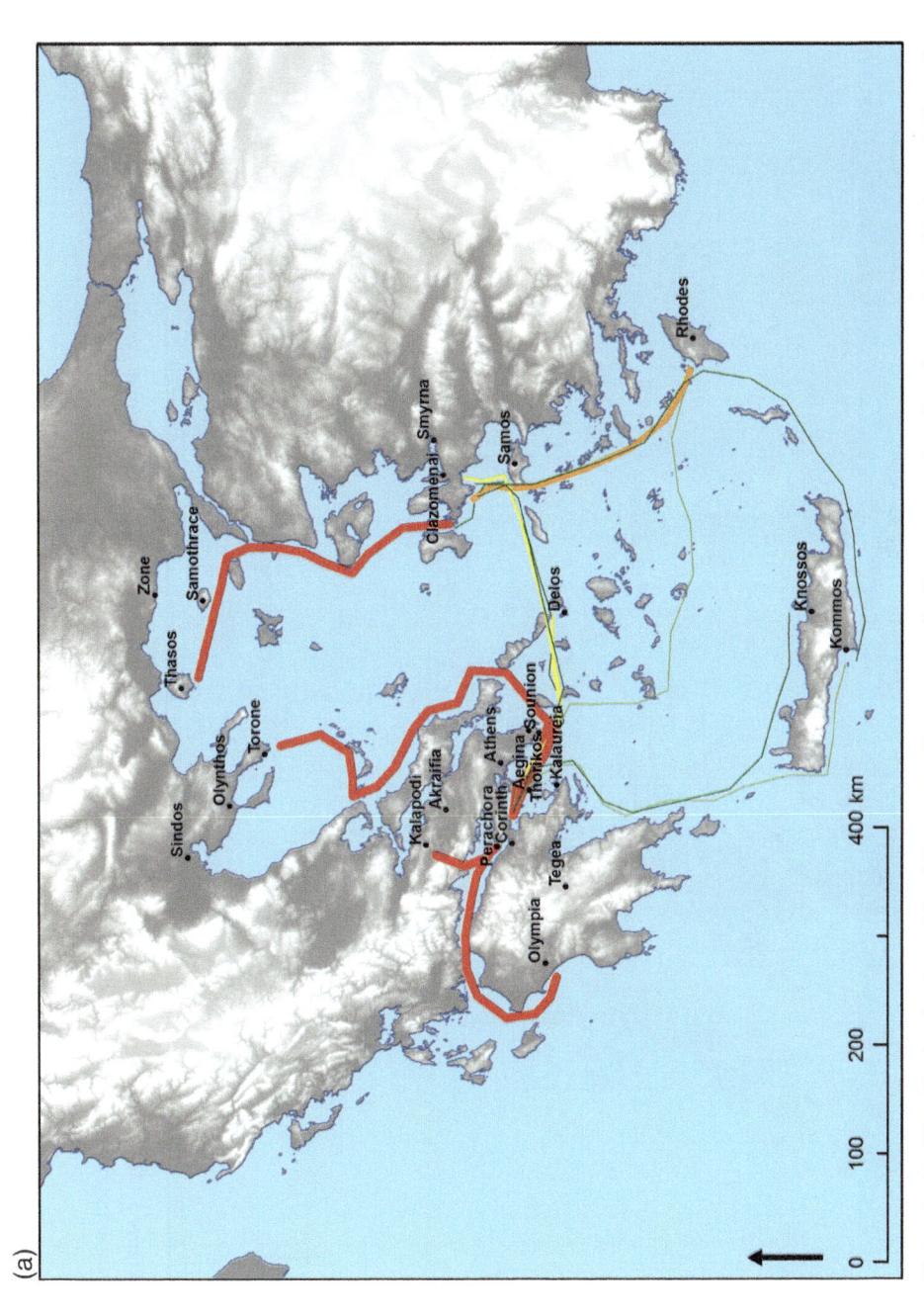

Figure 3.12a Visualisation for the weighted frequency of routes travelled between rough point of ceramic production and place of consumption, using PPA modelling. 700–650 BC Weight is a term relative to the total quantity of ceramic transported across the whole of the Archaic period as investigated in this chapter; the same colour-gradient scale is used as in Chapter 2.

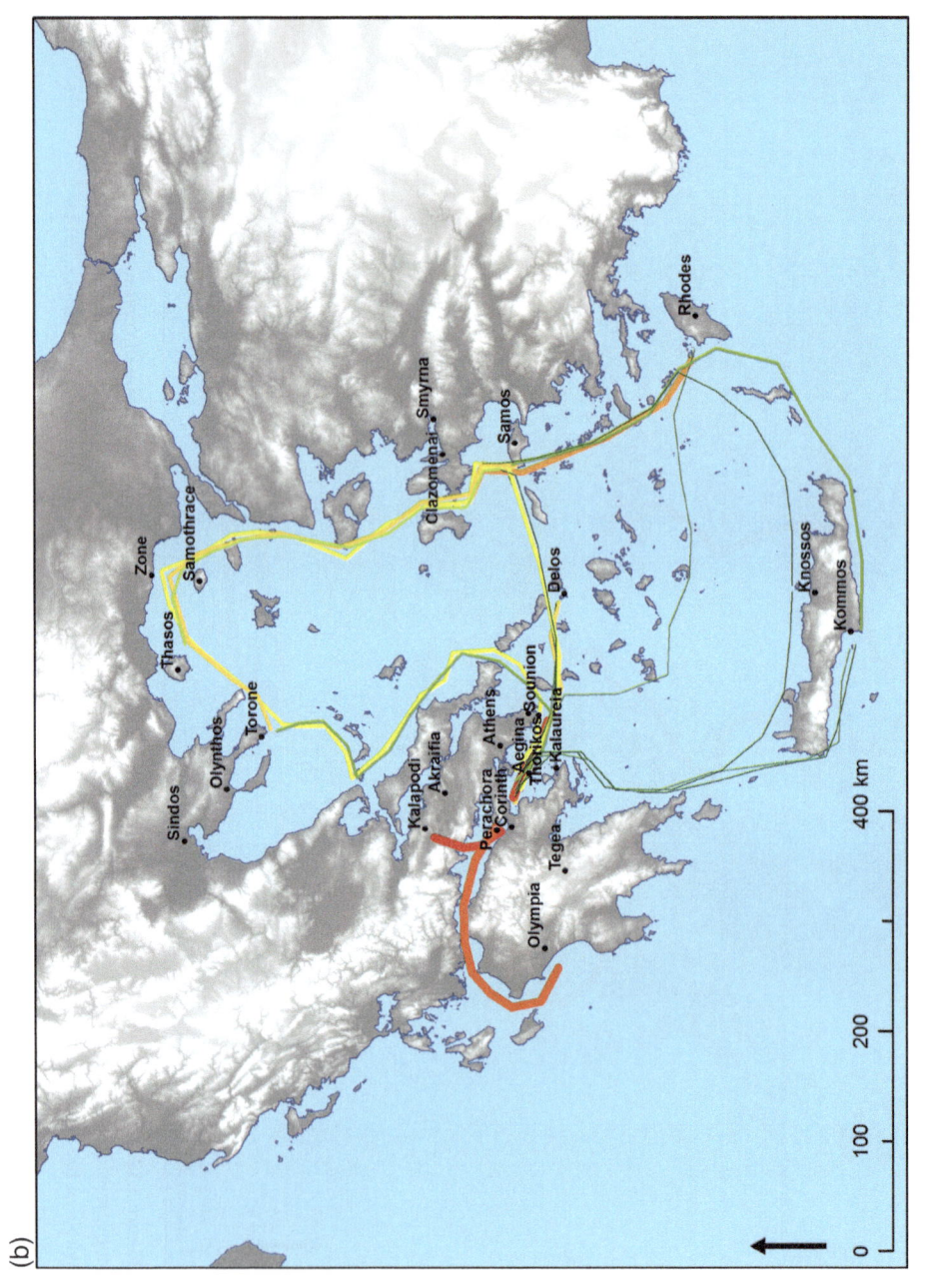

Figure 3.12b Visualisation for the weighted frequency of routes travelled between rough point of ceramic production and place of consumption, using PPA modelling. 650–600 BC.

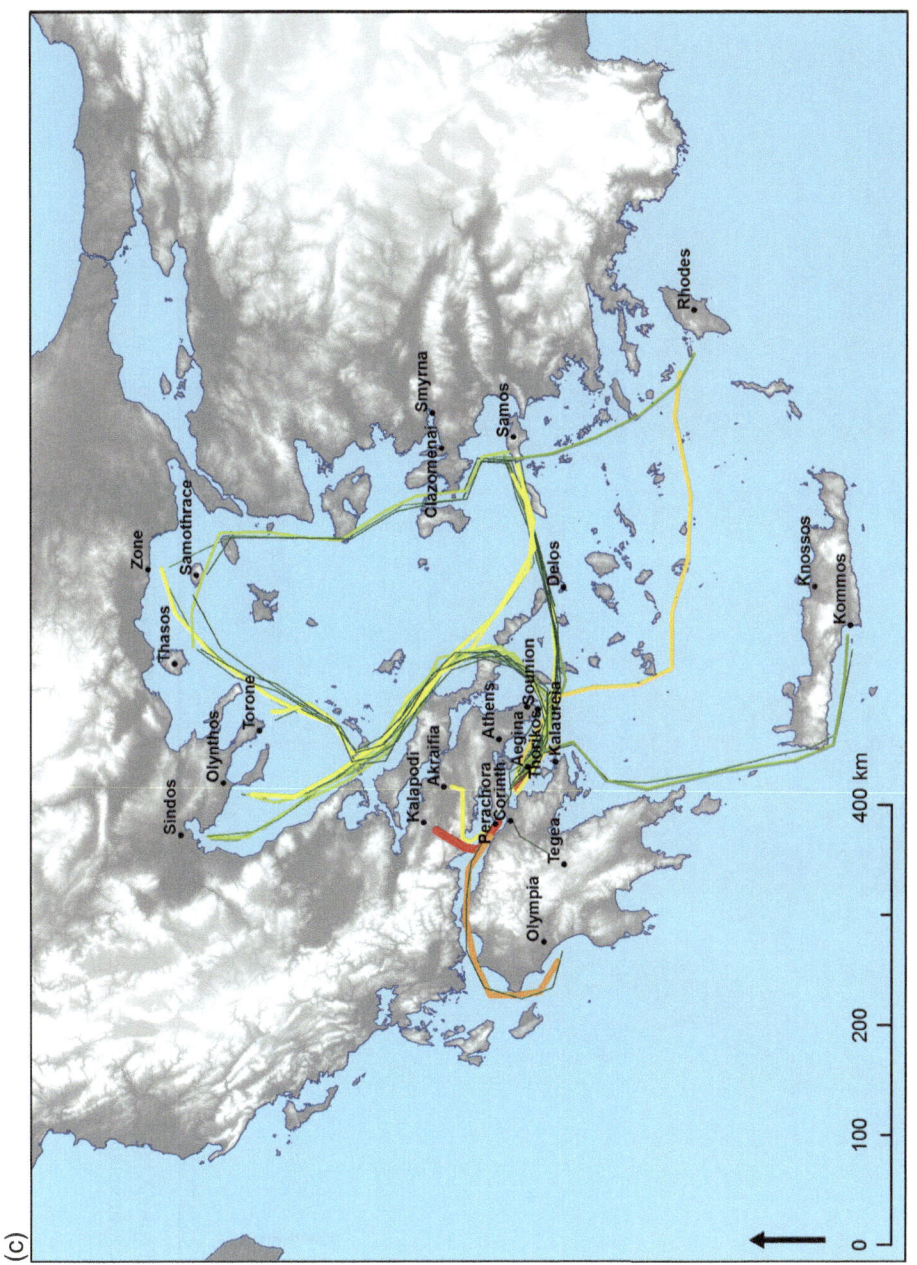

Figure 3.12c Visualisation for the weighted frequency of routes travelled between rough point of ceramic production and place of consumption, using PPA modelling. 600–550 BC.

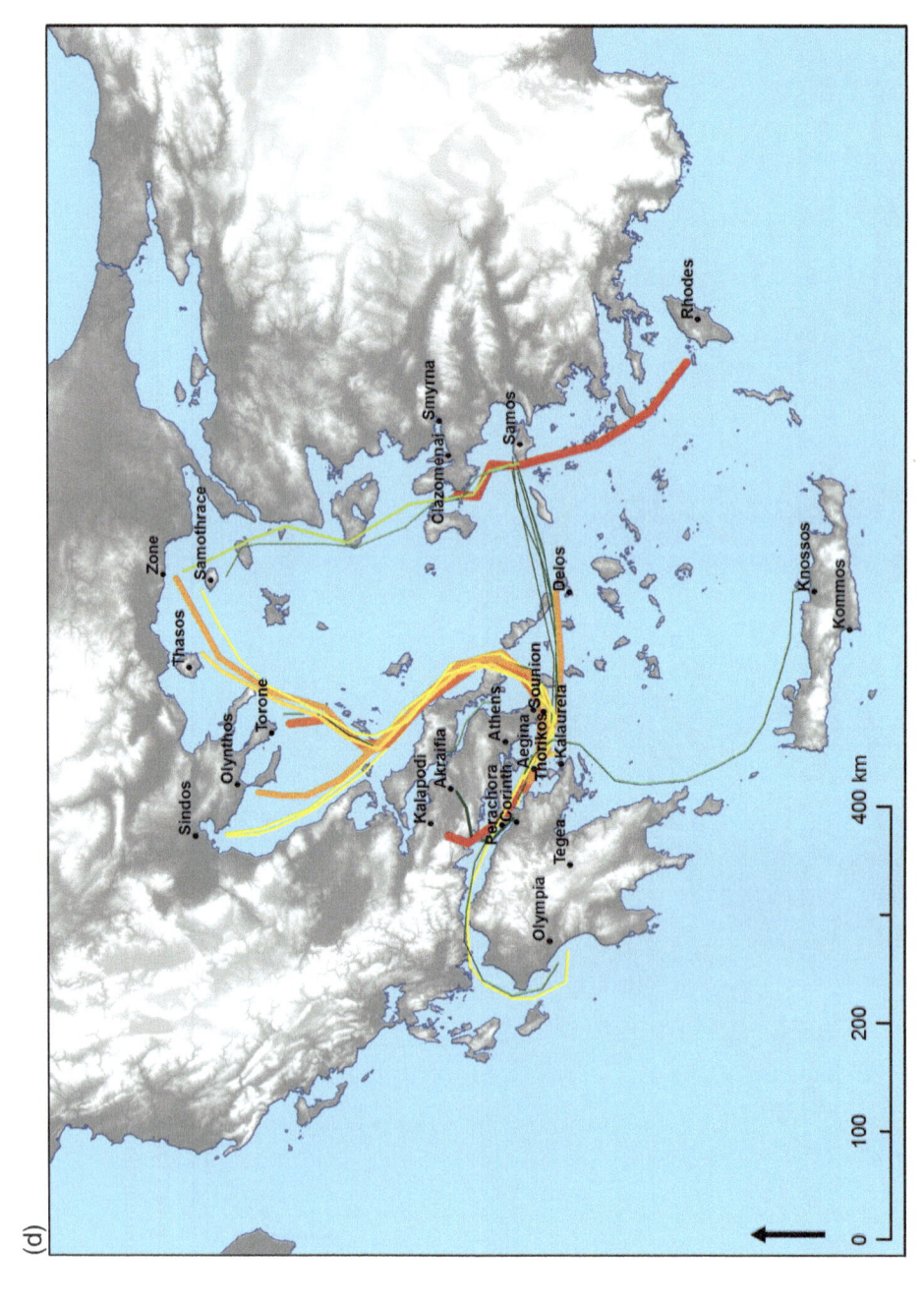

Figure 3.12d Visualisation for the weighted frequency of routes travelled between rough point of ceramic production and place of consumption, using PPA modelling. 550–500 BC.

The picture begins to change at the start of the sixth century BC. The number of routes connecting the Saronic Gulf to both the northern Aegean and to Ionia increased significantly, and it was along these channels that the largest quantity of material was shipped up to Zone. Ionia also connected itself with a small number of high-traffic routes to the north, specifically to Olynthos, Thasos and Torone. Once more, the number of routes across the Saronic Gulf was significant, both in terms of discrete number and for the quantities of material which were moved across them – on the basis of the present dataset, this was the most frequented part of the Aegean Sea, second only to the northern coast of Euboea. The number of routes originating in the Corinthia was less than for other regions, but high quantities of ceramics were shipped along the routes that did exist, notably still to Olympia, and across the Aegean to Rhodes. Fewer routes than before made their way to Crete, even though connections between Crete and Ionia *are* attested.

Finally, quite a different pattern emerges at the end of the sixth century BC. Namely, the routes which carried the greatest quantity of material originated in Attica and headed northwards across the coast of Euboea. The number of discrete routes counted within this corridor is numerous, and it was these channels that were responsible for the movement of large quantities of material. The links between mainland Greece and Ionia were still present (albeit used for shipping products in lesser quantities) and the link to Delos as a stopover in this route still a strong one. Routes connecting Crete with the rest of the Aegean became even weaker at this point.

As in Chapter 2, it is most productive to concentrate not on the individual lines themselves but on the general corridors that cut across the Aegean. Broadly defined, seven corridors can be identified across the four graphics produced. From the Saronic Gulf to the north Aegean; from Ionia to the north Aegean; between the Saronic Gulf and Ionia, across the Cyclades; from the Saronic Gulf to Crete; from Ionia to Crete; from Ionia to the Dodecanese; and along the Corinthian Gulf. Diachronically, there is evidence of all seven corridors being in existence right from the beginning of the seventh century BC. In the sixth century, though, there was more activity across the Cyclades, and there is less evidence of corridors in use to Crete. Corridors to the north Aegean were used variously; on the basis of the present dataset, it appears as if there would have been less movement along the Corinthian Gulf in the sixth century, but clearly the present data does not take account of large quantities of material that would have been shipped in this period along this channel towards Italy and Magna Graecia (e.g. 'Richter 182–9' as a representative sample).

To bring this back to infrastructure, a point raised already in Chapter 2: it was established that the widespread fashion for dedicating freestanding marble statues began extensively enough and in such quantities that there must have been some infrastructure for delivering marble overseas already in place in the seventh century BC, on the back of which such an intensive and extensive economic network could proceed quickly. To phrase this another way, there were some hundreds of ships every year involved in the shipping of raw marble for the production of *kouros* and *kore* statues, but this trade was already so well established by the start of the sixth century BC that the route corridors used in shipping marble overseas most likely pre-dated the actual marble trade.

It is entirely possible that the shipping routes of (luxurious) marble and the shipping routes of ceramics (and the commodity or semi-luxurious goods that they contained) were entangled with one another. That is, ships were already circulating the Aegean Sea in the seventh century BC packed full of ceramic goods, the shipment of these materials being responsible for the carving out of various route corridors across the whole of the Aegean basin. In the latter part of the seventh century and into the sixth century, fashions changed, and all of a sudden there was a desire by Greeks not just to consume small goods that came in ceramics but also to consume large marble statues. These same ships – hundreds of ships already circuiting the Aegean Sea – could be used for the movement of heavy marble, packages of both rough stone and semi-worked *kouroi* added to their mixed cargoes at one of the many stopover points. Quite simply, one economic network might have piggy-backed on the back of another.

By means of an entirely arbitrary example, the intersection of networks within the Cyclades is considered here. Ships must have been circulating between mainland Greece and Ionia in the seventh century to take small quantities of Attic ceramics to Miletos and Samos, while Ionian ceramics made their way back to Athens, the sanctuaries of Aegina, and to Perachora. These ships, if travelling most directly, would have passed through the Cyclades *en route*. Knowledge of a new tradition of freestanding sculptures in Egypt and in Ionia got back to mainland Greece, where demand developed among the aspirational elite to conspicuously consume similar sorts of products to mark out their distinctness. Given that ships were already passing by the Cyclades, a message could be conveyed to labourers and craftspeople on the islands of Naxos and Paros to prepare heavy blocks of marble and to have them loaded onto those same ships that were passing by between Ionia and the mainland. And herein the two types of economic network can be considered to have become entangled with one another.

Over time, this process became more regular and more systematised, and an economic network pertaining to the transport of these 'luxury' heavy marble products developed off the back of an earlier network. And going back to the data – as this chapter and Chapter 2 have done – this narrative is particularly compelling: when the results of the marble PPA are laid over the top of the ceramic results from the seventh century BC, a strong case can be made for the co-development of different networks each aligned to the transport of different types of products. Shipping around the Aegean Sea was already so well established in both range and intensity by the end of the seventh century BC that this new trade network could quickly 'piggy-back' on the existing network.

An Early Market Economy?

This is necessarily a simplification, but the picture presented here is an entirely plausible one. Early economic networks of the Aegean basin were entangled with one another – the desire for both luxury and commodity goods were interdependent – and, equally, they were subject to the shape of physical *route* networks. In a story about the interdependence of networks, moreover, chronology cannot be ignored. The notion that most corridors were already carved out in the seventh century BC is critical: the first network – for the shipment of broadly defined 'commodity' and 'semi-luxury' goods held within ceramic vessels – established itself early in the Archaic period, and this allowed the rapid deployment of a different but related network of luxury marble right from the start of the sixth century.

Crucially, though, it was the pre-existence not just of infrastructure but also of *knowledge* concerning the extent and nature of this infrastructure that allowed for the development of one economic network from another. This extends both to knowing what sort of ceramics were available from where and how they might be consumed for the activities conducted in various different spaces, but, also, to elite peers knowing about one another. This knowledge enabled those elites to drive processes of material acquisition and consumption to compete for status. To put this another way, *demand* for new products was a social transaction, and *supply* came in the form of access to a well-established shipping network: both supply and demand were necessarily *embedded* processes.

This narrative points towards a possible early market economy. That consumers knew what was out there and that they could target certain commodity (and, later, luxury) products requires a negotiation between producer and consumer. Central to these interactions was a knowledge of people's needs; economic networks enabled the transport of goods to be targeted, and these networks brought communities into close contact with their neighbours. This certainly attributes a greater sophistication of process to the early economy of Archaic Greece than has been traditionally conceded. Indeed, this model runs quite starkly against Finley's own model of a *purely* socially embedded economy, while now tending towards the standpoint of Bresson (and others), that there is room within an embedded economy for notions of comparative advantage and targeted acquisition. And, most crucially, this chapter has demonstrated that a model like this can be corroborated with primary material data.

To close, it is important to note that while discussion has been kept at quite a high level concerning 'luxury' and 'commodity' networks, the datasets analysed – marble and ceramics – were necessarily only small parts of much larger economic systems. Indeed, ceramics on their own tell us very little and they are in many ways the 'footprint' of commodity products like grain, oil and wine that could have been transported within pottery vessels. There is a compelling case to be made for the intersection of different types of networks, and even for the overlap of different types of *economic* networks. But to unpick this system even further and to evaluate its impact for the world of Archaic Greece much more broadly, we must widen the lens. It is now necessary to consider the entanglement of *other* sorts of objects within both economic *and* political networks.

4 | Entangled Networks
The Transfer of Technical Knowledge

The previous chapters have made the case for looking at one network from the point of view of two different datasets. That is, one can see different levels of economic connectedness between communities of the seventh and sixth centuries BC when reconstructing the network first through the dataset of freestanding sculpture and second with pottery. A critical point that has emerged is that these networks were entangled with other sorts of networks and cannot be so easily separated. The demand for various pottery types was dependent on the function that pottery vessels performed in everyday or religious activities conducted at urban and sanctuary sites; while the demand to produce freestanding sculpture was driven from a need to display and create markers of socio-cultural status. Having established the entangled nature of Aegean networks, this chapter looks at a material type whose very existence as either an economic or a political tool can be debated. The first part of this chapter deals with the problem of going from a single object to either economic activity of the Archaic period, while the second part looks at how a network reconstructed from a distribution of such objects might variously tell us about either, both or neither of those two worlds.

Value and Values

Objects are neutral and mute entities which gain their meaning through their position in the physical and social environment and through our interaction with them. In many cases, this meaning is assigned when an object is used (van Wijngaarden 1999: 2–3; Hildebrandt and Veit 2009; Borken and Rowan 2014: 4): an *aryballos* is just a lump of clay that happens to have been pulled into a particular shape, but we recognise that this object becomes part of a certain set of meaningful religious activities once it is filled with oil and left in a certain way at a sanctuary. To put this another way, meaning is ascribed to an object when it *performs* an activity (Gosden and Marshall 1999: 174; Joy 2009: 544). Value and meaning can be personal and subjective (*cf.* Bevan 2007: 12–6) but – as is more useful for the purpose of this discussion that looks at the ancient world at the level of the community – it is well understood that value and meaning can also be agreed (and also disputed) across social groups (Papadopoulos and Urton 2012: 1–21).

In conceptualising the value of statues and pottery as products, the previous discussion has focused to a great extent on *labour* value. A purely Marxist approach would emphasise that the value one should ascribe to an object is proportional to the effort and time expended in its creation – on this basis, one might assume that a *kouros* statue was more 'valuable' than an *aryballos* pot, that is, it tends more to being a 'luxury' rather than a 'commodity' – but a more nuanced view takes into account the notion that labour is a *chaîne opératoire* which also involves factors of exchange, desirability, accessibility and consumption (van Wijngaarden 1999: 3; Barrett 2009). One object can take on a multiplicity of different values in a number of different contexts too, a point long held by anthropologists but particularly emphasised over the past twenty five years by archaeologists who have engaged with this notion of value (Voutsaki 1997; Papadopoulos 2012; Iacono 2016). To put this in the language of connectivity, an object can simultaneously mean different things in different contexts, participating in a range of different and overlapping networks.

The target dataset of this chapter is coinage, and coins certainly have different meanings in different contexts. A coin in purely reductionist terms – a circular piece of metal of a certain shape, weight and design – has no intrinsic practical use until we imbue it with a particular sociocultural meaning. Perhaps the most obvious meaning that can be imbued is an economic one, wherein we use these objects as markers of wealth value,[1] that is, they can be exchanged for an equivalent set of objects or services. Sometimes this system of value is related to the amount and type of metal in the coin, (Seaford 1994; von Reden 1995, 1997; Crisà, Gkikaki and Rowan 2019: 4–6) but sometimes the images on coins and their shape are used as markers of wealth equivalency value: the images on coins in particular act as a sort of 'guarantee', communicating to us both the place where a coin has been produced and informing us of the places where it has direct economic value (*cf.* Howgego 1995: 95ff.; Seaford 2004: 125–46). A bimetallic coin emblazoned with 'ΕΛΛΗΝΙΚΗ ΔΗΜΟΚΡΑΤΙΑ' and an image of Europa and the bull we know has been produced in Greece, and owing to another label, '2 EURO', we know that this coin can be exchanged

---

[1] Bevan 2007: 17 suggests that value can be mapped onto objects by a scalar of quality, quantity and diversity. For coins, quality (i.e. the type of denomination of a coin) and the quantity apply as markers.

to the value of two euros across the Eurozone area. In this way, one can see how coins then represent a *contract* made between people and institutions, or an agreement made within communities for systems of wealth equivalency; and we understand how a coin can be used to participate in an economic network.

In addition, coins might acquire some additional – or alternative – cultural meaning. This might involve physically transforming the coin in some way: by cutting a hole in the metal and making the object a piece of jewellery, or repurposing the object as a gaming token.[2] We are quite familiar in the contemporary world with the idea that a coin, as an object marked with a date and a pictorial image that indicates its place of origin and production, can become a 'commemorative' object or an heirloom that people collect. Such coins become tangible things marking moments or events in history contemporary with production, a material reminder entangled with the memory of a past event:[3] a British coin minted in 1952 might be lent by some a particular cultural importance, as this object was created and in circulation at the time of Queen Elizabeth II's coronation. Yet another layer of meaning can be added when groups of coins become collections: depending on how complete, extensive or representative of certain sets of objects a collection is, an individual or a community with a shared set of socio-cultural values may attribute more 'meaning' to the collection itself than to each individual object. Most simply, it is clear to see that coins can acquire a special socio-cultural meaning beyond their primary economic role.

So, coins themselves are part of different interpretative systems: frameworks that variously prioritise their economic worth, and frameworks that amplify their role as culturally significant tokens. In scaling up this dataset from single objects to assemblages and in looking between assemblages to looking at networks of coins, it is not immediately clear whether one is dealing with an economic network or a network of socio-cultural meaning – or both, or neither. These 'meanings' and values of coins are entangled with one another, depending on the particular situation in which the coins are

---

[2] For a coin reused as a token, see those found in the 2020 excavations of the Mentor Shipwreck off Kythera: Mentor Shipwreck, Kythera – 2020, *Archaeology in Greece Online*, report 9615, created 1 February 2021, <https://chronique.efa.gr/?kroute=report&id=9615> accessed 15 December 2021. For coins that have been modified for use as pendants, see various in the BSA Museum Collection, MUS.C228, MUS.C233, MUS.C239, MUS.C247.

[3] On individuals reading or experiencing an object biography by interacting with the object, see Kopytoff 1986, Gosden and Marshall 1999, Joy 2002 and Whitley 2002. For a similar notion of *photographs* invoking memory for existing at the time of certain events, see Edwards 1999.

used, transforming the network and the nature of connections between the nodes within it.

Recognising this complicated and multi-layered nature of coinage as a material type, we might regard these *networks* of coins as *entangled networks*. In an attempt to disentangle those networks and to think about them in more specific historical terms, though, this chapter will focus on one particular historical event in the Archaic period, namely on the emergence of the first coinage. By looking at assemblages of the first coins minted in the Aegean and at the similarities and differences between various groups, this chapter aims to consider what exactly networks of coins meant for the Aegean basin, and to what extent the dataset can be used to help us think variously about issues of economics or of political affiliation, as this new technology emerged throughout the later part of the Archaic period.

Coins in the Archaic Period

During the sixth century BC, Greeks from all parts of the Aegean were minting coins (Fig. 4.1). Scholars continue to debate the date at which the *first* Greek coins were minted, and estimates range from as early as the end of the late seventh century to the mid-sixth century (Weidauer 1975; Furtwängler 1982; Kroll and Waggoner 1984; Wallace 1987; Carradice and Price 1988: 20; Williams 1991; Howgego 1995; Wartenberg and Fischer-Bossert 2016).[4] The problem with the dataset is that very few coins have been found in securely dateable archaeological contexts, and, indeed, very few have been found in archaeological contexts at all. Moreover, where archaeological information does exist, it is of poor quality. Of thirty-four hoards recorded before 500 BC, eighteen have unspecific find-spots, and others have only either been reported through secondary sources with little or no specific information on the coins themselves (Table 4.1).[5]

---

[4] On dating the first coinage to the sixth century using the hoard from Ephesos, see Bammer 1990 and 1991: 83, with a rebuttal from Weissl 2002: 313–21 and 2005: 365.

[5] The evidence of three hoards is of sufficient quality that they will be used to discuss further issues of coinage circulation (Ephesos hoard, start of sixth century BC [HOARD 9 and 10]; 'Cyclades hoard', mid-sixth century BC [HOARD 6]; 1893 'Western Asia Minor' hoard, sixth century BC [HOARD 21]). In addition, the context of the 'Kolophon hoard' [HOARD 32] will be discussed further below. This dataset is put together based on the synthesis of Thompson, Mørkholm and Kraay 1973, taking into account subsequent discoveries from the Archaic Aegean published in following issues of *Coin Hoards*.

Table 4.1 *Coin hoards dated to the seventh and sixth centuries. Sources are Thompson, Mørkholm and Kraay 1973 (TMK), and numbered editions of* Coin Hoards *(CH 1.3 = Coin Hoards 1, entry no. 3, etc.).*

ID	Reference	Site / Region	Discovery Date	Date (BC)	Contents
HOARD 1	TMK 1	Phaistos	1943	550–525	71 AR
HOARD 2	TMK 2	Athens	1788	525–515	26 AR
HOARD 3	TMK 3	Euboea	1935	530–510	6 AR
HOARD 4	TMK 4	Kythera	1925	525–500	AR
HOARD 5	TMK 5	Eleusis	1883	520–500	7–8 AR
HOARD 6	TMK 6	Cyclades	1889	500	145 AR
HOARD 7	TMK 354	Macedonia	1849	600–590	12 EL
HOARD 8	TMK 1152	W. Asia Minor	1947	Late C7	9 EL
HOARD 9	TMK 1153	Ephesos	1905	600–590	24 EL, 4 AR
HOARD 10	TMK 1154	Ephesos	1905	600–590	19 EL
HOARD 11	TMK 1155	W. Asia Minor	1935	600–590	11 EL
HOARD 12	TMK 1156	W. Asia Minor	1949	600–575	56 EL, 4 AR
HOARD 13	TMK 1157	Priene	1875	575–560	11 EL
HOARD 14	TMK 1158	Samos	1894	575–560	60 EL
HOARD 15	TMK 1159	W. Asia Minor	1933	575–560	24 EL
HOARD 16	TMK 1160	Didyma	1968	550	5 EL
HOARD 17	TMK 1161	W. Asia Minor	1969	550	49 EL
HOARD 18	TMK 1162	Sardes, Lydia	1922	546	30 AU
HOARD 19	TMK 1163	Rhodes	1941	525–500	10 AR
HOARD 20	TMK 1164	W. Asia Minor	1960	520	10 AR
HOARD 21	TMK 1165	W. Asia Minor	1893	520–500	1 EL, 75 AR
HOARD 22	CH 1.1	Asia Minor	1974	550–454	6 AR
HOARD 23	CH 1.3	Asia Minor	1935/1940	525	906 AR, 77 bullion
HOARD 24	CH 8.2	Western Asia Minor	1990	560	29 EL
HOARD 25	CH 8.5	Western Asia Minor	1988	540	30 EL
HOARD 26	CH 8.6	Western Turkey	1985	540	EL and AU
HOARD 27	CH 8.7	Western Turkey	???	530	3 AU, 14 EL
HOARD 28	CH 8.8	Lesbos	1991	525	6 BI
HOARD 29	CH 8.10	Western Asia Minor	1985	525	270 AR
HOARD 30	CH 8.12	South-west Turkey	1989	515	30 AU
HOARD 31	CH 8.13	Athens	1785	515	22 AR
HOARD 32	CH 8.14	Kolophon	1968	510	37 AR
HOARD 33	CH 8.15	Eleusis	1883	510	100 AR
HOARD 34	CH 8.16	Kilkis	1971	510	54 AR
HOARD 35	CH 10.2	Kythera	1920s	525–500	

Figure 4.1 Illustrative Archaic period silver coin from Corinth, a) obverse and b) reverse. BSA Museum MUS.C103. Photographs by author.

As becomes clear from the table of coin hoards, a large part of the dataset comes with insecure or unknown provenance, many 'turning up' in museum or private collections (e.g. HOARD 24–8 are reconstructed hoards that had been located by scholars 'in trade'; HOARD 29 turned up in Haifa Museum). And, as is the case with other datasets discussed within this book, where precise archaeological information is lacking, the dating of coins is frequently based on conjecture: through style, through literary references or through some other means (*cf.* Howgego 1995). This goes some way towards explaining the broad and imprecise date ranges for individual coin series, and, moreover, for critical 'fixed' points in coinage chronology – such as the date of the first coinage – being so greatly up for debate. Nevertheless, over recent years, particularly as the laws both recognising the archaeological significance of coins and regularising the reporting of ancient cultural material have been changed (particularly the 1970 UNESCO convention, and specifically in Greece law 3028/2002), the dataset of coins found in archaeological contexts is now growing.[6] As this material is more extensively published, it is likely that the date of the first coinage will be refined even further (*cf.* Wartenberg and Fischer-Bossert 2016).

These very first coins were made principally from electrum. A metal alloy comprising gold and silver, electrum was most probably used first as

---

[6] The *Archaeology in Greece Online* database currently lists 205 sites with Archaic period activity in the Aegean at which coins have been found over the past decade (correct on 15 December 2021), chronique.efa.gr.

a currency in Anatolia in the region of Lydia (Wallace 1987; Ramage and Craddock 2000: 19–20; Konuk 2012: 38–40; *cf.* Herodotus 1.50). Both gold and silver were available in abundance at the area of the Pactolus River, and there was surely no shortage of supply in raw resource for creating this alloy metal. The ratio of gold to silver within any block of electrum was variable, and there was no agreed standard to which the metal was produced (Meeks 2000: 145–8; Keyser and Clark 2001: 107; Konuk 2005: 49). Indeed, it is this very attribute that made electrum, perhaps, a good candidate for the first coinage: striking the metal into a coin would 'fix' its wealth equivalency value to a certain standard recognised within a community, irrespective of different material composition. This notion of 'facilitating' exchange and reducing friction within an economic network is discussed further below. Electrum coins were first produced in Lydia and then among the communities of Ionia. Thereafter, communities on the Aegean islands and mainland produced their own coins, choosing, however, gold, silver, bronze, lead and billon rather than electrum. Some Ionian communities continued to use electrum for their coinage throughout the Archaic period, even in addition to coinages of other metals (Ruschenbusch 1966; Kraay 1976: 20–238; Kroll and Waggoner 1984; Carradice 1987).

In appearance, these early coins were pieces of metal of a defined mass ('flans' of set 'weight standard'), struck with some defining visual characteristic. Mass was more important than shape of coin: as will be discussed further, coins of a certain denomination originating from a certain community would generally be the same weight, precise to the tenth of a gram. To ensure that the coins produced conformed to these agreed standards early coins were not necessarily perfectly circular in shape (*cf.* Kraay 1976: 11), and even within the same issue the shape of individual coins could vary. Coins were struck against dies, metallic tools which, unless they broke, could be used to impress some 10,000 individual coins.[7] These dies would imprint upon the flans either simple inscriptions or legends (as in the case of Klazonemai and Phokaia), incuse geometric patterns, or images (Kraay 1976: 5–8; Spier 1990; Howgego 1995, 62ff.; Spier 1998). Some images were specific to certain communities – some *combinations* of images were specific to certain communities – while the coins of some resembled those of another in subject matter but not in style (e.g. the difference between the profile view and frontal lions of Milesian and Samian coinage of the late sixth century BC).

---

[7] For a summary of the striking process and the notion of die-sharing in general, see Weidauer 1975: 66–8; Spier 1998: 331–3; and Fischer-Bossert 2018.

By using coins, Greeks were able to formalise pre-existing systems of wealth value and equivalency. A pre-money understanding of value that can be used for barter (*Od.* 1.430–431), compensation (*Il.* 1.184–186), gift-giving (*Od.* 11.355–361) and the award of prizes (*Il.* 23) is implied in the literary record, as is a system of standard measures for wine (*Il.* 23.741–747) and wool (*Il.* 12.433–437) (*cf.* Finley 1956; van Wees 1992: 228–32; Godelier 1999: 42–8; Seaford 2004: 68–72). But the evidence of the material record is even more compelling. First, there were in circulation in the seventh and sixth centuries pieces of silver – '*hacksilber*' – whose existence predates formal coinage (Kim 2002; Thompson 2003; Kagan 2006; Psoma 2016: 64 and 68). Hoard evidence from further east (Balmuth 1967; Bivar 1971; Gitin 1995; Gitin and Golani 2001: 38–9) and within Greek territories (*CH* 8, 35; *IGCH* 1874) has suggested that unbranded silver fragments were in circulation within and beyond the Mediterranean in the seventh and sixth centuries, and this is corroborated by both literary and scientific evidence indicating that the various silver mines were being heavily exploited *before* formal silver coinage had been introduced in the Aegean (Herodotus 6.46–7; Stos-Gale and MacDonald 1991). These tokens became markers of wealth that could have been exchanged for other commodities or services (Kroll 1998: 229–30; Kim 2001: esp. 15). Thus coinage allowed for this system to be regularised, and for a systematic production of these sorts of '*hacksilber*' tools.

Second, large objects must have had wealth equivalencies. This goes for objects that served no practical function themselves (e.g. iron spits: Herodotus 2.135; Waldstein 1902: 61–3; *cf.* Kraay 1976: 313–4; Haarer 2000; metal wire and scraps: Themelis 1981: 27) and objects that served some other function but could also be used to encode wealth-equivalency (e.g. tripods and cauldrons: IC 4.1, 4.8; *cf.* Whitley 1997: 649–60; von Reden 1997: 157–61). This made objects like these appropriate both to dedicate as votives in place of other objects of similar value and suitable to be used for the payment of taxes and fines; by extension, that means that there must have been agreement within a community that these objects, both large and small, had equivalent values. The introduction of any system of coinage, therefore, would not be responsible for inventing any new systems of equivalency but it would regularise – and, compared to the case of the iron spits and the tripods – provide a more convenient and portable alternative to exchanging tokens of wealth-value (Finley 1981: 236; Morris 1986: 9; Kroll 2012: 33–4).

The First Coinage in the Aegean

The first coins in the Aegean were struck just prior to the start of the sixth century BC, and thereafter the technology 'spread' rapidly across the rest of the basin. As has been noted above, the first electrum coins might have drawn inspiration from the region of Lydia, where a formal monetary system had been initiated in the seventh century BC. This, in turn, might have drawn inspiration from neighbours even further east in Mesopotamia and the Levant (see Kroll 1998: 229 for a summary of some of the evidence), who had been using formal systems of exchange employing weights and measures since at least the third millennium BC (*cf.* Powell 1990; Le Rider 2001: 1–24). But what may have begun as a technology that originated outside of the Aegean was soon reimagined as a Greek phenomenon, wherein over a period of only a few decades in the sixth century at least forty cities and island states from around the Aegean basin were already minting their own coins.

Greeks in Ionia and from around the coast of Asia Minor were the first to mint coins (Kraay 1976: 30–3; Boardman 1980: 97; Hanfmann 1983: 34, 69, 72–3; Konuk 2012; Kroll 2012: 38–9). At the beginning of the sixth century (Fig. 4.2a–b), coinage is attested in Ionia at (from north to south) Phokaia, Smyrna, Ephesos and Miletos, and also nearby at Mytilene on Lesbos, on Samos and Kos, and at Knidos. It is also possible that the first coin series of Ephesos, Miletos and Phokaia – all electrum coins with iconographic images on the one side and incuse geometric patterns on the other – were the first to be minted and can be placed at the end of the seventh century BC (Kraay 1976; Wallace 1987). Coinage was not taken up so quickly in other parts of the Aegean, and at the start of the sixth century, coin series are only attested for Corinth and up in the northern Aegean at Eion and Apollonia.

By the middle of the sixth century, by contrast (Fig. 4.2c–d), many more cities had begun to mint coins. On the Ionian coast, Smyrna, Chios and Klazomenai had also begun to produce coin series, but the main spread of coinage was around Central Greece. Akraifia, Mykalessos, Orchomenos and Phokis were now minting. The first coin series on Aegina were also struck, as well as on Andros and at Karystos on Euboea. This spread can be quantified as comprising 186 coin series from twenty-one cities. Indeed, this latter part of the sixth century saw the real acceleration for the rate at which Greek cities started to produce coins, and, by the latter part of the century (Fig. 4.2e–f), almost all regions of the Aegean – apart from Crete, the Peloponnese and parts of western and northern Greece – were producing coin series. It was during this period that coinage took off most considerably across the Cyclades, and the number of cities within central Greece minting would also increase once again.

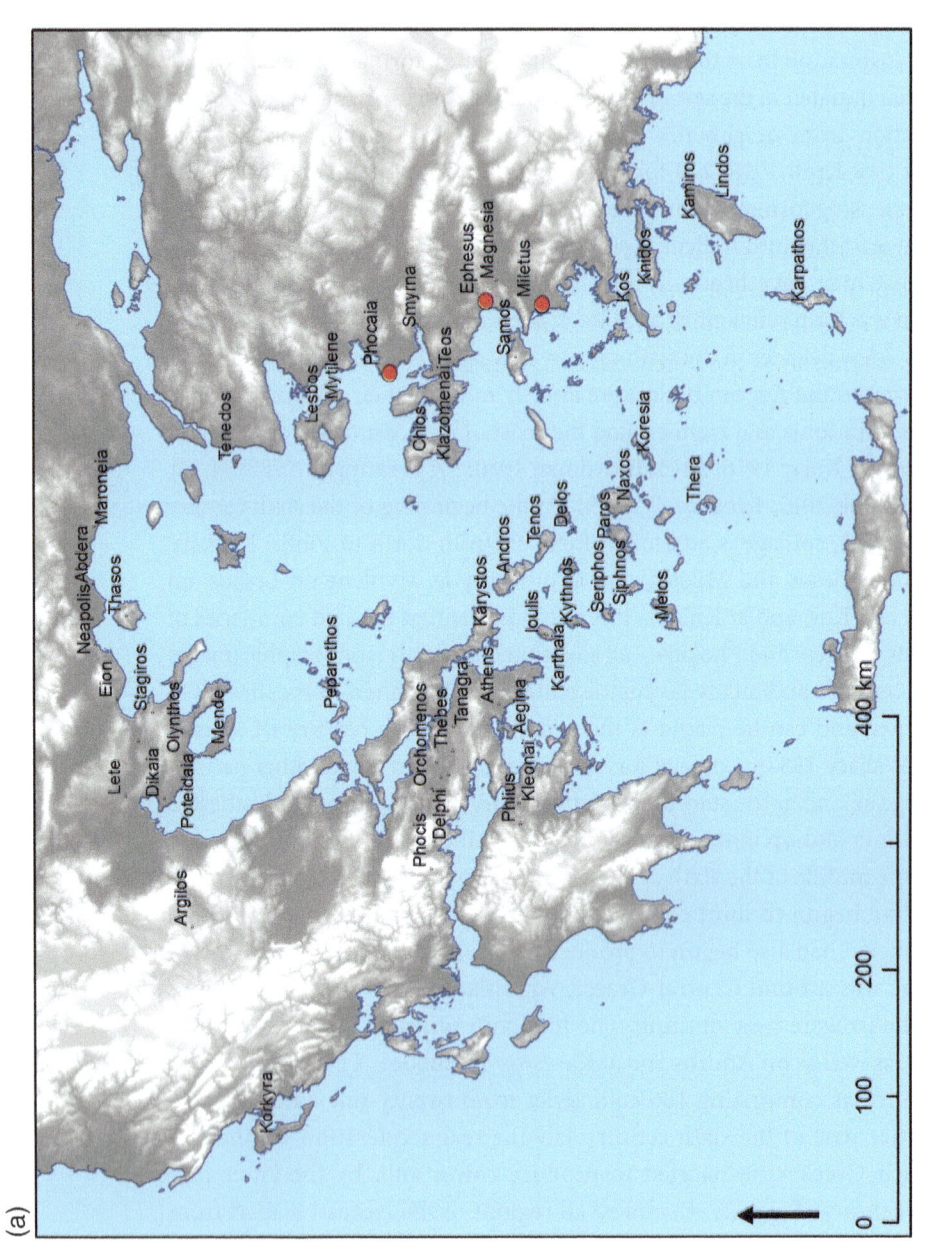

Figure 4.2a Distribution of sites for which there is evidence of coin minting. Pre-600 BC

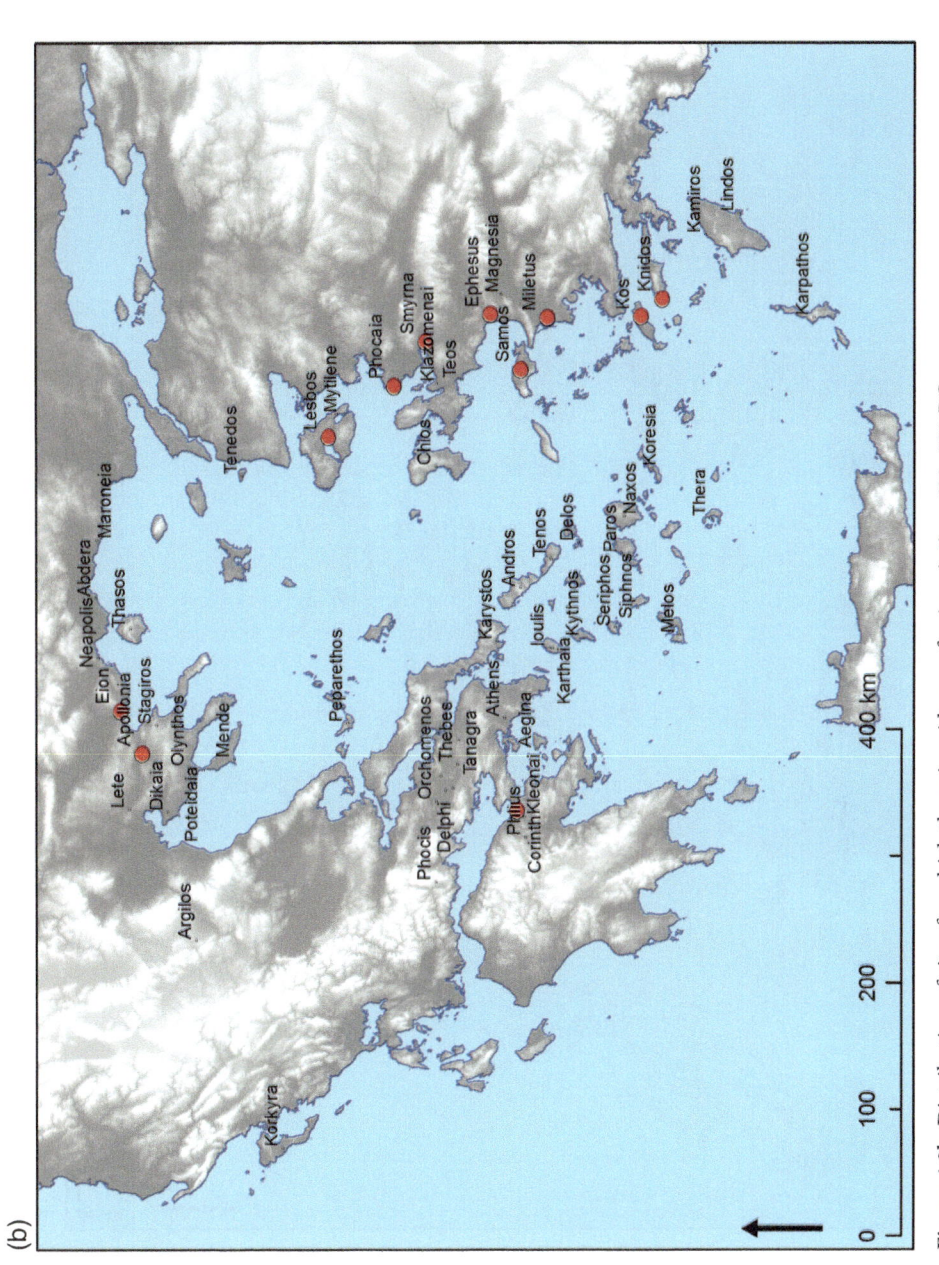

Figure 4.2b Distribution of sites for which there is evidence of coin minting, 600–580 BC.

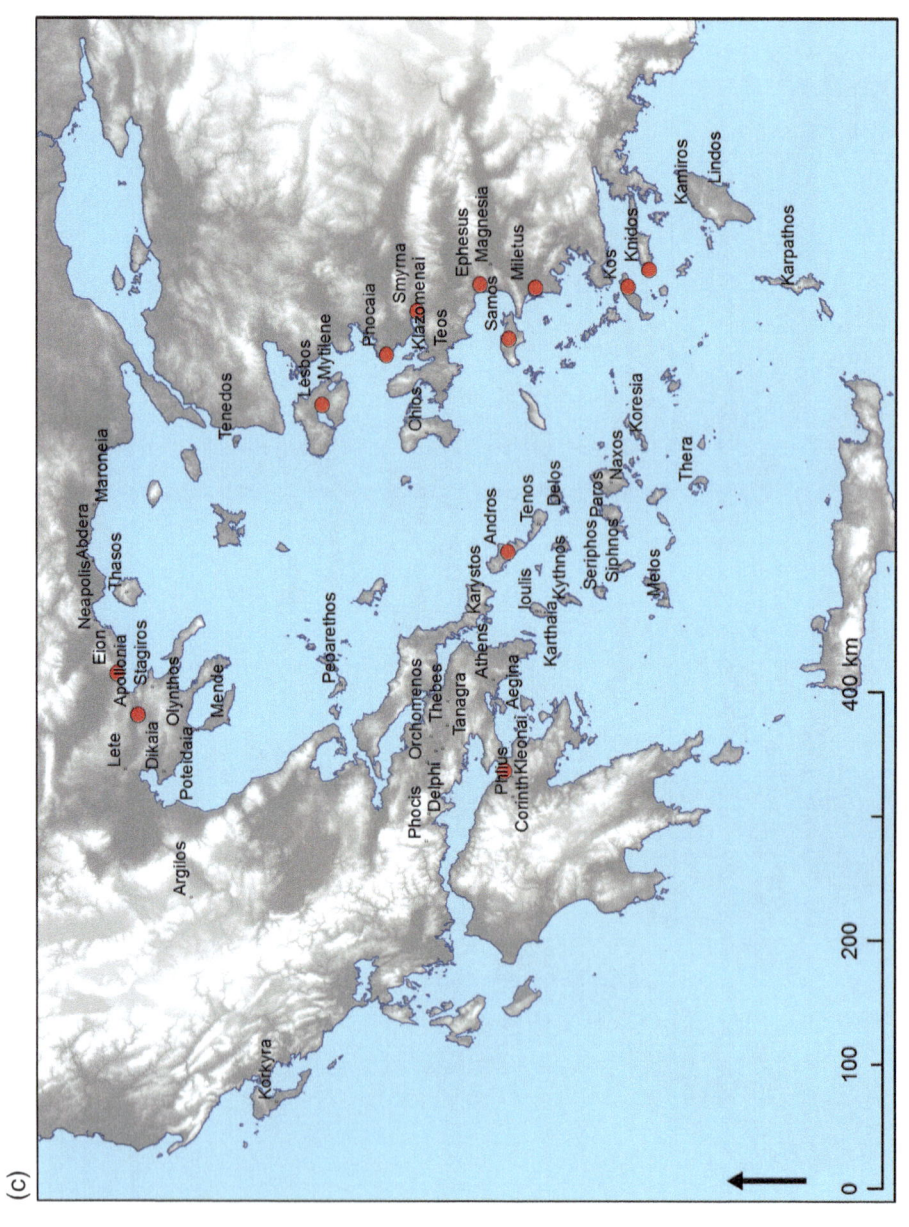

Figure 4.2c Distribution of sites for which there is evidence of coin minting, 580–560 BC.

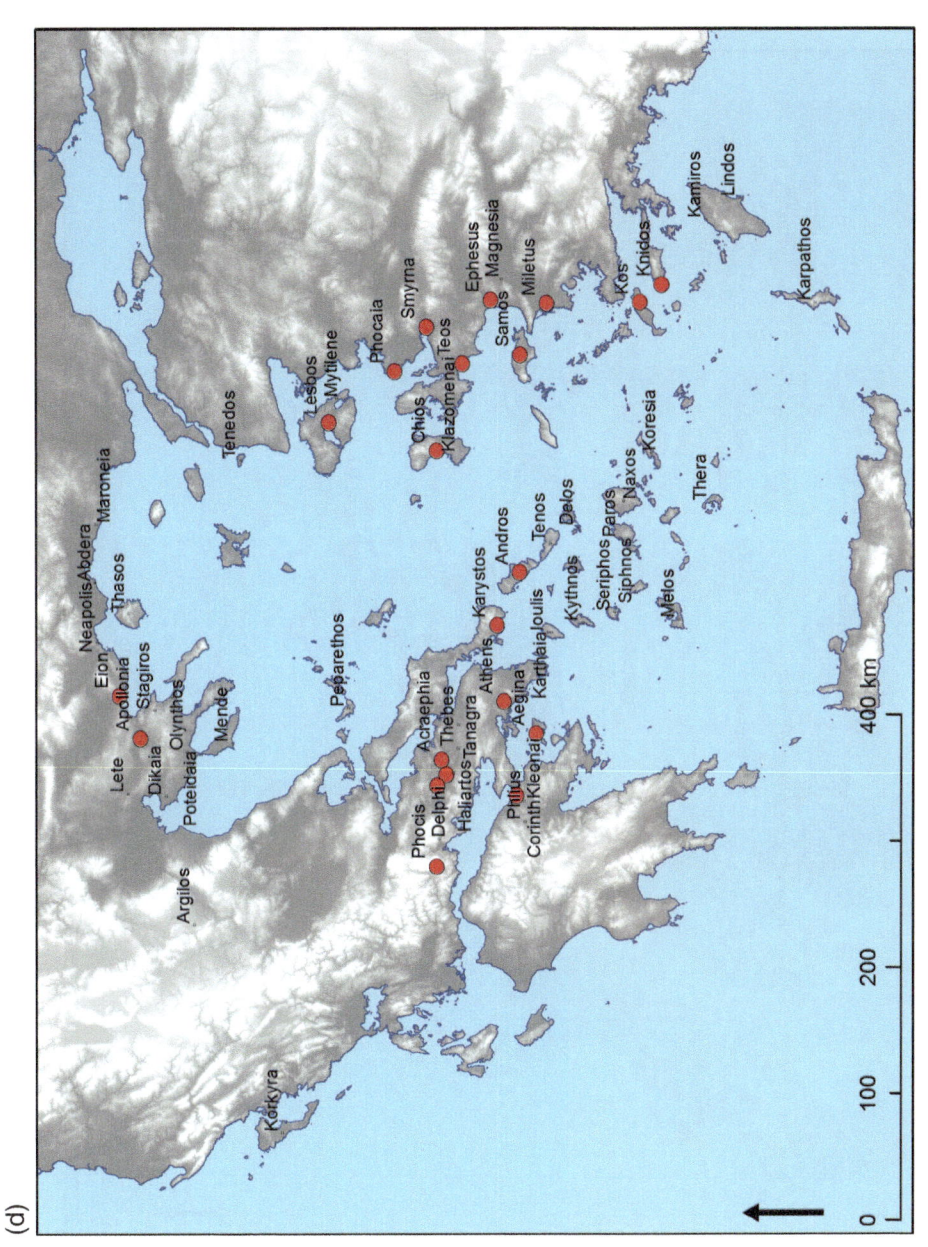

Figure 4.2d Distribution of sites for which there is evidence of coin minting, 560–540 BC.

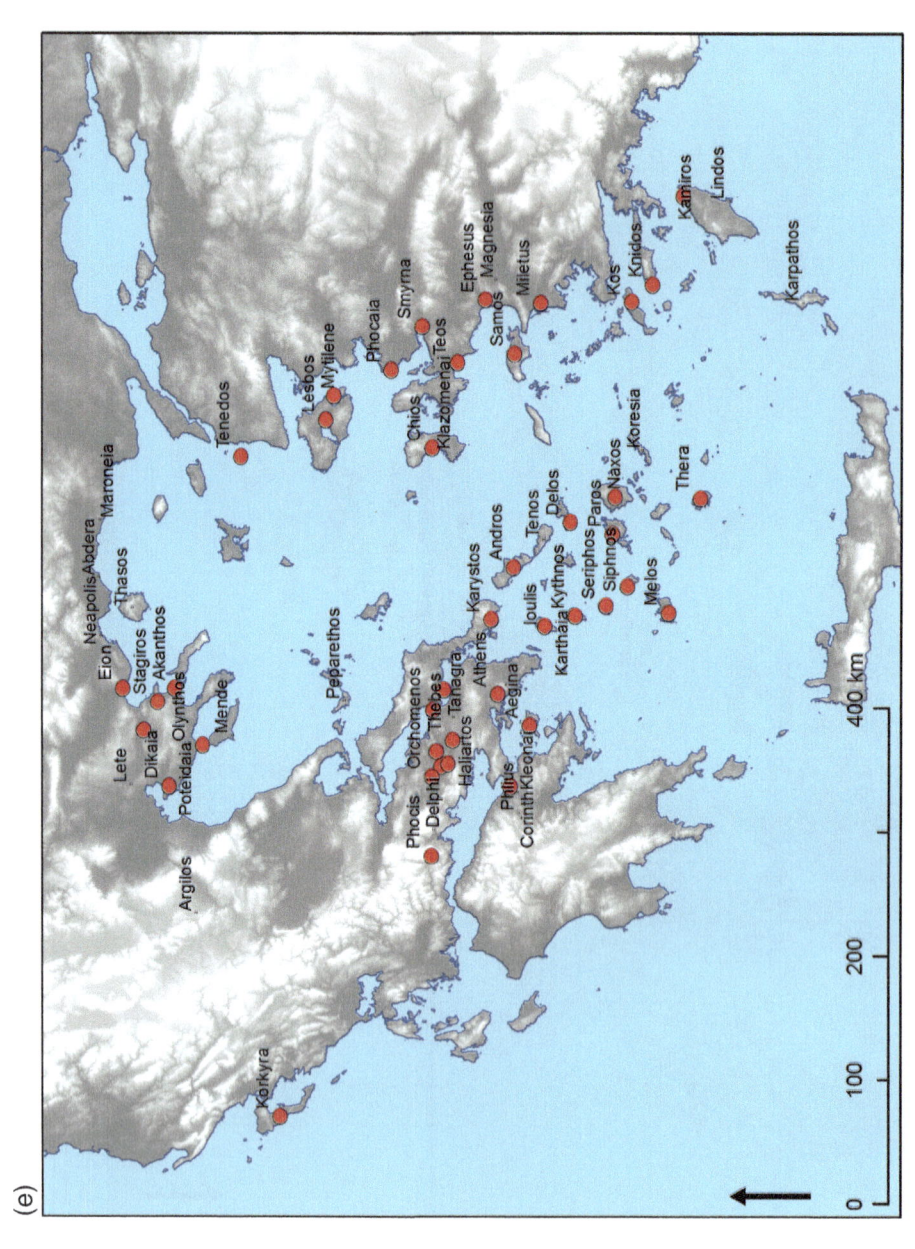

Figure 4.2e Distribution of sites for which there is evidence of coin minting. 540–520 BC.

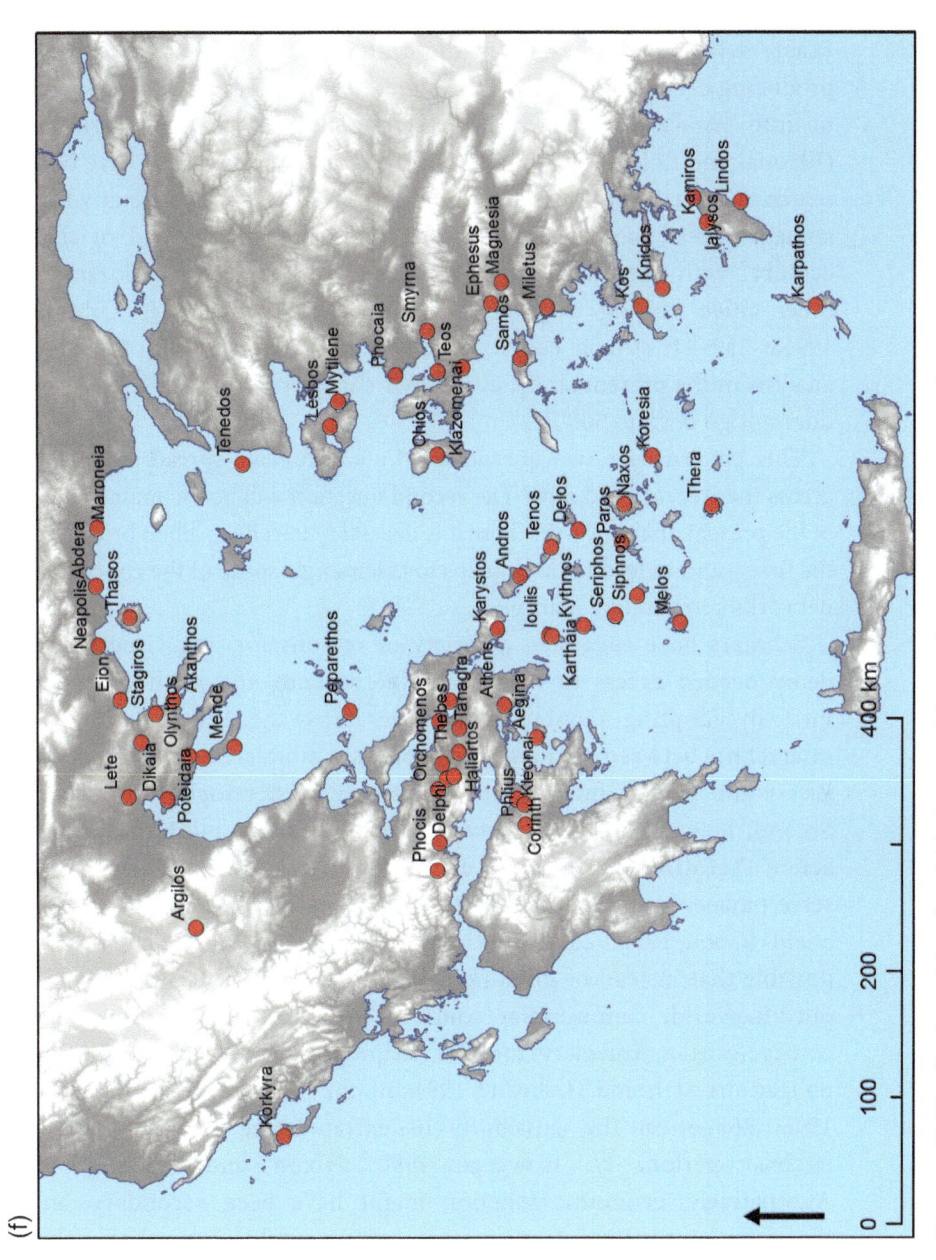

Figure 4.2f Distribution of sites for which there is evidence of coin minting, 520–500 BC.

By this stage, the number of cities minting coins had doubled over the course of just a few years, with now thirty-nine Aegean cities minting a total of at least 400 coin series.

This rate of increase continued into the end of the sixth century (Table 4.2), and by the end of the century sixty different cities were producing between themselves 631 series. Coinage was now being struck up into Thrace as well, with a greater number of cities in Corinthia (Kleonai and Phleious) now minting, and the first coinage to have been struck at the cities of Ialysos and Lindos on Rhodes. The rate at which coinage spread would continue even more beyond the end of sixth century, with the start of the fifth century seeing some dozens of other cities starting to produce coinage (*cf.* discussion in Osborne 1996a: 239–41; *cf.* von Reden 1995, and 1997; Kurke 1999); the main analysis in the present study, as in other chapters of this book, however, does not go beyond 500 BC.

This pattern begs two questions: *why* did coinage spread so quickly across the Aegean, and *how*? The second question will be the main subject of the present analysis, while here it is necessary to reflect, albeit briefly, on the first – and indeed to do so helps to disentangle some of the conceptual networks surrounding coinage.

Scholars have suggested a variety of reasons for why Greeks suddenly needed access to coinage in the seventh and sixth centuries. First, by adopting a system of coinage across the Aegean, economic interaction between various actors became simpler, and trade activities could extend further; this point will be developed more fully. Second, it is possible that it was not economic but *militaristic* interaction that drove the need, as a system was required that could help serve payments and finance military activities both locally and further afield (Cook 1958: 261; Mørkholm 1982; Kraay 1984). Third, it is possible that instead of thinking primarily about interactions with the outside world, communities considered their own operations, and coinage was a necessary tool for helping to pay legal or political obligations at home (Osborne 1991 on the Classical period; Martin 1996: 265–6 on the possibility of extrapolating evidence to the Archaic period. *cf.* Howgego 1990; Nixon and Price 1990). Alternatively, economic function might have been secondary, and the real motivation for creating coins might have been that communities required a form of portable token that could be used to advertise civic identities (Polanyi 1968; Price 1968; Murray 1980: 237–40; Picard 1989; Seaford 2004). That Greeks began not only to

Table 4.2 *Sites minting coins throughout the sixth century BC, with weight standards used for each.*

Site	Pre 600 BC	600–580 BC	580–560 BC	560–540 BC	540–520 BC	520–500 BC	Weight standards
Abdera						x	Abderite
Aegina				x	x	x	Aeginitan
Akanthos					x	x	Attic-Euboean
Akraifia				x	x	x	Aeginitan
Apollonia				x	x	x	Attic, Thraco-Makedonian
Argilos						x	Makedonian
Athens				x	x	x	Attic-Euboean
Chalkis					x	x	Euboean
Chersonesos						x	Attic
Chios				x	x	x	Chian, Milesian
Corinth		x	x	x	x	x	Corinthian
Delos					x	x	Attic-Euboean
Delphi						x	Aeginitan
Dikaia					x	x	Milesian
Eion		x	x	x	x	x	Phokaian
Ephesos	x	x	x	x	x	x	Milesian
Eretria						x	Euboean
Haliartos					x	x	Aeginitan
Ialysos					x	x	Ialysian
Ioulis						x	Aeginitan
Kamiros						x	Aeginitan
Karpathos						x	Milesian
Karthaia					x	x	Aeginitan
Karystos				x	x	x	Euboean
Klazomenai						x	Milesian
Knidos		x	x	x	x	x	Aeginitan
Koresia						x	Aeginitan
Korkyra					x	x	Korkyran
Kos			x	x	x	x	Phokaian
Kythnos					x	x	Aeginitan Attic-Euboean
Lesbos				x	x	x	Lesbian, Persic
Lete						x	Thasian
Lindos						x	Milesian
Magnesia						x	Milesian
Maroneia						x	Thasian
Melos					x	x	Milesian
Mende					x	x	Attic-Euboean
Miletos	x	x	x	x	x	x	Milesian

Table 4.2 (cont.)

Site	Pre 600 BC	600–580 BC	580–560 BC	560–540 BC	540–520 BC	520–500 BC	Weight standards
Mykalessos				x	x	x	Aeginitan
Mytilene					x	x	Phokaian
Naxos						x	Aeginitan
Olynthos						x	Euboean
Orchomenos				x	x	x	Aeginitan
Paros					x	x	Aeginitan
Peparethos						x	Attic-Euboean
Phleious						x	Euboean
Phokaia	x	x	x	x	x	x	Milesian, Phokaian
Phokis				x	x	x	Aeginitan
Poteidaia					x	x	Attic-Euboean
Samos					x	x	Euboean, Milesian, Persic, Samian
Seriphos					x	x	Aeginitan, Milesian
Siphnos					x	x	Aeginitan
Smyrna		x	x	x	x	x	Phokaian
Stagiros					x	x	Attic-Euboean
Tanagra						x	Aeginitan
Tenos						x	Aeginitan
Teos				x	x	x	Aeginitan
Thasos						x	Thasian
Thebes					x	x	Aeginitan
Thera					x	x	Aeginitan

associate certain places with images and styles or – and also – that they could recognise the 'brands' of other Greeks, is a notion that will be explored in more detail in Chapter 5.

The case for an economic function of coinage (i.e. one of the first three alternatives) is perhaps most compelling, based on evidence suggesting how coins were used. There is some indication that the *Hacksilber* that came before coinage and the first coins themselves were weighed on scales at the point of transaction (Kim 1994; 2001, 2002), after which the stamping of coins with recognised *insigna* replaced the need for weighing (Kagan 2006; Psoma 2006; 64, 68). So much is implied by the sequence of archaeological evidence. One of the earliest dated coin hoards found within the Aegean contained a combination of unmarked bullion and large volumes of low value coins, namely the 'Kolophon hoard' (Carson 1975; Kim and Kroll 2008) [HOARD 32]. This assemblage, located in 'western Asia Minor' between

1935 and 1940 (no other contextual information is available) contained 906 tiny silver coins and 77 pieces of unmarked bullion, dated to the sixth century. The marked coins seem to correlate to the Persic weight standard, while the unmarked bullion does not seem to be based on a standard.

The fact that both bullion and coins were found together suggests that both technologies could have been in use at the same time. And if bullion was still in use as a method of exchange, scales must still have been used during transaction, as weighing unmarked bullion provided the only way to establish the equivalent worth of a metal piece, whose value was proportional to its materiality; Kim and Kroll note too, that there would be no need for a weight standard to be used for the bullion if the intention was always that these pieces would be weighed when in transaction (Kim and Kroll 2008: 61–3) – a completely plausible suggestion. There is also the possibility that for the first coins – electrum alloys, whose metal composition was not fixed, and where two coins of exactly the same size and shape could contain quite different quantities of gold and silver – weighing at the point of transaction continued (Tselekas 1996; Kroll 2008: 18; von Reden 2010: 19). Later hoards, though, contain *only* coins, and unmarked bullion is no longer present. This implies that there could have been a change in the way that value was determined: in the pre-coinage system, the constituent metal composition and weight of a coin must have been linked to its economic value; but once the practice of coin stamping began, the *insignia* of coins could be used as a guarantee that a certain flan had a set value. The value of coin no longer had to be tied to its material worth, but a standardised and recognisable stamp could communicate the notion of equivalent value to both buyer and seller. Put simply, the presence of recognisable symbols and guarantors would *speed up* and *facilitate* any transactions. And it becomes clear to see, in this case, why the adoption of coinage would seem like a good idea to communities wanting to exchange more frequently or in greater quantity with one another:[8] a tool like this would reduce friction within the system.

Of course, these four alternatives stated above are neither limiting nor mutually exclusive. Different communities in different parts of the Aegean

---

[8] Some might even argue that it was not so much the intensification of trade but the growing size and complexities of communities that demanded a new way of establishing value and equivalency quickly. Noted in Chapter 1 is that Greek settlements were rapidly growing in size and in complexity at this time. Could it simply be the case that new demands placed on these communities required different sorts of tools. It is an observed phenomenon within the anthropological literature that once populations grow above a certain threshold, societies struggle to function unless there is some formalised method of economic exchange where coins (or similar tokens) can be used to represent units of fixed value (See Naroll 1956, Carneiro and Tobias 1963, Carneiro 1967 and the recent critique of this model by Vaesen et al. 2016).

subject to different sorts of economic or political pressures would have had different motivations. But what the wide-scale uptake of coinage does tell us is that there was *agreement* within and beyond communities about certain things. Naturally, impressed pieces of metal should be regarded within that community as having a specific value; and there was some *benefit* to the community in using this technology that they did not have before. Moreover, there was not just agreement, but *trust* within the community, such that members of a community, even if they had not met one another and had no prior personal relationship, could imbue these impressed pieces of metal with (economic or political) value, because they knew that the same values would be recognised elsewhere (Martin 1995: esp. 260ff).

The size of these communities is still debated. Some coins tell us the names of the communities who they served, most usually small or large cities. In either full or abbreviated form, various issues have legends on them that correlate to place names: Akraifia, Corinth, Delphi, Ialysos, Kamiros, Karystos, Klazomenai, Knidos, Mykalessos, Mytilene, Orchomenos, Phokaia, Tanagra. This implies that decisions concerning the production and design of coins were the concern of communities organised at this level – or, at least, a subset of individuals within this community who had sufficient authority to make a decision on behalf of the wider group. The community of the city of Corinth, for instance, decided among themselves to adopt this new tool, and in doing so emblazoned these new objects with the label 'Q' to indicate that they had been produced in and would be recognised by this community. But can we be certain of this bottom-up approach, that it was always agreement within the community that led to the production of coinage? Some have suggested that it was actually a top-down imposition by wealthy or powerful individuals that instituted the first mints (*cf.* Mackil and van Alfen 2006; *contra* Price et al. 1983; van Alfen 2012: 29ff.). Tyrants, it has been suggested – those who we know from public sanctuary dedications had a vested interested in promoting their own agenda and status – could have used a technology like coinage as another vehicle on which to communicate a message or identity. On this basis of the available evidence, this seems rather unlikely. Would one not expect then the name or image of these tyrants or wealthy individuals to appear on the coins themselves?[9] Coins served communities, and it is most likely that communities therefore chose to create coins to serve their needs.

[9] Compare, for example, the iconography of the coins of Ialysos, Klazomenai, Kythnos and Mytilene, all cities under the control of Polykrates of Samos in the late sixth century. All four have coin series that display a shared iconographic motif of the winged bull, but Polykrates himself is absent.

Coinage Networks

Given what we now know about the economic background to the first minting of coins, *how* did coinage spread so quickly across the Aegean in the sixth century?

The key attribute to focus on here is weight. As noted above with regards to the example of the Kolophon hoard, the mass of both uncoined bullion and the first coins was critical for the determination of wealth value. As coinage technology developed, standards were established for denominations within coinage series – that is, staters produced within the same community would always be the same weight (within a certain margin of error),[10] drachmas produced within the community would be a different fixed weight, and so on. In the sixth century BC there were some eleven different 'weight standards' in use across the Aegean: Aeginitan, Attic-Euboean, Chian, Corinthian, Euboean, Ialysian, Lesbian, Milesian, Persic, Phokaian and Samian. The names given to these weight standards are modern labels attributed to regions, islands or cities from which the greatest number of coins of each type were found, but they generally conform to the places at which the earliest coinage in a series that uses a certain standard are attested.

The following analysis looks at the distribution of coin series using these different weight standards in the Aegean across time, identifying shared standards and offering some explanations for the pattern. There is a large numismatic dataset to draw on for this analysis, thanks to over 150 years of very detailed encyclopaedic work on coins (going back to at least Head 1887), comprising a significant number of catalogues of coin issues and series, with painstaking work on establishing relative chronologies and identifying micro-variations in the dies used.[11] With the exception of archaeometry-based studies that look at the origin of the materials used in minting, and the absolute dates assigned to various coin series (e.g. XRF: Condamin and Picon 1964; Cope 1972; Carter and Carter 1974. NAA: Barrandon and Guerra 1998),[12] there has been less work done for Greek

---

[10] Kim 2001: 18 discusses variation in the weight of coins, plotting the distribution of weight within a single hoard comprising 906 silver pieces. The weight varies around a median of 0.02g, some 5 per cent and 10 per cent of the total weight of the two coin types analysed.

[11] See Martin 1995 for a discussion of the size of the dataset of coinage versus the resolution of information that we can get from relative dating

[12] Compared to neighbours in the study of Roman numismatics, in previous decades there has been relatively more disconnect between archaeological science and major numismatic studies within the Greek world, with scientific analyses of Roman coinage outnumbering those for the coinage of archaic and classical Greece by about ten to one: Metcalf and Oddy 1980, *cf.* Ponting 2012.

numismatics placing the dataset within broader historical framework, with some even commenting that while numismatists tend to look at micro-details, all historians want to do is to see the broad picture (Kraay 1964). This chapter aims to bring a greater historical focus to this rich and abundant dataset.

This study looks at 631 distinct coin series of the sixth century BC, from 60 different sites (Table **A3.1**). This represents roughly 60 per cent of the known numismatic data for this period, with some c. 200 unattributed coin series not analysed here.[13] Data were mined from Oliver Hoover's recent synthesis and restudy of Aegean coin series (Hoover 2010), verified against and supplemented with additional material sourced from online synthetic databases (*cf.* van Alfen 2012: 26). Accordingly, Hoover's chronological resolution is used, wherein the most precise coin series are dated within twenty-year slices. This chapter covers, therefore, five phases: 600–580, 580–560, 560–540, 540–520, and 520–500. Most coins in the database are silver, but there also exist in smaller numbers electrum, bronze and lead series, as well as the billon coinage of Lesbos. For each coin series, the denomination of the coin was recorded (e.g. 1/6 stater), as was the presence of any image or legend.

Data are visualised here via a series of successive SNA times lices, once more using Gephi. As discussed in Chapter 1, SNA can make visually explicit connections between entities of different scales visualised as nodes and edges. Here, a community minting coinage within a given twenty-year period (as indicated by the presence of a coin series in the material record) is visualised as a node. Any two communities who created coins on a shared weight standard have an edge drawn between them. Two abstract nodes are included, 'Attica-Euboea' and 'Persia': these represent weight standards associated with whole regions (communities of communities) rather than specific communities, using the agreed terminology as these standards are usually described in the numismatic literature. Some distinction in degree has also been made between nodes representing communities which produced coins set to their own standards (e.g. Aegina and Miletos, with regard to the Aeginitan and Milesian standards). Ties between nodes are unweighted, nor do they have direction.

For each of the five periods identified above, two visualisations of the data have been produced. The first is based around the 'force atlas' function of Gephi, which arranges nodes according to sub-networks clusters.[14] This

---

[13] *cf.* van Alfen 2012: 26

[14] Default settings of Gephi's 'force atlas' layout function were used, except the 'repulsion strength' was set to 12,000. The noOverlap function was then run under its default settings to improve the readability of the data, and the 'expansion' function was also run three times.

arranges together sites that share one or more weight standards and enables one more quickly to identify clusters of potentially interacting sites. One must note, though, that it is the number of connections that is important, rather than the place in the graph. The programme tries to sort more 'connected' nodes towards the centre and those with fewer connections towards the outside, but where there is an uneven spread of connectedness across the network, some more connected places will necessarily have to be sorted further towards the outside than they perhaps ought to be and *vice versa*. The second is a geographic visualisation.[15] All sites are set to geographic co-ordinates, with 'dummy' co-ordinates in the relative positions for the 'Attica-Euboea' and 'Persia' weight standards. In both visualisations, the nodes are of two sizes, relative to the different degrees described above.

At the start of the sixth century BC (600–580 BC, Fig. 4.3), five weight standards were being used by different communities across the Aegean: Aeginitan, Attic-Euboean, Corinthian, Milesian and Phokaian. Apart from the Attic-Euboean standard, all others were associated with cities or, in the case of Aegina, an island. And apart from Corinth, the same standard was shared by other communities who were also minting coins at this time: this was a small number of communities overall, and there was no preference within the Aegean for any one standard over any others. Some communities minted to the standards of others' who were geographically close: Ephesos to its Ionian neighbour Miletos; Kos and Smyrna with Phokaia, all communities in the eastern Aegean world. Others, however, were not close by: Samos used the same weight standard for its coinage as the Athenians; Knidos' coinage was based on that of Aegina; and Eion in the north used a coinage set to the same standard as the Phokaians. No other Aegean-based communities at this time minted coinage to the same standard as Corinth.

In the following twenty years (580–560 BC, Fig. 4.4), there were relatively few changes in the distribution of weight standards among Aegean communities as opposed to the previous period. There was at this time a beginning for the coinage being minted on the island of Andros, based on the standard of its neighbour Aegina. A very general distinction can be made already in this period between weight standards which served mainly a need towards local communities (the standard of Corinth was not used for any other neighbours; the Attic-Euboean standard served Athens, and the Aeginitan standard served Andros), and weight standards which were shared across the Aegean in both an east-west and a north-south direction (respectively, Samos used the Attic-Euboean standard, and Kos used the

---

[15] Default settings of Gephi' 'Geo Layout' function were used, except the 'scale' was set to 20,000.

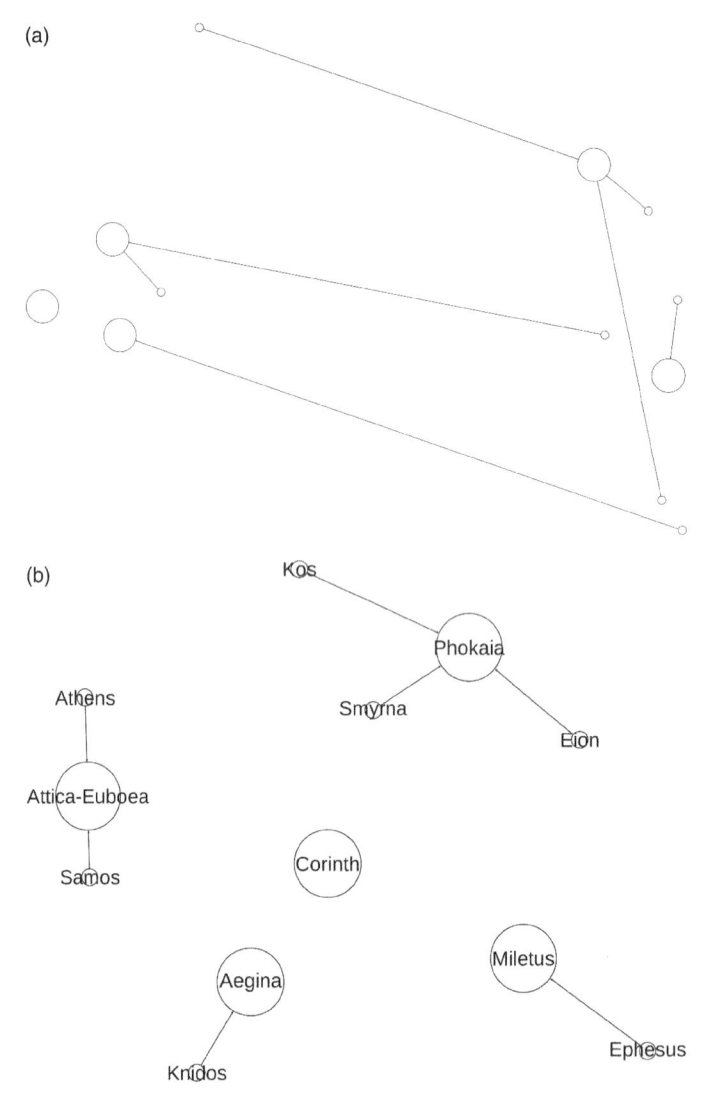

168   *Entangled Networks: The Transfer of Knowledge*

(a)

(b)

Figure 4.3 SNA visualisation of the sites minting coins 600–580 BC. Sites are represented by nodes, and ties are drawn between sites that share a weight standard: a) Nodes are placed according to their approximate geographic location in the Aegean; b) Nodes are distributed randomly in abstract space.

Phokaian standard). In general, there was a trend for those weight standards on the western side of the Aegean to serve more local communities and for those on the eastern Aegean to be taken up by a much broader network. But this is a trend that is still difficult to see in the second fifth of the sixth century BC, and it is something that will only become more apparent later.

(a)

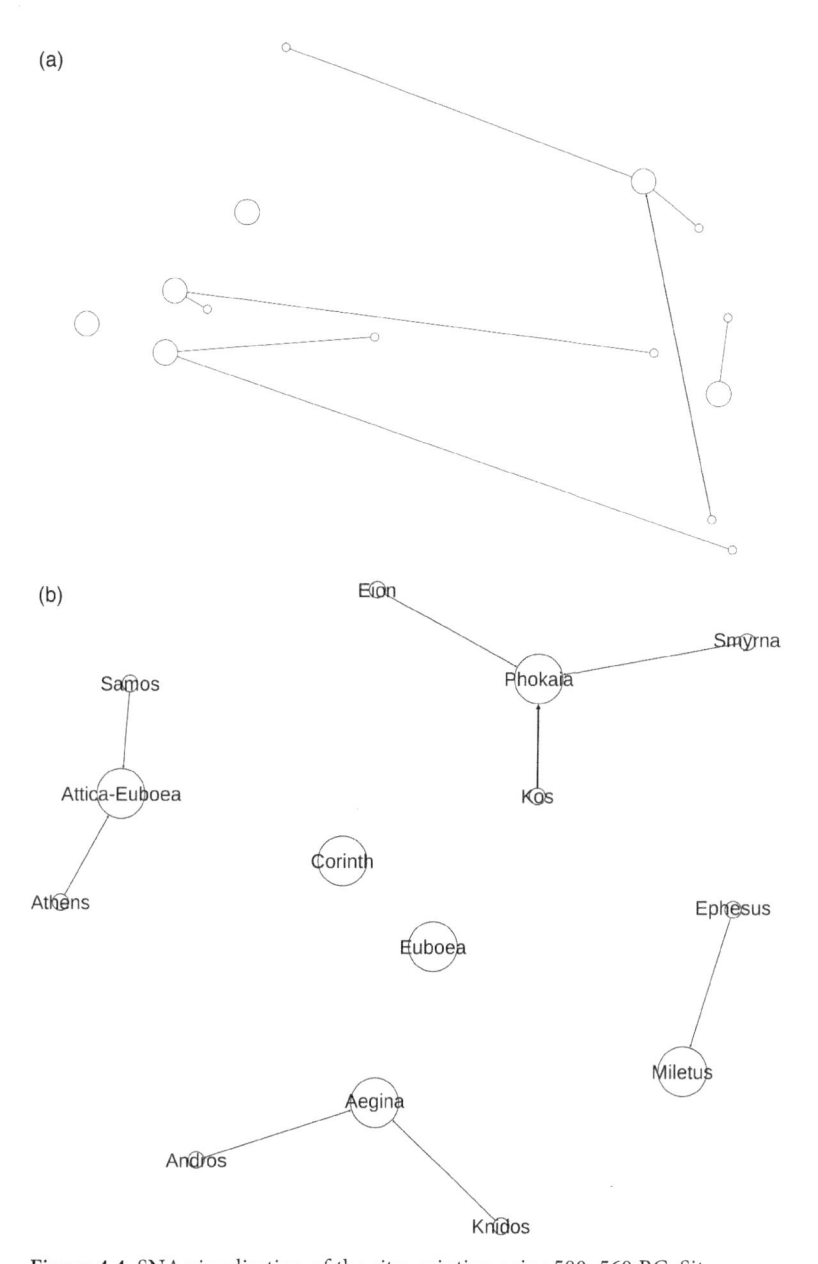

(b)

Eion
Samos   Smyrna
           Phokaia
Attica-Euboea   Kos
Athens   Ephesus
          Corinth
          Euboea
                Miletus
       Aegina
Andros
       Knidos

Figure 4.4 SNA visualisation of the sites minting coins 580–560 BC. Sites are represented by nodes, and ties are drawn between sites that share a weight standard: a) Nodes are placed according to their approximate geographic location in the Aegean; b) Nodes are distributed randomly in abstract space.

The middle of the sixth century BC (560–540 BC, Fig. 4.5) sees big changes in the eight-standard distribution as many more communities began producing coin series of their own. The communities minting to Aeginitan,

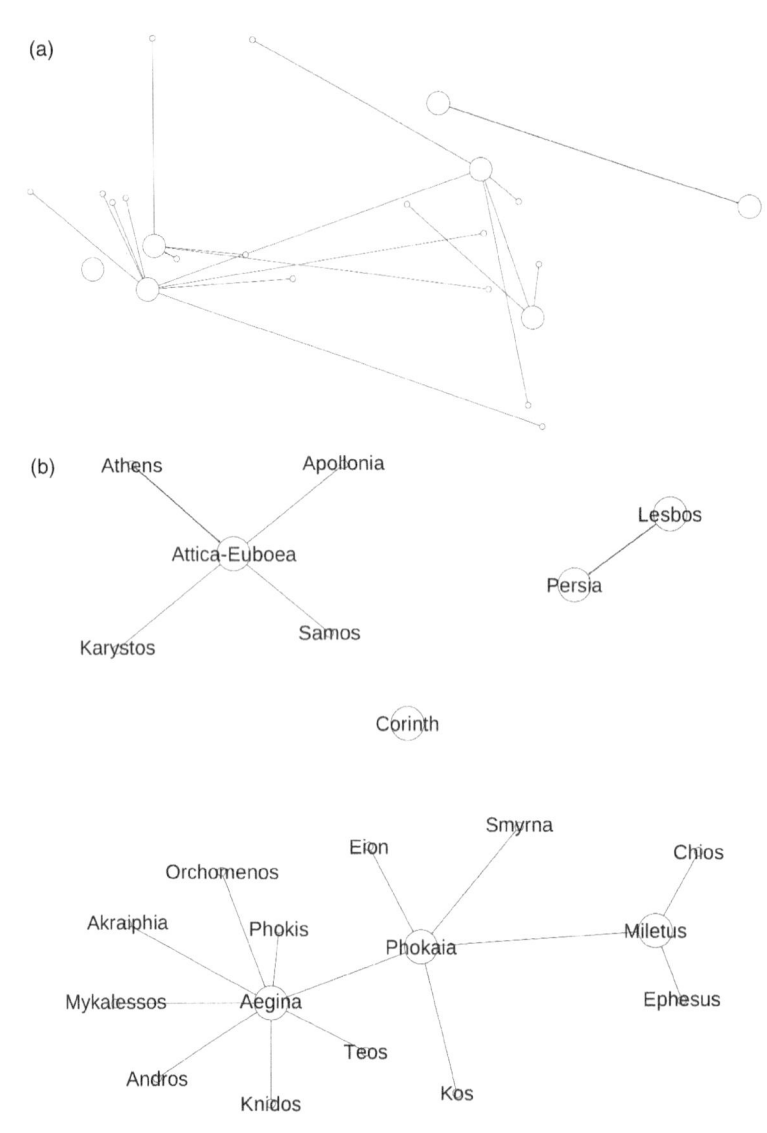

170   *Entangled Networks: The Transfer of Knowledge*

Figure 4.5 SNA visualisation of the sites minting coins 560–540 BC. Sites are represented by nodes, and ties are drawn between sites that share a weight standard: a) Nodes are placed according to their approximate geographic location in the Aegean; b) Nodes are distributed randomly in abstract space.

Phokaian and Milesian standards became linked, to an extent, as Phokaian itself produced coin series based on standards of all three cities. This produced a substantial network holding together several Aegean communities, as now a total of seven communities were producing coinage based on that of Aegina, while Chios had also started minting coins set to the Milesian standard. The

Aeginitan standard, in addition to reaching out towards the eastern Aegean (Knidos, Teos) continued to serve principally local communities, namely those in the Cycladic islands (Andros) but also those in central Greece (Akraifia, Mykalessos, Orchomenos, Phokis). The Attic-Euboean standard was also used by communities over a greater geographic reach, including some in the north (Apollonia) and in the Cyclades (Karystos) in addition to Athens and Samos who continued to use the standard. The Corinthian standard was not used by other Aegean communities; it would be taken by neighbours further west, but the boundaries of this current analysis do not reflect this usage of the standard. Lesbos, an island that is notable now and in subsequent generations for the great number of coin series that it would produce, based its coinage on its own local standard and drew inspiration from the Anatolian world. Finally, one might say in only the most qualitative terms that there was at this time more 'east-west' interaction between communities and parent weight standards than 'north-south' interaction.

As one moves towards the end of the sixth century BC (540–520 BC, Fig. 4.6), the patterns of the previous period become more pronounced. The Milesian and Phokaian standards continued to be used for local communities: the former for Chios, Ephesos and Melos; and the latter for Mytilene, Tenedos and Smyrna. The Aeginitan standard continued to be used by two main areas: the communities of the Cyclades (Andros, Naxos,

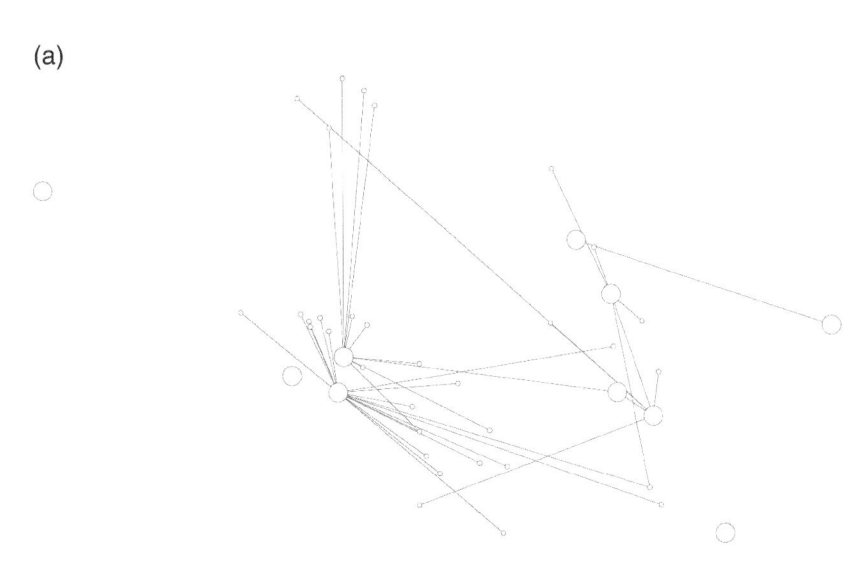

(a)

Figure 4.6a SNA visualisation of the sites minting coins 540–520 BC. Sites are represented by nodes, and ties are drawn between sites that share a weight standard: Nodes are placed according to their approximate geographic location in the Aegean. This image is available in a larger format online at www.cambridge.org/loy.

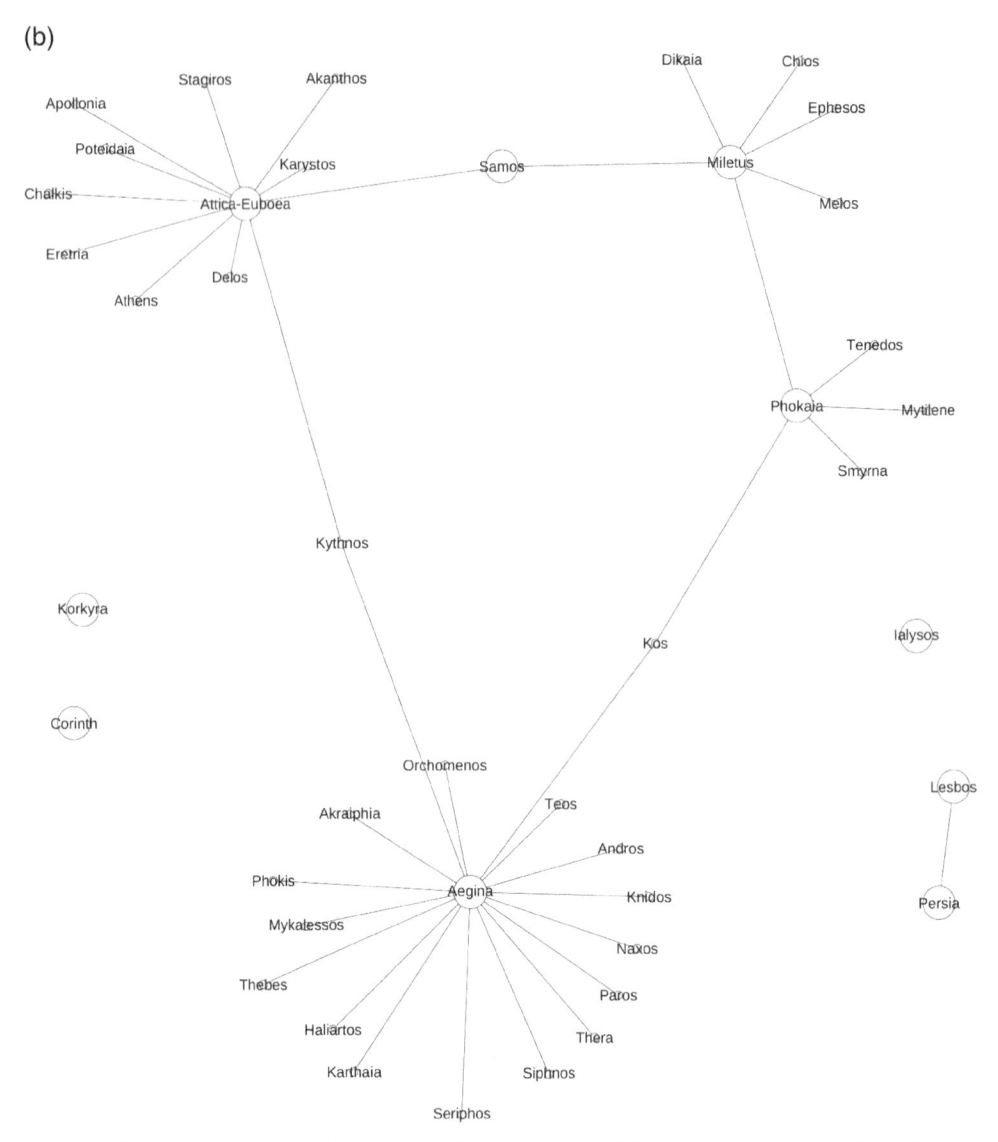

172 *Entangled Networks: The Transfer of Knowledge*

(b)

Figure 4.6b SNA visualisation of the sites minting coins 540–520 BC Sites are represented by nodes, and ties are drawn between sites that share a weight standard. Nodes are distributed randomly in abstract space. This image is available in a larger format online at www.cambridge.org/loy.

Paros, Seriphos, Siphnos, Thera) and those of central Greece (Akraifia, Haliartos, Mykalessos, Orchomenos and Thebes). In addition, the Attic-Euboean standard continued to serve two other groups: local communities based both terrestrially and on the islands (Athens, Chalkis, Delos, Eretria, Karystos) and up in the north Aegean (Akanthos, Apollonia, Poteidaia, Stagiros). What is particularly interesting in this period (and most evident when looking at the results of the network analysis visualised in abstract space) is that there is an Aegean-level connection. Many communities were connected to one another indirectly through the sharing of standards: all communities were part of a networked group apart from those that were already noted for being independent – that is, Corinth and Lesbos, now with the addition too of Korkyra and Ialysos.[16] A node of key importance to this network is Samos: not only did the community of Samos mint coins to its own standard, but it also produced other series that followed the Attic-Euboean and the Milesian standards. As will be discussed further, this was a key node in connecting together two main zones of interaction in the Aegean (the 'western' and 'eastern' parts).

Finally, at the end of the sixth century BC (520–500 BC, Fig. 4.7), the Aegean-level networking of communities had increased to an even greater degree. A majority of communities producing coinage were connected directly or indirectly to one another through the sharing of weight standards: the exceptions are the communities noted above (those either minting independently or linked to networks beyond the Aegean), and a number of smaller networks in the northern Aegean that took their own standards. Indeed, there was a flurry of production among communities of the northern Aegean starting to produce their own coinages at this time, particularly around Thrace: Abdera, Lete, Maroneia and Neapolis, while Argilos further to the west in the region of Macedonia also began minting. In forming the Aegean-wide network of communities, the key nodes for holding together these connections were Miletos, Phokaia and Samos. Moreover, the zones of connection become even clearer than they were in the previous period: a zone around central Greece and the islands held by the Aeginitan standard; a zone around Attica, Euboea and parts of the northern Aegean held by the Attic-Euboean standard; an independent zone of interaction in the northern Aegean; areas of connection across the Aegean sea in an east-west direction, held by the Aeginitan, Attic-Euboean and Milesian standards; and a zone of connection that ran up and down the coast of Anatolia, focused primarily around Ionia. With the exception of Chersonesos, minting to the Attic-Euboean standard, these zones of interaction had not reached Crete by the end of the sixth century. One final pattern to note, and one that I will return to: when looking at the distribution of weight standards displayed in abstract space, of the first standards established in the Aegean (Aeginitan, Attic-

---

[16] Unlike Mytilene that used coins on a local standard but also had coins on other standards (in this case, the Persic and Phokaian), Ialysos used only its local standard and did not mint additional coins. The Ialysian standard is, however, similar to the Milesian standard: the silver stater of the former weighed 14.8g while the latter was 14.2g; and the Ialysos' silver diobol weighted 0.95g while the Milesian was 1.15g.

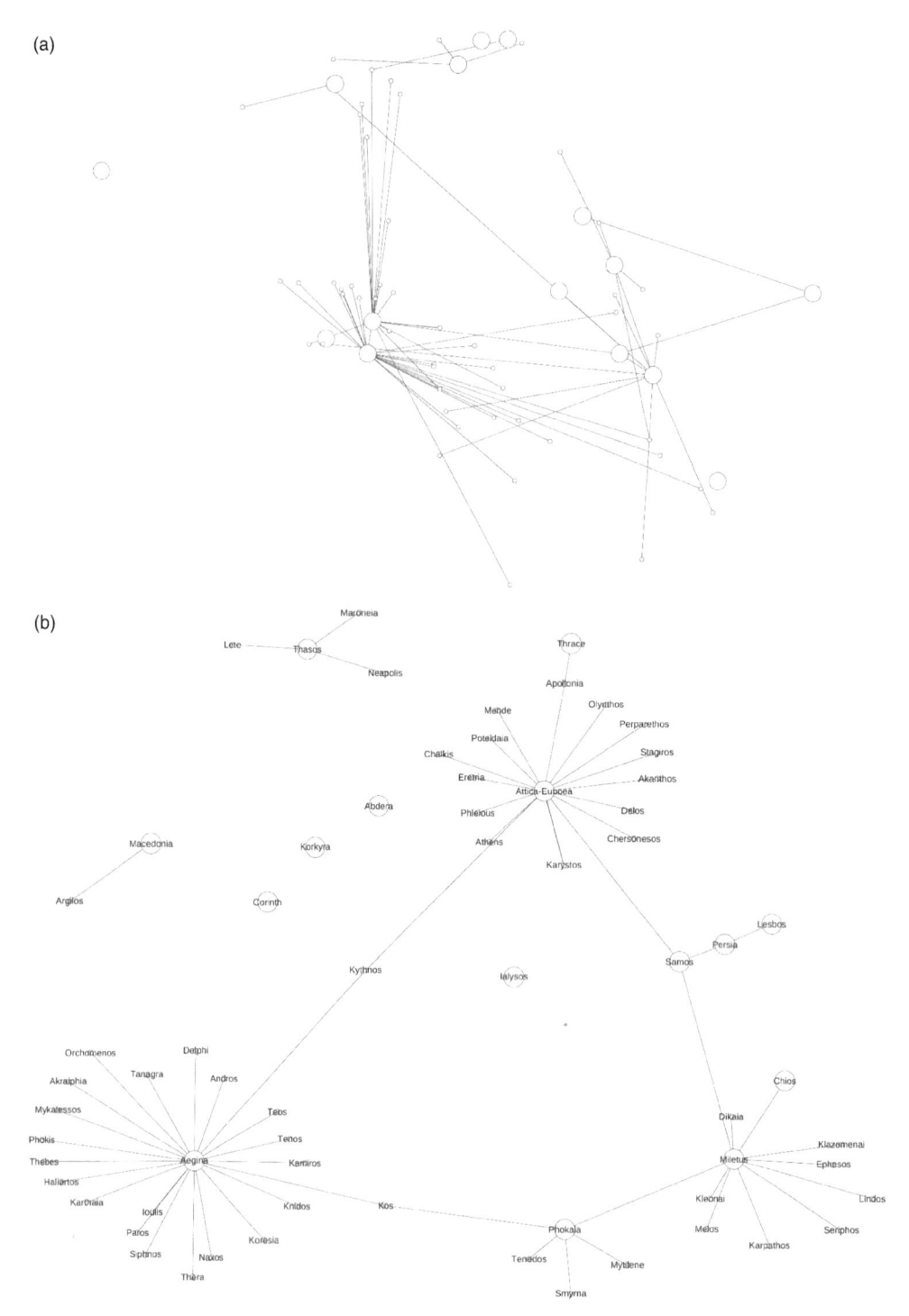

174 *Entangled Networks: The Transfer of Knowledge*

(a)

(b)

Figure 4.7 SNA visualisation of the sites minting coins 520–500 BC. Sites are represented by nodes, and ties are drawn between sites that share a weight standard: a) Nodes are placed according to their approximate geographic location in the Aegean; b) Nodes are distributed randomly in abstract space. This image is available in a larger format online at www.cambridge.org/loy.

Euboean and Milesian), one can see a 'halo' of sites around each of these standards. Twenty-two sites minted to the Aeginitan standard, fifteen to the Attic-Euboean, and eleven to the Milesian. Across each twenty-year time slice, an increasing number of communities had been taking up these standards. The Phokaian standard, by contrast, had relatively less uptake, with only six communities adopting this standard by the end of the century.

Distribution and Production

Having established the shape of the network for shared weight standards, it now remains to decide what this means. In this section, two alternatives are discussed: first, that this is a pattern about the use of coins; and, second, that this is a pattern about the production of coins.

Distribution

It has already been suggested that having coinage of a similar standard facilitated economic activities between communities. So much might seem obvious if we use an (anachronistic) analogy with our own contemporary coinage system:[17] using commonly recognised coins allows one to participate without the barrier of currency exchange in an economic system. However, as noted, one cannot immediately presume that coins fulfilled in these earliest times *only* an economic function. There were pre-existing value systems that did not use coinage, and even systems that co-existed alongside coinage, albeit for a short period (e.g. *Hacksilber*). What is more, as seen in the data cited, Corinth was not networked with the same weight standard group in the Aegean and there is substantial evidence of Corinthian trade within and beyond the Aegean throughout the sixth century BC.

So how can one make the case that this *is* an economic pattern? The most obvious solution is to try and align this pattern with other patterns of economic activity that have already been identified – namely, with the ceramics pattern. Here it is most useful to look synchronously at the data from the end of the sixth century BC: as has been observed, these networks grow over time and their shape becomes clearest in the latter periods.

Five 'zones' have been identified which may or may not be 'economic zones': an area in the north Aegean linked to the Attic-Euboean standard; another area in the north Aegean linked to various local standards, namely the Abderan, Thasian, and Thracian standards; parts of central Greece

---

[17] The comparison is anachronistic given that some ancient coins had not purely token value but also innate wealth value relative to their metal composition, on which see above.

linked to the Aeginitan standard; a large cluster of communities within the Cyclades linked to the Aeginitan standard; and Ionia, linked (mainly) to the standards of Miletos and Phokaia. In addition, Samos was noted for its exceptional role in connecting various networks together; and both the Attic-Euboean and Milesian standards were responsible for bridging the 'east-west' across the two coasts of the Aegean.

These 'zones' map quite roughly onto areas identified in the previous chapters. Attic pottery was noted to have spread up towards the north Aegean in quite considerable amounts by the end of the sixth century BC, when communities in the region also began to scale up production of their own local ceramics too. And Ionia was consuming for the most part its own local potteries, with an exception from Samos that also consumed a considerable number of Attic pots. The mapping of zones is less consistent, however, when looking at the Cyclades and at central Greece. On the one hand, there are fewer data points for the ceramics from these areas of the Aegean, and so it is difficult to ascertain whether this is a pattern about absence or just a gap in the dataset. On the other hand, ceramics might not be the most useful dataset to map here, and one could look instead at the economic network made evident through the proxy data of marble statues. Although marble was not originating from Aegina, it has been observed that the Cyclades were quite tightly bound in a network of marble exchange, held together by Naxos and Paros (both islands that would, by the final quarter of the sixth century BC, take up the Aeginitan coin standard). In addition, parts of central Greece were importing marble from Naxos and Paros, even though they had more local alternatives nearby in Boeotia.

The mapping of these patterns does not prove a direct relationship between possible economic networks for marble, ceramics and coins. Nor does it necessarily suggest that these networks intersected to the same degree in each of these different zones. What it does suggest, however, is that these networks were *entangled* with one another. Attica was already supplying, for example, ceramics to the north Aegean in the sixth century BC, so there was some motivation for the north (or a push from Attica?) to adopt a similar set of weight standards when using coinage. To take another example, the islands of the Cyclades participated in two different but overlapping economic networks simultaneously: one that involved the production and export of marble statues, and another that was facilitated by a shared coinage weight standard. Different types of economic activity were separate from one another and driven by different needs; but participation in one network

Table 4.3 *Sites for producing amphoras throughout the Archaic period, according to the dataset used in the previous chapter*

Site	700–650 BC	650–600 BC	600–550 BC	550–500 BC
Athens	x	x	x	x
Chios	x	x	x	x
Corinth	x	x	x	x
Delos	x	x	x	x
Kalaureia		x	x	x
Klazomenai	x	x	x	x
Lesbos		x		
Miletos	x	x	x	x
Olbia		x	x	
Paros	x	x	x	x
Rheneia		x	x	
Rhodes		x	x	x
Samos		x	x	x

seems to have increased the possibility that a community would participate in another economic network *in addition*.

However, the comparisons drawn here between loosely defined 'zones' are quite general. It is worth subjecting a subset of the ceramic data to the same sorts of analysis conducted in this chapter in order to see the patterns more precisely using a unit of analysis which includes just one shape (and one function) but which is ubiquitous across regional wares. Here, the amphoras from the ceramics dataset are analysed, comprising a set of 652 datapoints (Table 4.3). This shape has been chosen for analysis given that, compared to other shapes of vessels, amphoras of the Archaic period often had the highest level of inter-regional mobility (Sezgin 2012; Monachov and Kuznetsova 2017; Lawall 2019); as expected, much of this relates to the exchange of the products contained within amphoras. Furthermore, they have been well studied to the extent that we can see the pattern of their production and distribution with a high level of precision. This material has been periodised by the time slices used above in the ceramics chapter: 700–650 BC, 650–600 BC, 600–550 BC and 550–500 BC.

SNA is used here once more to visualise the pattern of *amphora* distribution. Nodes represent places at which *amphoras* have been found, and edges are drawn between nodes indicating a co-presence of *amphora* types. This might indicate some level of (economic) networking that is more precise than the general ceramics study in Chapter 3. The Delian pottery presents problems for modelling, owing to the absence of technical scholarship. Recent work on the Cycladic *amphoras*, however, has suggested that material once thought of as exclusively made at one workshop on Delos was in fact manufactured across multiple different island workshops (Alexandridou et al. 2017: 135–48); restudy of the material is ongoing. Moreover, there is substantial evidence to suggest that the 'main' workshop of the Cyclades was located on Paros (Zaphiropoulou 2017). Thus, for the purposes of this analysis Delos has been understood as a consumer of large quantities of pottery, and 'Paros' has been designated as a node which represents not only the Parian ceramic workshop, but also as a more general label which represents all local production in the Cyclades. The result of this is that there is less precision in the analysis of the Cycladic island internal networks than those in, for example, the region of Ionia. But on the macro-regional scale, the data is still fit for purpose, and they can illustrate well the shape of the Aegean as a whole.

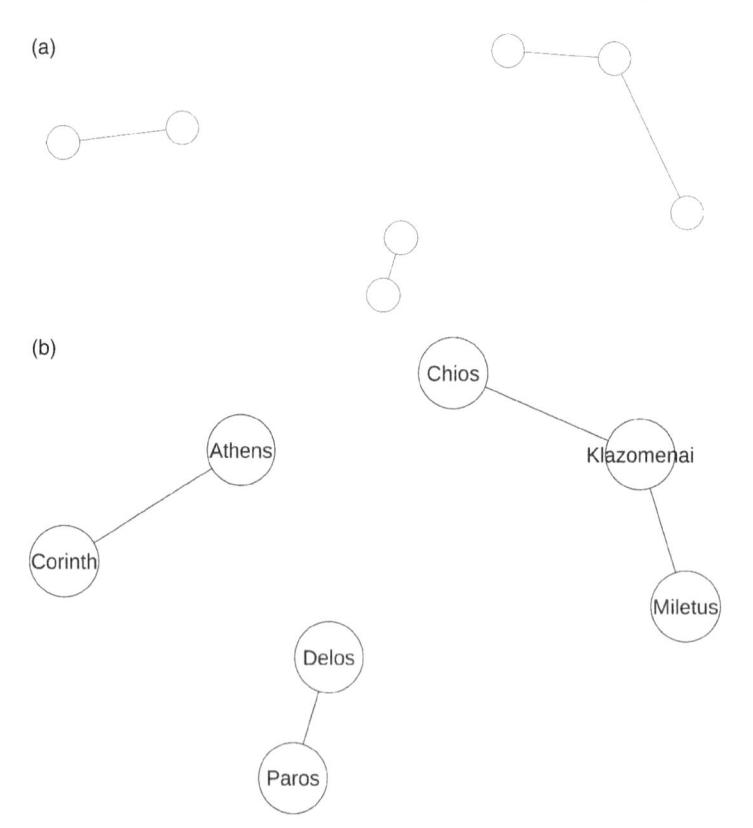

Figure 4.8 SNA visualisation of the sites producing amphoras 700–650 BC. Sites are represented by nodes, and ties are drawn between sites at which amphoras produced elsewhere are found: a) Nodes are placed according to their approximate geographic location in the Aegean; b) Nodes are distributed randomly in abstract space.

(a)

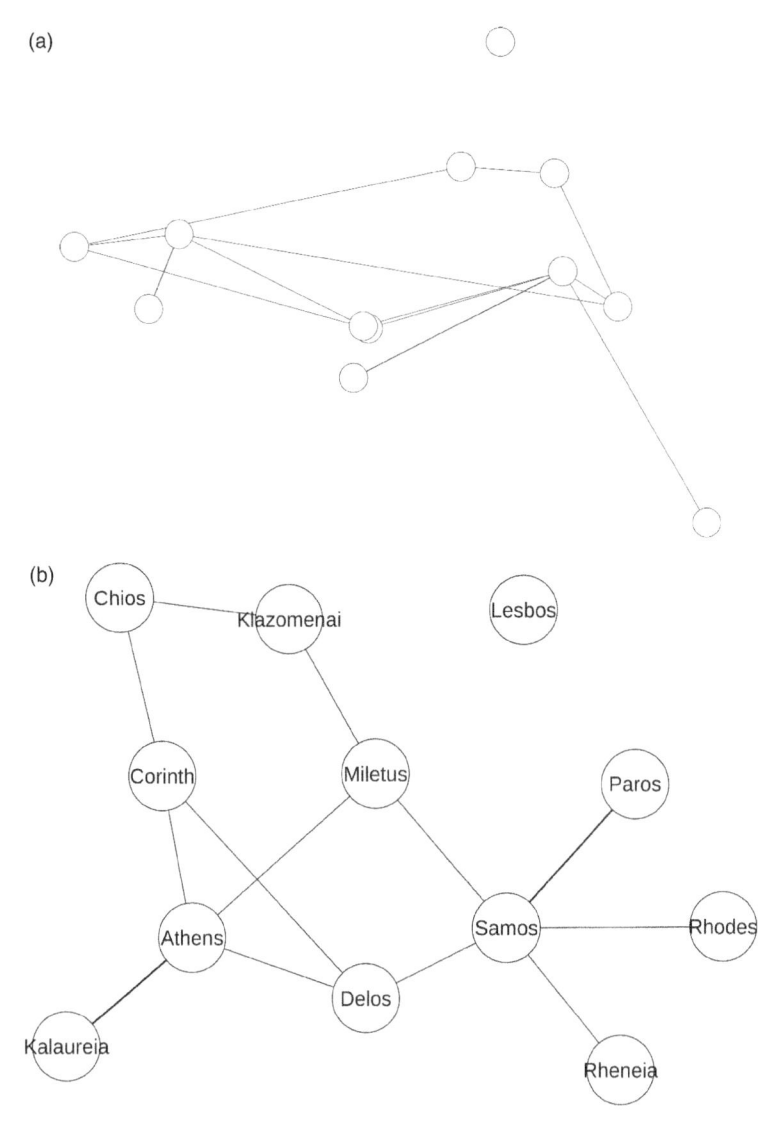

(b)

Figure 4.9 SNA visualisation of the sites producing amphoras 650–600 BC. Sites are represented by nodes, and ties are drawn between sites at which amphoras produced elsewhere are found: a) Nodes are placed according to their approximate geographic location in the Aegean; b) Nodes are distributed randomly in abstract space.

The data indicate that in period one (700–650 BC, Fig. 4.8), the Aegean was divided into three zones based on *amphora* exchange networks: the Greek mainland, the Cyclades, and the east Aegean. Only the closest neighbouring sites of the largest size for the period were involved in the exchange of *amphoras*. By the end of the seventh century (period two, 650–600 BC, Fig. 4.9), there was, however, significant networking across the

(a)

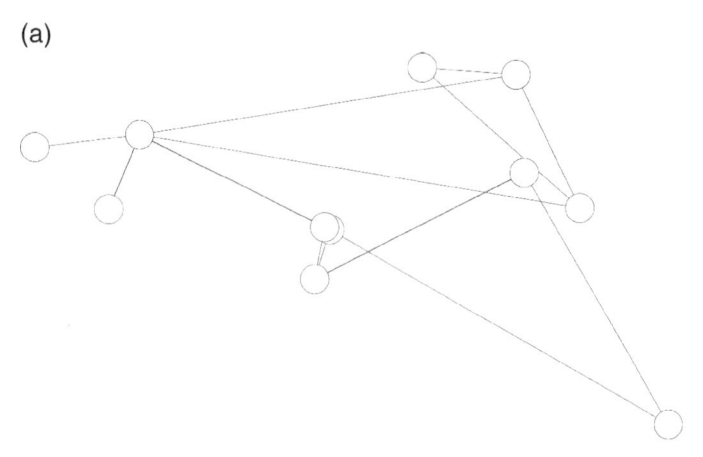

Figure 4.10a SNA visualisation of the sites producing amphoras 600–550 BC. Sites are represented by nodes, and ties are drawn between sites at which amphoras produced elsewhere are found. Nodes are placed according to their approximate geographic location in the Aegean.

Aegean. In particular, there was a high level of exchange between the sites of Ionia – including between sites that produced 'north Ionian' and 'south Ionian' amphoras. By contrast, Corinth and Rhodes were on the periphery of Aegean networks of exchange – though these sites would have been further involved, respectively, in networks further west and east. Samos exhibited high levels of connectivity with neighbouring and disparate sites. By this stage, almost all sites for which data are available were connected to one another, with the central connecting nodes at Athens, Miletos and Samos. In the third (600–550 BC, Fig. 4.10) and fourth (550–500 BC, Fig. 4.11) periods investigated, this pattern of the end of the seventh century BC repeats: one sees an integrated network, where all parts of the Aegean connect either directly or indirectly with one another. The only significant change is that there is now a connection between Rhodes and the island ceramics; and that Kalaureia exhibits some further connections with Corinth and with the Cyclades. However, upon visualising the data in non-geographic space, we see that while the *amphora* exchange network of the late seventh century is cyclical across the Aegean, that of the sixth century is linear. This indicates that amphoras and their commodities were exchanged on a 'local' basis, where individual cities each interacted with a limited set of economic contacts.

The shape of the *amphora* pattern is similar to that of coinage, even if developing at a different pace. In both cases, there was in the earliest phases little communication between the eastern and western sides of the Aegean,

(b)

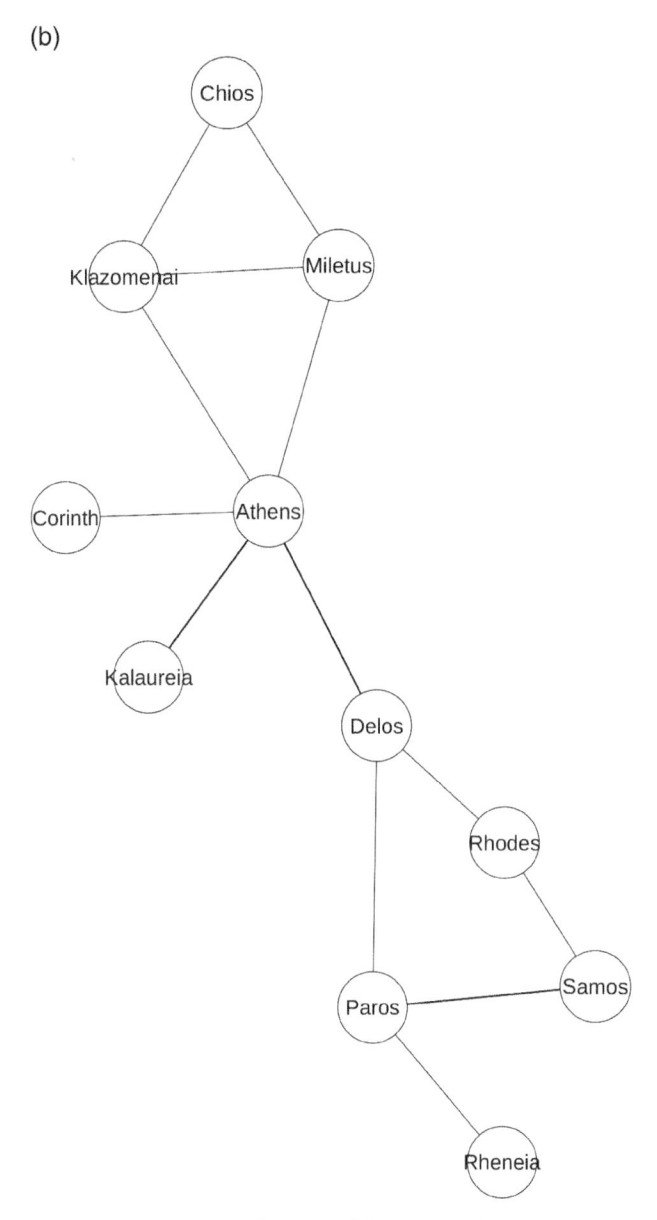

Figure 4.10b SNA visualisation of the sites producing amphoras 600–550 BC Sites are represented by nodes, and ties are drawn between sites at which amphoras produced elsewhere are found. Nodes are distributed randomly in abstract space.

but small clusters of interacting communities around a few key sites of each mainland (e.g. Athens, Corinth, Miletos). Subsequently there was a rapid change of pace in Aegean-level networking, where most if not all communities investigated were connected either directly or indirectly through the

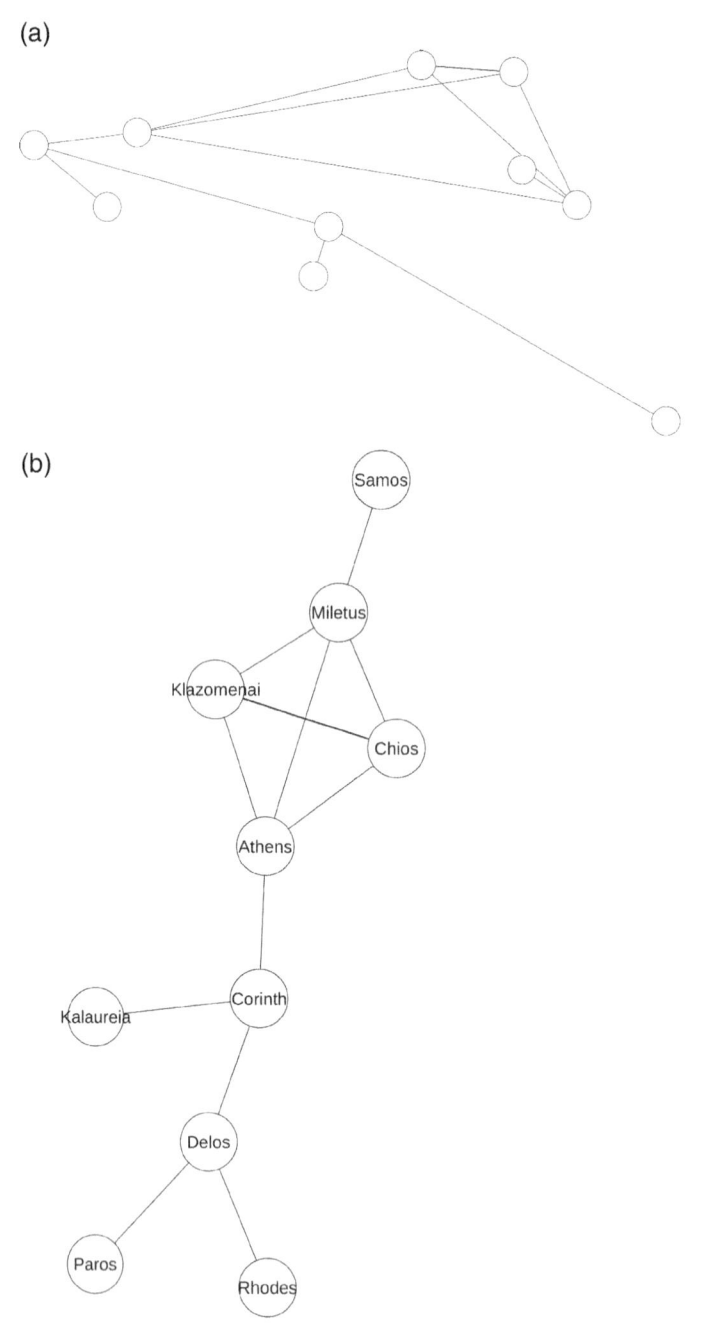

182 *Entangled Networks: The Transfer of Knowledge*

(a)

(b)

Figure 4.11 SNA visualisation of the sites producing amphoras 550–500 BC. Sites are represented by nodes, and ties are drawn between sites at which amphoras produced elsewhere are found: a) Nodes are placed according to their approximate geographic location in the Aegean; b) Nodes are distributed randomly in abstract space.

sharing of weight standards or the trading of *amphoras*. The shape of these connections was either as a cyclical or as a linear network, but the most important factor is that the communities were all connected to one another. Critical, though, is that these changes were not co-temporaneous. The first trans-Aegean *amphora* networks were in place some time between 650–600 BC, whereas it was not until 560–540 BC that there was a similar phenomenon for coinage.

This is a similar scenario to that which was seen when comparing the data for the marble statues with the ceramics. Qualitatively similar economic networks emerge in the material record, but with some time lag. This could imply one or both of two things. First, that one type of economic network (e.g. an economic network represented by shared weight standards) formed on the back of another (e.g. a network of *amphora* distribution). Communities already had a set of (economic) contacts established through trading goods in *amphoras*, and so they could learn quickly from one another the technology of coinage and start minting to the same weight standards.[18] Second, that the pre-existence of one type of network helps to explain the rapid spread of another network across the Aegean. As noted above, scholars have long maintained that for the spread of coinage to have been possible in such a short space of time there must have been an economic network already well established off the back of which coinage could 'piggy-back' – the evidence of coinage provides just one possibility, in the same way that the network of 'commodity' trade could have formed the basis for a 'luxury' marble network. It is also possible that networks not investigated here played a crucial role in forming other systems, or that the networks investigated here only became materially visible at certain times, even though they existed long before. But the key issue remains the same: the early networks of the Aegean were entangled with one another. The contacts that communities made by interacting in one way could be used to form new types of connections, and they allowed for the rapid development of new economic networks.

Four key points emerge that will be revisited in subsequent chapters. The first and most salient point is the one just made above, that networks depended on one another, with the result that in the material record we can see a 'time lag' in the development of similar networks based on different products. Second, there is a difference between geographic centrality and network centrality in the Aegean: most notably, in the case of the weight standard usage, Ionia and the eastern parts of the Aegean

---

[18] See also Forsyth 2021 on innovation flowing along physical trade routes.

were towards the centre of the economic network, even if geographically they are on the 'periphery' of the Aegean basin. Third, there *are* patterns of geography. East-west connections across the Aegean developed earlier than north-south connections. Certain places were key links in the structure of the overall Aegean network, both large regions (the Cyclades) and individual islands (Samos). Finally, the terrestrial areas of mainland Greece that faced away from the Aegean (notably Corinth and the Peloponnese) participated to a lesser degree in the Aegean-level networks, as their focus was directed towards other places.

Production

The network analysis might also tell us something about the sequence of production for coinage among communities. That is, coinage was taken up first by a small number of communities, and, in subsequent years, an increasing number of communities began minting coins to the same weight standards used by these first few coinage pioneers. In the abstract network graphics, this is quite neatly represented in the final periods by 'bursts' or 'haloes' of several sites radiating around central nodes, (e.g. the island and central Greek communities around the Aegina node). Not only does the sequence of network graphics illustrate that the number of communities that knew how to mint coins grew in every subsequent generation, but it might also tell us where they got this knowledge: either from the nodal community, or from one of the other closely associated communities in that small network. The network models could also reflect the spread of coinage and the transfer of knowledge between different city communities.

This notion is best illustrated by means of an example. Within the period 540–520 BC, the island of Siphnos began to mint silver coins to the Aiginetan weight standard. Two series are attested within the material record: a stater weighing 12.2 g bearing an eagle flying upwards on the obverse side and an incuse square with a 'union jack' device on the reverse side; and a triobol weighing 2.95 g and bearing the same motifs. These coins weigh the same as coins of the same denominations struck on Aegina,[19] and they are therefore of a common weight standard. The Aeginitans had been minting coins since the beginning of the sixth century BC, and so it is

---

[19] At the very least these coins weigh the same as the Aeginitan denomination *within a margin of error*. Triobols of Aeginitan standard coins vary between 2.90–3.00g; but this is clearly of a very different ballpark to Attic-Euboean (2.15g), Phokaian (2.01g), or Samian (1.62g) coins of the same material and denomination.

conceivable that the knowledge of minting transferred to the Siphnians from the Aeginitans (either directly or from an intermediary node), with the result that when Siphnians began minting, they made coins that *resembled* Aeginitan coins in appearance, size and weight, and, therefore, they made coins that were minted to the same weight standard.

This would explain two features of the network graphics produced. First, that weight standards were used within zones. Communities may have had more immediate access to the knowledge and technologies of their nearest neighbours as opposed to those on the far side of the Aegean, and so once coinage has been adopted by at least one community within a region, then others would have greater access to this idea and might be more likely to follow suit. Here the example of central Greece is useful. Between 560–540 BC, Akraifia, Mykalessos and Orchomenos all began to mint their own silver coins set relative to the Aeginitan weight standard. There was likely an initial contact with Aegina, its people, or its products that allowed for the transfer of minting knowledge to move from Aegina to central Greece. Over the next twenty years, Haliartos and Thebes began to mint silver coins of the same standard too. By this stage it was unnecessary for either Haliartos or Thebes to have direct contact with the Aeginitans to learn about and acquire knowledge of minting, but the same information could flow from neighbours at Akraifia, Mykalessos or Orchomenos.

Similarly, this model would help to explain the overall shape of the network graphics produced. The networks generated show a linear connection of communities: A is connected to B, is connected to C, is connected to D, etc. This succession could be indicative of the sequence in which the knowledge to mint moved across the Aegean, where the type of weight standard adopted would be proxy for the place at which one learnt to mint. What one cannot discern from this macro-view, however, is *where* the process of coin striking took place:[20] did communities further down this chain of coin production use the facilities of other communities who had begun minting first, or was it merely the idea and knowledge of the technology that moved from place to place? To answer this question, one would need to look at the specific dies used for the striking of issues of series of coins in the Archaic period to establish whether or not dies might have been shared between different communities – but that is beyond the scope of this study.

Is this a plausible story? There would need to be both motivation and facility for the knowledge of coinage to transfer across the Aegean. The case

---

[20] There is, so far, little to no evidence that indicates where minting took place in the Archaic period.

for motivation has been discussed extensively here; as for facility, this requires that communities were either in contact with one another or with one another's materials in great enough intensity for there to be opportunity to recognise, choose and adopt a new technology. The case for widespread mobility has been made above: the mobility of the free-standing statue artists certainly attests to individuals with specialist technical knowledge being in circulation in the sixth century BC, if not earlier. Again, the case for widespread mobility in the sixth century BC has been made, and the geographic route networks discussed in the previous two chapters help to support this notion. More critical is the need to demonstrate that coinage itself was in circulation, both within and beyond communities.

At this point, then, it is productive to return to the evidence of hoards again – namely the three hoards previously mentioned briefly – to assess the extent to which coins were in circulation. The hoard from Ephesos, found at the Artemision and dating to the sixth century BC (Head 1908, Robinson 1951a) was discovered over subsequent seasons, with eighteen specimens found in 1904 under the stone slabs thought to be the centre of the earliest temple of Artemis, and nineteen more specimens found in 1905 in a small jar in a similar area to the west near the temple's central platform; a further forty-nine coins were found in fill around the western edge of the structure and beneath the foundations of the south wall. Comprising mainly electrum coins with four bronze coins, communities represented by this hoard included Ephesos itself, Miletos and Phokaia, as well as Lydia through the presence of fourteen coins (the largest number of coins originating from any one place). The second hoard, recorded as having been found in 'the Cyclades' (HOARD 6) dated to the end of the sixth century and contained both a greater total of coins (145) and a larger number of communities represented by them (8). Within this hoard are issues from Aegina, Chios, Delos, Keos, Kos, Miletos, Paros and Siphnos; no information is given on the context of this hoard, beyond the very simple fact that it was 'lately found' (Greenwell 1890: 13), but some conjecture is made that the hoard might have come from somewhere in the sphere of Aegina, given that most of the coins in it are based on the island's weight standard; Greenwell also notes similar hoards having been found in previous years on Thera and on Melos. The final hoard is labelled as 'Western Asia Minor' (HOARD 21). It contains seventy-six coins from at least eight different places, including Athens, the islands (Andros, Kos) and communities of Ionia (Ephesos, Miletos, Phokaia, Teos), and those further afield (Abydos). Very little contextual information is available for this final hoard – there are not even details of its exact find spot beyond 'Western Asia Minor' – but the history of trade and identification of coins from this group is given by Thompson, Mørkholm and Kraay (1973).

These mixed hoards clearly indicate that coins circulated away from home. All hoards contain material from a variety of communities; moreover, while the Ephesos hoard contains coins mainly from the Ionian 'zones', the Cyclades hoard contains coins from the Cyclades and from Ionia, while the hoard found in Anatolia contains coins not only from these two areas but from Attica as well. These mixed assemblages suggest that coins were moving both within and beyond their local areas, and this inter-zonal movement of objects supports the notion stated above that the Aegean became a network that linked together different zones of interaction through common nodes. Moreover, each of these hoards contains coins of at least two different weight standards – Ephesos (Milesian and Phokaian), Cyclades (Aeginitan and Milesian) and Anatolian (Aeginitan, Attic-Euboean, Milesian and Phokaian) – further supporting the notion that coins not only moved between geographic zones, but also around different economic zones. It is possible, then, that a community using coins of various types could quickly establish contacts with a greater number of communities using different weight standards in exchange, and thus it becomes clear that another tool in reducing the friction within an economic system is to circulate and use coins of different values.

While this second point might be conjecture, the main issue is clear: coins circulated away from their point of production. And if coins were circulating, knowledge of coinage technology could reach non-minting communities. This point has been rather coarsely defined, but the story fits with and makes sense of the dataset: through circulation of knowledge, objects and people in motion, the new technology of coinage could spread across the Aegean according to serial networking between communities and dependents.

These were economic networks through and through; but economic networks that inform us *both* about distribution *and* about production.

Entanglement and Intersection between Economic and Political Networks

This chapter began by considering how multiple networks can be manifested across the same dataset. Small coins present big challenges in relating them to socio-cultural processes, partly because there are so many issues at stake in how exactly coins were used in Archaic Greece. What is clear, though, is that weight standard provides a good starting point in identifying any patterning. It can be linked with practice, the defining attribute of the community: discussion on both proto-currencies and on hoards has suggested that scales were used at the point of coins' transaction, and this in turn indicates that the weight of coins was proportional to the perceived economic value. With myriad weight systems in operation throughout the world of Archaic Greece, the implication is that there were different *value* systems at play and different networks of coins. And looking at the shape of these value systems across the Aegean basin, two particular stories emerge: one about economics (i.e. by sharing weight standards, it became easier for communities to trade with one another) and another about transfer of knowledge (i.e. the pattern shows us where and how communities first learnt to mint coins for themselves). One tells us about how communities engaged with one another in ongoing interactions, while the latter tells us a history of past interactions.

As with the previous case study on luxury and commodity networks, chronology is important. The luxury network could spread across the Aegean at such a pace because it was based on a pre-existing network; here, too, the coinage network appears to have been enabled by an earlier pottery network, an example of one form of economic network giving space for another. Qualitatively, the coinage network is like the amphora network but with a time lag. Networks provided infrastructure on which new connections could be made and formed the channels along which individuals and communities could come together. But the time lag also has important implications methodologically for the study of networks more broadly. The network of coins and the network of ceramics look qualitatively similar, though they date some 100 years apart. If it is correct that they refer to *the same* economic system, then this raises the question of how *visible* those same types of networks might be at different times when recovered through different datasets.

And so it has been argued that it is the weight of the coins – not the symbols on them – that shape their network distribution in the Archaic period. These networks help to make the case for economics rather than politics being the primary determinant of coin use. To dig deeper into issues of political affiliation, therefore, it becomes necessary to shift the focus from whole communities onto those few elite peers whose activities were geared towards *representing* whole communities. What is required is a discussion that looks more closely at markers of political affiliation from the moment of production, where agency can be ascribed to certain individuals at the point of creation – a dataset such as the corpus of inscriptions.

5 | Political Networks

Expressions of Political Affiliation

This chapter is about how communities expressed themselves consciously and unconsciously, and about how other communities responded to such acts of expression. An entanglement between collective identities and epichoric alphabets will be analysed, looking across the corpus of inscriptions for the seventh and sixth centuries.

Identity and Expressing an Identity

Identities, in the ancient world as today, were situationally defined. So much was brought firmly onto the agenda for anthropologists in the late 1970s through early 1990s (Bourdieu 1977; Anderson 1983; Bhabha 1990), but it was not until the late 1990s that these issues were adopted within classical archaeology, largely through the work of Jonathan Hall (1997) and Sian Jones (1997), and also more generally through the anthropological work of Geoff Emberling (1997, 1999). It was not so much that where one came from defined who one was, but rather the things (or people or places) that individuals saw, heard, spoke, tasted and experienced constantly made and remade one's own identity (*cf.* Mac Sweeney 2009; Mullen 2013: 4–5). That is, habitual practices either similar to or different from those of others are thought to be largely responsible for defining feelings of closeness or distinctness. And as is widely discussed elsewhere (Morgan 2003; Crielaard 2009; Demetriou 2012; van Dommelen 2014), groups acquire identities based on those things that they experience as a *collective*: the identity of the whole is defined by the similarities that exist between the sum of their parts.[1] In many cases, the strongest catalyst for either creating or reinforcing group identities comes from a moment of encounter with *different* sorts of groups – such as war (Hall 1997) or settlement (Morgan 1999; Malkin 2001) – as this forces a group to confront the differences

---

[1] In addition to individual identities, communities might have expressed collective identities to signal to their own members or to others notions of particular cultural, social or political importance, (Patterson 1975, on which Morgan 2009 reflects further. *cf.* Hall 2004: 46, revisited specifically in Hall 2009). This discussion will be developed further.

between 'us' and 'them' (Cohen 1985; Cohen 2002; Mac Sweeney 2013: 1–6). Some groups identified for antiquity correlate to names of groups that identified themselves in this way (*cf.* McInerney 1999), other groups might not. Both individuals and groups of individuals have their experiences of the world shaped by the people, places, things and circumstances around them, and this informs notions of personal and shared identity – and the ways in which these identities are expressed.

One's identity, then, is entangled with the way in which one interacts with the world, both consciously and unconsciously.[2] The way one speaks, the way one dresses, the things one produces, even one's participation in certain types of communal events may become *markers* of one's membership or non-membership of certain groups. Clearly, many such traits will be observable only in the contemporary world, and the archaeologist (or the ancient historian) looking for expressions of an individual or collective identity in the material record has a much smaller dataset than the anthropologist. What the archaeologist needs is a set of markers that persist.

Some of the best surviving visual markers of variation and difference in the material record are those objects produced in different styles (Hastorf and Conkey 1990; Carr and Neitzel 1995; Whitley 2018b: 178–83; *contra* Neer 2010: 6–11). A large and diverse dataset such as the record of painted pottery clearly has areas of difference and similarity within it that can be grouped together in ways that are meaningful from the point of view of aesthetics (e.g. [as in Chapter 2 of this book] the group of Attic pottery versus the group of Corinthian pottery; individual hands of 'artists' identified by Beazley *ABV*; see also Lynch 2017) – but do these stylistic markers mark out particular groups? Archaeology is far beyond the crude generalisation that '(types of) pots = (types of) people', and the compartmentalisation of visual culture to a strict structuralist framework is considered by many as too reductive. Objects made to look similar to other objects must say *something* about the people who produced and consumed them – but to move this towards a framework of *identity* requires a more nuanced view.

The issue of style standing proxy as some sort of symbol has been discussed extensively over the past half-decade, particularly in light of a more critically engaged post-processual archaeology. Ian Hodder (1982) was one of the first to interrogate style – in the sense of 'a

---

[2] The word 'entangled' is quite appropriate here. Taking language, for example: if one speaks in a certain dialect – using particular sets of words or a particular accent – then the idea of speaking in a similar way to others might also *create* and *reinforce* a collective group identity, rather than strictly *vice versa*. The formation of an identity and the expression of an identity are clearly reflexive processes that feedback into one another.

categorisation of visually similar material culture' – against the social groups in which certain styles were found. By exploring this issue through the lens of ethnoarchaeology in the context of contemporary groups in Africa, he argued that style and group identity are entangled in a complicated nexus of conscious production and unconscious reproduction: style is both a passive reflection and a by-product of social organisation. A similar approach was taken by Shanks and Tilley (1987; *contra* Taylor and Whitley 1985; *cf.* Conkey and Hastorf 1990; Carr and Neitzel 1995), while James Whitley's own explicit handling of *Style and Society* (1991) adopted a more hermeneutic and contextual approach, setting up a framework in which – contrary to universalist assumptions that linked together style and the worlds of Early Iron Age Greece – a 'work of art' was taken as 'the outcome of particular historical conditions, and as being inextricably linked to the culture of which it was a part ... ' (Whitley 1991: 22. *cf.* similar approaches taken in Snodgrass 1980: 27–8 and Morgan and Whitelaw 1991). One could put these concepts side by side, he argued, as long as one acknowledges the messiness of the issues involved and puts them within the framework of certain assumptions. Catherine Morgan, too, has argued that these issues are compatible as long as one remembers context, as an exploration of style '[requires] us to search beneath simple classifications for fine-grained shifts in style and shape preferences which are more likely to hold social meaning' (Morgan 1999: 94). Style, for all of the above, is something connected with society, even if that connection is complicated and must be approached via quite particular frameworks.

The reaction to (or development from) these problems of style was to adopt a different sort of theoretical approach from the early 2000s. The conversation had already been begun by Bourdieu (1977), Giddens (1984) and others concerning the *agency* of art and the effect that style might have on a viewer interacting with it in not only contributing to but even creating certain facets of identities. However, it was Alfred Gell's *Art and Agency* (1998) that was most effective in stimulating change among the thinking of archaeologists.[3] This framework indicates that an object created or marked in a certain style is not simply a proxy indicator of some person or idea, but – taking Gell's own model of the art nexus – one can consider that there

---

[3] For very early receptions of agency theory, see Dobres and Robb 2000 and Dornan 2002; the bibliography for all those who have responded to Gell explicitly is vast. Osborne and Tanner (2007) considered the initial uptake of Gell's work by archaeologists slow; their volume grew out of first a Theoretical Archaeology Group session and thereafter a series of seminars at King's College, Cambridge, organised with the explicit intent to get more archaeologists thinking through Gell's work.

is a complex relationship to be negotiated by the person ('artist') creating the idea behind an object ('prototype'), something that becomes realised ('index') and communicated to a viewer: depending on one's own contextual and situational position within this chain, different ideas and identities can be communicated and adopted by means of similar markers.[4] And, more recently, drawing from both Gell and Bourdieu, this nexus has been expanded further towards material entanglement theory (Hodder 2012),[5] towards frameworks that look not only at the formation and expression of complex identities when people create and view objects of certain styles, but also at the participation within these complex webs of meaning of people interacting with one another and with objects affecting the meaning or understanding of other objects. It is beyond the scope of the current study to reassess the nature of these conceptual frameworks: needless to say that art, style and identity are entangled in all sorts of ways. Art, style and identity represent and create one another, and to unpick one we need to keep in mind the others.

Iconography, Writing, Identity – and Everything in Between

This chapter is largely about what writing looks like. In some senses, writing and iconography need not be kept so separate from one another, as they both (albeit writing in a more formal way) comprise symbols representing something else (Bennet 2021). When an object is marked in some way with either iconography or writing, at that moment that 'simple mark become[s] an arbitrary sign for people to think with' (Malafouris 2013: 234). And a written symbol can be treated just as semiotically as a drawn symbol if we consider, as discussed, that there is a complex relationship of meaning and understanding between the person who created the sign, the person who sees the sign, and, of course, the sign itself. It is not controversial to suggest that the *content* of things written – that is, words, phrases, or even whole texts – conveys meaning such that language frequency can be plotted against collective identities (Loy and Slawisch 2021). But to go a step further and say that the signs used to record writing communicate aspects of identity requires more.

That type of writing can be used to communicate aspects of identity depends on two things. First, writing and inscribed objects are agents.

---

[4] *cf.* the permeability of cultural boundaries and the different levels of identities that can be communicated through the same objects, as discussed by Demetriou 2012, 10–2.

[5] For a critical assessment of the development of these frameworks, see Van Oyen 2016.

That writing has agency should come as no surprise (*cf.* Keane 2003; Preucel 2006); the clearest demonstration of this for the Archaic period has come from James Whitley, who has drawn attention to pieces of writing that speak directly to the viewer and that refer to themselves in the first person – the *oggetti parlanti* (Whitley 2021b). Second, that there was enough variation concerning the way in which things are written down such that different sorts of messages can be communicated. That there was variation was certainly the case for Archaic Greece, and a fuller discussion on the phenomenon of the epichoric alphabets will follow. That these symbols could be comprehended – both recognised as writing and as vehicles that could communicate meaning – seems likely, given the growing evidence for a wide literacy among Archaic period communities (Langdon 2015; Matthaiou 2021: 257ff.). It follows, therefore, that in investigating such phenomena it is critical to treat writing as proper material culture (*cf.* Whitley 2017): to think about the sorts of objects writing appeared on, how people would have looked at these objects, and, most obviously, what the writing itself looked like; it is not enough just to think about writing as transcription or printed text.

The practice of creating art or of creating writing in a certain style conveys some sort of an identity, either individual or collective, given that the act of creation is an active process where the one creating the symbol has to make choices. They have to choose how similar or how different to create their work relative to other groups', and this distance and similarity express the extent to which they associate themselves with or distances themselves from the work of others. To measure the network of similar and different identities expressed through practice, therefore, a large and diverse dataset of things is required: and the proposal here is to work with the dataset of writing from the Aegean basin of the Archaic period.

Writing in the Aegean Basin, 700–500 BC

People in the Aegean Basin were writing the Greek language using an alphabetic system throughout the seventh and sixth centuries BC. Inscriptions were made on pottery, stone and bronze, and while the corpus of the earliest writing comprises principally short graffiti, the same writing system was used later in the Archaic period to record religious dedications and laws, among other texts (*cf.* McCarter 1975: 65ff.; Wachter 2010: 49–50).

The record of writing for the seventh and sixth centuries BC spans different types of site and context. The largest groups in the *corpus* of inscribed objects are personal dedications, painted or incised on pottery or stone. The typical length of such inscriptions is short, comprising only a few words: most often a name or a dedicatory formula in the style 'X set me up to Y' ([Name of person in nominative] μἀνεθήκε [name of deity in dative]). Much of this evidence comes from sanctuaries (Fig. 5.1), but longer legal texts (particularly in Crete) were displayed within urban centres.

The inscriptions discussed in this chapter are drawn principally from *Inscriptiones Graecae* (*IG*), supplemented by the regional corpora for Asia Minor and *Inscriptiones Creticae* (*IC*), through the Packard Institute (http://epigraphy.packhum.org/regions/14), and also by those

Figure 5.1 The 'Nikandre *kore*', indicative of a piece of freestanding sculpture that has been inscribed using an epichoric version of the Greek alphabet. The inscription on the left leg is printed below. Photograph by author.

inscriptions in Anne Jeffery's *The Local Scripts of Archaic Greece* (*LSAG*) (now widely available with additions via the website for the Oxford *Poinikastas* project) which do not appear in *IG* (the significance of *LSAG* to this study is discussed further below). Clearly this is 'secondary data collection', which although not completely representative of *every single inscription* published to date in the Aegean, is highly *representative* of the material that is available: there is no reason to doubt that coverage from *IG* and from the other corpora listed above skew the data in favour of any period, any region or any style of writing: in other words, this study is not based on a completely comprehensive dataset, but on a dataset that contains sufficiently full and diverse data as to reflect the same patterns that would not change through the inclusion of more data. Were this study to include additional sources the amount of data for analysis would increase, and by a substantial amount for the eighth century (Dakaris, Vokotopoulou and Christidis 2013; Strauss Clay, Malkin and Tzifopoulos 2017); however, so that the analysis conducted in this chapter can be mapped onto data presented in the other chapters, and in the interest of avoiding problems with the comparability of data from multiple sources, the decision was taken to explore only the data available in *IG* and *LSAG*. As there currently exist no mineable digitisations of the target *corpora* with letter-shape meta-data, the database was compiled manually.

Data were recorded at the level of the site: Attic demes were thus recorded as separate data-points; for smaller islands with only single sites yielding data, the 'site' is equivalent to the island name. 'Sites' were recorded with respect to the places where inscriptions were found, not necessarily where they were made. This key decision was made for two reasons: first, the interest of this study is in how Greeks would have read and understood various inscriptions, and so the find spot gives a clearer indication of where ancient people might have used and engaged with these inscribed objects. Second, there is limited data available on place of production for the inscriptions studied, and the place of origin of some pieces of writing is based, circularly, on the style of writing used. So deciding simply to take the find-spot of writing avoids this issue of agnosticism and possible circular reasoning that would have to be unpicked on a case-by-case basis. These parameters gave a workable dataset of 1356 inscriptions (Table **A4.1**, summarised in Table 5.1 and Table 5.2, Fig. 5.2).

As defined earlier, the chronological range of this study (as for other chapters) is 700–500 BC. Inscriptions were included which had been dated in *IG*, by Jeffery in *LSAG*, or in another *corpus* as coming from the period

Table 5.1 *Sites for which writing containing the target lettersets for analysis has been found.*

Site	700–650 BC	650–600 BC	600–550 BC	550–500 BC
Abai			x	x
Abydos			x	x
Achaea				x
Aegilia			x	x
Aegina	x	x	x	x
Aigiale	x			
Aixone				x
Akovitika			x	x
Alope				x
Ambryssos			x	x
Amorgos				x
Amyklai		x	x	x
Anafi	x			
Anagyrous	x	x		
Antissa			x	x
Apollonia				x
Apollonis Hyperteleatae			x	x
Argos	x	x	x	x
Arkades			x	x
Arkadia				x
Arkesine			x	x
Asea				x
Assos				x
Athens	x	X	x	x
Axos				x
Brauron			x	
Cephale				x
Chalkis			x	x
Chersonesos				x
Chios		x	x	x
Corinth	x	x	x	x
Cynus			x	x
Delos	x	x	x	x
Delphi	x	x	x	x
Dichova				x
Didyma			x	x
Dodona				x
Dreros		x		
Dyme	x	x		
Elateia			x	x
Eleusis			x	x

Table 5.1 (cont.)

Site	700–650 BC	650–600 BC	600–550 BC	550–500 BC
Eleutherna				x
Eltynia		x	x	x
Emporio				x
Ephesos			x	x
Epidauros				x
Erchia				x
Eretria	x	x	x	x
Erythrai				x
Galaxidi				x
Gargettos				x
Gortyn		x	x	x
Halai			x	x
Halai Araphenides			x	x
Hyperteleaton			x	x
Ialysos		x	x	x
Ikarion				x
Isthmia			x	x
Ithaka	x	x	x	x
Ixia				x
Kalapodi		x		x
Kalavryta				x
Kalydon			x	x
Kalymna	x			x
Kamiros	x	x	x	x
Karystos				x
Keos			x	x
Kephallenia			x	x
Klaros			x	
Klazomenai				x
Knossos			x	x
Kolophon		x	x	x
Korkyra		x	x	x
Koropi			x	x
Kos		x		x
Kosmas			x	
Krommyon			x	x
Kythera			x	x
Larisa	x	x	x	x
Lemnos				x
Lete				x
Leukas			x	x
Limnai				x

Table 5.1 (cont.)

Site	700–650 BC	650–600 BC	600–550 BC	550–500 BC
Lindos			x	x
Lousoi				x
Magnesia				x
Magoula				x
Megara			x	x
Melie				x
Melos			x	x
Melpeia			x	x
Methana		x	x	
Methymna				x
Miletos	x	x	x	x
Mount Mavrovouni			x	x
Mycenae			x	x
Mykale			x	x
Myli			x	
Myous				x
Myrrhinous			x	x
Mystras			x	x
Mytilene		x		
Naupaktos				x
Naxos	x	x	x	x
Neandria				x
Neapolis			x	x
Nemea			x	x
Oinoi	x	x		
Oitylos			x	x
Olympia	x	x	x	x
Opous			x	x
Orchomenos			x	x
Orminion			x	x
Oropos			x	x
Paiania			x	x
Palairos			x	x
Paros	x	x	x	x
Penteskouphia		x	x	x
Perachora	x	x	x	x
Phaistos	x	x		
Phleious			x	x
Phokikon				x
Pleiai				x
Praisos			x	x
Prasiai			x	x

Table 5.1 (*cont.*)

Site	700–650 BC	650–600 BC	600–550 BC	550–500 BC
Priene			x	x
Prospalta			x	x
Ptoion Sanctuary			x	x
Rhizenia	x	x		
Samos	x	x	x	x
Samothrace		x	x	x
Sangri				x
Selinous		x		
Sellasia		x		x
Setaia			x	x
Sigeion		x	x	x
Sikinos	x	x	x	x
Sikyon			x	x
Siris			x	
Skione				x
Smyrna	x	x	x	x
Sounion			x	x
Sparta		x	x	x
Sphettos				x
Stiris			x	x
Stratos			x	x
Styra			x	x
Syros	x			x
Tanagra		x	x	x
Tegea			x	x
Tenos			x	x
Teos			x	
Thasos		x	x	x
Thebes	x	x	x	x
Thera	x	x	x	x
Thermon		x	x	x
Thespiai			x	x
Thessaliotis	x	x	x	x
Thorikos			x	x
Tiryns			x	x
Triteia				x
Troezen			x	x
Troy			x	x
Tyros			x	x
Vlachomandra	x	x		
Zacynthos				x
Zarax			x	x

Table 5.2 *Number of inscriptions analysed by period. Inscriptions that are dated across two 'periods' (e.g. 600–525 BC) are counted more than once.*

	Number of inscriptions analysed
Period one (700–650 BC)	207
Period two (650–600 BC)	339
Period three (600–550 BC)	574
Period four (550–500 BC)	900

700–500 BC. Given the variable resolution to which inscriptions had been dated – some had a suggested precision of ten years (e.g. 570–560 BC), while others were dated to a whole century (e.g. sixth century BC) – the compromise decision was made to analyse the data in fifty year time slices. This does not work at the broadest common denominator of inscription date range, but it does provide enough sample periods with which to generate meaningful results. The four periods chosen were 700–650 BC, 650–600 BC, 600–550 BC and 550–500 BC. Further information is given below regarding the apportioning of inscriptions to different date categories.

Looking for Patterns Across the Corpus

Various attempts have been made over the past 150 years to map writing styles in the Aegean basin onto ideas of collective identity or political affiliation. For the Archaic Period, this relies on the notion, as discussed, that there was no fixed Greek alphabet at this time but a number of epichoric alphabets, resulting in a group of different lettersets that could be used to represent the same sound value. As will be discussed, the general idea was that if one wanted to represent a certain sound value and had a choice of, for example, three different letter shapes that could represent that sound value, then the choosing of one (either consciously or unconsciously) would say something about oneself: if this person were choosing to write in a similar or different way to others, then they were showing or denying some notion of affiliation. This has most usually been mapped against (regional) geography, based on the idea that groups of Greeks from the same places wrote in similar ways, while others who came from elsewhere would be more used to using different lettersets to represent the same values.

One of the first and most literal attempts was Adolf Kirchhoff in 1863, using the inscriptional record as he knew it to identify three regions of the

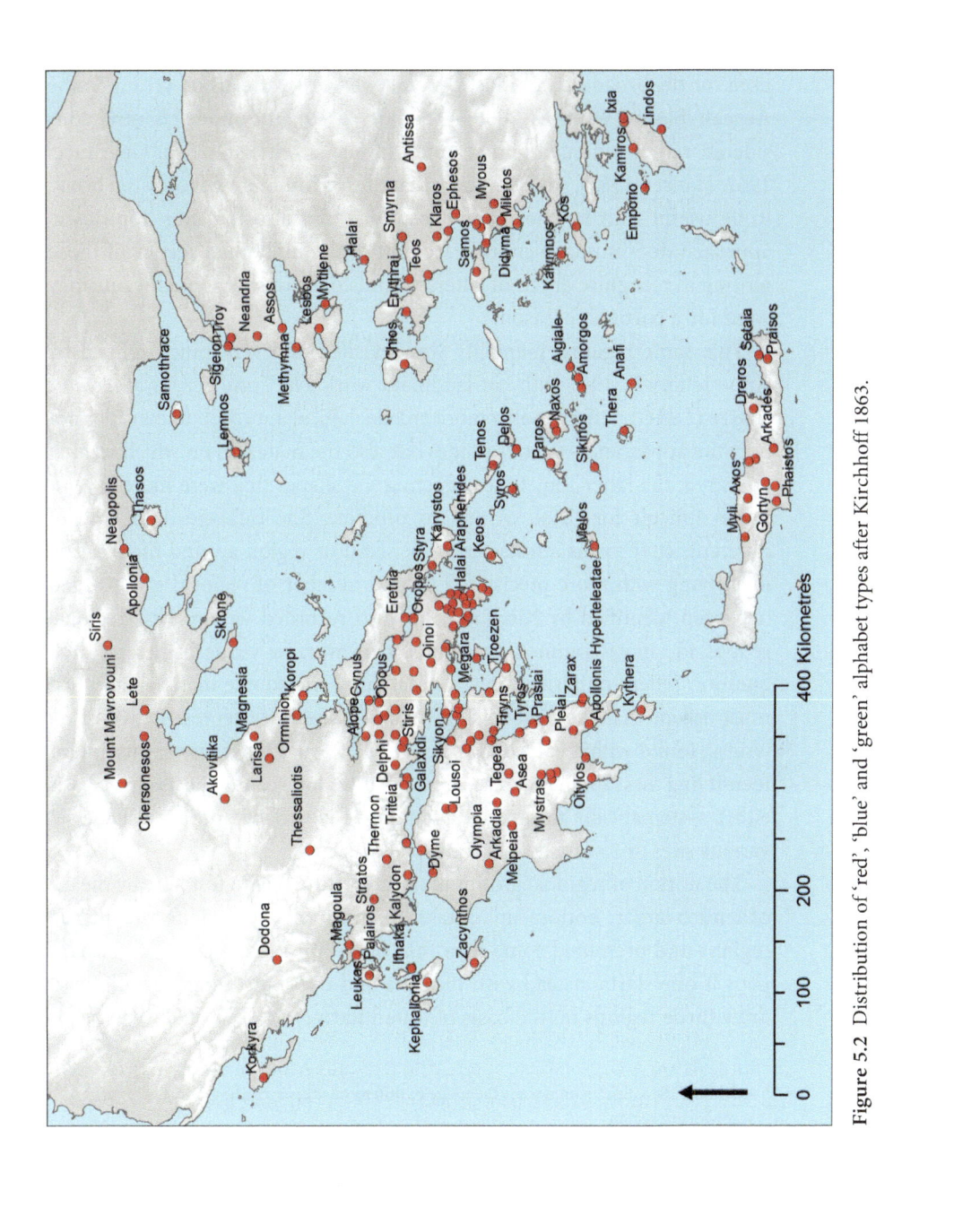

Figure 5.2 Distribution of 'red', 'blue' and 'green' alphabet types after Kirchhoff 1863.

Aegean Basin in his *Studien zur Geschichte des griechischen Alphabets*. He labelled these regions 'red', 'blue' and 'green' (Fig. 5.3, Table 5.3),[6] noting that Greeks who came from a 'red' region would use the set of 'red letters' and so in this way one's very broadly defined regional affiliation could be identified from the way one wrote. Although the Kirchhoff model is still used for the broadest and most general overview patterns of writing in the Aegean Basin (Voutiras 2006; Woodard 2010), the model is now considered rather outdated and is not without its criticisms (e.g. Guarducci 1967; Hansen 1983),[7] most notably that these groups are not only too broad to be useful with far too many exceptions, but also that this 'top-down' approach does not take enough account of the individual agency of those writing to recognise different lettersets and consciously choose the one they want for a particular reason.

This same regional mentality was revisited and very much refined by Anne Jeffery in 1961 with her landmark work *The Local Scripts of Archaic Greece* (LSAG). Jeffery took a more archaeological approach to consider not only the appearance of letter shapes but also the materials on which writing appeared, the latter sometimes affecting the shapes that were more easy or more difficult for those writing to produce. She catalogued the use of different letter forms attested in each island or region around the Aegean, identifying with more precision a greater number of regional groups than had been identified by Kirchhoff; she also recorded within these regional groups the most common variations. However, by virtue of her research question Jeffery published only a selection of the source material, and one must accept that the generalising examples used are representative of *all* writing found within each of these regions.[8] Clearly Jeffery is very useful for identifying these different areas, but her study alone cannot be used as a basis either systematically to test the quantitative covariance of letter shapes at various sites or to reveal diachronic patterning.

The notion of regional groups is an interesting one to test here by means of a much larger, 'bottom-up', dataset. Both Kirchhoff and Jeffery identified regions and presented some data that fit within these regions; what happens if one starts instead with the data and uses clustering algorithms to draw those regions on the basis of (quantitative) data? Would 'regions' or

---

[6] Kirchhoff 1863. taf. 1 summarises the usage of different letters according to site, and taf. 2 according to region.

[7] Woodard 1997 takes a different approach on classifying lettersets by comparing letter shapes and possible sound values with earlier Iron Age and Bronze Age forms.

[8] This model and its application of systematic and non-systematic data has been re-evaluated in recent scholarship by Elvira Astoreca 2021.

Table 5.3 Alphabet groups after Kirchhoff, organised by most frequently occurring shape and approximate sound values. Letter shapes under investigation in this chapter are highlighted.

Sound value	a	b	g	d	e	w	z	h	ɛː	th	i	k	l	m	n	k_s	o	p	s	k	r	s	t	u	k_s	p_h	k_h	p	oː
Green alphabet	A	B	Γ	Δ	E	Ϝ	I		B	⊕	I	K	ʌ	M	N	⊞	O	Γ	M	φ	P	⧗	t	Y	X	φ	Y		
Red alphabet	A	B	Γ	Δ	E	Ϝ	I		B	⊕	I	K	ʌ	M	N	⊞	O	Γ	M	φ	P	⧗	t	Y	X	φ	Y		
Blue alphabet	A	B	Γ	Δ	E		I		H	⊕	I	K	ʌ	M	N	⊞	O	Γ		P	⧗	t	Y		φ	X	Y	Ω

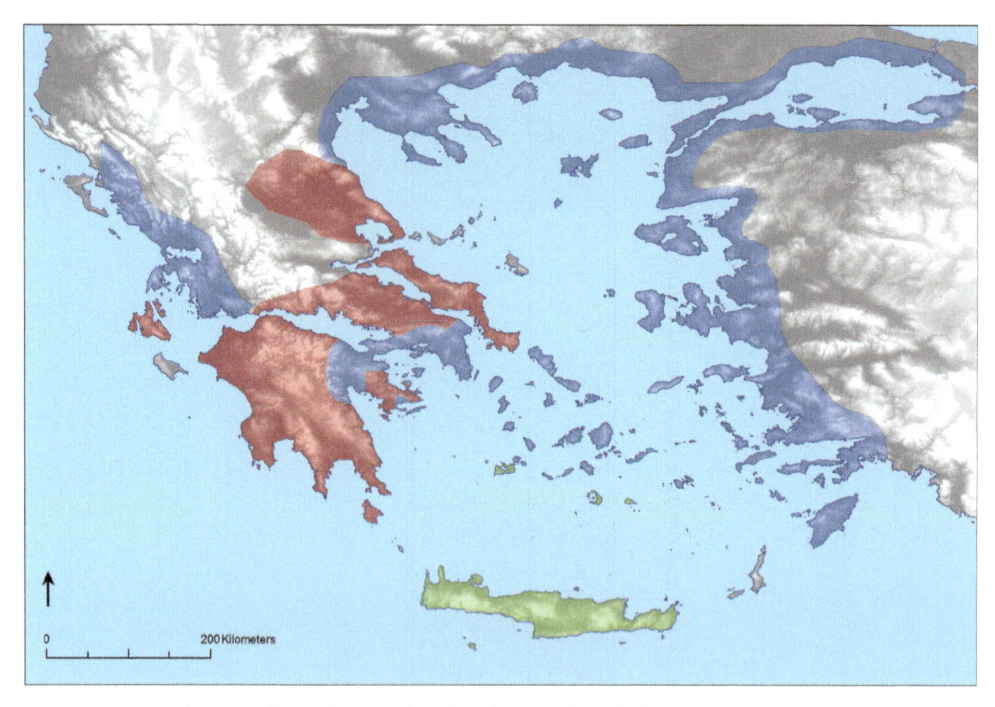

Figure 5.3 Distribution of sites discussed in this chapter, for which writing containing the target lettersets for analysis has been found.

groups even emerge? This chapter will consider the dataset of Archaic period writing in a fairly comprehensive way, aiming for a more complete coverage of the total material than either Kirchhoff or Jeffery's more selective case-study approach. By measuring the co-variation of different types of writing in different places at a different times, analysis will reveal areas of the Aegean that adopted similar writing practices to one another throughout the Archaic period; and, therein, the discussion will move from distribution of writing types to the practices and local identities that those sorts of practices embody for the relevant communities.

The Data

What is required is some index against which similarity or difference can be measured. Here the co-variance of five different types of letter groups will be used to measure the variation between inscriptions found at sites all over the Aegean basin: aspirates, sibilants, long vowels, iota and additional letters.

i) Aspirates

Two of the three regional variants of Archaic Greek contained the phoneme /h/ in the Kirchhoff division of the Aegean. The 'blue' alphabet of Attica, Ionia and the islands and the 'green' alphabet of Crete and Thera were said to contain /h/ while the 'red' dialects did not contain this sound value. /h/ was variously designated by the graphemes <H>, <B>, or less often <☐>.

ii) Sibilants

Two main grapheme variants of the sibilant /s/ are attested for the Archaic period: the three-stroke <ϟ> and the four-stroke variety <ϟ>, the latter of which could be rotated 90 degrees thus <M>. In this analysis, the first two of these varieties have been grouped together, as the main questions relate to the patent recognisability of letter forms, rather than to the specifics of grapheme morphology. <ϟ> and <ϟ> are used somewhat interchangeably between sites, whereas <M> is restricted to Crete, Thera and Corinth.

iii) Long vowels

This category deals with both the quality and orthography of the letters /ɛ/ and /o/. Specifically, regional dialects of Greek variously distinguished between short and long vowels (/ɛ/ vs /ɛː/, and /o/ vs /oː/), and also with the diphthongs /ei/ and /ou/. Where the sound /ɛː/ existed within the dialect, it was denoted by one of five letters <☐>, <B>, <ß>, <Ɛ> and <H>, while /oː/ exists within only two varieties <O> and <Ω>. Where one would expect /ei/ in later koiné Greek there are eleven options <☐>, <ß>, <ßI>, <ßϟ>, <Ɛ>, <ƐI>, <Ɛϟ>, <H>, <I>, <ϟ>; and for /ou/ there were four options <O>, <OI>, <Oϟ> and <OY>.

iv) Iota

Two main discernibly different ways of writing /i/ existed within the Archaic period alphabets: <I> and <ϟ>. The first of these is the most common, and the second correlates with alphabets which use <M> for /s/ and therefore do not confuse <ϟ> for /s/.

v) Additional letters

The final set of letters for analysis relates to the sounds /ks/, /kh/ and /ps/, which are designated by a number of regional variants. /ks/ is rendered by eleven graphemes or digraphs <◻𐤎>, <+>, <H𐤎>, <KM>, <K𐤎>, <𐤎>, <X𐤎>, <𐌅>, <ϕM>, <Y> and <Y𐤎>; /kh/ by six <+>, <KΘ>, <KH>, <𐤎>, <X> and <Y>; and /ps/ by three <Γ𐤎>, <ΓM> and <Y>. These sounds are attested in no great quantity throughout the corpus (n_{ks}=106, n_{kh}=264, n_{ps}=20).

Methodology and Nature of the Data

In measuring variation in community affiliation by using the inscriptional record in this way, two immediate objections might be made. The first concerns the issue of simplification. In relating the distribution of lettersets too closely to identity, one risks reducing conclusions to essentialism and culture history.[9] Indeed, some (or all) of the etic categories that we observe through the use of clustering algorithms might not have made any sense to ancient people (*cf.* Miller 1985; Lucy 2005).[10] A robust methodology is required that puts emphasis on the connections and continuities in the material record rather than simply on the data itself. As outlined in Chapter 1, network analytical perspectives offer this approach, since formal network analysis can partition networks visualised into smaller units based on the sum of ties or edges drawn.

In this chapter, sites at which writing was found are represented by nodes, and then ties are drawn between any two sites at which the same letter shape was used to represent the same sound value. This method creates a similarity distance network between sites, where the strength of the tie between sites is relative to the number of shared letter shapes for expressing the same sound values. Data for each of the four periods are analysed here separately, giving four separate descriptive statistical outputs. Sites are treated as *abstract* nodes, and for each variant letter form identified within the database, the presence or absence of such a shape on inscriptions from the site is recorded in a non-quantitative binary ('present' or 'absent'). The measure of connection between each site (i.e. the weight of a tie between two nodes) is equal to the number of shared letter shapes; this is measured by using a Brainerd-Robinson similarity matrix (Brainerd 1951; Robinson 1951b).[11] This produces a numeric value for the

---

[9] For reactions against culture history in light of the rise of computational spatial analysis, see McNairn 1980, Trigger 1980 and Shennan 1989.
[10] A fuller discussion on etic categorisation is offered in the next chapter.
[11] On using R to calculate the Brainerd-Robinson matrix, see http://www.mattpeeples.net/BR.html, accessed 15 December 2021.

connection between any two pairs of sites, relative to all other connections between all other sites. And having the data in this form – as a matrix of sites with values designating the strength of their connections – allows for one to visualise these sites as nodes and their ties as edges in a network environment.

The second objection concerns the nature of the inscriptional record itself – is the dataset actually good enough to identify culturally significant large-scale patterns? Can we be sure that there are no selective biases in our dataset? The issue is explored more generally in this book as a whole, but this particular case study interrogates the concept of representativeness further. In some senses, the patterns identified by Kirchhoff and Jeffery relied on their understanding that the data they were using was representative – in other words, that the data available to them reflected perfectly the historical patterns of reality, and that if more data became available there would be no need to adjust the story that was being told.

A worked example illustrates well why we cannot assume that the archaeological record is representative of the variable under investigation here. Let us assume that at one site ('A') we have ten occurrences in the inscriptional record of letters that would be sounded /e:/. Six of these are written <H>, and four of these <Ƕ>. Therefore, we might suggest that the probability of /e:/ being written as <H> at 'A' is 0.6. However, there are all sorts of uncertainties surrounding the material dataset, and although the probability of 0.6 is the most likely, there is a lack of precision and in a small sample the chance of, for example, the probability being 0.9 or 0.3 is still comparatively high. The nature of the evidence and its discovery is such that we cannot be certain our sample perfectly represents an original population. First, we cannot be confident that the materials excavated at 'A' are representative of all the material which was originally to be found on that site. Furthermore, we must consider the case of broken or fragmentary inscriptions. If an inscription is broken, the lost section may have contained a set of letters expressing /e:/, and we are now uncertain as to how that sound would have been expressed in writing. (Moreover, even if an inscription is not broken, it may be so short or brief in nature that it does not even contain our target letter sound /e:/). Second, given the sporadic and occasional publication of the inscriptional *corpora* from Greece, we cannot even trust that the data we have represent all the objects discovered. The nature of our sample – and, therefore, our proposed probability of 0.6 – is uncertain.

One might choose to deal with this uncertainty in two ways: dealing with the raw input inscriptional data before it is processed; or dealing with the output connection. Here, the second solution is adopted,[12] to adjust for and experiment with the similarity matrix. Once the similarity matrix has been generated for each pair of sites using the Brainerd-Robinson algorithm, the sites in this study are visualised as nodes, and ties are drawn between sites with the strength of their edge being given by the similarity value. Next, groups of nodes are sorted together into 'clusters' or 'neighbourhoods', based both on the number of common ties between groups of sites and the strength of the ties exhibited between them. This sort of modularity analysis can be used to good effect to identify groups of nodes within much larger networks (Blondel et al. 2008), and alternative algorithms used to identify clusters within a network might variously render similar or different results (cf. Clauset, Newman, and Moore 2004; Pons and Lataby 2006; Su et al. 2010). Here, the native modularity tool of Gephi is used to identify those clusters, calculated through using the exploratory statistics panel and taking account both of the number of edges but also the weight of edges shared by any pair of nodes.[13] For each of the four periods, the algorithm was run with three different resolution values (0.5, 1.0 and 1.5), wherein the lowest value forces the programme to identify a greater number of clusters or neighbourhoods in the same dataset; while the greater value sets the similarity threshold for forming clusters much higher (compensating for the fact that there are so many gaps in the data that only the strongest connections visible should be deemed in any way historically meaningful). Clusters will then be tagged and projected both in the abstract and geographically. If those clusters identified map onto geography, this would suggest that the approach taken by Kirchhoff and Jeffery stands up to the empirical data – but one might also see where regions identified computationally do and do not overlap with those previously found. If the clusters do not map onto geography, however,

---

[12] The PhD thesis on which this book is based adopted the opposite approach, that is, to 'buffer' data before the main Brainerd-Robinson analysis. A Bayesian framework was used (cf. Lavan 2019 and McElreath 2016: 19–70), taking the position that Bayesian inference is the process of estimating the parameters that might inform a population or probability distribution, based on both a core dataset and our personal beliefs about that dataset. A Bayesian statistician would argue that there is no 'true' or fixed interpretation of the dataset – that is, the probability of a fragmentary inscription containing certain lettersets in its more complete form – but only 'personal' beliefs. Here, the matrix output by the analysis has been buffered: pilot tests indicated that the same substantive historical conclusions could be reached regardless of whether one buffered the input or the output data, but that processing output data was significantly quicker and simpler.

[13] https://github.com/gephi/gephi/wiki/Modularity, accessed 15 December 2021.

that is also interesting, and some other explanation must be given for the divergent pattern.

Before presenting the patterns generated by the clustering algorithm it is necessary to add a disclaimer on the methodology. Clustering brings together site nodes based on the similarities between them: we might usually expect these to be similarities of presence, but, in this case, they might also be similarities of absence. If, for instance, a group of sites have very few inscriptions attested from each, at which only a small handful of letters match, there would quite clearly be for a majority of lettersets investigated a 'similarity' identified by the clustering algorithm that a majority of letters are not present. Such a cluster is still useful to identify as, instead of showing us a group of sites whose writing is similar to one another, it shows us a group of sites whose data is so poor that these sites cannot be usefully allocated to other meaningful groups. These are clusters based on an absence of evidence, not necessarily on an evidence of absence. Where appropriate, the following discussion will identify clusters that might usefully be classified as these 'clusters of absence'.

Results

The 1.0 resolution modularity identifies three clusters of site nodes (Fig. 5.4c–d) for period one (700–650 BC): a group that maps across Crete, the southern Cyclades and parts of the mainland; a second group that covers the Saronic Gulf, north Cyclades and parts of Ionia; and a third group that mainly covers central Greece and Ionia. Although for this first group there are similarities in the way that fairly common sounds are written (particularly with <I> for /i/ and <ϟ> for /s/), this group is mainly about absence. More becomes clear when looking at the data for the same period using the 0.5 modularity resolution (Fig. 5.4a–b): the fairly large cluster is consistently identified once again, while there are in addition smaller clusters based on actual similarities of lettersets, for instance: a group comprising Athens, Corinth, Delos and Thebes, all sharing <Ɵ> for /h/ and <Ɛ> for /e/; a group of Naxos, Samos and Smyrna who use <H> for /ɛː/ and <Kϟ> for /ks/. On balance, it is in fact these additional lettersets and the aspirates that seem to have most weight in grouping sites into their respective clusters. Geographically, there is some organisation to these clusters: a group that covers north Ionia, a group that touches the Saronic Gulf and north Cyclades and a group in central Greece – but equally there

(a)

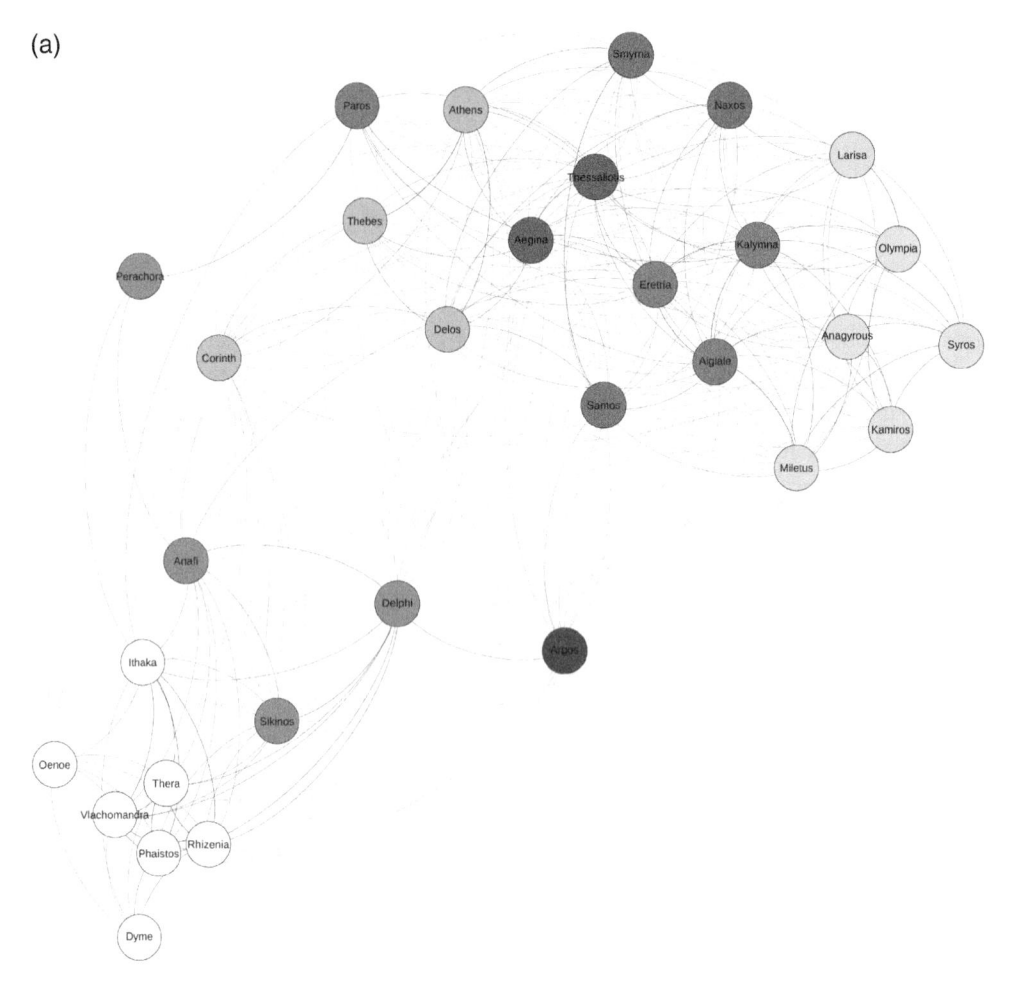

Figure 5.4a SNA visualisation of the sites clustered according to similar writing styles, 700–650 BC. Nodes are distributed randomly in abstract space, clustered under 0.5 modularity parameter. This image is available in a larger format online at www.cambridge.org/loy.

are clusters (e.g. the cluster comprising Anagyrous, Kamiros, Larisa, Miletos, Olympia and Syros) that have little to do with geography. The 1.5 modularity resolution (Fig. 5.4e–f) suggests that the strongest patterns of all divide the Aegean between the south and west and the north and east. The differences between these groups of sites are most clearly characterised by the ways in which they write the vowels and aspirates.

For period two (650–600 BC), the 1.0 modularity analysis identifies again three clusters of sites nodes (Fig. 5.5c–d). These groups are very similar in their geography to the previous period, with the addition of sites from the north Aegean that are part of the same cluster as those sites in

(b)

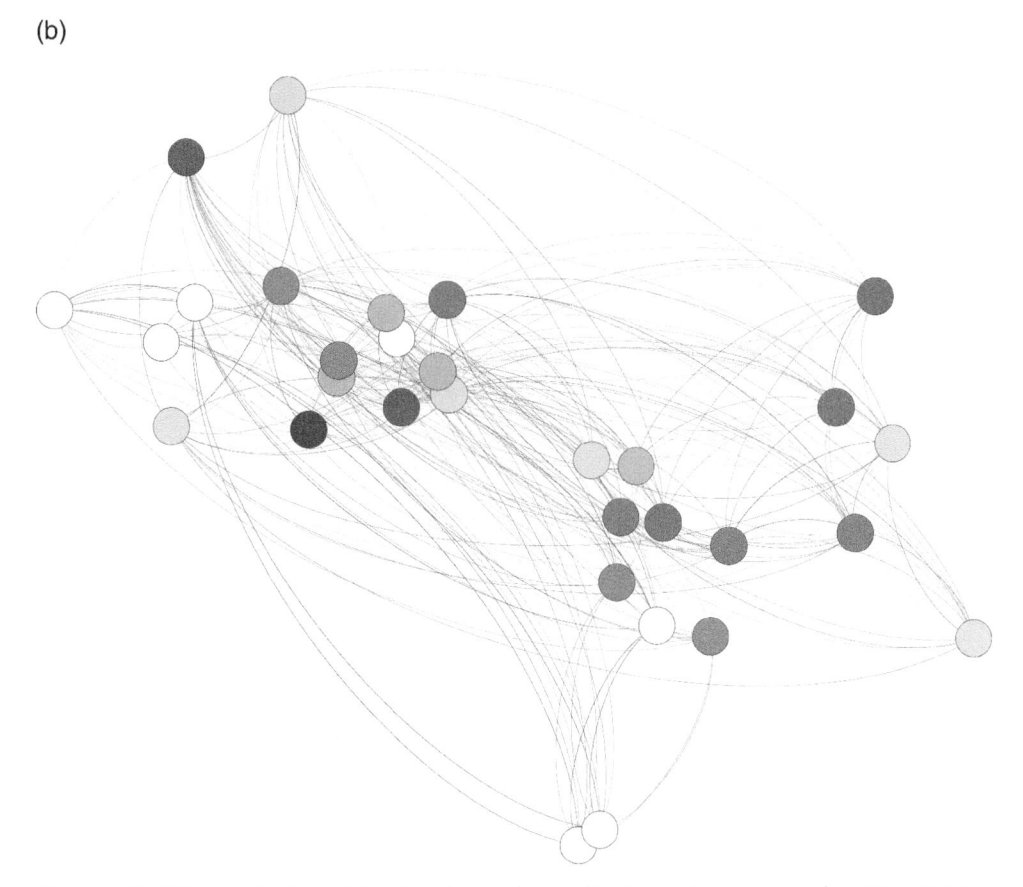

Figure 5.4b SNA visualisation of the sites clustered according to similar writing styles, 700–650 BC. Nodes are placed according to their approximate geographic location in the Aegean, clustered under 0.5 modularity parameter. This image is available in a larger format online at www.cambridge.org/loy.

south Ionia and around the Saronic Gulf. This cluster certainly contains the sites with the richest data – both the longest inscriptions and those that express on them more letter forms. As an example, Corinth in this group has within its dataset inscriptions using two different symbols to express the same sound value /h/ (<В> and <H>), two symbols for /i/ (<I> and <ϟ>), two symbols for /s/ (<ϟ> and <M>), and all attested Archaic period symbols for both /ɛː/ (<H>, <Ʀ>, <ƦI>, <BI> and <I>) and /oː/ (<O> and <Ω>). Clearly by having a greater range of letters used at this one site, there is potential for connection with many other sites. There is little change when looking at the 1.5 modularity analysis (Fig. 5.5e–f) when compared with the 1.0 analysis, beyond the addition of more sites to the north of the Aegean. In fact, given that for those sites on Crete and in central Greece we might justifiably

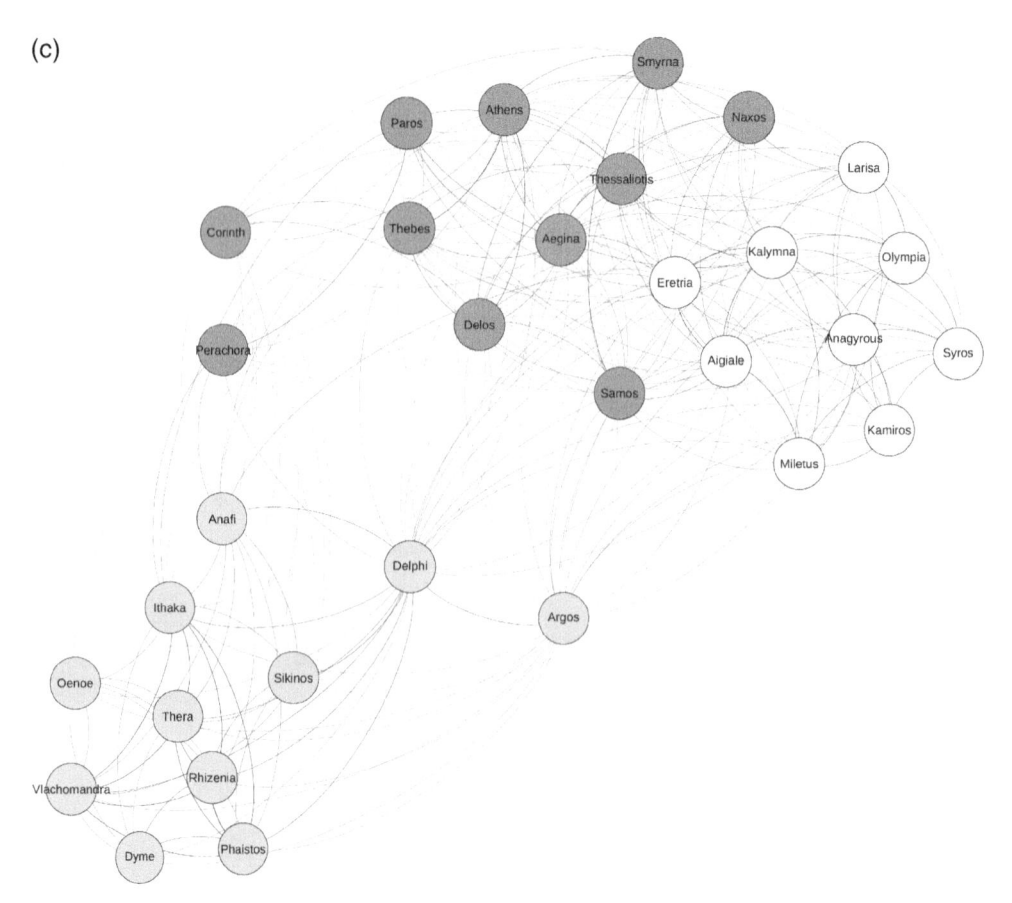

Figure 5.4c SNA visualisation of the sites clustered according to similar writing styles, 700–650 BC. Nodes are distributed randomly in abstract space, clustered under 1.0 modularity parameter. This image is available in a larger format online at www.cambridge.org/loy.

identify the group as a 'cluster of absence', these two clusters could quite easily be labelled as 'sites at which there is evidence for more lettersets used in writing' and 'sites at which there is evidence for fewer letters used in writing'. For the 0.5 modularity analysis (Fig. 5.5a–b), by contrast, eight groups can be identified. Some of these clusters appear to be consistent with the geography of the Aegean Basin – there are two clusters that broadly take in the Cyclades and Ionia, while there is a smaller cluster that focuses around the Saronic Gulf. On the other hand, there are groups that are nothing to do with geography: a cluster that comprises Corinth, Korkyra and Thera, and that same group that takes in Athens and Aegina also includes Ialysos on Rhodes. Even by forcing the algorithm to search more intensively for clusters in the data of this period, the largest group is still that which covers Crete and parts of central and western

(d)

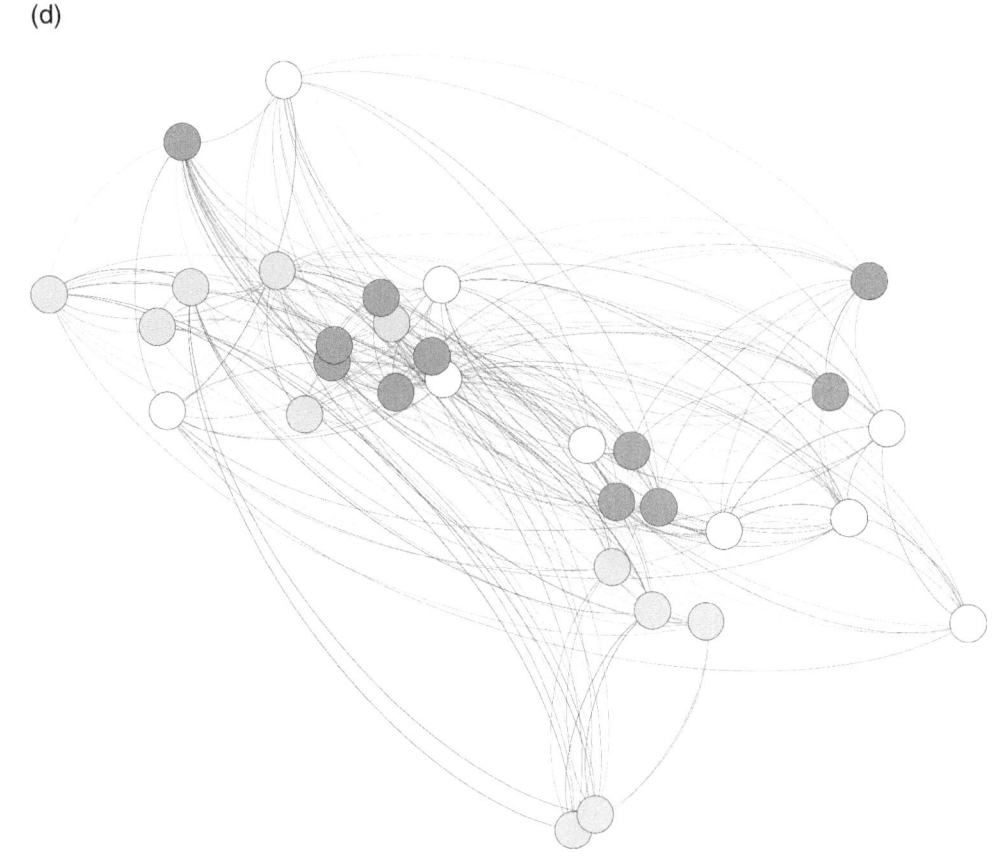

Figure 5.4d SNA visualisation of the sites clustered according to similar writing styles, 700–650 BC. Nodes are placed according to their approximate geographic location in the Aegean, clustered under 1.0 modularity parameter. This image is available in a larger format online at www.cambridge.org/loy.

Greece – possibly a group that relates to a 'cluster of absence', an artefact of the particular methodology used.

It is in period three (600–550 BC) that the picture starts to change. The 1.0 modularity analysis returns another graph characterised by three different clusters (fig. 5.6b–c); however, this time their geographic scope is different. One group stretches north-west from Crete across the Saronic Gulf to central and western Greece; a second group covers the Peloponnese up to the north Aegean and parts of Ionia; while a third group, the smallest group, falls mainly over Ionia. In contrast to the previous two periods, this smallest group seems to be a true cluster and not one of absence: the Ionian sites are characterised by a similar use of <⊟> and <H> for /ɛ/, <Ω> for /oː/, either <+> or <⌿> for /kh/, and an

(e)

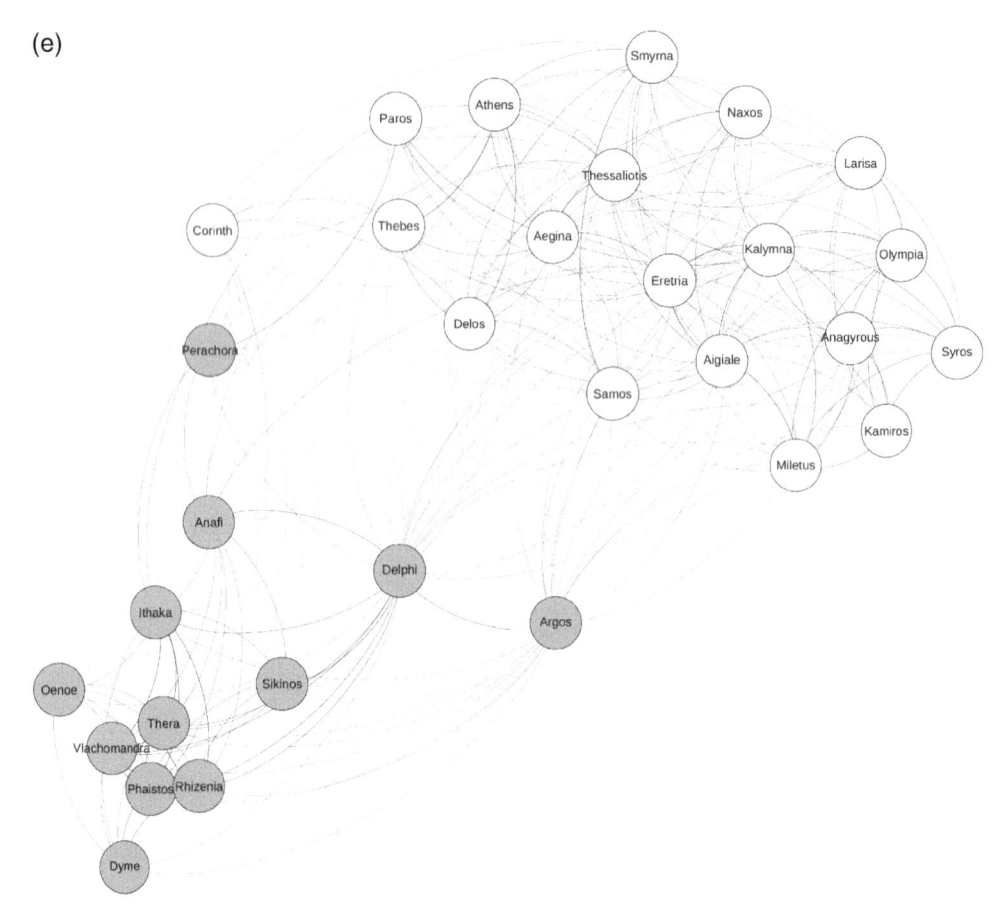

Figure 5.4e SNA visualisation of the sites clustered according to similar writing styles, 700–650 BC. Nodes are distributed randomly in abstract space, clustered under 1.5 modularity parameter. This image is available in a larger format online at www.cambridge.org/loy.

absence of signs for aspiration. The 1.5 modularity analysis (Fig. 5.6d–e) absorbs this Ionian group into the second of the groups identified above (that which covers the Peloponnese, north Aegean and other parts of Ionia): here it is just Crete and western Greece that are deemed by the algorithm to show sufficient deviation from the pattern used by the rest of Aegean sites to be considered a separate cluster. The lettersets used at this site are different for sure, taking <ϟ> instead of <I> for /i/, and <M> instead of <ϟ> for /s/. But taking the resolution value for modularity in the other direction and setting it to 0.5, one creates quite a different sort of graph (Fig. 5.6a).[14] Twenty-seven separate clusters are distinguishable here. The

---

[14] The data are only visualised here in geographic view. The abstract view was deemed too visually complex to helpfully identify separate groups.

(f)

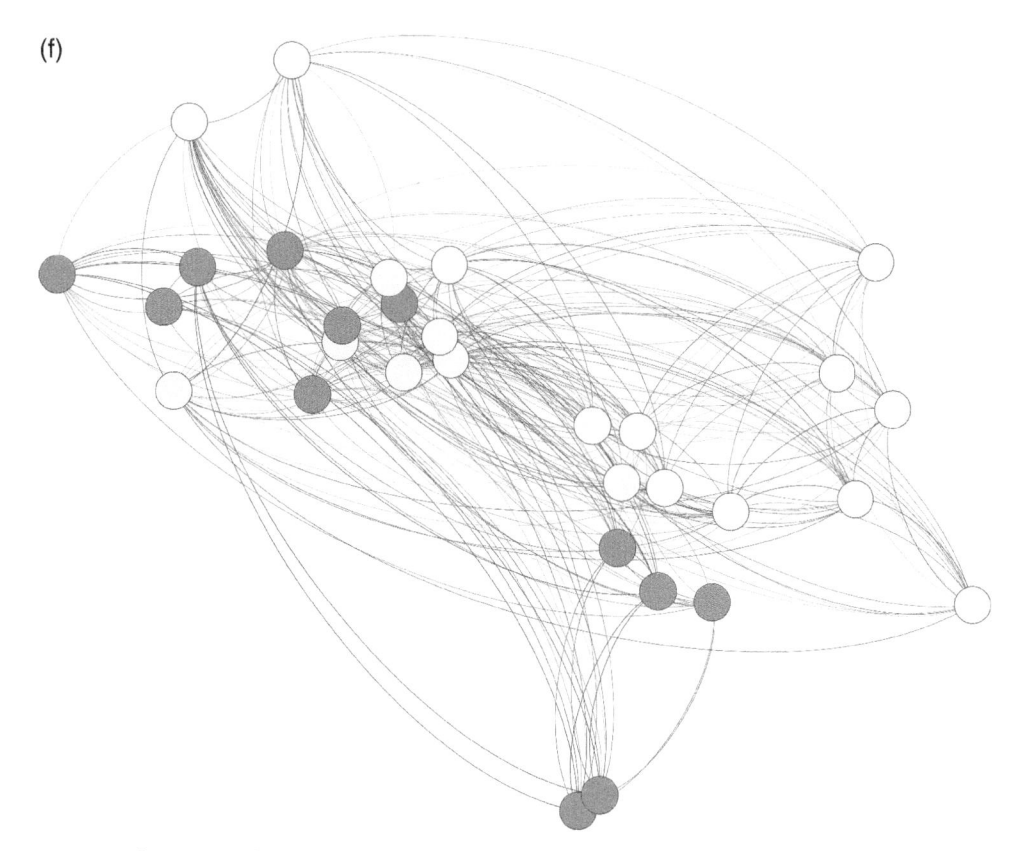

Figure 5.4f SNA visualisation of the sites clustered according to similar writing styles, 700–650 BC. Nodes are placed according to their approximate geographic location in the Aegean, clustered under 1.5 modularity parameter. This image is available in a larger format online at www.cambridge.org/loy.

largest cluster is that discussed previously, extending from Crete to western Greece. Other clusters, however, are only a few sites in size, and some only a single site. Where do there seem to be clusters of sites together mapping onto geography? The three *poleis* of Rhodes form a tight cluster together, as do groups of sites in both the north and south of Ionia. Parts of the north Aegean behave like other parts of Ionia, while the Cyclades, Saronic Gulf and Peloponnese show the greatest number of site clusters, and the most individual sites ranked as clusters in their own right. At these sites the inscriptional record might be much richer and, therefore, the algorithm for modularity used here might be more likely to pick out patterns of difference: but it really is striking that, using the exact same technique, this pattern of the start of the sixth century is so different to that of the end of the seventh century, and that the level of clustering for similarity seems to be in general at the level of the site rather than the region.

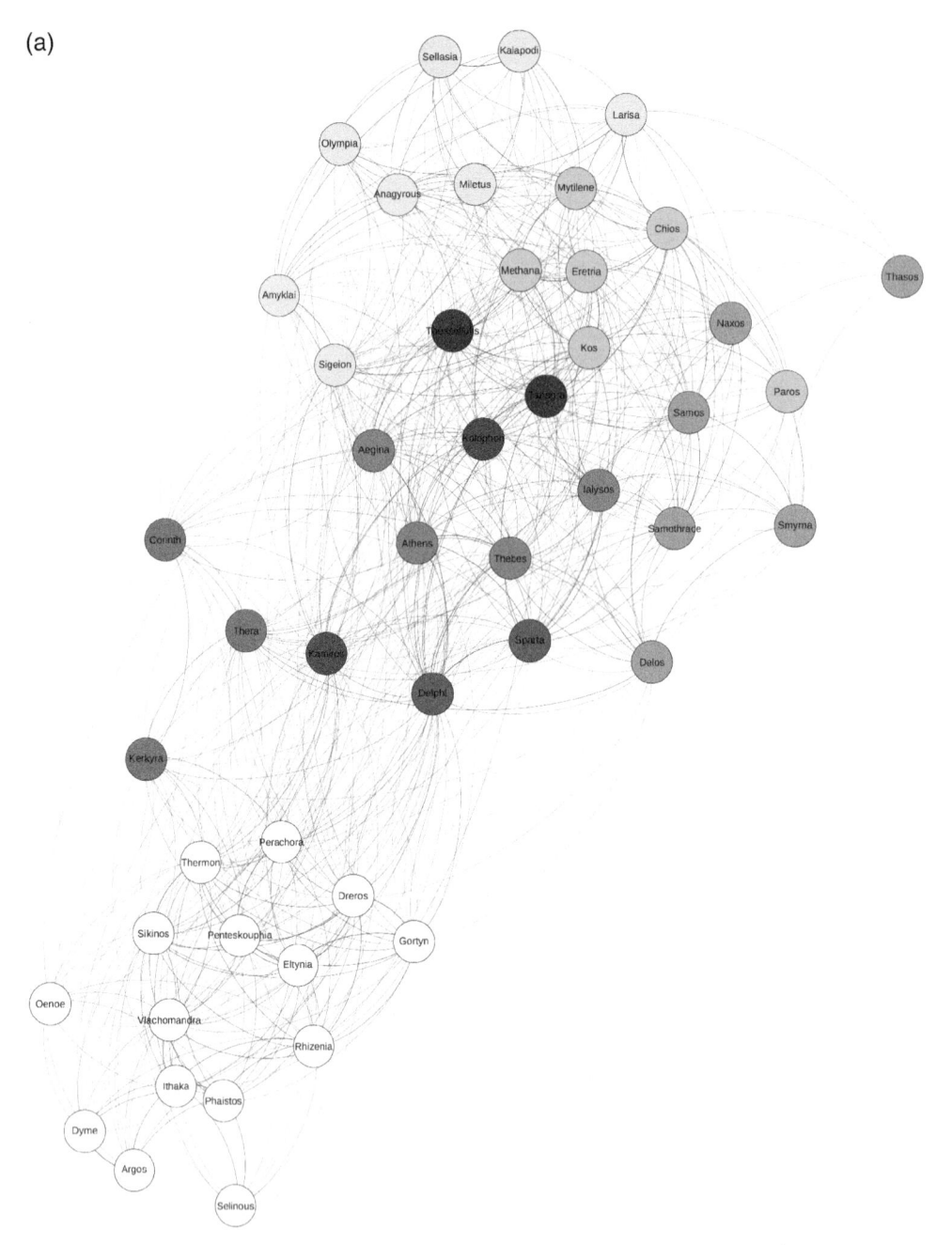

216   *Political Networks: Expressing Affiliation*

(a)

Figure 5.5a SNA visualisation of the sites clustered according to similar writing styles, 650–600 BC. Nodes are distributed randomly in abstract space, clustered under 0.5 modularity parameter. This image is available in a larger format online at www.cambridge.org/loy.

(b)

Figure 5.5b SNA visualisation of the sites clustered according to similar writing styles, 650–600 BC. Nodes are placed according to their approximate geographic location in the Aegean, clustered under 0.5 modularity parameter. This image is available in a larger format online at www.cambridge.org/loy.

It is much the same case for period four (550–500 BC). The 1.0 resolution modularity analysis – for the first time across these time periods – identifies *four* different clusters (Fig. 5.7b–c). It is very difficult to map these clusters on to regional groups at all. Each cluster cuts across all parts of the Aegean (with the exception of Crete, which is bisected east-west into two different clusters). On the one hand, the dataset in terms of its number of sites is just so much bigger for this period than for the previous (compare 151 sites in period four to 111 in period three, 48 in period two and 31 in period one); on the other hand, there are some lettersets of the Archaic period that are barely attested during this time slice, including <☐> for /h/ only at Apollonis Hyperteleatae and on Thera, only one instance of <☐ϟ> for /ks/ at Setaia, and not a single <O|> or <Oϟ> for /ou/. But adjusting the parameters for the other two modularity analyses renders two quite

(c)

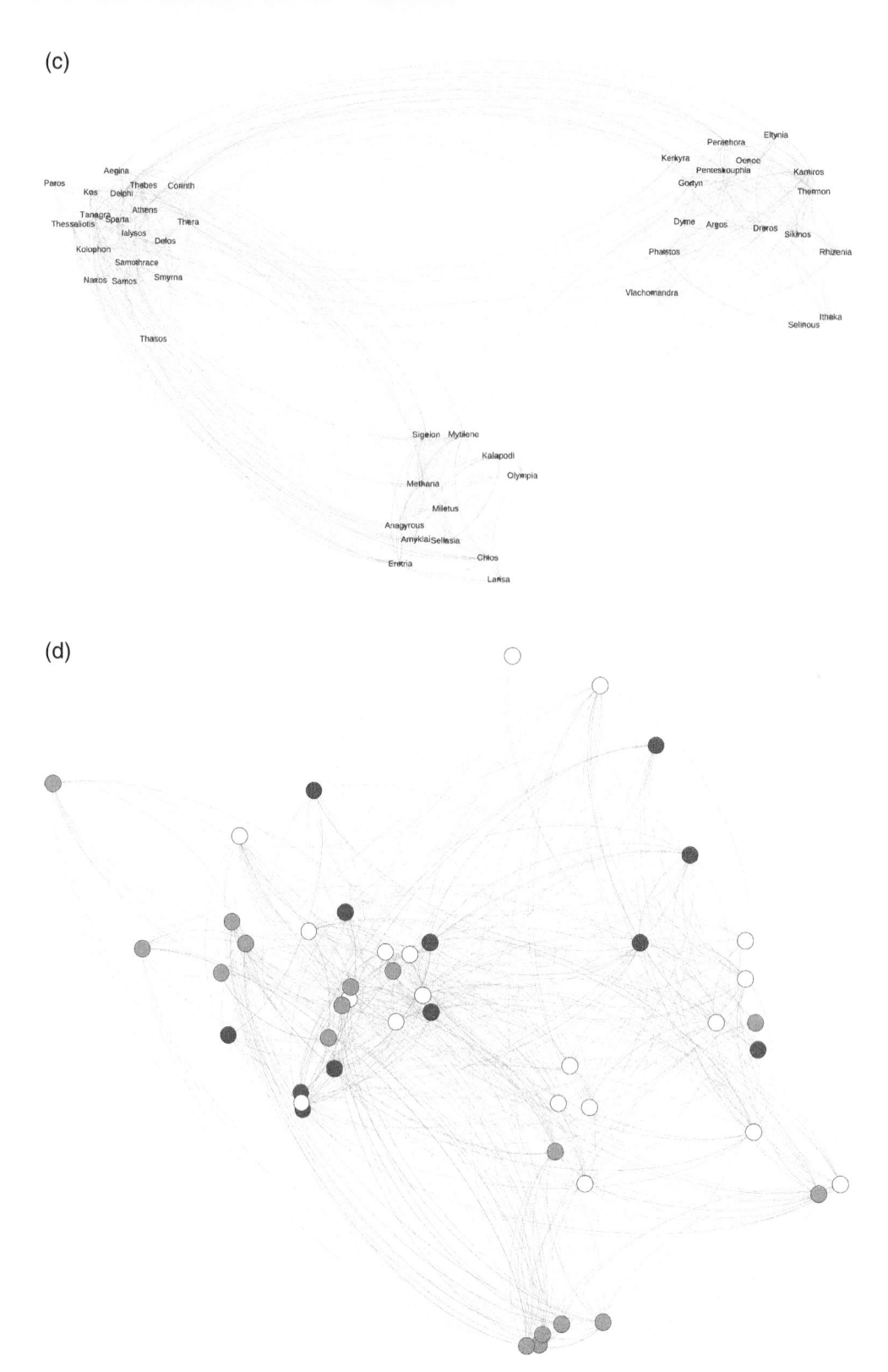

(d)

Figure 5.5 c) SNA visualisation of the sites clustered according to similar writing styles, 650–600 BC. Nodes are distributed randomly in abstract space, clustered under 1.0 modularity parameter.
d) SNA visualisation of the sites clustered according to similar writing styles, 650–600 BC. Nodes are placed according to their approximate geographic location in the Aegean, clustered under 1.0 modularity parameter. This image is available in a larger format online at www.cambridge.org/loy.

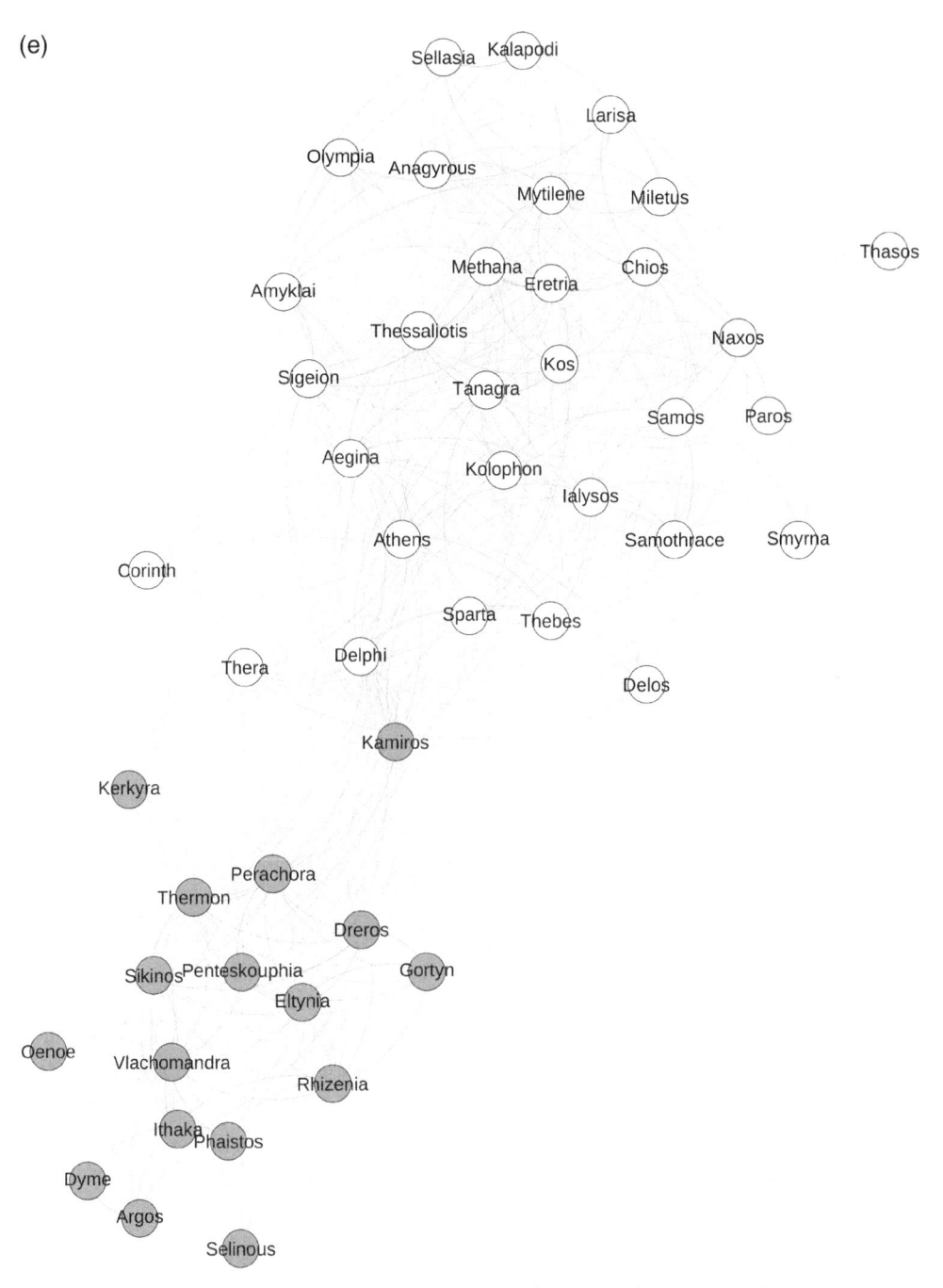

Figure 5.5e SNA visualisation of the sites clustered according to similar writing styles, 650–600 BC. Nodes are distributed randomly in abstract space, clustered under 1.5 modularity parameter. This image is available in a larger format online at www.cambridge.org/loy.

(f)

Figure 5.5f SNA visualisation of the sites clustered according to similar writing styles, 650–600 BC. Nodes are placed according to their approximate geographic location in the Aegean, clustered under 1.5 modularity parameter. This image is available in a larger format online at www.cambridge.org/loy.

different patterns: the 1.5 modularity analysis (Fig. 5.7d–e) puts all of the site nodes into the same cluster, while the 0.5 resolution modularity graph (Fig. 5.7a), like that of period three, renders a panoply of thirty-five different clusters. Once again, there is very little geographic organisation to these clusters – except for a group around central-west Crete. Where there appeared in the analysis of the period three data to be more unity on Rhodes and around Ionia, this is not the case in period four. There are high levels of variation between clusters in all areas of the Aegean.

(a)

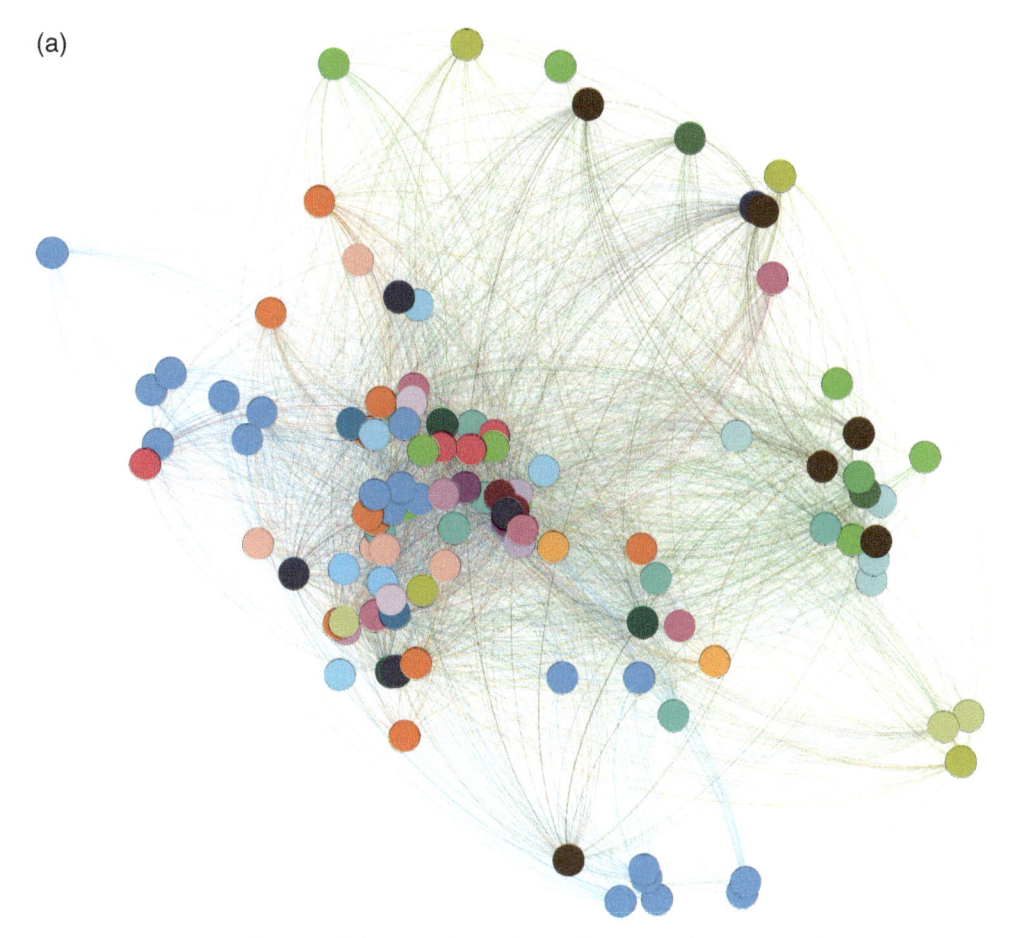

Figure 5.6a SNA visualisation of the sites clustered according to similar writing styles, 600–550 BC. Nodes are placed according to their approximate geographic location in the Aegean, clustered under 0.5 modularity parameter. This image is available ina larger format online at www.cambridge.org/loy.

Discussion

The network analysis makes it clear that there are patterns and changes in the way that writing was used in different regions in different parts of the Archaic period. If one accepts, as argued above, that both an act of writing undertaken in certain way and the producing of letters that others can read and recognise are significant factors for an entanglement with issues of identity, then one might logically infer that these changes in the pattern of writing distribution reflect not only changes in *what sorts* of identities were being expressed in the Aegean Basin, but also changes of *how* these identities were being expressed. Writing is, after all, a material expression of certain

(b)

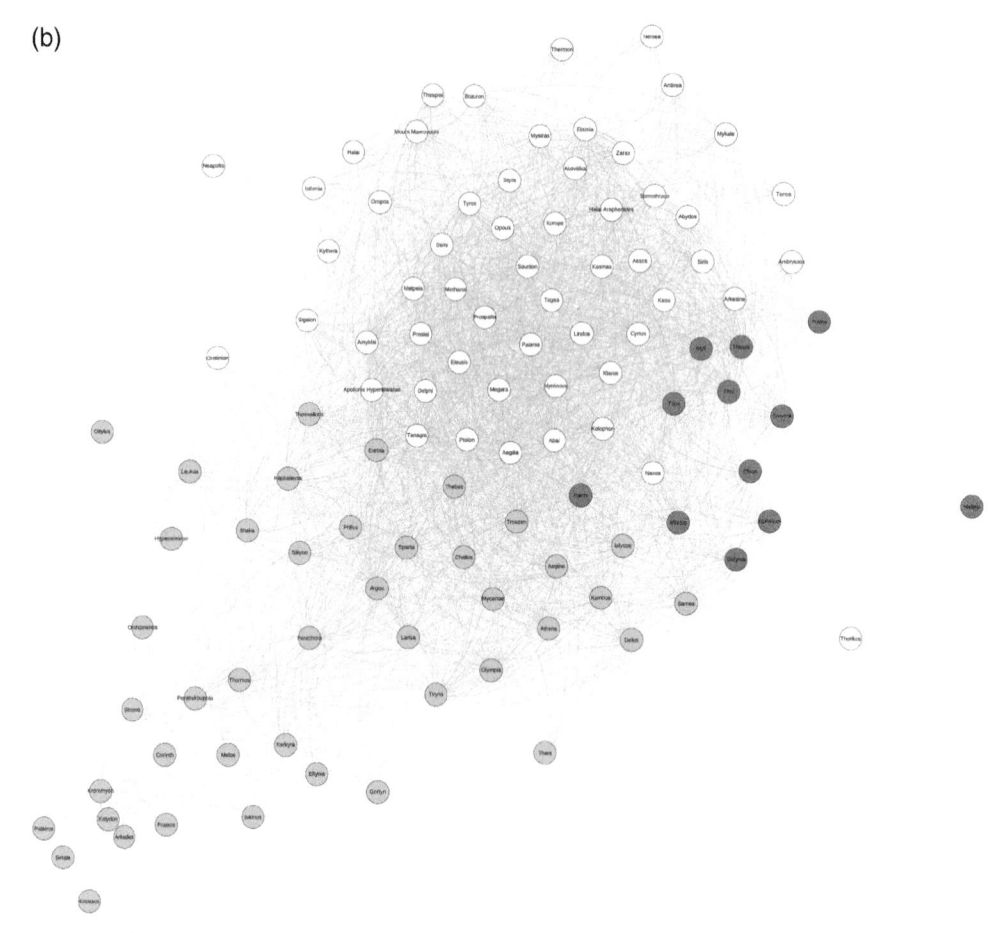

Figure 5.6b SNA visualisation of the sites clustered according to similar writing styles, 600–550 BC. Nodes are distributed randomly in abstract space, clustered under 1.0 modularity parameter. This image is available in a larger format online at www.cambridge.org/loy.

ideas, and the (conscious or unconscious) decision to write in certain ways must tell us something about the people who produced that writing.

Three particular patterns of interest will be discussed here – patterns that can be identified clearly in the data, independent of which algorithmic lens we look through. First, there is the chronological pattern. Between the seventh century and sixth century, the distribution of site clusters changes fairly drastically, and it is necessary to suggest a reason for there being so much more variation across the Aegean by the start of the sixth century. Second, there is the regional pattern. Compared to the regional units defined by Anne Jeffery (or even to those of Kirchhoff), this analysis suggests that, on the basis of the presence of similar lettersets, there were

(c)

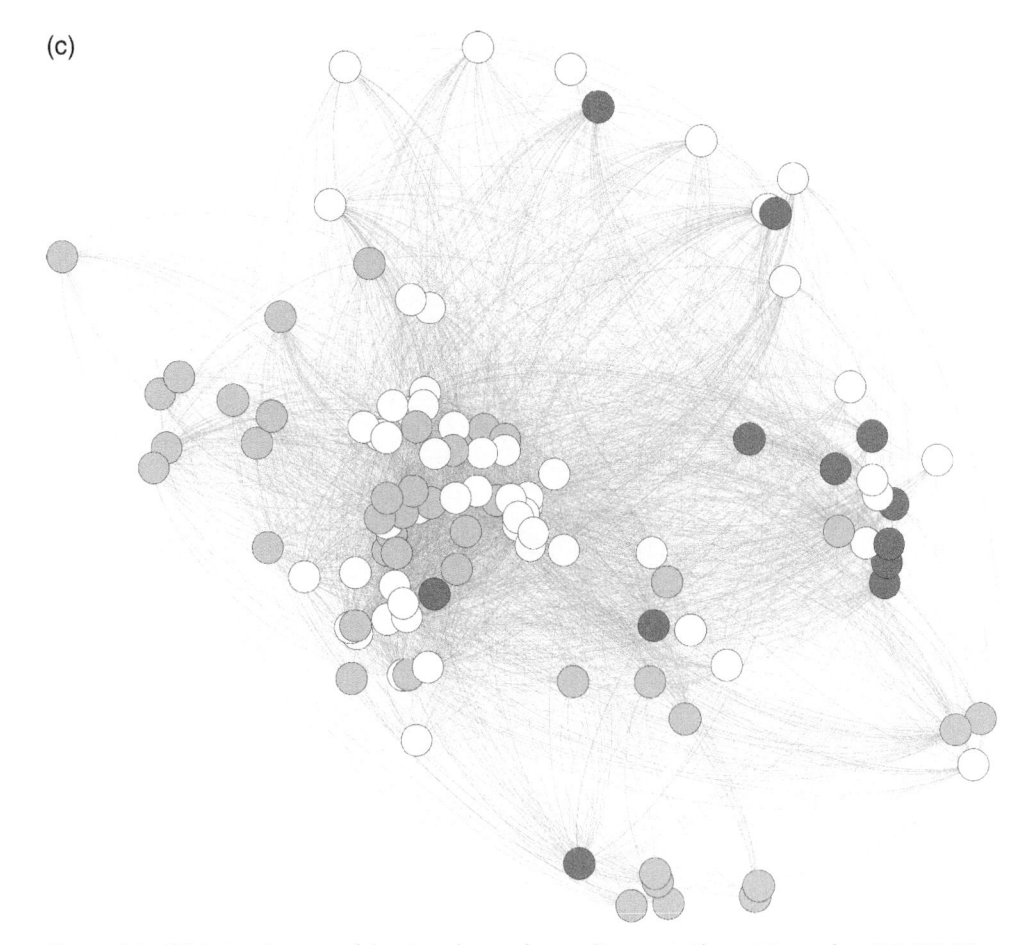

Figure 5.6c SNA visualisation of the sites clustered according to similar writing styles, 600–550 BC. Nodes are placed according to their approximate geographic location in the Aegean, clustered under 1.0 modularity parameter. This image is available in a larger format online at www.cambridge.org/loy.

clusters of sites both larger and smaller across all periods than one might expect. Finally, it is necessary to consider also that the patterns generated by this analysis are the result neither of time nor of geography, but rather from the context in which writing was produced. Different sorts of contexts demand different sort of writing (e.g. formal legal texts versus informal personal dedications); so, even though the interest of this chapter is at the top-level and a broad-view analysis, a more contextual-based approach cannot be neglected.

(d)

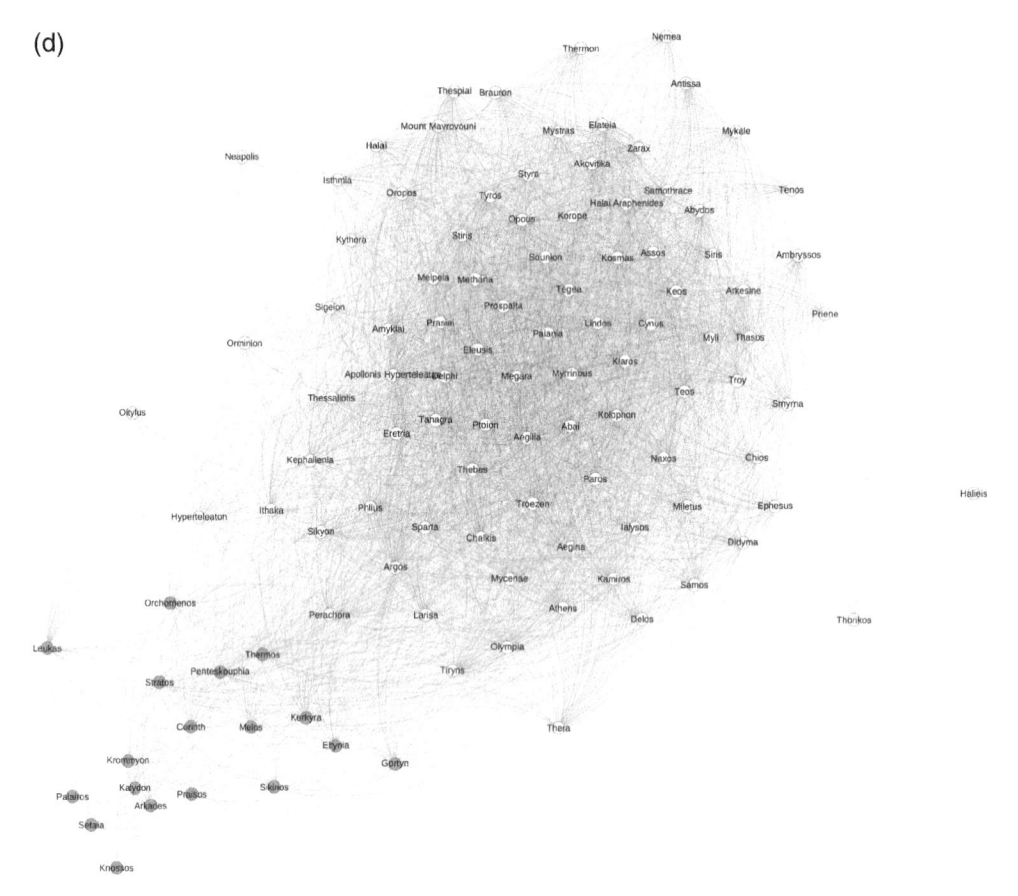

Figure 5.6d SNA visualisation of the sites clustered according to similar writing styles, 600–550 BC. Nodes are distributed randomly in abstract space, clustered under 1.5 modularity parameter. This image is available in a larger format online at www.cambridge.org/loy.

Changes in Writing Practice Over Time

Chronologically speaking, there are two main patterns to note from the modularity analysis. First, that between the start of the seventh century and the end of the sixth century the story becomes much more complicated; second, that despite broad-brush patterning there are some sites that do not form clusters with their geographic neighbours – and this variation is quite evident in the data regardless of the resolution factor used in identifying the clusters.

The pattern of complexity is easier to justify. As noted above, using the 1.0 resolution on the modularity analysis, three clusters of sites can be identified for the first three periods (i.e. 700–550 BC); and at the end of the sixth century BC, four clusters of sites can be found. The geographic spread

(e)

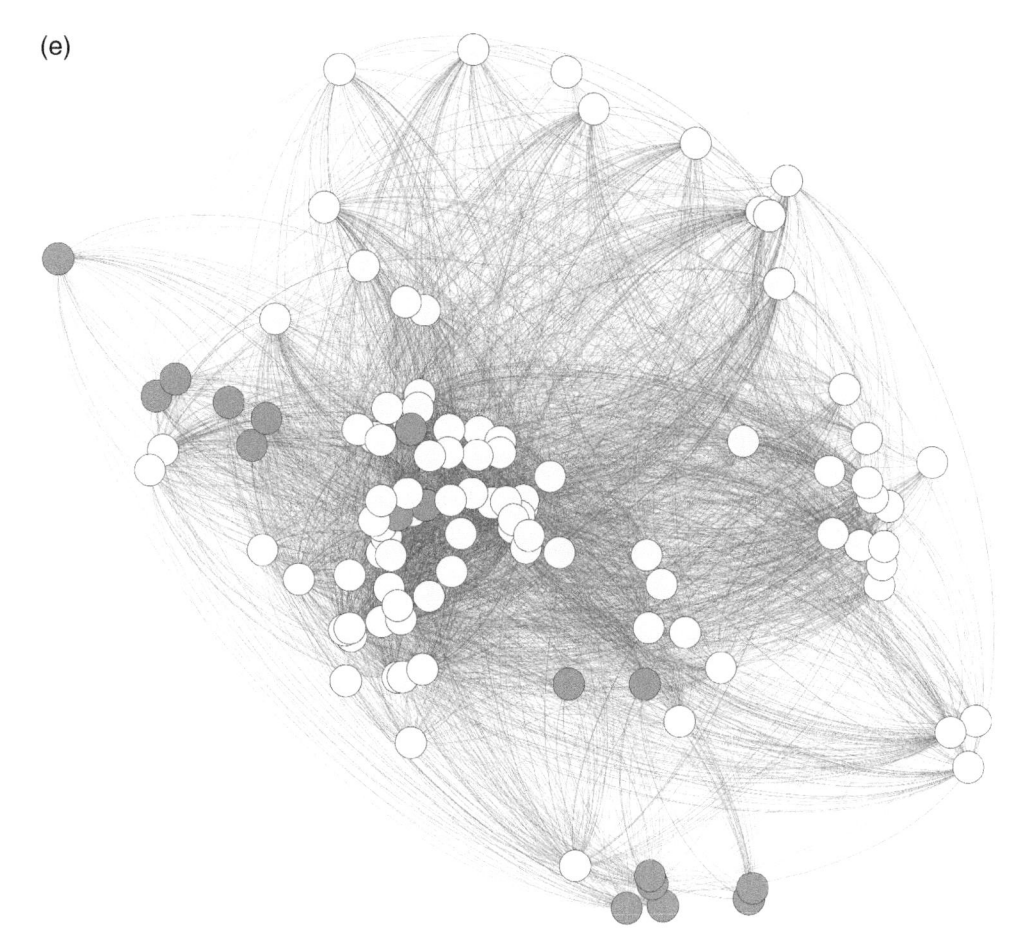

Figure 5.6e SNA visualisation of the sites clustered according to similar writing styles, 600–550 BC. Nodes are placed according to their approximate geographic location in the Aegean, clustered under 1.5 modularity parameter. This image is available in a larger format online at www.cambridge.org/loy.

of the clusters in the seventh century is quite consistent, with one group covering Crete and the Peloponnese, and two other groups moving across from central and western Greece via the Cyclades to Ionia. Things change in period three, as there are two main groups (the Peloponnese and central Greece vs Saronic Gulf, islands and Ionia), with a third much smaller group touching parts of Crete and also sites elsewhere. Crete will be dealt with separately, as this is quite a different case. But for the other parts of the Aegean, this distribution does map (albeit loosely) onto the division of writing-set regions demarcated by Adolf Kirchhoff. The 'red' alphabets of the Peloponnese and central Greece map to one cluster, while the 'blue' alphabets of the Saronic Gulf, islands and Ionia are another cluster.

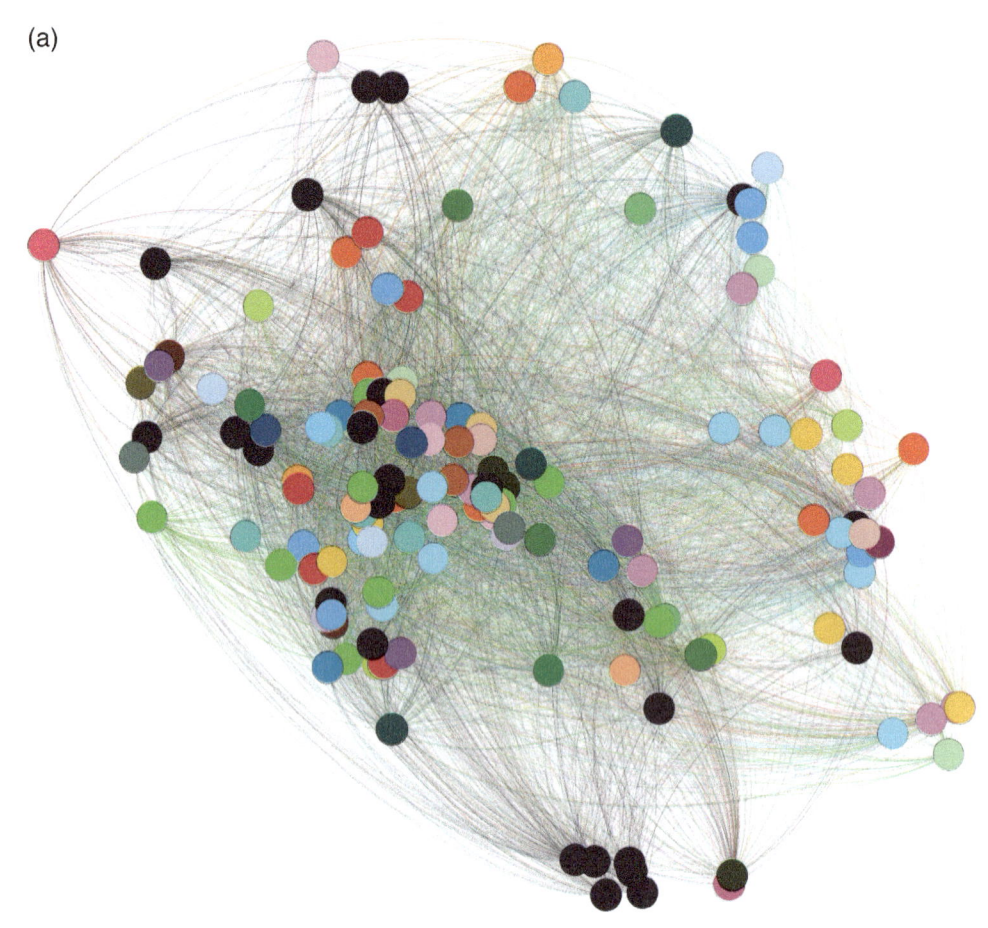

Figure 5.7a SNA visualisation of the sites clustered according to similar writing styles, 550–500 BC. Nodes are placed according to their approximate geographic location in the Aegean, clustered under 0.5 modularity parameter;.

Nevertheless, by period four the clusters identified are too many, too complex, and too overlapping in their geography to look anything like the Kirchhoff pattern. The Saronic Gulf and Peloponnese in particular contain a subset of sites within all cluster networks, such that it is too difficult to call this a unified locale in terms of the writing sets used. But, on the other hand, it is notable that the Kirchhoff pattern – a pattern 'eyeballed in' nearly 150 years ago on the basis of some quite low-grade data – can be recreated using here a more scientific methodology.

There are two principal implications on recreating the Kirchhoff pattern. First, there is an issue about chronology. The Kirchhoff pattern can only be

(b)

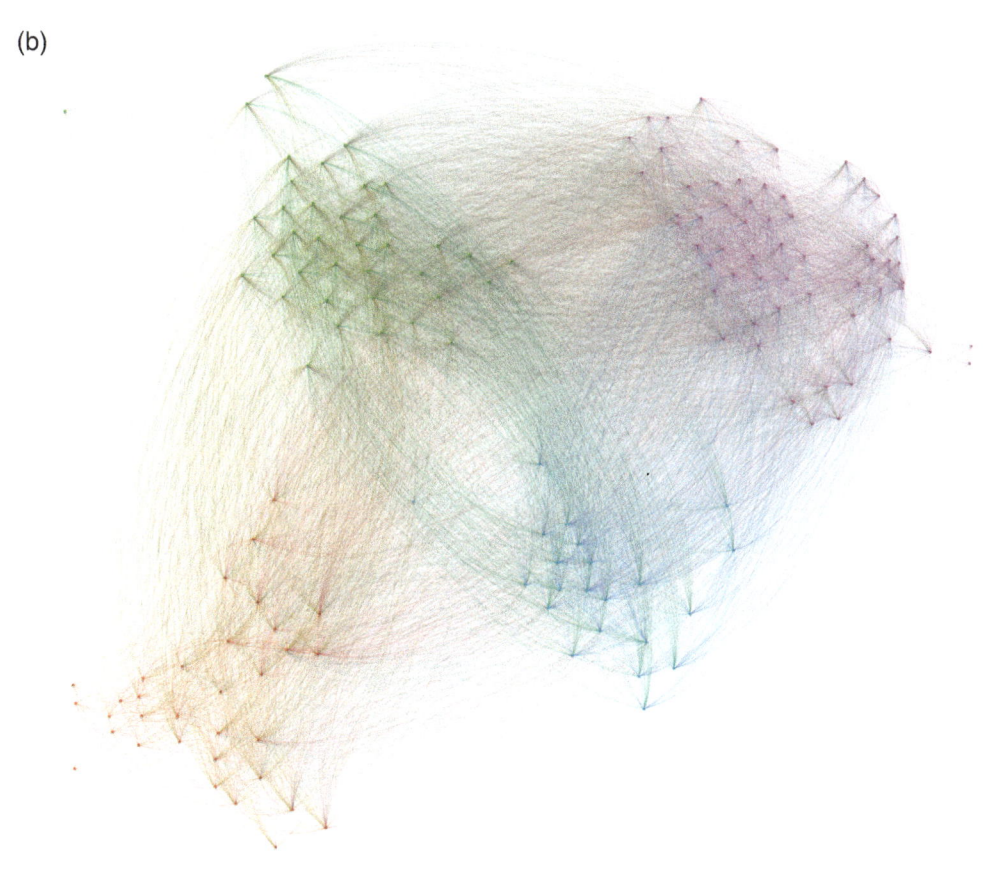

Figure 5.7b SNA visualisation of the sites clustered according to similar writing styles, 550–500 BC. Nodes are distributed randomly in abstract space, clustered under 1.0 modularity parameter.

recreated reliably in one of the four periods investigated, that is, at the start of the sixth century BC. As Kirchhoff had it, his distribution of alphabet types was a model that could be applied to the Archaic period in its entirety. That is clearly not the case here, and at best his model seems to be perfectly appropriate only (at most) for a fifty-year time slice. A lot of things have moved on since Kirchhoff, and it should be absolutely no surprise that a single model for the whole of the Archaic period is quite inadequate: but this point does serve to remind that things were changing *so quickly* within the Archaic period, and that any sort of explanatory model becomes inadequate *so quickly*. The second implication, though, is more methodologically significant. The Kirchhoff pattern can only be recreated – even in one period – when applying the 1.0 resolution modularity analysis. What precisely does this mean for our understanding of the data? The 1.0 setting

(c)

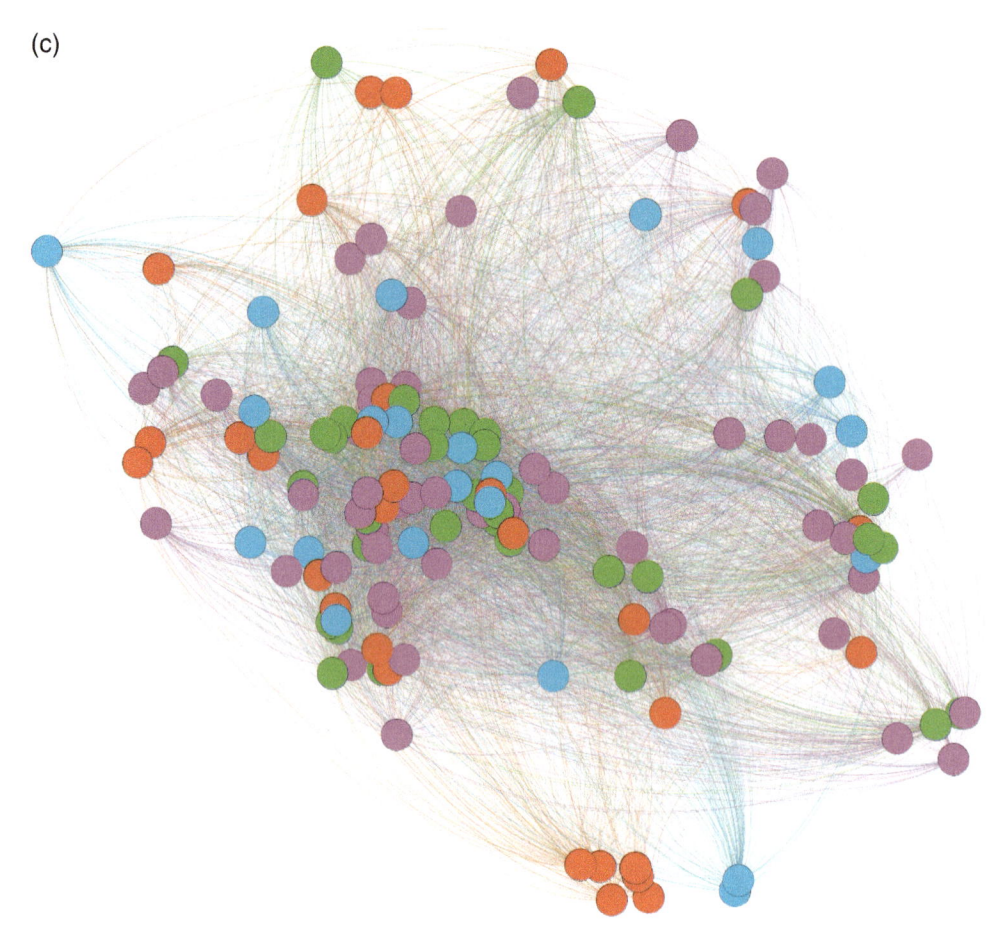

Figure 5.7c SNA visualisation of the sites clustered according to similar writing styles, 550–500 BC. Nodes are placed according to their approximate geographic location in the Aegean, clustered under 1.0 modularity parameter.

assumes that the dataset is fairly balanced, complete and representative: 0.5 models for a scenario where the dataset is fairly incomplete, and the algorithm must compensate by forcing more connections between sites when there are weaker links in the data; and 1.5 suggests that even though the data is complete, divisions between clusters of sites are not in fact that meaningful unless there are many similarities between sites. So by saying that it is significant to identify Kirchhoff's pattern in using only one of these resolution settings, we are also making a statement about the data itself: that the dataset is complete enough and representative enough to find patterns, and that those patterns one can see in the data are themselves

(d)

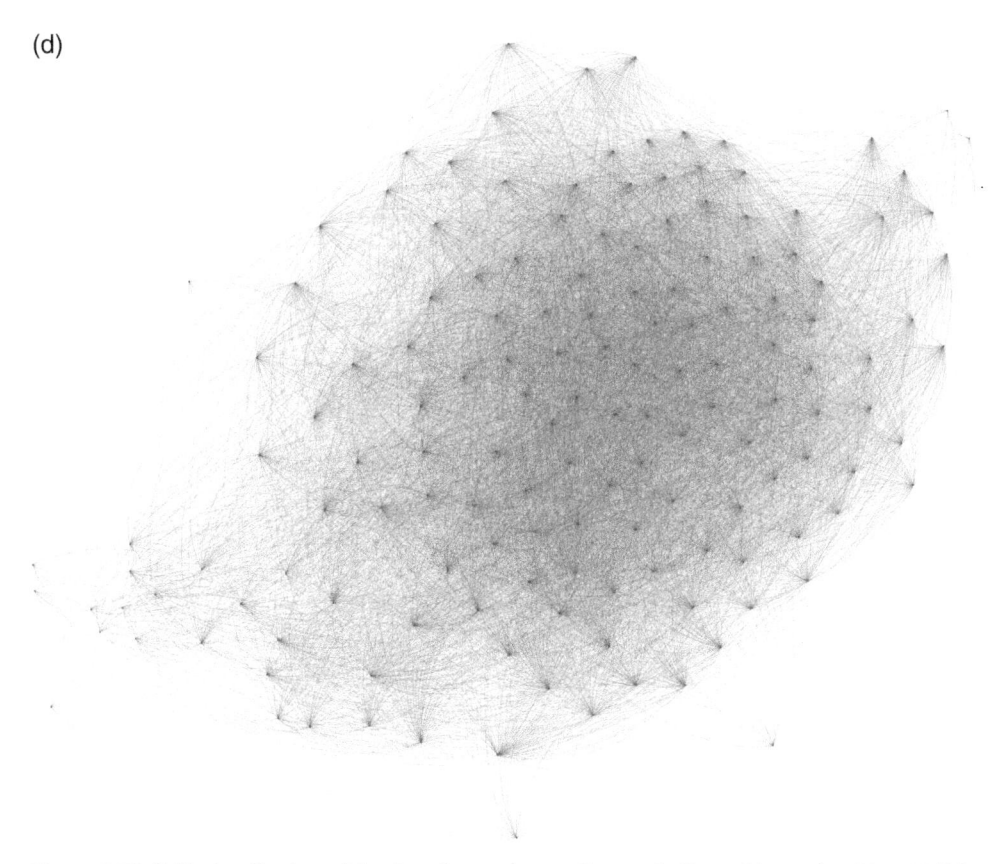

Figure 5.7d SNA visualisation of the sites clustered according to similar writing styles, 550–500 BC. Nodes are distributed randomly in abstract space, clustered under 1.5 modularity parameter.

both statistically and historically meaningful.[15] These are big statements, and indeed they are notions that many ancient historians would argue against qualitatively: thus, it is necessary here not to jump too quickly towards pattern identified quantitatively, as it also might assume fallacies that can be easily contested about the data.

That the situation becomes more complex in the space of 200 years can be taken quite patently from the quantity of data that is available from each period. In every fifty-year block, both the number of sites for which writing is found and the number of co-occurring lettersets increases by a substantial degree, and therefore there is no surprise that the patterns of site clusters change so drastically. In period one (700–650 BC), the

---

[15] While the first issue is one of methodology, the second is more relevant to the notion of identity and of demarcating communities or groups of similar individuals. It is not necessary to repeat here the complexity of this second issue, and on where to draw the boundaries around similar groups on the basis of some shared characteristics or expression.

(e)

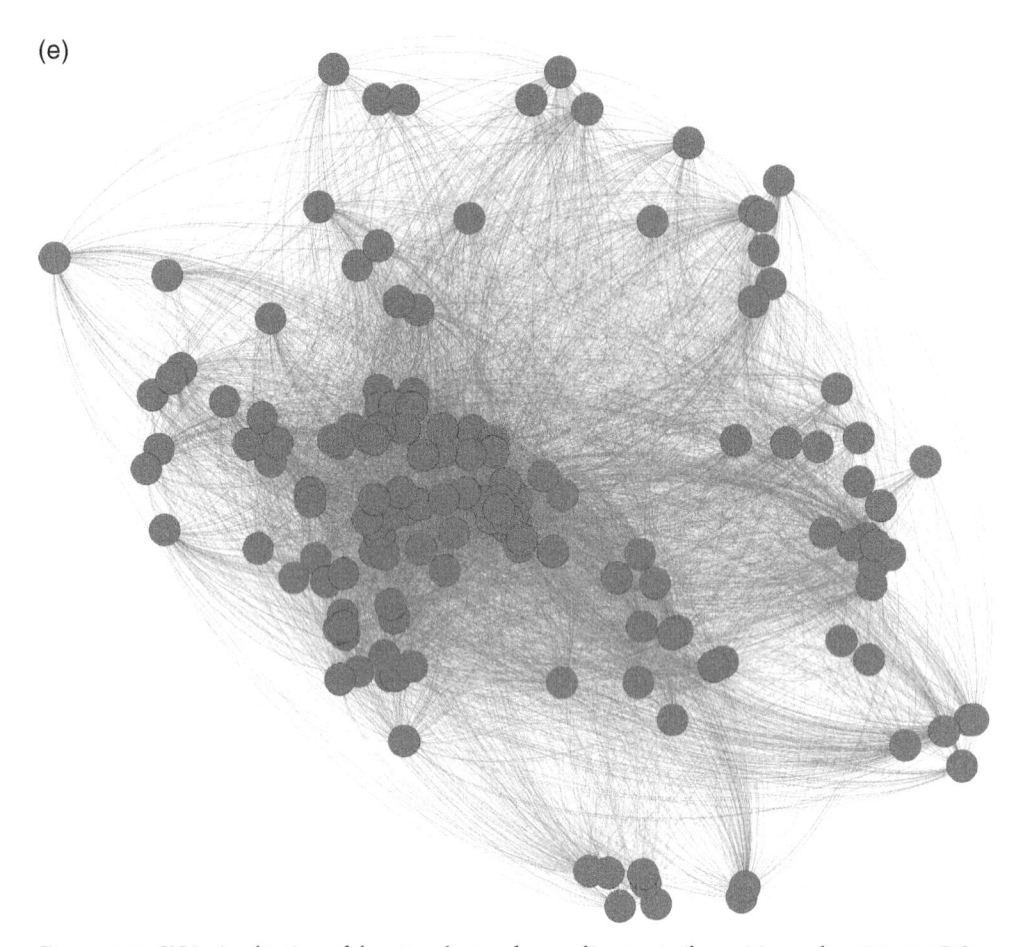

Figure 5.7e SNA visualisation of the sites clustered according to similar writing styles, 550–500 BC. Nodes are placed according to their approximate geographic location in the Aegean, clustered under 1.5 modularity parameter.

dataset comprises only 31 sites and 137 co-occurring letter shapes, while already by period two (650–600 BC) these numbers have grown to 48 sites and 242 co-occurring lettersets. For period three (600–550 BC) there are 111 sites with 555 co-occurring lettersets, and for period four (550–500 BC) 151 sites with 744 lettersets. As both the number of sites and the number of lettersets grows by five times between the start and end of the Archaic period, it is no surprise that in using the same algorithms, different sorts of patterns will emerge.

But there *are* sites that, regardless of period, regardless of the size of the dataset, and regardless of the algorithm used, tend to look different to their geographic neighbours. Notably, right from the start of the seventh

Figure 5.8 Sanctuary of Apollo at Delphi, view from the theatre looking down the mountain. Photograph by author.

century BC, Delos, Delphi and Olympia appear in different clusters to their neighbours (in 1.0 and 0.5 resolution analysis). In period one, for example, Delphi is in different clusters to neighbours at Thebes and Larisa; in period two, Olympia is in different clusters to neighbours of the northern Peloponnese at Corinth and Perachora; and Delos, although in some periods in the same cluster as both Paros and Naxos, for others is quite distinct from its neighbouring islands.

Quite obviously the thing that these sites have in common with one another is that they are sanctuaries, that is, sites receiving a high volume of traffic of both local and non-local visitors (Fig. 5.8). It has already been mentioned that among the transformations that took place in the Aegean in the Archaic period, there was an increase in the use of pan-hellenic sanctuaries.[16] Owing to the increased use of these spaces, more people

---

[16] There is a problem with the notion of pan-hellenic space, as a concept for which there is relatively little direct evidence for collective pan-hellenic identities in the Archaic period, and to talk about pan-hellenism in the Archaic period might actually be a back projection, *cf.* Spawforth and Walker 1985: 81–2; Said 1990; Hall 2002, 131, 2007: 272–4; Romeo 2002: 21, 31, 24–5; Mitchell 2007. On participating in notions of pan-hellenism consciously vs consciously, see Nagy 1979: 7. Nevertheless, there is sufficient evidence for an increase in the number of Greeks *gathering* at these sorts of places from 700 BC

were passing through;[17] and, as became clear in the discussion on identity, when there are more people from different places in a space, there might be more motivation to show off one's own identity (*cf.* Raschke 1988; Morgan 1990; Eder 2001; Kyrieleis 2006; Nielsen 2007; Smith 2007). How does one do that through writing? The most obvious way is to say, using words, where one is from: and, at Delphi for instance, the dedicatees of various monuments during the course of the sixth century identified themselves as Knidian (*FD* III I 289), Corinthian (INSC 178), Tyrrhenian (INSC 179), Parian (INSC 1079) and Spartan (INSC 1287). But it was not simply enough to *say* where one came from: in doing so, the people who put up these inscriptions wrote in lettersets uncharacteristic of Phokis but characteristic of the place from which they came. Whoever inscribed these dedications seems to have reproduced the letter forms associated with the place of origin of the dedicatee, and they did not assimilate these dedications to local Phokaian writing tradition. In fact, the letter forms were used help to communicate a self-identity as much as the words inscribed.

And, if one adopts the hypothesis that it is not sanctuaries *per se* that are special but merely spaces at which lots of people gather, we might look, too, at ports and harbours (Horden and Purcell 2000: 391–5; Feuser 2009: 127–8; McClain and Rauh 2011: 148). It was noted already in Chapter 4 that Rhodes played a role in connecting east and west, and that the island was an important stepping-stone for various commodities and people moving in, out, and around the Aegean. As one might expect, therefore, we find in the textual record strong statements of local identity made at sites on Rhodes, at places that would have experienced high volumes of non-local traffic. Some of those producing writing found on Rhodes explicitly say that they are local, and two in particular name themselves as natives of Ialysos (INSC 1041, INSC 1042). But non-locals also passed through and left their mark at these sites: the inscriptions from the sites on Rhodes contain a greater number of letter forms used to express the same sound values as those of any other single site across the rest of the Aegean. At the end of the sixth century BC, both <Ŧ> and <Χϟ> appear for /ks/; <Χ>, <Υ> and <+> for /kh/ (while <Υ> can also mean /ps/ on Rhodes); and <H> and <Ɛ> are employed in almost equal proportion to signify both /h/ and /ɛ/. If one accepts, again, that those writing chose to write in a certain way to express a certain facet of their identity through leaving a symbol on the visible landscape that others could see and recognise, this is evidence that multiple identities were being communicated across the island.

[17] On the relationship between games in particular and the effect that they had on the changes in layout of sanctuaries, see Gardiner 1925; Drees 1968; Mallwitz 1972; and Holmberg 1979. See Scott 2010: 8–10 and 260–5 for activity at Delphi and Olympia specifically.

The implication here is twofold. First, Greeks had knowledge of various different lettersets – perhaps even of *all* the various shapes for each different sound value – and that those producing writing *consciously* chose which set of letters they would use for a given piece of writing (*cf.* Luraghi 2010). This was the mechanism that allowed individuals not only to select which letterset would be most appropriate for conveying the identity that they intended, but also for ensuring that the writing they produced could be meaningfully understood by others. Second, regional identities were so embedded within the world of Archaic Greece that writing could be deployed as an effective tool in flagging up where one was from. For example, a Phokaian at Delphi, rather than just perceiving non-local writing as some unintelligible array of signs, would recognise Corinthian writing as having been written by someone who had come from Corinth. Writing would become an important tool therefore, not only in creating but also in *communicating* regional identities. The specific symbols used to represent certain sound values were variant according to different parts of Greece, and this level of variation was so well known that certain symbols recognisably originated from certain places; seeing these symbols would communicate an identity of place by association.[18] For the sanctuaries themselves, and harbours and ports also, in the Archaic period were specific contexts within which issues of writing and identity played out differently than they did elsewhere.

Explaining Regional Variations

So certain types of sites behaved differently when it comes to those producing writing wanting to express local identities in more visible and more direct ways to areas of high traffic; but that still does not explain the regional patterns – or lack thereof.

The case of the Ionian cities provides an example for where an entire region displays little geographic patterning in the choice of letter forms. Consistently across all time periods, the inscriptions from the sites within Ionia are characterised by different lettersets. The output of period four

---

[18] Of course, some (more mobile) Greeks would have seen more regularly different types of 'local' writing styles than others: those who participated within activities at sanctuaries like Delphi where many different Greeks gathered might have been more plugged in to these issues of regional identity. However, given that this is a broad-level analysis, this multi-scalar differentiation is not discussed in detail here. In any case, this is not necessarily a comment on the social distribution of *literacy;* but it suggests that different parts of society were more or less engaged at various times with using writing to express their identity.

(550–500 BC) makes this point most clearly. In Kirchhoff's model, we would expect all Ionian states to use the 'blue' alphabets, employing, as indicated by Jeffery, a range of regional forms such as <Ω> for /o:/, <H> for /e:/ and additional letter forms <Ŧ>, <X> and <Y>. But, in actual fact, we actually see three main clusters of sites. The first includes Didyma, Ephesos, Erythrai, Mykale and Priene; the second includes Klazomenai, Kolophon, Melie and Miletos; and the third includes Myous and Samos. The first of these uses only <X> for /kh/, while the second uses a mixture of <X>, <+> and <Y>, and the third <X> and <+>; the first uses <ΕΙ> for /ei/, the second <ΕΙ> and <Ε> and the third <Ε>; for /o:/ the <Ω>, the second uses both <Ω> and <O>, but the third only uses <O>; and concerning the aspirate the first group uses various <H> and <Ө>, the second only <H>, but the third <H> and <□>. Quite clearly even though we might usually think of this area as a cohesive 'region' with all sorts of similarities between sites, difference is also important here. If one accepts the hypothesis proposed above – that Greeks recognised different lettersets but chose which ones to use for showing off certain identities or affiliations – then that would imply that for sites in Ionia, the lower order configuration of the community (the site, the city, the settlement) was more important as far as this dataset is concerned than the region. This issue is of crucial importance when it comes to understanding the history of Archaic Greece more broadly, and the point will be discussed in greater detail in Chapter 6.

Some of the regional patterns identified by the cluster algorithm are an artefact of the quality of the dataset used, namely at Attica and on Crete. In Attica, this is to do with the number of sites modelled: the dots on the map here do not represent separate cities (as they do in Ionia) but demes of the *same city,* and for the most part, the same set of letters is used at all the different sites: <Ϻ> for /s/, <Ε> for /ɛ:/ and <O> for /o:/. The main variation occurs with the writing of /h/ (<H> at Ikarion in *IG* I³ 1015, and Paiania in *IG* I³ 1266 but <Ө> at Aigilia, *IG* I³ 972, 1242) and /kh/ (<+> at Aigilia in *IG* I³ 1241 and 1242, Paiania in *IG* I³ 1267 and Thorikos in *IG* I³ 1271; <X> at Aigilia in *IG* I³ 972 and 1243 and Oropos in *IG* I³ 1475). But by having so many sites – and, particularly in the case of the 0.5 resolution modularity analysis where the main *desideratum* is to identify even slight difference – these small variations seem to be much more significant in the clusters identified,[19] and, while not perhaps completely historically significant, the algorithm which looks across all of the Aegean in the same way shows

[19] One could argue the opposite: that perhaps this level of regional variation was in fact normal in the sixth century BC, and similar patterns of diversity elsewhere are somewhat masked by the paucity of data available from other parts of the Greek world

a different sort of output for Attica where the data are more numerous than everywhere else. That is to say, a strong case can be made for the sites of Attica acting as a 'region', and where one looks at the data on a case-by-case basis, as here, there are many more similarities than differences. It just so happens that the method used identifies just as strongly the differences as the similarities: and this somewhat masks the picture of the writing of Attica expressing a strong regional-level pattern. So this is a pattern consequent on having more data than the average site; the converse, however, is true of Crete.

To put it another way: one might be surprised at how Crete appears to be a very homogeneous cluster of sites during some periods, and a mix of different site clusters in others. Eight sites are included in the analysis for Crete at the end of the sixth century: Arkades, Axos, Eleutherna, Eltynia, Gortyn, Knossos, Praisos and Setaia. Of these, there are some very strong similarities between all sites that make this group a sensible cluster against other parts of the Aegean, most notably for the use of <M> for /s/ (at all but Knossos, where no /s/ is recorded), <ϟ> for /i/ (for all sites except Eleutherna, where <I> is also attested), <ʀϟ> for /ei/ and <O> for /o:/. These similarities clearly account for the clusters that spread across the whole island, as these sites are using lettersets that are very rarely used elsewhere in the Aegean, and so rightly the sites of Crete belong together as a cluster. But there are also differences too: Setaia uses <□M> for /ks/, while Praisos uses <Ŧ> and Axos, Eleutherna, Eltynia and Gortyn use <KM>; Eleutherna uses <□>, <B> and <H> for /ɛ:/, Axos uses <ʀ> and <H>, Gortyn only <ʀ> and Eltynia only <B>. As there are so few sites available for this analysis on the island and given that there are 'blanks' where certain letters are not represented in any form (aspirates, only one /kh/, only one /ps/, very few long vowels and no instances of the diphthong /ou/) even slight differences such as these might become exaggerated in the cluster analysis. This is certainly the case for the 0.5 resolution modularity analysis, and even in the 1.0 modularity analysis in period four (550–500 BC); Praisos and Setaia seem to be doing something different to their neighbours. The algorithm weights difference for each letterset the same, so here a more contextual approach would be useful in evaluating the data too: is a 'cluster' more historically meaningful if it brings together all of those sites using <M> for /s/ and <ϟ> for /i/, or are those additional letters more important in drawing culturally meaningful groups? Clearly, this is a subjective question that the automation of the algorithm masks over; and it is in fact the paucity of data points and letters available for analysis that might bring out surprising patterns.

At least for the seventh century BC, the islands behave in this analysis as one might expect on looking at the patterns of Kirchhoff and Jeffery. In period one, there is some division between the islands of the north Cyclades – Delos, Naxos, Paros – and those towards the south – Thera and Anafi. The writing on these islands to the south contain letter sets that more usually appear on Crete than in the north Cyclades or on either mainland, notably <ϟ> for /i/ and <M> for /s/. Such is enough difference already in period one to mark this set of islands out as part of a cluster separate from other sites of the Cyclades. In period two, there is similarity between the islands of the Cyclades and parts of the Saronic Gulf and Ionia: the most common lettersets between this group of sites relates to the way that these places deal with vowels, and particularly long vowels, containing letters that express the sound /ɛː/ (most usually <В> or <H>) or /oː/ (most usually <Ω>). Certainly in the case of the 1.0 resolution analysis, these lettersets have the greatest effect in shaping the clusters: sites that write these sounds in different ways (or do not express these sounds in writing) are necessarily part of different clusters. But in the sixth century BC the complexity of the clustering of sites means that it is very difficult indeed to identify any meaningful groups across or between the islands. This is apparent even when looking at the 1.0 resolution modularity analysis, but this is even more clear with the 0.5 resolution algorithm. The number of clusters that are created towards the end of the sixth century BC is significantly large, and this seems to imply that there are few meaningful geographic groups that could be drawn in this period.

A picture like this has two implications, one historical and one methodological; and we must decide which one (or both) to accept (or reject). The first, historical, implication is that if these groups have been identified in a methodologically sound way, the region at the end of the sixth century becomes less important and the site becomes more important. So much has already been suggested, that the sorts of regional boundaries that someone like Kirchhoff was drawing might only be applicable for certain time slices within the Archaic period; and, in the case of places like the sanctuaries discussed, it is conceivable that sites were doing something completely different to other sites around them. But the alternative is that this is down to the algorithm. By lowering the resolution in the modularity analysis, one is encouraging the computer to look for differences between sites – and suggesting that such differences might be meaningful. Clearly the amount of variation necessary to demarcate clusters at the start of the seventh century is very different to the amount of variation required at the end of the sixth century: this implies, at least, that the Archaic period cannot be viewed as a homogenous time period, and that the story of these two centuries is very different in terms of data, in terms of writing distribution, and in terms of the complexity and variation of different identities expressed through the written form. The same algorithm might not actually be that usefully applied to different time slides of the Archaic period. It might in fact be more productive not to look only at this data across a large period – but to adopt in addition a more contextual approach.

Differences Between Writing Contexts

In some ways, the neat Aegean-level framework that has been presented conceals the nature of the problem: context. On a top-down view of the data, striking contrasts between the alphabets of proximate geographic areas are distinctly more in evidence in the second half of the sixth century. For this period, and as discussed, the inclusion of additional letters within various inscriptions and the presence/absence and shape of the aspirate seem to play the greatest part in influencing (the lack of) regional patterning. But context is just as important: this is not a homogeneous dataset, and the differences in who is dedicating what, where, to be read by whom, and in the types of materials used for writing and the typology of inscriptions are all factors that are at play.

Period four (550–500 BC) exhibits the most variation, and those differences might usefully be explored further by considering the different conditions under which writing was produced. Each 'dot' on the map of the Aegean in each period represents writing created in very different ways, different lengths of texts and different quantities of material available. Thus, a more contextual view of the inscriptions themselves must also be given, and we need some means of classifying the data, even coarsely, if we want to make any sort of meaningful comparisons.

Table 5.4 *Number of inscriptions in period four (550–500 BC) by finds context category. Bin one: small personal objects. Bin two: dedications. Bin three: short texts giving information intended to be read (e.g. boundary stones,* stelai*). Bin four: longer texts for record (e.g. building records). Bin five: public law codes.*

	Bin one	Bin two	Bin three	Bin four	Bin five
Period four (550–500 BC)	382	376	57	40	46

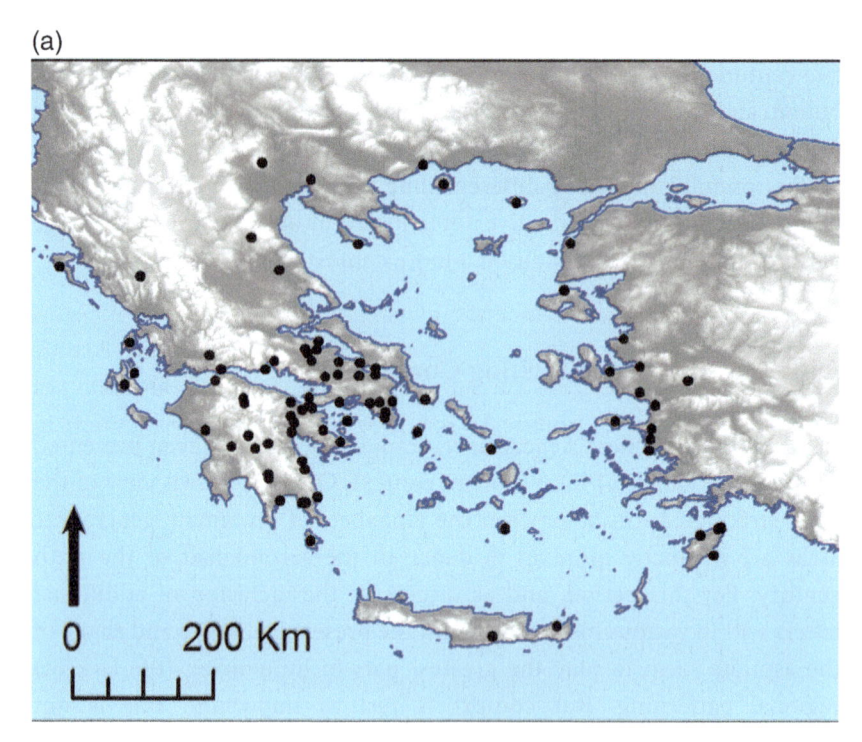

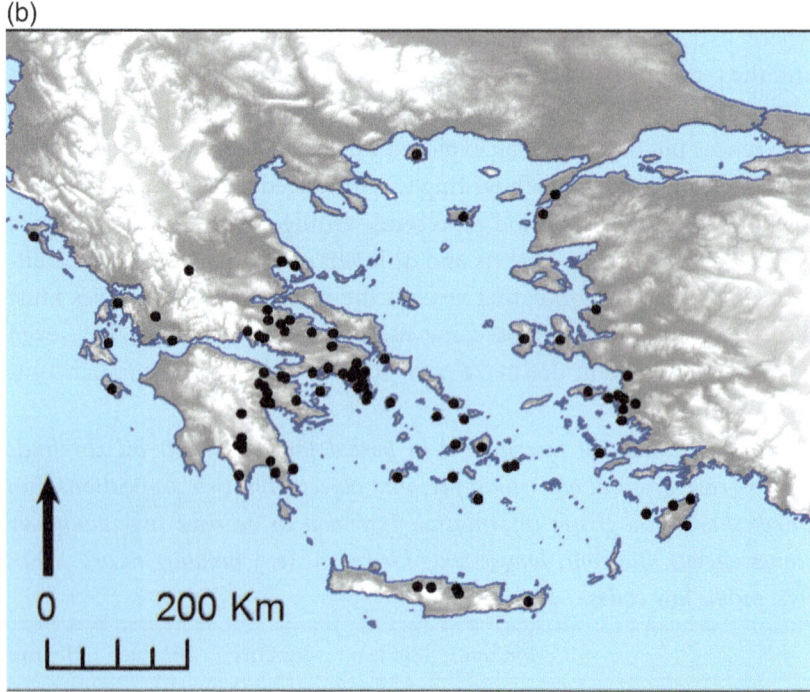

Figure 5.9 Sites at which writing was found 550–500 BC by context category: a) bin one, small personal objects; b) bin two, dedications; c) bin three, short texts giving information intended to be read (e.g. boundary stones, *stelai*); d) bin four, longer texts for record (e.g. building records); e) bin five, public law codes.

(c)

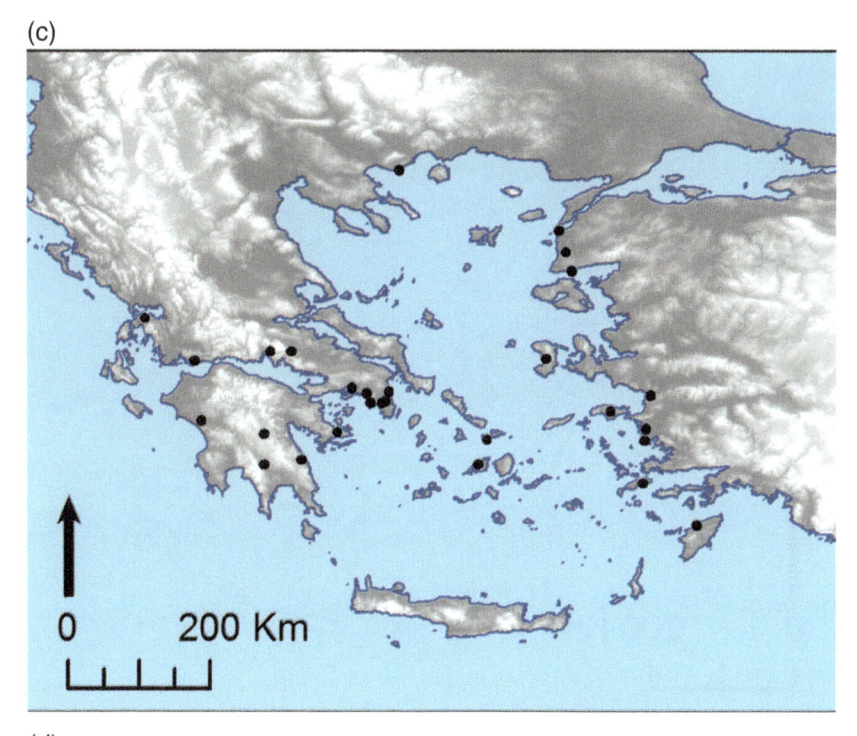

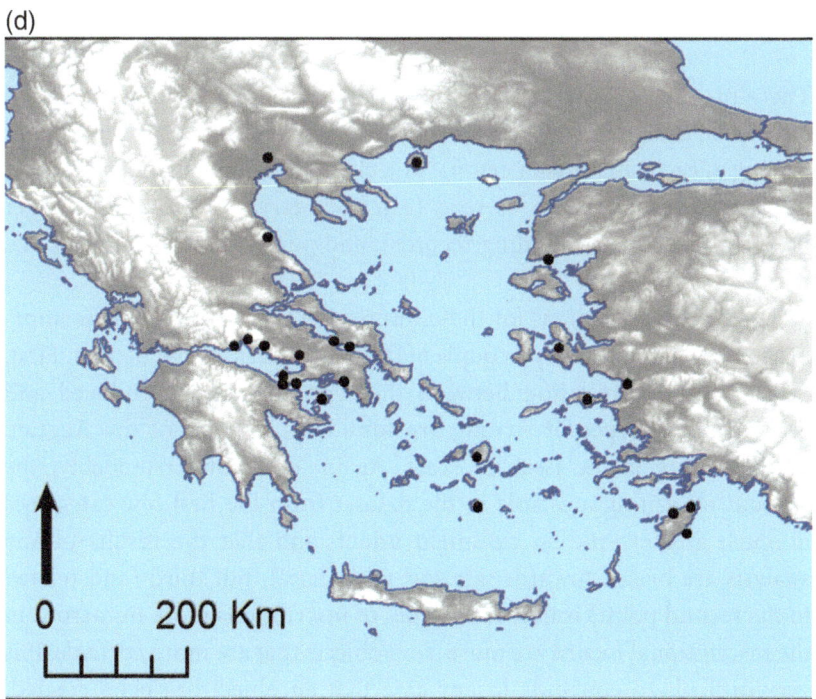

(d)

Figure 5.9 (cont.)

(e)

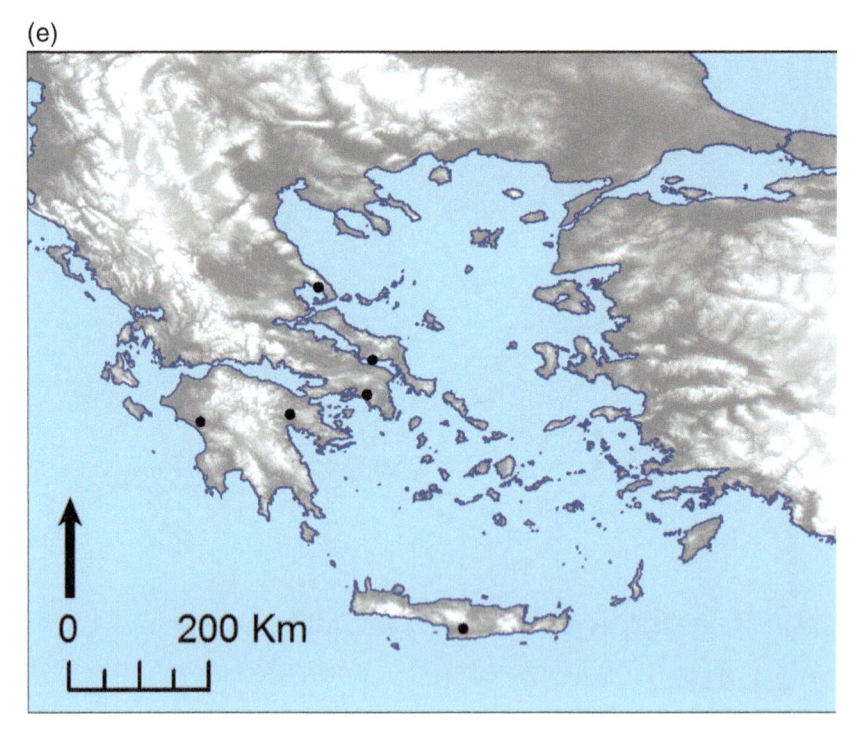

Figure 5.9 (cont.)

Therefore, purely as a heuristic, each of the inscriptions from this period have been assigned to one of five categories descriptive of the type of writing at each site: small personal objects; dedications; short texts giving information intended to be read (e.g. boundary stones, *stelai*); longer texts for record (e.g. building records); and public law codes (Table 5.4, Fig. 5.9).

The distribution maps for these inscription types add little new information but help to clarify a couple of factors concerning the dataset. First, there is little correlation between the type of writing produced and geography: all types of writing are found in all parts of the Aegean. Second, there is the issue of scale. Again, quite understandably, the amount of writing available in the dataset from the first few categories is much greater, and so we might understand that the results of any analysis are biased towards this sort of material. But third (and related to the second point) is that those types of inscriptions more numerous in the inscriptional record are more from objects that are more *portable*. It is very difficult to conclude in any case that an object has been created, written on and dedicated all in the same place – nor can we so easily say that the place where an inscribed object has been found and recorded is the place where that object was originally meant to have been left in antiquity. These categories are very loosely defined: they are not meant to overly inform conclusions; they merely help to sort the data and make sense of the dataset.

Changing the scale of analysis to a case study of two roughly contemporaneous *corpora* suggests that the letterset chosen may have indeed depended on the context of the writing. Inscriptions from both Corinth and from Gortyn are analysed here;[20] both are sites that appear as single dots on the distribution map, but the writing from these two places was created in two very different contexts.

The writing from Corinth comes from a set of early sixth-century *pinakes dipinti* (painted clay votives) which were dedicated on the Acrocorinth to the god Poseidon (*IG* IV 269–94) and discovered in the late nineteenth century in a single-sealed (refuse?) context (Rayet 1880; Wachter 2001: 275–7). Given the nature of this context, it is likely that these *pinakes* were all disposed of during the same event – and there is, in a sense, some possibility that they could have been *created* within a relatively short time span of one another. This set of objects gives us the chance to evaluate, therefore, how much variation there might have been at the same time, in the same place, between a set of objects written on by different people: and, indeed, the inscriptions of the *pinakes* suggested that those inscribing these objects had a certain degree of freedom in how they wrote. In particular, those who wrote on these *pinakes* chose a range of options for the rendering of the sound /ɛi/ in the name 'Poseidon', and within this corpuscle one finds five different letters or lettersets used to express this same sound value:[21] <Β>, <Ε>, <ΒΕ>, <ΕΕ> and <Ε>.

How can we explain the variation in writing practice between all of these objects? As stated above, this is unlikely to be an issue of space or one of chronology, given that all objects were disposed of together in one place. We are left, therefore, with two options. First, there is possibility that these pieces of writing were written by individuals who were not local to Corinth: <Β> or <ΒΕ> or <Ε> might have been these individuals' preferred way of writing the sound /ɛi/ at the place where they came from, and they brought

---

[20] These two sites are chosen because they have at them writing created in two very different contexts for two very different intended audiences. The fact that they are from such different geographic worlds complicates the picture: one might argue for comparing, for example, Corinth with its neighbour Sikyon, *cf.* above where proximate sites of Attica and Ionia were compared. But the difference in writing *types* is not so great between these two sites, and their comparison would not so strongly illustrate the point being made here.

[21] See some discussion by Amyx 1988 and Wachter 2001: 261, 273.

this writing practice with them to Corinth. The notion of itinerant crafts-people and itinerant writers is not new, but the implication here is pertinent to the current discussion. The lettersets chosen relied to a greater extent on those *producing* the writing, rather than those *reading* anything written: on the one hand, those writing in a way considered 'non-local' to Corinth may have accepted that it was more important for them to write in a way that was normal for them as the writer than to create writing understandable for those at this place who may not have been familiar with these different lettersets;[22] on the other hand, we might take the same assumption that Greeks were familiar with all types of writing from different possible lettersets, and that those reading something written in a non-local letterset would signal to them something about the geographic identity or political affiliation of the one who had created the writing. The second alternative is similar: that these inscriptions were made *not* by itinerant or non-local people, but by local people who were choosing to write in a way that was not characteristic of Corinth. That is, they had knowledge of all lettersets, including those not from Corinth, and they were free to *select* which set of letters they should use. Whose freedom was this exactly: a freedom exercised by those inscribing the objects (i.e. the artists, *cf.* Wachter 2001: 275–7), or by those who bought and used these products (i.e. the customers)? In some senses, it does not matter to the argument: the important thing is that there was choice by *someone* to commit to one form of alphabet rather than to another and, more crucially, that these people had the *agency* and the *freedom* to choose how to write. The knowledge of both those writing and those reading aside, what this case study demonstrates is that in certain contexts there was freedom to write in different ways.

On the one hand, this case study helps to support the position that the site is more important than the region: inscribed objects could be moved between places, and, even if created in a regional writing style in one place, they could be moved and deposited at a *site* further away (e.g. at a pan-hellenic sanctuary) that was in some way more meaningful to the object and to what was written on it. But on the other hand, this also muddies the waters: for the sake of this analysis, it has been assumed that objects have been found in places where they were intended to have been read – but this may not have been true. Must the whole of this analysis be disregarded as invalid, in that case? Not necessarily. As stated earlier, when the scale of the analysis becomes

---

[22] Of course, there is also possibility that this writing was produced not so that it could be read and understood by people at Corinth, but that dedications like these were meant to be read and understood only by the god.

much bigger, the precision of each individual data point becomes less important: to see the general patterns more clearly one must accept that the 'fuzziness' of the data is greater. So while the portability and specific object biographies of some of the inscriptions analysed within this dataset could be contested, this should not affect the *general shape* of the results generated, nor, more crucially, the thrust of the *story* that one can tell with that general picture, since it is beyond the scope of this study to examine in detail individual inscriptions.

So much for the first option – what happens in cases where there is *less* freedom for those creating writing? The *pinakes* can be usefully compared to a more 'formal' writing context, namely the early sixth-century Gortyn code from the steps of the temple of Apollo Pythios (Fig. 5.10).[23] This boustrophedon inscription, displayed in a prominent part of the city of Gortyn,[24] whose letters were likely picked out with red pigment for an even greater visibility, deals with fines and punishments, judicial procedures and laws containing officials and family property. Even if it was not displayed to be understood (i.e. even if there was not a widespread literacy

Figure 5.10 Slabs of the law code, Gortyn. Photograph by author.

---

[23] On recent finds of archaic Cretan inscriptions more generally, see Tsipopoulou 2005, Haggis et al. 2007 and Kritzas 2010. On the public and monumental nature of Cretan inscriptions, see Raubitschek 1972 and Perlman 2004.
[24] Gagarin and Perlman 2016: 265 remark that the position of the law code on the walls of the temple indicate that this was done 'to invoke the support of the god for this legislation'.

that everyone within the local community could read precisely what had been written), it was made to be seen. Within the text of this inscription, there is a completely consistent mapping between sounds and letter shapes for all of the letters sampled: <ϟ> for all instances of /i/, <KM> for all instance of /ks/, <M> for all instances of /s/, <B> for all instances of /ɛː/ <Rϟ> for all instances of /εi/ and <O> for all instances of /oː/. The lack of variation in letter shapes used within the law code is striking, particularly for a document that contains over 200 lines of full and partial length text, along with shorter fragments.

Perhaps this lack of variation should not be so surprising: the Gortyn lawcode is a *single document*, and in some senses it would make no sense to have internal variation within the text. Conversely, we can also use this case study to say something about those writing and reading texts like these. If we assume a widespread literacy among the local population, we are again left with the alternative that those writing and reading had knowledge of just one letterset or of all lettersets. If their knowledge was limited, then this reaffirms our idea that this is an avowedly local inscription, written by local people for local people, giving locally pertinent instructions. If they had knowledge of all lettersets, this is also important: those writing consciously *chose* a letterset that was relevant to the local population (i.e. it was a letterset entangled with their local political affiliation), to affirm the idea that this text was important to the local community. It would also signal to those non-local people visiting the site of Gortyn the importance of such a text to the local community, as it was written in a way that was a little bit different to what that visitor would be used to. Whichever of these alternatives we choose, we have to accept that the context in which pieces of writing were produced had a direct effect upon the freedom with which those writing could choose to use various lettersets. There was less freedom in more 'formal' contexts such as these, but more freedom in the 'informal' contexts discussed. We might suggest, therefore, that even though in both cases writing in certain local styles was a marker of identity, the circumstances surrounding the practice of writing in each of these two scenarios was different – a difference that is not immediately visible when the data is analysed at the level of the site.

Writing, Identity, the Individual and the Community

This chapter began by raising the problem of reconstructing individual and collective identities. Writing was understood to help shed light on these issues, as the symbols created during writing are formed through the agency of those writing: letters drawn are linked to the practice of those who wrote. Different clustering techniques have been used to group variant lettersets together, revealing first a point about methodology and handling data like this and, second, a point about political affiliation and ancient identity.

Sorting 'types' of lettersets using computer models helps to solve one set of problems, but it creates new problems. In building on previous attempts to classify types of writing, computerised clustering techniques allow both for a larger and more comprehensive dataset to be handled, and also for the rules-based allocation of writing sets to different groups rather than the simple 'eyeballing in' of patterns. So while 'writing group' patterns drawn over the past 150 years by people like Kirchhoff and Jeffery are useful heuristics, new analysis reveals that generalisations like this do not tell the whole story. That story is a bit more complicated to untangle than might be first thought, however. Strong patterns emerge around the start of the sixth century BC on which 'regional groups' within the Aegean Basin can be easily distinguished; but before this date the dataset is too small and afterwards too complex to reliably identify the same sorts of groups using the same methodology. This also carries the implication that 'regional groups' considered by people like Kirchhoff and Jeffery have more time depth to them, and that regional patterns shifted at a fairly rapid rate throughout the Archaic period as identities were challenged, identities shifted and political affiliations were put on show in new arenas. Places like Attica and Corinthia express a strong regional pattern, whereas on Crete and in Ionia, areas that one might expect to look quite 'regional', there are more differences between sites than common features throughout the region. A further note on methodology is necessary: the sorts of patterns that we see are also dependent on the variables that we use for analysis. And so the broader implication here is that the overall story that we can tell depends on how *we* want to treat the data – one must guard here against creating self-fulfilling prophecies of analysis and interpretation. This notion should not be surprising for scholars of the ancient world who are so frequently confronted with partial and messy datasets: but the challenge is made explicit here.

Patterns about political affiliation have been noted too. The sites which appear as the most prominent 'nodes' of connection between different regional alphabet traditions are the pan-hellenic sanctuaries at Delphi, Delos and Olympia, the emporia on Rhodes and certain of the Cycladic islands. As is entirely evident from the data, these sites became progressively more prominent throughout the sixth century BC as spaces within which mobile individuals communicated their native identities through their own local scripts. This also suggests that in the sixth century Greeks who could read could commonly recognise a wide variety of lettersets and have knowledge of a variety of different alphabets. Therefore, the choice of lettersets which the scribes themselves made was something very conscious. Scribes chose to retain their home alphabets when they put up writing in non-local contexts, and they chose lettersets in order to signal where they had come from, or alternately to suppress their regional identity in favour of a state-level message. The variation in alphabetic symbols used between sites can therefore not be explained purely in terms of geographic position of these sites, but rather in terms of Greeks making choices to communicate individual identities.

Although this suggestion will not come as a surprise to scholars who have discussed individual instances of non-local alphabets in pan-hellenic sanctuaries, nevertheless the analysis here confirms the degree to which the practice was generalised. Observing pieces of writing inscribed in different alphabets from the same site, this phenomenon is by no means unusual. The rich diversity of local alphabetic traditions in use at non-local spaces indicates the importance to the scribe in the seventh and sixth centuries BC of selecting certain variant sets of letters for marking identity. Indeed, the importance of the relationship between the use of writing systems and expressions of identity for this period has been hitherto somewhat underestimated. The political networks with which states were involved in the Archaic period were clearly associated with different local and communal identities, and the way in which people chose to write demonstrates to us how people expressed these identities.

6 | Political Networks

State Alliance and Amphiktyonies

This chapter synthesises the results of the quantitative studies from the previous four chapters and situates them within a broader historical framework. The analyses conducted have demonstrated that the material record, if approached with the right tool kits, contains clear evidence that particular places within the Archaic Aegean were linked in networks. The nature of those networks differed according to context. It now remains to test this model against historical data, and against long-held assumptions about the role of politics in determining other forms of connection, and the nature of economic communication in the ancient world.

Summary of Networks Identified

The results of the marble study indicate that there existed in the sixth century an extensive network for the export of raw stone and worked sculpture. This connected all corners of the Aegean Basin overseas, and it depended on two things: a large labour force; and a pre-existing network for the transport of commodity goods (such as grain, oil and wine) on which the export of these prestige goods could piggy-back. The mobility simulation indicated that, even with the simplifications made and with the assumptions taken, the export of a single product connected various parts of the Aegean in a number of ways. Places that both produced and received marble were directly connected by a network of other clients and customers; furthermore, by virtue of the sailing routes in the Aegean, certain places – particularly those in the Saronic Gulf – were highly integrated into this network, even though they themselves were not directly involved in the actual production and consumption of marble statues. This case study also indicated that even where local resources existed, those who commissioned statues might still look elsewhere for their source marble: something about the quality or prestige of the product won out over pure utilitarian availability of resources and compels us to consider the agency of elite peer dedicators in our model of the ancient economy.

Turning to ceramics, the data supported the long-held claims not only that urban and sanctuary sites consumed different sorts of pottery (in both shape and ware) but also that individual sanctuaries 'specialised' in the types of pots consumed. Whether we think that enterprising salesmen sought out likely markets and persuaded suppliers to manufacture appropriately or that enterprising consumers sought out appropriate sources for the particular goods they wanted, we are dealing with a world in which knowledge of who was making what (and where) and who needed what for their particular activities was widely distributed. The change in the proportion of ware types at urban sites suggests that there was a widespread shift between the seventh and sixth centuries from the consumption of locally produced pottery to the importing of pottery from a greater number of networks, and this pattern is consistent across all parts of the Aegean basin.

The coin networks yielded two significant patterns. The first was a pattern of production, and the second was a pattern of the spread of technology. Aegina, Athens, Corinth, Miletos, Ephesos and Phokaia – the first states to mint coinage – were the 'pioneers' for minting in the Greek world, providing a template for communities which later minted their coins to the same weight standards. By contrast, Ionian cities ended up with seven different weight standards thanks to peer competition and a desire to stand out: this suggests that these communities learnt coinage technology directly from their Lydian neighbours rather than from one another. Second, data revealed that coinage technology did not just spread passively from this network of pioneers to new communities, but that the pattern was entangled with a pattern of pre-existing economic contacts. It is likely, therefore, that connections visible in the distribution of weight standards from the sixth century reveal economic networks already formed in the seventh. In fact, this coinage pattern can be explained with greater precision once it is put side-by-side with the ceramics pattern. The network of *amphora* distribution in both the seventh and sixth centuries was qualitatively very similar to the weight standard pattern. By the mid-seventh century, then, the entire Aegean was already united in one network, but, individually, each community had a limited number of direct contacts. Such a network was a prerequisite for the rapid spread of coinage in the sixth century.

The letter shape pattern has important implications for how we handle historical data. The methods used demonstrated how we can quite easily reconstruct 'eyeballed in' patterns using statistical models, provided that we assume the data we possess are perfectly representative of an original population. If we acknowledge, however, the patchiness of the data and subsequently we move to adjust or to buffer the data, different patterns emerge. In terms of the substantive patterns, the quality of the data are such that we cannot identify 'regional' groups in the seventh century which shared writing practices in the same way that we can for the sixth century. Important for the role in displaying political affiliation were changes in sixth-century writing practices, largely shifting through the increase of writing produced at sanctuaries and *emporia*. The communities of both Ionia and the Cyclades exhibited a great internal variety with respect to the letter shapes they chose; and those who produced writing in different places in Attica wrote in very similar ways.

As noted in the introduction of this book, patterns have been brought to light as a result of both lumping *and* splitting. Further discussion will be offered on lumping, but as far as splitting goes – this is a natural consequence of using a network analytical approach. Networks are non-specific and overlapping, and, as has become clear, one entity, one individual, one community can simultaneously be part of different networks operating at different levels. To take the example of the Nikandre *kore* once again, one can 'split' this single object to be analysed as a piece of freestanding sculpture and as an object with a piece of writing in an epichoric alphabet. As a piece of stone, this statue was moved along a very short-range shipping network from neighbouring Paros to Delos, a route that was part of a much broader Parian-marble shipping network serving the needs of pan-hellenic sanctuaries right across the Aegean. But as an inscribed object, the Nikandre *kore* was part of a network of Cycladic islands in close communication with neighbours in the Saronic Gulf and in Ionia. So at these different levels, this one object simultaneously connects the people who created it to local- and regional-level communities. The creation and dedication of this object brings together the people who demanded, created and consumed stone statues, but also the people who chose to write in a way that advertised the local Cycladic communities. The Nikandre *kore* is just one rather choice example – but for ceramics painted with the names of potters and painters, for other statues that advertised the name of a sculptor or a dedicator, for coins emblazoned with the name of their parent city, these objects (some portable, some not) all participated in these different levels of network and spoke to different types of communities. And 'splitting' the same object into two or more categories for analysis helps to uncover the shape of these networks.

What then do these patterns mean for the community, and for the shape of Archaic Greece as a whole? To answer this question it is useful to take a step back and to consider what the data actually show – and what they do not. The distributions investigated in the previous chapters lump together individual acts of some quite specific processes: the commissioning and putting up of a statue, the consuming of pottery, the deposit of coins and the writing of Greek. Analysis has revealed patterns caused by the repetition of these activities undertaken in certain ways; and it is this accumulation of individual activities in specific places that has been called a 'behavioural' community. In fact, it is these activities – and these alone – that define what has been understood by the community here, and no further (distorting) factors have been considered, nor any preconceptions about the nature of these groups or their members. The next step, as will be discussed, is to determine whether the communities identified through the material record map onto anything known from ancient sources. More specifically, do these communities map onto things that we might have names for: the *polis*, the *ethnos*, *komai*, or the pan-island *koina*? And are these units equally visible, in all places and at all times? More simply, if we have other (literary and historical) datasets that tell us that groups of Greeks did things in common with one another, are those the same groups that we can find through reconstructing communities of activity in the archaeological record?

The community, as a simple unit of behaviour, was adopted for its flexibility in that it can refer to different sized units and to different types of units.[1] Sometimes we might conclude that the place and the community intersect, when we see different types of networks intersecting at the same place. But at other times it is either a smaller or a larger unit that matters. Particularly at sanctuaries, as became apparent in the discussion on writing, context was more important, where, depending on the particular type of writing being produced, different sorts of communities were present at the same place. On the other hand, sometimes there were enough commonalities between places that a behavioural community might extend more broadly, that collections of places together resemble things that look like regions – albeit more in evidence in the (later) sixth century than in the seventh century.[2] The boundaries between these levels are fairly flexible, and this is why it is helpful to consider here activity rather than simply place or landscape. Particularly unhelpful is the view that geographical proximity

---

[1] *cf.* Morris 2005, esp. 102–4, on keeping the models critically focused on the data at hand, while also being broad-brush enough so as to make useful comparisons.

[2] Regional material culture *style* is a separate issue, of course: the 'Attic' regional style is different to the 'Corinthian' regional style, both widely attested, and both useful heuristics for the modern scholar in sorting data quickly into broadly defined bins – and into groups that are historically attested and that might have made sense to ancient people.

and division of territory according to geographical features heavily shaped all networking; the data very clearly indicate that this was not the case, and that networks very often cut across the Aegean Basin. Put simply: what story can be told when those networks themselves take centre stage?

In looking at the activities underpinned by these networks, it is useful to put emphasis not just on the activities conducted by communities but also on the range of *different activities* that took place. Here another theoretical framework is useful for the discussion, one that draws on the work of Thomas Hall and Christopher Chase-Dunn (1997).[3] These two prominent American anthropologists aimed in their landmark study to refine the model of world systems theory, the paradigm instituted by Immanuel Wallerstein in 1974, positioned to explain contemporary global inequalities within and between states.[4] Variously taken up and adapted by a number of archaeologists, world systems theory promotes that idea of how systems of polities operate together to contribute an overall network. Hall and Chase-Dunn took this notion further by positing that large systems of connected states interact in various ways, and that these interactions can be broken down into four separate categories: networks for the bulk transport of goods; networks of political and military association; networks associated with the movement of prestige or luxury goods; and networks that transmit cultural or technological knowledge. Quite clearly, 'networks' might comprise different sorts of interactions. These 'networks' are non-equivalent to one another, nor do they overlap uniformly. The network framework does illustrate, however, that although there might have existed between communities similar material flows and object distributions, the activities that defined those networks and caused their material patterning might have been quite different. It is possible, for example, that a particular place might be an important node in the overall web of communities even though it participated in only one network. It is similarly plausible that a community might 'join' the wider system through participation in one network (e.g. for commodity goods) and then progressively become integrated in other forms of network. It thus becomes evident that one cannot use one set of material data to discern every network which linked groups: the generic label 'network' becomes too broad a brush, and greater specificity becomes necessary.

---

[3] A concise summary of their argument as far as networks are concerned is given in Hall 2006.
[4] See recent world-systems work in Sherratt and Sherratt 1993 and Schortman and Urban 2011: 28–33, while Kardulias and Hall 2008 and Hall, Kardulias, and Chase-Dunn 2011 offer a more explicitly theoretical perspective. For recent critique, see Hall 1987; Hollis 2005; Hall 2012; and Carlson 2012.

Two Test Cases

Having established above what it is that we think a network might look like in terms of the modelling of its material culture distributions, it is useful to test that model against historically attested networks that other sources tell us existed in the seventh and sixth centuries. The first test case here is the Kalaureian *amphiktyony*, and the second is the Ionian League, both allegedly collectives of city states that had some cultural and religious significance.

The Kalaureian Amphiktyony

The Kalaureian *amphiktyony* was a network that tied together the communities of Aegina with Athens, Epidauros, Hermione, Kalaureia, Nauplion, Orchomenos and Prasiai (Fig. 6.1). The existence of this collective is attested in the literary record by Strabo (8.6.14 c374) who, speaking of the *amphiktyony* in the past tense, seems to imply that the network existed *at some point prior* to the first century BC: Strabo notes that Kalaureia became sacred to Apollo in exchange (with Leto) for Delos, but more importantly for present purposes he indicates that there was a network *based at the temple of Kalaureia* in which the communities that he lists participated in communal sacrifice. Similarly, an inscription of the Hellenistic period found at Kalaureia (IG IV 842) offers a not too different story, that there existed an *amphiktyony* and that Poseidon was at its centre; the identities of individual communities are not given here. Little more can be said on these two small pieces of evidence, in particular, nothing of chronology. That this network existed in the Archaic period (or earlier) cannot be deduced on the basis of textual evidence alone:[5] much more productive is to look to the archaeological record (*cf.* Kelly 1966, Forrest 2000: 284–5).

Given that the Kalaureian network supposedly centred around the cult site of Poseidon at Kalaureia, the archaeology of Poros is the best place to start. Excavations by the Swedish Institute at Athens brought to light the first architectural remains from the sanctuary more than 100 years ago (Wide and Kjellberg 1895), and research at the site continues

---

[5] This has not prevented scholars from hypothesising the chronology of this network on the basis of philological evidence alone. Kelly 1966: 113–5 offers an overview of (mainly nineteenth- and early twentieth-century) scholarship taking this approach, of whom are to be noted: Müller 1817 and 1820 (for a Bronze Age foundation of the *amphiktyony*), Curtius 1876 (Archaic period foundation) and von Wiliamowitz-Möllendorff 1896: 102–3 (fourth-century foundation).

Figure 6.1 Sanctuary of Poseidon at Kalaureia, as it can be seen today. Most of the standing remains across the site date after the end of the Archaic period. Photograph by author.

today.[6] Apart from some Mycenaean graves and a single Geometric period sherd (Coldstream 1968: 341–2), the first substantial archaeological remains from the site, including a temple and *peribolos* wall, originate in the sixth century. From this period, too, terracottas and bronzes have been found in significant number – objects that might actually reveal a great deal about the activities that took place at this site (*cf.* Kelly 1966: 115–17) – but the majority of which still await publication. The quantity of pottery from the seventh century indicates that there might have been significant activity at the site before the construction of the temple, even if it might be difficult to conclude on this basis alone that the that activity was cultic (*cf.* Constantakopoulou 2007: 35).

---

[6] See Berg 2016 for an overview and cultural history of the 'Big Dig' history of Kalaureia, and the involvement of the Swedish Institute. The most recent programme of research was launched in 2015: for a summary report of the most recent season's excavation see https://www.sia.gr/en/articles.php?tid=546&page=1, and on the new programme of research and affiliated research activities, see Loy 2020b: 162–3. For the results of the excavation period 1997–2001, see Wells, Penttinen and Billot 2003.

That there was a temple here with religious activities being conducted in (at least some part of) the Archaic period appears well documented archaeologically. But whether that mere existence of a temple also implies the existence of an *amphiktyony* whose member communities could come and use this space – not to mention the problem of *what else* it was that these communities in alliance were meant to do with one another – is harder to construct.

Both the purpose and function of the Kalaureian network are to a large extent the subject of guesswork. This network might have been purely a religious network for the shared participation of its members in cult activities (Shipley 1996), or it could have had its basis in a military (Foley 1988: 148–9) or political alliance (Sourvinou-Inwood 1979: 20) whose shared character took on additional meanings at some later date. A common feature of all of these supposed member sites (apart from Orchomenos, curiously) is their proximity to the sea,[7] their definition as 'maritime' or 'coastal' sites. This might have afforded network members some socio-cultural significance,[8] that there was some connection between the network members' perception and experience of the sea and its cults; but it is also possible that there was a more practical reason for this network (*cf.* Figueira 1981: 186, 220 [n. 34]; Constantakopoulou 2007: 37). It might be that, given dangerous and uncertain sailing conditions in the Aegean Sea, these sites could be used to mark points of safe transit (Schumacher 1993; Mylonopoulos 2006; Kowalzig 2018; Loy forthcoming), as possible points of refuge between which travellers could stop (Marinatos, Hägg and Sinn 1993; Morgan 2003; Osborne 1996a: 231–2). And while recent archaeological study does indeed indicate that there was movement of people in and out of Kalaureia by people coming from reasonably far away (Mylona et al. 2013) and that the space had to be reorganised during the lifespan of the sanctuary to accommodate cult participants (Alexandridou 2013), this notion of how and why people were moving between sites of the Kalaureian *amphiktyony* is still largely a point of conjecture. If the existence of a temple in the Archaic period implies the existence of a network at the same time, we still do not know what it did.

So can the network approach help shed some light on this question of the Kalaureian *amphiktyony*? The results of the analyses conducted in this book

---

[7] Early modern travelers to the Saronic Gulf, including Spon, Wheler, Chandler and Gell, all commented on the strategic importance of this group of sites, located in prime-position between the Saronic Gulf and the Peloponnese. Athanasiou 2014 has recently synthesised and commented on this early modern data.

[8] This is an issue explored by the Swedish Institute's research programme 'The Sea, the City and the God', 2007–2012.

actually further complicate the picture. The proximal-point luxury and commodity shipping routes modelled in the first two case studies do not even get close to Poros, seemingly taking a more direct route through the Saronic Gulf north of Aegina and out towards the *isthmus*. If one were concerned with long-range shipping, this would suggest that the most efficient route would avoid going near the Temple of Poseidon at Kalaureia, and indeed one might not even stop for all that long within the Saronic Gulf. Of course, this might be an issue of scale: the shipping analysis was conducted at the level of the Aegean, and did not consider much smaller 'local' movements around a smaller 'pond' like the Saronic Gulf; Figueira (1981: 220) did actually suggest that, even if the Kalaureian *amphiktyony was* a network associated with movement and sea travel, it was probably only local, concerning, for instance, the local marketing of agricultural goods. This 'local' network is very different to the long-range networks of marble discussed in Chapter 2. When we consider 'commodity' goods, however, the ceramic shapes found at Kalaureia in the seventh century are similar to assemblages at Aphaia (another network member), but also those from Lindos and Delos; and in the sixth century there was similarity with Chios. Given that pots can be interpreted as markers of practice, could this be an indication of similar practices – a network of cult practices? – shared between Kalaureia and Aphaia? That seems unlikely given the range of other disparate sites included within this group, many of them from the other side of the Aegean, and most of them not in the Kalaireian group. It really appears more to indicate simply that things were in circulation, rather than there being some sort of tight network at play. In terms of coinage, there are many gaps in the dataset for the Kalaureian *amphiktyony* sites, owing in part to the dearth of coinage from the Peloponnese in the Archaic period. Orchomenos does adopt the Aeginitan standard, but so do myriad other sites: there is nothing remarkable here that shows a special link between two sites part of this same network (unlike the specific coinage of the Boiotian League of the Classical period), not least of all because Athens, another participant of the *amphiktyony*, uses its own Attic standard, breaking any sort of network unity. Crucially, Kalaureia, at the centre of the network, was not minting coins in the Archaic period. The inscriptional record does not add much either. There are bronze inscriptions from Epidauros, Orchomenos and Prasiai, all using a similar <I> for /i/, <ʖ> for /e/ and <O> for /o/: but while Epidauros and Prasiai use <ϟ> for /s/, Orchomenos uses <M>; the fact alone that these are bronze inscriptions is nothing special in the Argolid region, other examples having been found from sites which are not even part of the Kalaureian network. Aegina and Athens are obviously different beasts, with stone and pottery inscriptions that use <H> where Orchomenos uses <ᗺ>. And there is the recurring problem of an absence of data from Kalaureia. Put simply, in the material datasets analysed, there is little evidence of the sorts of similarity that have been understood as characteristic of economic or political networking between disparate communities.

It would seem, therefore, that these network analyses have very little to offer for shedding light on the Kalaureian *amphiktyony* – and in fact the data highlight more differences than they do similarities. Sadly, there appears to be no unity of activity between these communities in the datasets explored, neither at an economic nor at a political level. Even though this could be an issue of scale, in analysing the data at the level of the Aegean rather than in looking up-close at the Saronic Gulf, the complete absence of *any* sorts of connections between *amphiktyony* sites is striking and this suggests that it is not such an issue. If, as would seem to be the case, it really is impossible to locate substantial connection between these communities from the datasets analysed here, we must consider the alternatives. Was the Kalaureian *amphiktyony* some sort of military alliance where its constituent members were *only* in communication with one another against a common threat, but in all other ways (i.e. at the political and economic level) independent from one another? Or was this a conceptual network, a network of the mind, a network that, although linking places together by means of a common sailing route or through shared cult practices, was not materialised in any detectable way?

Or is it the case that a temple does not a network make? The fact that there was an Archaic temple of Poseidon at Kalaureia does not necessitate immediate collective action from neighbouring communities; it could simply be that the *amphiktyony* of which Strabo wrote, began some time *after* the end of the Archaic period. This is certainly a possibility when looking at the network analysis: there is nothing particular in the data to mark out collective *activity* between member communities of the Kalaureian *amphiktyony*. We must conclude, therefore, either that a network of this sort is not visible in the archaeological record with the data and methods used or that the very existence of an Archaic period Kalaureian *amphiktyony* itself can be called into question.

The Ionian League

According to Herodotus, the Ionian League was a collective comprising twelve cities from the coastal region of western Anatolia (Fig. 6.2): Miletos, Myous, Priene, Ephesos, Kolophon, Lebedos, Teos, Klazomenai, Phokaia,

Figure 6.2 View from Samos across the Mykale strait to the Anatolian mainland, comprising part of the region of Ionia. Photograph by author.

Samos, Chios and Erythrai (Herodotus, *Histories* 1.142). This network had supposedly formed in the seventh century BC (*cf.* Roebuck 1955a; Cook 1962; Kowalzig 2005; Herda 2006) in response to a collective effort of 'Ionian' cities in military alliance against the city of Melie (the source for this narrative, however, is Roman: Vitruvius, *De architecture* 4.1.4); others have dated the beginning of this network even earlier to 1087 or 1077 BC (Bearzot 1983; Shipley 1987: 29–31), in part based on a date given by the (Hellenistic) Parian Marble (IG XII.5 444). The Ionian League was, according to Herodotus, a loosely defined network, given that member communities spoke different dialects of the Greek language. They expressed their own local identities and political alliance, and they rejected the forming of some centralised political unit, opting instead to maintain their independence (Herodotus, *Histories* 1.170). Member cities would congregate, though, at a 'Panionion' sanctuary located near Myous in the Mykale mountains,[9]

---

[9] Two candidates have been suggested as the location of the Panionion sanctuary. The first, identified by Theodor Wiegand and Hans Schrader (1904: 24ff.) and excavated by Gerhard

participating in shared festivals and rituals dedicated to the god Poseidon (Herodotus, *Histories* 1.148).

Our textual sources – both those fairly contemporary and those from generations later preserving some sort of memory of the Archaic period – seem to indicate that there was a network of Ionian states: what was that network meant to do? Let us consider the activities that might have been undertaken by such a network. Inspired in part by the narrative of the Meliac War – and noting, in addition, another story from Herodotus that the Ionian communities met at the Panionion in 546 BC to plan collective action against the Persian invasion – scholarship of the early twentieth century emphasised the militaristic and political importance of an Ionian League (von Wiliamowitz-Möllendorff 1906, Caspari 1915, Judeich 1933). The League permitted members, so it seems, to come together and to plan for co-ordinated military movements like the Ionian Revolt at the start of the fifth century BC. But over at least the past seventy years and since the suggestion from Carl Roebuck (1955a) that membership to the Ionian League also had something to do with the ethnic identities of constituent communities, the conversation on the nature of the Ionian League has changed somewhat. The League was not a strict political alliance, but a socio-cultural symbol of collective identity (Tausend 1992: 70–4; Hall 2002: 67–73; Mac Sweeney 2017: 394–5), a social and political term adopted by choice (Kowalzig 2005: 48ff.). That is, membership of the Ionian League helped to create (and to re-create) communal bonds between communities within the region of Ionia, while participation in some of the cultic and religious activities previously discussed helped to physically bring these communities together, to let them see one another and to reinforce these bonds. This begs the question, therefore, whether it is possible to see this sort of collective activity in the material record.

Once again, it is necessary to consider the results of the network analysis for informing our view on the activities of the Ionian League. Although, as

Kleiner, Peter Hommel and Wolfgang Müller-Wiener Hommel (1967), is located at Otomatik Tepe near Güzelçamlı, a site that comprises a terrace wall and council chamber, dated to around the sixth century BC. The second, discovered by Hans Lohmann first in the early 2000s through extensive field survey at Çatallar Tepe and later excavated (Lohmann 2005, 2007; Lohmann, Kalaitzoglou and Lüdorf 2014; *cf.* Herda 2006), comprises a building of the first half of the seventh century BC overlaid by a temple of the mid-sixth century BC. The second candidate, although more plausible, presents the problem of being a small site, perhaps not offering sufficient space for a Panionion gathering on the scale of 546 BC to have taken place. In some respects, the exact identity of the building does not matter; moreover, the location of the cult might have moved around Ionia in subsequent generations (*cf.* Mac Sweeney 2013: 177, 187). What is important here is that there appears to be evidence of *at least some sort*
of building from the Archaic period that could help to verify the existence of the Ionian League and its activities at this time.

noted earlier, the *kouros* was a sculptural form that seems to have found its origins at least in part in Ionia, the model run in Chapter 2 indicates that there were few ships moving around Ionia for the shipment of this product. When it came to shipping 'commodity' ceramics, though, it appears that in all parts of the Archaic period there were a fair number of ships moving north and south along the Ionian coastline, linking together sites of the Ionian League with areas for export in the north Aegean and on Rhodes. As to the composition of the ceramic assemblages themselves, there is not such a substantial number of data points mined from across Ionia, and so only a few broad-level comments can be made. Sanctuaries on Samos and Chios have similar assemblages in that they were consuming a large number of *kraters*, while both Samos and Miletos shared a high consumption of *amphoras*. This latter point is particularly unsurprising, given what is known about both Miletos and Samos as major producers of amphoras throughout the Archaic period. And, just as unsurprising, the general ware type for Chios, Klazomenai, Miletos and Samos was in all cases Ionian, which, at this broad-brush level, tells us little more than pottery was being both produced and consumed locally at the level of the region. One might say, quite reasonably, on the basis of these datasets, that there is some *limited* regional level economic networking going on among the communities of Ionia.

With the coins, though, it is a different story. Ionia was split between those communities who were minting to the Milesian standard (Chios, Ephesus and, later, Klazomenai) and those who are using the Attic-Euboean standard (Samos and Teos). And that is to say nothing of the fact that by the end of the Archaic period Samos was minting coins on its own standard, and usage of the Milesian standard was by no means a local phenomenon, being the standard used in coinage as far away as on Melos and Seriphos. As was also (not) the case with the Kalaureian *amphiktyony*, there was no League coinage. So while these results are somewhat disappointing for our idea of a unified Ionian League, the degree of similarity when it comes to the lettersets is more encouraging. All sites represented within the Ionian League used similarly <H> for /e:/, <⌒> for /s/ and <Ω> for /o:/. Similarity is one thing, but there is nothing distinctly Ionian about usage of these particular lettersets (with many of those lettersets being shared by sites in Attica), nor, as noted, does this imply that there is some linguistic homogeneity between communities of Ionia given that we know there were different dialects in place across the region. Difference is important, too, and as highlighted in Chapter 5 there were also smaller groups within Ionia that had adopted different letterset practices to one another. But what *is* shown here is that there was *some* sort of cultural unity between sites – unlike the case with the lettersets of the Kalaureian *amphiktyony* sites. So while on the one hand there appear to be only very loose economic or political links between communities of the Ionian League, on the other, there does appear to be some sort of much broader socio-cultural collective.

How does this map onto what we know about the Ionian League? The network analysis would seemingly confirm the notion put forward by many that there is evidence for neither strong economic nor political ties between Ionian communities. Geography does seem to play some part in how the group of sites interacted with one another, but geography was not the deciding factor: that is, Ionian sites were consuming broadly similar types of ceramics, but the evidence of the weight standards would suggest that they were participating in a range of different economic and political networks from one another. The evidence of lettersets indicates that the region is leaning towards some sort of socio-cultural network, the sorts of shared ideas and practices that cannot be measured so easily. This is exactly the sort of notion that recent scholarship has emphasised for the existence of the Ionian League: this was a group of sites that had shared ideologies and a shared set of identities, even though these are intangible ideas that leave very little material trace. In essence, the communities of Ionia were displaying both a unity with one another, but, at the same time, a sense of independence. The Ionian League, on the basis of these datasets, was to a greater extent an emic-network that was experienced by its participants, rather than the sort of etic-network that can be quite easily measured by the material record.

What is the lesson that can be learned here, from both the situation with the Kalaureian *amphiktyony* and the Ionian League? In the case of the former, where one would expect to find evidence of a network, there was no evidence at all; in the case of the latter, only weak links suggestive of a socio-cultural network could be found. And yet text – and scholarship – would have us believe that there might be much closer connections between constituent members of both of these networks, or at least close enough that those links would be made more visible in the material record as analysed here. Quite simply, the moral to take from this story is that we must guard against the evidence of texts overstating the level of connection within historically attested networks.

It is worth considering why this should be the case. As previously noted, most of the 'primary' textual evidence for these networks comes from non-contemporary sources, written generations after the Archaic period. It is not new (nor surprising) to suggest that we should treat sources like these with a certain amount of caution, and indeed with reference to these particular case studies it has been argued that there could be an element of 'back-projection': writers of the Classical or Hellenistic period casting back the image of a more unified present onto a less closely networked past. Naoíse Mac Sweeney (2013: 176–87, 2017: 394–5) and Jan Paul Crielaard (2009) have each argued that writers of later periods used the idea of an early Ionian unity to galvanise collective identity in the fifth century, and it is entirely possible that this is the same story with Kalaureia. The retrospective creation of networks – or, at least, the idea of presenting a network as more unified than it might in fact be – would certainly account for the disparate material patterning in the record for these regions. With no or little formal network holding together communities of the Saronic Gulf or Ionia, it is difficult to argue the case for close political or economic ties between these regions' communities. Communities communicated their own localness and independence through the use of various lettersets and coinage weight standards, and any affiliations that they felt with one another were more ephemeral, the sorts of connections that leave little trace in the material record.

And so we must regard with caution the identification in literature and history of 'known' Archaic networks: not only, as will be argued, because military and religious alliances do not always map closely onto material culture; but also because the authors who speak of these networks might have had an agenda in making communities appear more historically connected than they actually were.

What Was the Reality?

So we have not got very far in starting with the historic/literary record and in trying to validate it with the network data. What happens if we start working from the network data, in taking a 'bottom-up' approach instead?

Since the same places are linked to *different* networks in *different* contexts, networking between communities cannot be attributed to single factors. What we have is a large web of places connected by *different* means, and variously growing and engaging with other groups. The connections between communities of Archaic Greece might have been of an order unprecedented for this part of the world at this time, but their reach can hardly be called 'global' or 'macro'; furthermore, the present study has suggested that states operated individually (and in fact provides a case against the idea of 'regionalism'), and that inter-polity groups and leagues existed only in a very weak sense at this time.

Even though political interaction does not necessarily lead to other forms of communication between communities, some of the strongest patterns that emerge relate to political networks. The case of Rhodes is particularly noteworthy, since it was an island that was home to three independently defined communities, namely Ialysos, Kamiros and Lindos. All were firmly established by the start of the Archaic period, and all were already engaged with external networks (Thucydides 6.4.3; Pindar, *Olympian* 7.13–4; Coldstream 1968: 262–7; Kourou 2003). These communities had distinct identities: they were listed as separate members of the Dorian Hexapolis league of states,[10] with Herodotus (1.144) listing the six cities as Lindos, Ialysos, Kamiros, Kos, Knidos and Halikarnassos. As demonstrated in the previous analysis, these communities used different lettersets in their inscriptions. Furthermore, Ialysos and Lindos minted coinages on different standards, respectively on a local 'Ialysian' standard and the Milesian standard; and all attested Lindian coins bear the motif of the lion's head, giving them a further association with the coinage of Miletos. Being distinct from one's close neighbours was clearly a concern for the Rhodian cities, and *individual* community identity was something far more important than geographical proximity or shared membership of the same *island* community.

And yet there *are* elements of similarity in their material record. Art historians have long recognised that in ceramics found on the island, a distinctive 'Rhodian' style of pottery is well attested and appears to be specific to no one of these sites (Cook 1933/1934: 2; see Bouzek 1987 for a concise summary of some existing challenges of scholarship). Although it is the case that recent scientific analysis confirms that many of these ceramics were made on Kos and not on Rhodes (Villing and Mommsen 2017; *cf.* Kerschner 2017), the point still stands that there was a material *koiné* of sorts across the island when it came to consumption, and it is still striking that – on a macroscopic view, a quick glance afforded by either a present-day or ancient viewer – all of these three separate communities each with their own separate identities drew on a *common visual language* and a set of motifs for their ceramics. These communities were similarly involved in corresponding trade networks: when the pottery market shifted

---

[10] Information on the Dorian Hexapolis is scarce, but a *terminus post quem* for the league can be dated to the time of Herodotus.

for one of the Rhodian communities (e.g. when there was an increase in the volume of Ionian ceramics or a decrease in Cypriot ceramics imported, *cf.* Bourogiannis 2017) this same phenomenon is observable in the material record across the whole island. For pottery – a dataset that reflects to some degree processes of production and import – there actually seems to have been a single economic network for the whole island. The communities of Rhodes exhibited points of similarity and points of difference in their networks, but they all participated within the same political entanglement.

To use the model of Hall and Chase-Dunn, Ialysos, Kamiros and Lindos were all clearly part of the same group of communities, but they participated in economic networks and networks of political association in distinct and different ways. The communities were part of the same commodity markets for ceramics (and the goods they contained), but these communities formed different political alliances and expressed different identities at the level of the community. Economics and politics were not entirely separate but entangled in a mesh of cause and effect. The commercial activities of Rhodes extended the reach of the island's coastal communities, and by coming into contact with a wide-range of competing neighbours and peoples overseas these communities felt the need to express their own differences and form distinct identities. The Rhodian communities were in close (peer polity) competition with one another, and their proximity in fact drove the desire to express distinctness and communicate their local identities.

In addition to this intra-island network, communities also operated inter-island. The sanctuary of Apollo on Delos throughout the latter part of the sixth century attracted considerable interest from visiting dedicators and was a place where the networks of various islanders intersected (Constantakopoulou 2007: 38–58; Angliker 2017: 29–31). Significant monuments were erected on behalf of the states of both Naxos and Paros (such as the terrace of lions, colossal *kouros* and the Monument of the Hexagons: Santerre 1959: 35–6; Bruneau and Ducat 1983: 153),[11] and

---

[11] Historians acknowledge that, on top of this socio-cultural rivalry exercised by elite peers, there was some sort of more formal rivalry exercised between these two islands in the Archaic period (Kondoleon 1963 and Parker 1997) – but knowing what exactly was the nature of that rivalry is more difficult to decipher. There is very limited evidence for political or militaristic disquiet: at some indeterminate point during the Archaic period, Miletos attacked Naxos (Andriskos *FGrH* 500 F1). Paros was a known ally of Miletos (Archilochus fr. 192, Herodotus 5.28–9) – and so this was assumed to be 'rivalry by association'. The only other piece of evidence is that Parian Archilochus (*Fr* 89) writes about various battles with the Naxians, and supposedly died when in battle against an army from that island – so, presumably, there must have been formal rivalries *at some stage* between the two islands, contested through battle.

the island also attracted the attention of both Athenian Peisistratus and Samian Polykrates.[12] Perhaps the greatest material representation of inter-island connectivity is the Nikandre *Kore*, the early sixth-century BC Parian marble statue, dedicated on Delos by a Naxian woman, indicated with an inscription of an alphabet characteristic of the island of Naxos.[13] Delos could act as a meeting point for the traffic of elite peers, the sorts of wealthy elites financing monuments like these, and the island as a key node in facilitating the circulation of these ideas. But the results of the present analysis also indicate that a similar phenomenon was also taking place at the micro-level. In analysing the lettersets, Delos, like Delphi, was the recipient of many more inscribed dedications than its neighbours, and many written in non-local forms too: this was interpreted in light of the sanctuaries' positions as key nodes for mobile non-local scribes. As was stated earlier, it is entirely logical that at a place where there was a greater number of monuments dedicated, there was a greater volume of writing. And yet Delos still had its own distinct identity: unlike the neighbouring islands, it chose to adopt the Attic-Euboean weight standard for its coinage, and it was the only island state to have emblazoned on its coins the iconography of the *kithara* as opposed to the more usual dolphin. Delos was thus both a meeting point for other identities, and a place with its own very distinct identity – a node that operated two functions in a much wider Aegean network. More crucially, however, this implies that an island sanctuary's immediate networks were not bounded by its own coastline; they extended to one or more other islands.[14]

The opposite is true of Crete. The first thing that becomes apparent when looking at the data from Crete is that the island is (as was predicted back in Chapter 1) different in so many ways to the rest of the Aegean. Indeed, it is difficult to put Crete side-by-side with other parts of the Aegean on the basis of such difference. Crete was not part of the *kouros* tradition, nor were its communities engaged in the production of coinage until after the end of the sixth century BC – and this has largely kept Crete excluded from much of the synthetic discussion of this volume.[15] But other parts of the Aegean too have been relatively silent, notably the Peloponnese and central Greece. Very few data points for analysis have emerged from

---

[12] See Thucydides 3.104 for both the purification of the island by Peisistratus (543 BC), and for the dedication of Rheneia by Polykrates.

[13] This sculpture and inscription is discussed more extensively in Chapters 2 and 5.

[14] *cf.* Boomert and Bright 2007, for the idea that the study of archipelagos should also include neighbouring mainland communities.

[15] The issue of 'clusters of absence' was discussed in Chapter 5. But, as outlined in Chapter 1, this is not entirely an issue of absence but one of profound difference.

this area, and, while this is in part an issue of data availability and data quality, it is worth reflecting on these 'blackspots' of Aegean-level connectivity.

The common factor here is the sea. For the most part the Peloponnese and central Greece comprise communities that settle inland away from coastal areas – in many instances mountainous or relatively inaccessible locations – far away from a sea that has been argued as a crucial vehicle for facilitating the connection between Aegean communities. And, yet, for Crete the sea does *not* act as an opportunity for connection, but more as a barrier.[16] The sea, so often conceptualised as a tool by which island communities could interconnect, actually rendered Crete to the same degree of relative isolation as the landlocked Peloponnese and central Greece (*cf.* Dawson 2019, 2021: 214–20). Why should this be the case, and what was the effect? First, it would appear that distance does matter, and that the position of Crete, slightly out of the close orbit of the rest of the Aegean islands afforded it a position outside of its main route networks;[17] and, second, Crete's large size allowed the island to be subject to its own regions, populated by different and disparate communities who, through connection with one another, removed the need for these communities to look overseas in their networking. Indeed this notion of intra-island regionality is particularly convincing when looking at the evidence of the lettersets, given that certain parts of western Crete seemingly followed different patterns to the rest of the island. And it is not new to suggest that Crete operated a world of 'regions within regions' (Whitley 2021a), an island whose own internal networks expressed such differentiation without looking too heavily outwards to the Aegean Basin. If we accept the reading that differentiation in lettersets provides evidence for political competition and a need to express identities, this would also suggest a further fragmentation of the island between competing peers. And so the reverse is true here to that posed for the Cyclades: rather than the sea giving opportunity for individuals to form communities across islands, the sea could also isolate to the extent that multiple communities could form and compete even within the same island.

This notion of the local community versus the island community is an important one, and it has crucial implications for how we think about communities and insularity in the Archaic period. Archaeologists have long been interested in the island as a unit of analysis (Broodbank 2000: 16–8; Spriggs 2008; Dawson 2016: 323–9), asking to what extent

---

[16] On the fluidity of the sea between connection and isolation, see Rainbird 2007, esp. 1–25.
[17] Note too that this was at a time when shipping technology was still rather rudimentary and the capacity for long voyages was limited.

islanders decide to or are forced to behave differently from their mainland neighbours in response to a combination of natural and cultural factors.[18] In thinking through an alternative – as becomes necessary given that the networks of the Archaic period cannot be well explained by using a model of islands as distinct and bounded entities – it is important to consider that islands were not necessarily places of isolation: this is an idea that has received significant attention in scholarship of recent years, and discussion in previous on shipping routes for both 'luxury' and 'commodity' goods has made the case for high-level connectivity between islands and other parts of the Aegean. Even at quite a superficial level, one can clearly note that there was a greater number of communities located on the coast than inland, and this has been suggested as a strategic move to accommodate the needs of outward-facing communities who needed the sea to reach their neighbours. The sea was used as a means to connect to other communities: the sea was a vehicle responsible for helping to materialise some of those networks already discussed.

Economic networks are also patently visible. A good place to start is in Ionia where the data are both so plentiful and so well studied that we can see with great precision how these networks changed over time at quite a specific level. In particular, the study of *amphoras* – vessels whose distribution is a good proxy for economic activities – has sufficient chronological resolution to chart these changes over the period 700–500 BC. From the start of the seventh century there were such close similarities in the shape and decoration of Chian, Klazomenian and Milesian *amphoras* that it is likely that they all stemmed from a common place of production in northern Ionia (Monachov 1999; Sezgin 2012). But in the last quarter of the seventh century, these communities adopted distinctive styles for their *amphoras*. Production rates at Chios and Klazomenai altered significantly, whereby at the midpoint and in the final twenty years of the sixth century there was a sharp increase in the number of *amphoras* made, something that might indicate that a more visibly distinctive product was required to compete in non-local markets. Similarly, production of Milesian *amphoras* took place at a number of workshops both within the city's hinterland and also at the Hellespont, such as was necessary to meet demand of trading posts all around the Aegean and Black Sea area.[19] It appears that, despite

---

[18] To some extent, this line of thinking employs a somewhat culture-historical perspective and it is based on deterministic ideas of geography and environment (Braudel 1949: 160–1; *cf.* Irwin 1992; Kuklick 1996: 625; Whittaker 1998: 7; and Fitzpatrick 2004).

[19] See Hind 1995 for a list of trading posts named around the Black Sea area. Most of the catalogue is based on evidence of the fifth century, but some of the attestations are from Herodotus, and it

political instabilities in the area, the ambition of these cities to reach into Aegean markets could still expand undeterred: the success of economic networks – for this region, at least – was not directly dependent on political prosperity (Slawisch 2013, *contra* Cook 1961, Balcer 1984, 1985). This is all consistent with the evidence of coinage. It has already been noted that the dense network of economic relationships shown by coinage in the sixth century must have relied on a pre-existing economic network – that is, one that was in place in the seventh century.

Is this a plausible story? The case for pre-existing economic networks can be made more strongly when the evidence of coinage is also considered. The variety of coinage standards in use in Ionia in the sixth century has been interpreted as proxy evidence for the pre-existence of multiple markets in competition with one another. Separate communities of Ionia looked to the example of coinage begun by the Lydians and adapted the technology onto their own models, which was to the benefit of each community. As argued, the fact that coinage could emerge so quickly in this area in the sixth century strongly suggests that networks were in place already, and the evidence of both *amphoras* and coinage sits together particularly well in this region. But it is not just at the level of the region that the coinage data corroborates this narrative, but also at the level of individual communities. The number of non-Ionian communities using the Milesian weight standard both at the beginning of and throughout the sixth century BC attests to a fairly broad and successful economic network, just the sort of reach that is also shown through the amphora dataset. Communities adopted coinages based on the Milesian model so that they could participate in these networks more readily, networks whose foundations had already been well laid before those sixth-century coins were minted.

In contrast to this rather neat economic framework, evidence indicates that economic and political networks in Ionia operated quite independently. As has been noted, economic and political *prosperity* were not interdependent. Previous discussion has indicated that the end of the sixth century was a time of economic boom for the Aegean, and this is particularly consistent in Ionia: many communities adopted several weight standards to align with multiple economic networks, and the production of *amphoras* increased in rate because of the activities of centralised workshops. Chian and Klazomenian *amphoras* at this time looked similar and

is not impossible to suggest that some of the later trading posts had their origins in the sixth century or earlier.

might have been produced at a centralised regional production centre. Similarly, 'southern' Ionian *amphora* production of the later sixth century centralised around Samos. Should this be surprising? Two points are worthy of note: the first at the regional level, the second at the level of the community. First, one must consider that throughout the latter half of the sixth century, Ionia as a whole region was standing directly in the shadow of the Persian Empire, as Darius I grew his forces and prepared to move towards the Aegean. This was a time of significant instability and unrest for the region that would erupt into the Ionian Revolt in 499 BC (Herodotus 5.28ff.). And yet this does not appear to have altered *significantly* the reach or operation of certain economic networks originating in Ionia; in fact, networks appear to have developed apace at this time. Shared production centres produced *amphoras* of many different local varieties, and they served to extend the reach of each city's market much further across and beyond the Greek world: a stronger economic network was the answer to a turbulent political situation. Second, there is also the notion of inter-community rivalry. Of all 'regions' in the Archaic world, Ionia showed one of the greatest degrees of diversity, and individual communities in this area each had strong local identities. This was communicated both through the use of individual and distinct coinage motifs (the bee, the boar, the griffin, the lion) and in the choice taken by those producing writing to indicate the same sounds with distinctive letter forms. These distinct iconographies and writing practices were entangled with very distinct, local, community-based identities: the notion of the community was strong here, perhaps more so than the region. But where the communities of this region displayed a *distinctness* in the display of their political identities, they also appear, quite by contrast, to have fostered a notion of economic *collaboration*.

In both cases, there is evidence of the same idea: economic networks took priority over both inter-regional and intra-regional political networks, and the operation of one did not depend directly on the other. The implication is twofold. First, economic and political networks were separate and non-overlapping, something which is consistent with the Hall and Chase-Dunn model. And second, and as was the case with Rhodes, one might argue that close economic collaboration drives further political competition. As participants of the same economic network, the communities of Ionia were aware of one another and brought into close contact. They were knowledgeable of their peers – their competitors – and this knowledge is what drove peer competition. It is therefore of no surprise that communities should be part of different economic and political networks, as participation in the first drives the desire to exert status and individuality in the second.

Another prime example where networks did not overlap with one another comes from the north Aegean. This is most simply illustrated by looking separately at the 'luxury' and 'commodity' shipping lanes: beyond Thasos, the north Aegean was not involved in the tradition of dedicating large marble statues, while, by contrast, large amounts of (mainly Attic and Corinthian pottery) made its way north. In fact, this 'commodity' pattern for economic trade networks is a strong one, such that it is evident in the coinage dataset too: just as in the early seventh-century sites of the north Aegean are involved in Athenian and Corinthian pottery networks but by the end of the sixth century local production takes priority, for coinage, sites of the north were using the Phokaian and Attic-Euboean standards early in the sixth century before adopting all of their own weights by the end. So while there is little evidence of a 'luxury' economy developing in this region, there is strong evidence of a robust 'commodity' network developing.

This story of the north Aegean raises interesting points. There is the implication here that the operation of one network does not necessarily lead to the formation of another: the 'commodity' network does not have to become a 'luxury' one. This should not be surprising. Participation in games of competition and status building – that is, in the commissioning and erection of marble statues – was at the discretion of elite peers. While in the southern Aegean the desire of aspirational individuals to compete with one another through conspicuous consumption was so great that it drove a widespread production of statues, in the northern Aegean elite peers were simply not doing this. Their own preference was to compete in other sorts of ways, either less archaeologically visible or in ways not analysed here. Indeed, we should view the absence of large marble-based 'luxury' production networks in the north not as a failure of commodity networks to transform into a new type of economic network, but rather that individuals in these communities simply interacted with one another in a different way to their neighbours elsewhere in the Aegean Basin. The other point is that there was clearly a circulation of people around the north. Not only is this evident in the widespread movement north of southern Aegean material types in the seventh century, but it can also be seen to the extent that the region has attained enough economic power to set up multiple local networks of its own by the end of the sixth. This pattern will be of no surprise to commentators of the north Aegean who have noted the richness of natural resources in this area (Dimova 2019: 134; Tsiafaki 2020), emphasising in particular that the economic incentive of pursuing these resources was what drove people north not just now but across subsequent periods of Greek history (Archibald 2013: 249ff.). A desire for timber, wood, fuel and raw minerals brought people to this region and allowed local networks of substantial size to develop here. The clear indication is that the desire for specific economic products drove the circulation of certain ('commodity') economic networks, while the different types of activities of elite peers in these communities – different sorts of socially embedded practices – restricted the development of other ('luxury') networks.

Another noteworthy example for seeing how this tension between economic and other types of network plays out comes from Aegina. Of the data explored here, there are significant differences in the small finds of the two major sanctuaries of the island – Aphaia and Kolonna; in the seventh century, the ceramics from Aphaia were principally Corinthian, but Kolonna's ceramics were mainly Ionian, with a larger number of Attic ceramics from the sixth century. For two sanctuaries so geographically proximate to be part of two such different networks requires some sort of explanation, and it is possible to conceive of that difference here in terms of how those two sanctuaries were used. As discussed in Chapter 3, the presence of Corinthian material does not indicate that these things travelled on the back of political, cultural or other sorts of ties between Aphaia and Corinth; rather, since the ceramics demanded by cult requirement (*aryballoi* and *pyxides*) were readily available only from Corinthian potteries, the participants of religious activity at Aphaia necessarily turned to this city and to these networks in order to satisfy their need. Is it going too far to suggest that the people of Aphaia were recognising and identifying different markets? Not necessarily, and the *location* of the sanctuary on the island helps to make this point. At 176 m above sea level, the temple of Aphaia is certainly visible across the eastern part of the island, but it is hardly accessible (Fig. 6.3). The movement of imported ceramics up to the temple would have required investment in terms of time, people and infrastructure – even though the goods themselves would have been light-weight.[20] By the principle that individuals will (generally) follow a path of least resistance unless there is some compelling reason not to, it would not simply be a case of taking whatever imported material happened to arrive on Aegina. Rather, the participants

---

[20] *cf.* Berg 2010 and Archibald 2016 for the notion that scholars have paid less attention to the movement of commodities between harbours and inland sites. Bonnier 2014 goes some way to discussing this phenomenon for the Corinthian Gulf.

Figure 6.3 View from the Sanctuary of Aphaia on Aegina indicating both the distance from the sanctuary to the sea and the steep topography that must be traversed to reach the site from the coast. Photograph by author.

of cult at Aphaia had to *plan* the transport of ceramics up to the site, and had to determine which materials were worth the effort of the journey between port and temple. That is, given the overall cost in time and energy that must have been spent to transport ceramics up to the temple of Aphaia, it is conceivable that consideration was given to ensure that those were the *right sorts* of ceramics.

By contrast, the temple of Apollo at Kolonna lies right on the western shore of the island, and there is evidence back into the prehistoric periods that this shoreline was used as a place for boats to moor (Welter 1938: 39; Knoblauch 1972).[21] As already discussed, shipping technology of the Archaic period was such that sailors would navigate along the coast from harbour to harbour, and on journeys taken in tempestuous or unpredictable conditions, intermediary stops might have been required along the way. Aegina, as a prime node positioned geographically at the

---

[21] It is irrelevant to this argument whether there was substantial infrastructure for mooring and launching at Kolonna, as literary evidence suggests that a beach and a few props of wood were all that were required. Rankov 2013 presents a substantial volume of literary evidence from Homer and Hesiod for these sorts of activities taking place without formal infrastructure.

heart of the route between the Saronic Gulf and the Cyclades, would have been a good and visible point for sailors to aim for. And Kolonna – positioned in a conveniently accessible location on the west of the island facing in towards the rest of the gulf – might have provided just the sort of space for sailors to stop. Why should this affect the composition of ceramics found at the site, though? If ships were to stop here somewhat unexpectedly, one assumes that there was less targeting of specific goods, and that it was necessary to dedicate simply whatever happened to be in the existing cargo. This story makes sense in considering that there are at Kolonna high proportions of Ionian and Attic ceramics: ships taking routes between these regions would have cut by Aegina and, if necessity required one to stop at Kolonna, then those Attic or Ionian wares held on board for long-range transit could be given at the sanctuary, dedicated at the port's temple, as a means of thanks to the gods for a safe voyage (*cf. Od.* 3.178–9). It comes as no surprise, therefore, to find higher proportions of Ionian and Attic ceramics at this site; these items came from ships making longer voyages in the Aegean which only happened to pass by Aegina (*cf.* Watson 2011: 89–113). While the assemblage at Aphaia was more targeted by virtue of its nature as an inland site, coastal Kolonna had greater access to the extensive trade networks of Aegina in the Archaic period.

And on this notion of the entanglement between physical routes and conceptual socio-cultural and economic networks, another prime example is the case of Euboea. Two central points have emerged in the previous chapters that are relevant to Euboea and its networks. First, Euboea (and, more specifically, the north coast of Euboea) was in a central prime location for the shipment of goods around the Aegean, sitting right in the middle of the shipping lane from Attica up to the north Aegean. Although this shipping lane was used less intensively for the transport of marble (owing to a lesser demand for statues in the north of the Aegean) than for ceramics, this trade route was well established at the start of the seventh century BC. Second, Euboea's own networks had considerable geographic reach, with the Attic-Euboean coin standard being one of the most widely used (and one of the first to be adopted widescale) by the end of the sixth century BC. It has also been noted that Euboea played a particular role in connected networks on the east and west sides of the Aegean. In essence, Euboea was both physically and economically connecting right across the Aegean.

Are these two factors related? A good case can be made that they are. The idea is now well established that shipping lanes provided opportunity for ships to stop *en route*, to trade by cabotage and to interact with coastal communities. It is a pity that there are not more sites available with data available of the quality sufficient for the present study such that this notion could be explored to a greater extent across the island, but – if we accept that island sites are located at coastal points where people might want to stop – the idea at least of site *locations* supports the idea that ships could stop frequently in moving past the island (Boffa and Leone 2017; Kowalzig 2018). As ships moved along this coast on much longer journeys into the north Aegean, the communities of Euboea benefited from interactions with their transient crews,[22] were able to learn and spread ideas, and to learn new technological knowledge as it arrived on their shores from elsewhere. It is even conceivable that the technology of coinage arrived at Euboea in this way, knowledge of minting coming to the island (and being taken to neighbouring communities) via ships that came to Euboea for other reasons. To put this another way, Euboea exploited traffic coming past its shores to extend its own networks,[23] and both the existence of physical routes and the circulation of people and ideas around the Aegean was put to good use. To put this in less historically specific network terms, the high betweenness centrality of the network afforded by physical location could be exploited and used to place the island at the centre of other (conceptual) networks (*cf.* Déderix 2017, Crawford 2019; Loy 2019: 378–80; Seifried and Gardner 2019).

Finally, a coda to this necessarily broad-level discussion brings things back to a more contextual view of the people involved in some of these macro-systems. After all, clear evidence has emerged that it was the actions of people – elite peers – communicating with one another and their competition for status that underpinned many of those economic and political connections observed. And to ground this notion back into the reality of Archaic Greece, evidence has indicated that the prime nodes where this sort of competition played out were the religious sanctuary sites. Indeed, the greater the infrastructure for people coming together (i.e. at larger pan-hellenic sanctuary sites like Delphi and Delos), the greater the opportunity for competition and connection has been observed. It is quite clearly not new to suggest that sanctuaries were hotbeds of competition for the Greeks,[24] and over recent years this idea

---

[22] Knodell 2021 notes that many of these structural changes on the island of Euboea were already in play during the eighth century, but it was not until the seventh and sixth that they become more visible in the archaeological record. *cf.* Leone 2012.

[23] Euboea's strategic geographic centrality allowed individuals not just to converge on the island, but also to disperse from this point: the issue of Euboean 'colonisation' is not dealt with here.

[24] See for example Snodgrass 1980: 52–65; Morgan 1990; de Polignac 1994: 11–3; Osborne 1996a: 231–2 and Agelidis 2017. Nor is it new to suggest that other gathering places, such as harbours,

has received even more attention through extended discussion of the relationship between sanctuary as physical place versus socio-cultural space, as seen now in the prominent idea that physical places facilitate competition and exchange (*cf.* Huber, Jacquemin and Laroche 2015).[25] Put simply, sanctuaries allowed people to come together to do things[26] – and, as argued right from Chapter 1, it was communities doing things that informed the overall shape of the Archaic Greek world.

This final point highlights the whole irony of looking at networks in this way. This whole network framework was adopted to put the emphasis on outward-facing connection: to look in detail at activities and at the edges of a network, to consider the possibilities of elite peers 'reaching out' into the wider world. The irony, then, is that if sanctuaries – single nodes – are the places where these sorts of embedded behaviours are more prominently defined, then this is actually the reverse of network analysis.[27] This is people *closing in* on single spaces to compete with one another, because it was only when people came together that these exchanges could take place, and it was only when individuals and communities confronted one another that their identities were so completely challenged. The edges of the network might define the important activities that took place shaping economic and political networks, but it is the *nodes* of places like sanctuaries that make those communal activities an historical possibility. To put this another way, once we move from abstract economic and political processes back to actual places and to people converging on these places, it becomes clear that place and activity are entangled with one another in more ways than might have initially been thought: that the things elite peers did in informing the communications of their communities were not only socially embedded but also spatially embedded. There can be no network without nodes, and, although this study began by professing to shift the focus away from sanctuaries and religion back to an archaeology of communities, it is completely impossible to exclude these places from a broader discussion on the network of Archaic interactions.

---

allowed Greeks to come together and to compete in new ways: *cf.* Reger 2016. Both Tandy 1997 and Kaplan 2002 and 2003 apply this theory to the case study of Archaic period mercenaries.

[25] Facilitation is given by means built structures within sanctuaries (Ma 2013: 144; Hollinshead 2015; Kristensen 2018) but also by the very layout and large spaces within sanctuaries (Connelly 2011; Aurigny 2020: 97–100).

[26] These 'things' might include feasting, festivals (Phillips and Pritchard 2003; Miller 2004), or even just simple consumption of material goods (Aurigny 2020: 104–12).

[27] *cf.* Kistler et al. 2015, Whitley *pers comm.*

Networking in the Archaic Period

The previous two sections have outlined different ways in which the results of the network analyses can be interrogated: from the 'top-down', going from 'known' networks to networks identified in the material record; and going from the 'bottom-up', starting with the networks that emerge from the analysis and attempting to explain their shape using other historical data. In doing so, it has been possible to add a new layer of interpretation to specific regional histories and to evaluate individual case studies. What remains is the final step of looking beyond individual case studies and considering what the implication is for the Aegean Basin as a whole.

Do the communities of activity identified through the distributions of material culture correlate to known political communities? Lettersets give the most plausible option here, given both that there is a strong case that different types of writing were selected to communicate meaningful communal identities and that there was an absence of common lettersets in the 'temporary' community that is constituted by the dedicatees at a panhellenic sanctuary. Indeed lettersets were useful for identifying, in the case of Rhodes, the known political units of Ialysos, Kamiros and Lindos as distinct. The second clearest mapping for activity to political units was in the production of coinage, because of possible 'political' intervention likely regarding weight standards – particularly evident at places like Corinth or Miletos. Neither the community of statue production nor the community of pottery has much to do with a claim on forming a distinct political unit.

As has also been noted, the size of the groups operating with commonality is flexible. There is some regionality to patterns, where the letterset data from Attic demes is so uniform that it might as well be aggregated into the single Athenian 'community', while in other places, like in Ionia, there is not; islands – particularly large islands like Crete or Rhodes – are comprised of separate and distinct communities of activity, while for others, like Naxos or Paros, it is easier to equate the island as a whole with the community. Even the pan-hellenic sanctuaries are communities of sorts, albeit playing by slightly different rules. Given that networks did not map onto geography, it was not merely a case of communities being left with no better alternative than to interact with other communities who happened to be located nearby; but, if there would be a significant benefit to the local community, one could actively choose to communicate with groups who lived further away. For example, to those operating Ionian markets, there was some benefit in extending networks beyond the local, something that we can see clearly in the abundance of Ionian ceramics in the assemblage at 'non-local' sites like Kolonna on Aegina. This implies that Greeks recognised that some courses of action were more beneficial than others, that it was better to be part of one network rather than another. Greeks, both individually and in groups, recognised all sorts of advantages and disadvantages in interacting with other communities here rather than there, and they actively made *choices* to be part of certain local- and long-range networks.

There were decisions to be made both about economic transaction and also about expressing political affiliation. On the former, in minting coins, communities had to choose, when adopting weight standards, which other communities they would interact with most closely. By utilising the same standard as a neighbour, a community could trade more readily with this group. Equivalency provided the smooth flow of information around the network, but difference put up a transactional barrier, bringing the risk of isolation from other networks. Lindos, for instance, plugged itself into Miletos' extensive exchange networks by minting its own coinage on the Milesian standard, while Ialysos could not so easily participate in those same networks in using its own Ialysian standard. On the other side of the coin, the communities who chose to acquire certain types of ceramics (both for the shape and for their ware) became more closely aligned with the commodity trade networks that spread far beyond the physical communities themselves. And these commodity networks, seen already in Chapters 2 and 3 of this book, were not just abstract networks but shaped the very ways in which people would move around the Aegean Basin. The case for this has been made in previous chapters, and a prime example concerns the construction of the *diolkos* to move cargoes like heavy marble blocks up the *isthmus* and between the Saronic and Corinthian Gulf: a demand for marble in the northern and western Peloponnese, for instance, necessitated the construction of a structure like this, indicating quite clearly how the desire for certain material products had an effect on the way in which people moved (and constructed new pathways to move) through the Aegean. Communities were making decisions all of the time, and these decisions had very real impacts on the ways in which their members lived in and interacted with the rest of the world of Archaic Greece.

Ironically, though, it was sometimes actually away from home that the community became most visible. Not just anywhere, but specifically at sanctuaries and ports – areas of high traffic at which many Greeks were meeting one another – political identities were on show, and communities, by being present in these contested spaces, chose to engage in dialogue with one another. To put up an inscription was to participate in this dialogue between communities: to decide on the size of that inscription, what it said, and what lettersets were used dictated the way in which that communication played out. Dedicatory practice at Delphi provides good evidence of this. By dedicating a stone treasury near the entrance of the Sacred Way, the community of Knidos indicated that it wanted to advertise its presence in the sanctuary to other communities; and by appending to this treasury a dedicatory inscription naming the Knidians explicitly and using local non-Phokaian lettersets, that message of personal identification was amplified. This was done not just with writing but with sculpture too: the widespread availability of marble for producing freestanding sculptures provided an arena for communities to compete with one another, and the choices made on the style, size and materiality of those sculptures were the tools chosen by individuals and communities for how to compete with one another. This was about generating recognition through performative actions, activities that worked across networks and between communities – about advertising a sense of individual or collective identity in a non-local environment. And the basis of that sort of communication was in knowing what sorts of messages other Greek communities would recognise.

Thus, participating in the community was about performing activities through choice: the implication here is that choosing to perform one sort of action rather than another depends on knowledge. It is not controversial to suggest that Greeks could only choose the most effective strategy for extending their own economic reach if they knew where to find these networks, and they could only communicate their local identities so effectively through knowing how others would respond to their strategies. What is a more novel suggestion concerns both the *amount* of common knowledge that there was and the wide *extent* to which this was in circulation around the Aegean, facilitating the formation, coordination and transformation of all manner of networks. The whole premise of a 'luxury' network piggy-backing on a 'commodity' network depends on the notion that those commissioning, producing and dedicating statues knew enough about ceramic supply patterns that a whole new type of network could be built on top of existing shipping lanes. Indeed, the evidence discussed appears to support the claim by Osborne and others that not only was there knowledge and targeting of certain networks in the Archaic period but also that a (proto-)market emerged out of these systems. The main core of early Archaic period economic activity in the Aegean Basin was the transport of bulk goods; but because of the circulation of knowledge that arose *as a result of these expanding networks*, competition and prestige markets developed in synergy. Knowing what other people wanted encouraged Greeks to reach out towards other networks, and, in doing so, their communities learned strategies for competition with one another in different ways.

What is the implication of the assertion that it was a careful targeting of markets that led to the formation of other types of networks? On the one hand, it points to the rather unsatisfying notion that all types of community activity oriented for networking were entangled to the point of indivisibility. Even though Greeks knew what was going on in the wider world, one sort of knowledge was not distinct from another. But, more usefully, given that dividing between different sorts of knowledge and different sorts of activities is not entirely helpful, the notion of indivisible knowledge moves us forwards on a different theoretical debate, namely on the 'embeddedness' of Archaic Greece. The Aegean world that emerges is one in which there was a significant intersection between networks of economics and politics, one in which the activities undertaken by communities in connecting with one another were various and overlapping. Shipping routes were carved out for the benefit of both luxury and commodity products; the production of coinage was geared towards the utility of shared weight standards, but this also gave an opportunity to advertise one's community identity using visual (iconographic) attributes as one might do in using certain lettersets. Greeks were neither entirely *homines oeconomici* nor *homines politici*. The 'economy' as a total entity comprised a number of different (religious, social, cultural, militaristic) networks – with varying levels of economic or political priority.

Networks, then, were non-specific and variously overlapping, but they were also crucial to the overall formation of the Aegean world. Networks reconstructed from the distribution of objects in the material record might not map onto what we think we know about alliance and rivalry from the literary and historic record, stories told about the interactions between communities that oftentimes turn out to be anachronistic. Much more productive is to take a bottom-up approach. This makes clear that the activities of communities aligned towards networking were largely motivated by the desires and ambitions of elite peers within those groups, variously expressing their identities and affiliations in high-traffic locations, and that the mechanisms for advertising oneself subtly changed over time. This socially embedded desire for status and competition drove large-scale shipping networks for moving goods around the Aegean, networks that built on an earlier generation of commodity trade that was more systematically oriented towards the needs of its consumers in a proto-market. All of these networks intersected at different levels: the Aegean comprised different types of network at various levels that were variously entangled, constructed and co-ordinated at various times throughout the Archaic period; and, while they did not overlap directly one-to-one with one another, each network depended on another and they developed in synergy.

7 | Conclusions

This book has used the 'big-ish data' that are an important product of the particular archaeological history of Greece to investigate the political and economic interactions of communities from the Aegean Basin in the seventh and sixth centuries BC. It has argued that it is possible to use different modelling techniques to engage the vast material record of Archaic Greece to map the networks of interaction between communities and to define the nature and role of connectivity in the overall formation of the Aegean world.

To evaluate the effectiveness of these methods, it is important here to return to the research questions defined at the start of the book. Namely, what does this analysis of big data tell us about the 'big questions' that have exercised historians of early Greece? Those questions have been both political and economic: politically, scholars have wanted to know how formally organised the political communities of early Greece really were, and what role elite peers played within these communities; economically, scholars have debated whether the methods of modern economics can appropriately be used to analyse the ancient economy.

Economic Networks

The case has been made for an economy based around the bulk transport of commodity goods. Many of these commodity products – grain, oil, wine – are archaeologically invisible, their cultivation and trade inferred through other sources. The distribution of excavation pottery across the Aegean Basin, however, is suggestive of a widely distributed economic network in operation as early as the seventh century BC. While these networks operated initially very locally, by the end of the Archaic period they linked together, either directly or indirectly, sites from all corners of the Aegean Basin. Similarly, the spread of weight standards facilitated economic transfer between different communities, and those whose coinages adopted several different weight standards enjoyed the advantage over their neighbours of participation in several different economic networks. Those communities who were the among the first to adopt coinage gave themselves a position of advantage by providing a 'template' for a number of smaller communities to subsequently adopt 'their' standard.

Space and time are important too. Early shipping technology provided an effective means for distributing commodity goods around the Aegean Basin – but this was both a timely and a risky process. Short 'harbour-to-harbour' shipments were made along coastlines where key stopover points became nodes at which quantities of non-local potteries (and non-local commodity goods contained inside them) could be consumed. On the issue of time, many of the networks discussed in this context had their roots in the eighth century and earlier. But these networks developed at an unprecedented rate in the Archaic period, and certainly by the end of the sixth century BC the irregular and opportunistic exchange systems of the Early Iron Age had become increasingly organised.

Large quantities of things were consumed in the Archaic Aegean, including commodity goods, semi-luxuries (like textiles and perfumes) and larger luxury products (like marble statues). When it comes to ceramics, consumption (particularly at sanctuary sites) has been linked to practice: certain types of vessels were required for certain activities. Ceramic shapes are not independent of ware, nor, by extension, place of production, and so the requirement for certain types of vessels demanded that the users of sanctuaries looked towards specific places to fulfil that need. Here there is the problem of push-pull: were consumers selecting certain types of products, or did producers force different vessels in certain directions? In some sense it does not matter which explanation one accepts: both alternatives suggest there was an element of choice and selection in ceramic consumption – the sort of process characteristic of early market behaviour.

At a macro-scale it is possible to make the case for one type of economic network laying the foundation for another. Not only did a pre-existing commodity network enable the rapid development of a marble statue network, but an early economic network based around *amphoras* – and, necessarily, the consumable products stored within them – helped to set the stage for the first coinage. The transfer of knowledge for minting coins flowed along a network of similar shape to the ceramic distribution network, indicating for us that it is particularly useful in identifying network intersections when we find qualitatively similar networks separated by a time lag. And, indeed, as the compartmentalisation of an economy into different products (or into different classes of product like 'commodity' and 'luxury') is a somewhat arbitrary, generalist and anachronistic exercise, it is in fact not altogether surprising to learn that these economic networks were so closely related (but not necessarily identical) to one another.

More difficult to align are economic and *political* networks: the extent to which this alignment is possible varies on a regional basis. On Rhodes and in Ionia, there was economic networking between communities who more consciously marked themselves as politically independent. This contrasts with Attica where there was greater political and economy homogeneity – different corners of the Aegean just did economics and political affiliation differently. Geography helps in explaining the variation: Aegina and Euboea lie at the heart of two routes that cut across the Aegean Basin, their position having been used to explain both the volume of non-local ceramics consumed on Aegina and the potential for Euboea to link itself to so many other communities for sharing its coinage weight standard. But this is not deterministic. As illustrated in the case of the northern Aegean, local trajectories are just as important: an early interest in (the natural resources of?) the region by Athens and Ionian cities accounts for pottery consumed here and the sharing of weight standards with northern communities, after which, towards the end of the sixth century BC, both the consumption of local ceramics and the operation of independent coinage networks had developed throughout the region.

The main 'value added' in adopting this data modelling approach has been that it has enabled various economic products to be analysed separately. That is, discussion has not just focused on 'commodities' but on *different types* of commodities, thus enabling one to see the extent to which the exchange of different goods was 'embedded' to various degrees. The distribution of different goods was associated with the effects of different social values, and the desire to target these specific goods reveals more about the varying priorities of the communities of Archaic Greece. Although this emphasis on different goods (and different economic activities) helps to reiterate the point made that it is unproductive to take a modernist view of a singular 'economy' comprising rational economic actors, the existence of various, overlapping and long-lasting economic *networks* suggests that the desire for different types of products was indeed targeted. Encouragingly, this is a data-driven conclusion that resonates fairly strongly with models from the current trend in theorising the ancient economy, that the division between economic activity strictly for profit and activity embedded within society might not need to be so stark.[1] Generally, this Bressonian view

---

[1] Archibald and Davies 2011 and Harris and Lewis 2016 both argue for the case for later periods, but much the same theoretical can be applied to the Archaic period.

advocates an ancient economy that both performed social and cultural functions, but which also specialised in the production of certain products, ultimately enjoying growth throughout the seventh and sixth centuries.[2]

Political Networks

It was in comparison to the literary-historical record that there was least intersection with material networks. As seen in the case of both the Kalaureian *Amphiktyony* and the Ionian League, non-contemporary sources present problems, as does the issue of back projection. But even when making allowances, the archaeological data are simply not substantial enough to map onto these patterns. Particularly lacking was any sort of coinage network for the communities of Ionia or for the Kalaureian *Amphiktyony*. While one could argue that the material record analysed in this way can only get us so far and that the sorts of interactions one might expect from communities in formal alliance are *not* easily distinguishable from the present dataset, there is also the issue of non-detectability. It is not just that there are weak patterns, but there are almost *no* connections between communities expressed in the way that we would expect. And so the reasonable conclusion to make is that the sorts of networks that one finds looking through text and the sorts of networks that emerge through an analysis of archaeological history are separate and non-overlapping.

Although the main focus of this study has been on the community as a unit of analysis, a case has also been made for looking at individuals in light of competition between aspiring peers. The actions of an individual are not separate from one's own community, nor are they separate from the communities of others: an individual might choose to dedicate a statue for their own benefit, for example; but the presence of that statue within a sanctuary space is also tied back to an individual's home community, and a community of craftspeople quarrying the stone, transporting the stone, shaping the stone into the statue that it becomes. The ambition to create more elaborate statues, more sizeable statues – just *more* statues – kept turning the wheel to crank up the extent and scale of the marble network until the net sum of marble shipped around the Aegean on an annual basis to meet the needs of a few became truly vast. The desires and ambitions of just a few to consume

---

[2] Ironically, then, the picture that emerges here of the economy of Archaic Greece is of a system 'embedded' in the social activities entangled with many different commodities, yet – and contrary to the objections of someone like Finley (1971: 174) – this position has been reached through a reasonably formalist treatment of the data.

created a ripple through the Aegean on large-scale production processes, linking together people, places and practices.

Mobility and circulation set the stage for interaction: once Greeks came together, the need to advertise one's community affiliation became so much greater. For thinking through these issues of affiliation, the practice of writing is particularly useful, given that the agency to *express* affiliations rested with individuals: those who were doing the writing had to make decisions about which of several variant lettersets they would use, thus indicating something to those reading the writing about their place of origin. And even stronger is the notion of choice and selection, if we accept those who produced writing could read and had knowledge of *all* variant lettersets in use in the Archaic Aegean. Writing was a form of practice that linked the individual to the community, and it was a practice that left a mark in a prominent way for others to come and read.

Pan-hellenic sanctuary sites were microcosms for this sort of competition and connection. In fact, compared to a *polis* sanctuary, a pan-hellenic sanctuary did competition and competitive display in quite a different way. On the one hand, there were pan-hellenic spaces where, as shown by the data, a range of different identities were put on show through use of distinctive lettersets. On the other, this variation is *not* there when we look at other urban sites that have their own sanctuaries, and where writing took on a more predictably 'local' form. One might therefore conclude that there was a greater degree of competition at pan-hellenic sanctuaries than at other sanctuaries. But at these 'local' sanctuaries there *was* still a degree of competition, as seen through the deploying of large and elaborate votive objects such as *kouroi*. The critical difference here was that the aim was quite different. That is, the idea was to show off one's own power, wealth and status with a *kouros*, while the aim of leaving words written in a certain way in a pan-hellenic space was to show a different aspect of one's identity, that one is from a given *polis*, that they came to this sanctuary, and that they left a record of themselves. This was still elite competition but of a different sort: it was competition that was predicated on connections made with individuals or collectives from other places to have the intended effect.

The importance of the sanctuary also demands that one reflect on the nature of the community. More specifically, this study set out to look at the interactions between *economic* and *political* units of different sizes – and yet the critical patterns bring us back to *sanctuaries*. In some ways, this should not be surprising: the dataset for this analysis is drawn from big digs, which by their very nature have featured more sanctuaries than any other type of site. But do the patterns drawn go further in making the case that the most important type of community in Archaic Greece was actually based around the religious – or that the principal variety of community was the 'community of cult'? Both. On the one hand, this study has underlined the well-recognised importance of sanctuaries and religious activities for bringing together Greeks of all affiliations to network and to compete on a stage where economic and political dialogue could take place. But, on the other, it has also demonstrated that there *were* other critical types of network informing the shape of the Archaic Greek world, networks that are perhaps less immediately detectable. It has been argued that the character of economic interactions in the seventh century BC had a profound effect on shaping further economic and political interactions in the generations to come, but that this is a network whose shape is more inferred (or, indeed, 'back-projected') than is immediately visible. So, although economic activity is less detectable in the archaeological record, that does not necessarily mean that it was less important than religious connectivity owing simply to a pattern of visibility. Similarly, while the networks for competing politically and for advertising status were certainly *enabled* by bringing people together in sanctuary spaces, this study has also demonstrated that networks can be overlapping but quite separate. Political and economic interest did intersect with the world of the gods – but they existed independently, too.

Sanctuaries also cause the most disturbance when we attempt to reconstruct the regional patterns (particularly of lettersets) across the Aegean. That is, sanctuaries acted like basins that drew all sorts of writing produced by people of different origins, expressing a whole range of community affiliations; but in using clustering algorithms to sort the letterset data, the noise created around sanctuaries obfuscates clear-cut regional patterns. On the one hand, we can take this to be a pattern of the data: and, for the seventh century BC – at least where the quantity of the data available for analysis restricts the extent to which we can discern patterns to the level precision possible for the sixth century BC and its world of extreme diversity – this might be the case. Alternatively, it is also the case that, not just at sanctuaries, but in general across the Aegean the community has been a more useful unit of analysis than the region. Classical archaeologists and ancient historians are trained to see regions: some groups consciously identified themselves as Attic, Boeotian or Corinthian, some styles are particularly characteristic of certain places; and even the geography and political organisation of (modern) Greece encourages one to see the Aegean as a patchwork of different regions. What this study has indicated, though, is that regions and networks do not map perfectly. Ironically, taking a broad view has underlined the importance of some quite small geographic units, for instance, the sanctuary. Moreover, it has been demonstrated that community-level networks spread across islands (and larger islands contained multiple smaller community units), and yet regions like Ionia were composite for a diverse range of smaller parts. The crucial turning point was around the start of the sixth century when networking between communities looked most 'regional-like', though somewhat obfuscated by diversity and complexity thereafter. And, even more importantly, when we adopt a chronological view focused on the activities of communities, the size of region networks changes considerably over even fifty-year periods. That not only borders but that *regions themselves* were just as flexible in such a short space of time raises a new set of challenges.

With the analysis having provided a way of describing the behaviour of various political units, the question is how this might relate more specifically in the Archaic period to what Greek historians have referred to as the 'rise of the *polis*'. Without reopening the debate on the nature of a *polis*, it is sufficient to say that the conversation now is not one of definition alone, but one that focuses on the activities of certain units and their members. What we have is a set of non-equivalent units of different sizes whose communications, competitions and exchanges were crucial to the expansion and operation of the Aegean world in the seventh and sixth centuries. Whereas the 'rise of the *polis*' model would have it that there was a set of early sudden changes or a renaissance throughout the Archaic period, what the data have in fact demonstrated is that communities underwent gradual change, and it was only right at the end of the Archaic period that the shape of the Aegean world was being reconfigured significantly throughout the networking activities of its constituent units. Moreover, given that those units were of various size – sometimes individual political units, but sometimes much larger or smaller units – it is in fact the case that place does not straightforwardly correlate with *polis* or any other particular Greek term. If one is to embrace the 'diversity of the Greek situation' and to put the emphasis on the activities of its constituent units, it is then the 'community of activity' and the 'community' alone that one can speak of.

This resonates with the central notion of Peer Polity Interaction (Snodgrass 1986, *sensu* Renfrew and Cherry 1986), that communications of various kinds take place between autonomous and independent geographically proximate political units (e.g. competition, warfare, or exchange of goods), and the motivation to *increase* these interactions is subject to an intensification of contact with and knowledge of one's neighbours. That is, when communities become more aware of one another, they are motivated to find new ways of displaying their own status or power. And where almost forty years ago this model, although regarded as an eminently sensible description of the realities of Archaic Greece, suffered from a lack of supporting data – from the numbers crunched by Snodgrass in his analysis of Greek temple sizes being rather small – the much larger 'big data' analysis conducted here strongly suggests that the model holds up both across the Archaic period and across *different parts* of the Archaic period. In other words, the data analysed have revealed that the development of both substantial economic and political networks were subject to pre-existing connections – competitions and exchanges – which themselves were enabled by knowledge of who else was out there and what they wanted.

And it is that knowledge of others that is essential to the formation of all these networks. Knowledge enables an individual or a collective to gain the material goods that they desire (i.e. they know what exists and how they would be best placed to obtain these items), and knowledge also enables one to distinguish themselves within the community – or in other communities. Knowledge is not something that can be measured empirically through the datasets chosen, but its existence is strongly indicated through a sequence of networks enabling one another. Most strongly, the case has been made for a succession of economic networks,[3] that the trade of commodities enabled a system by which luxuries could also be traded; and this network also allowed the knowledge of a minting technology to be adopted wide scale over a short period of time. But this same network, and the knowledge that underpinned it, might also have been necessary for the formation of other sorts of networks: was it perhaps the same knowledge of a wider Aegean world launching the marble trade that also enabled a network for the expression and competition of political identities, leading more formally to the formation of political communities? Was it not knowledge of who else was out there that could have transformed the minimal community of people in a particular place into a political community, uniting to meet their needs and desires?

Connecting Communities Beyond Archaic Greece

Although this book has been about 'big data', in many ways it is just a 'small pilot study'. Vast quantities of archaeological data have been used to draw the historical conclusions outlined – but there is still plenty of material left

---

[3] On knowledge and economic networks too: the element of specialisation visible in the pottery record attests a high volume of traffic enabling potential consumers to have a greater level of in-depth knowledge for what might be acquired.

to be utilised. The 'Greece' of 'Archaic Greece' has only looked to the Aegean Basin, and a very different picture might emerge once one draws in Greek settlement overseas, the broader extent of the Greek-speaking world, or even if one did away with the notion of 'Greek' settlement entirely and turned instead to patterns of all kinds of communities interacting right across the Mediterranean. The notion of an arbitrarily defined 'Archaic Greece' might also be understood by what came before and what came after. Indeed, many of the things that this book has argued were happening in Archaic Greece were also happening a century or two earlier in the Early Iron Age. A logical next step is to look for those networks, but particularly challenging is the possibility of doing this with 'big data' techniques owing to a paucity of high-quality published data covering large geographic areas. And in the other direction, too, the question of whether networks of the Archaic period set the stage for the Classical world remains open. The network of the fifth-century Aegean world *par excellence* was the Athenian 'Empire', and still up for debate is the extent to which the foundations for this network were laid in the Archaic period. While the dataset is much larger, much richer, much more complicated and more entangled than the dataset of the Archaic period, the fifth-century Aegean world provides an enticing case study with which to explore further from an archaeological historical approach the notion of connectivity.

Unashamedly, this book has taken a far more processual and 'etic' approach than many other current studies in Archaic Greece. As outlined in the Introduction, the intention has not been to fly in the face of more recent 'emic' approaches, but, in side-stepping some of the problems of definition and precision for each individual datapoint, the goal has been to run some *experiments* on assemblages of data – to see what questions one might ask in taking a very literal understanding of a 'network'. And while a data-driven approach like this does not claim to be a panacea that can present a picture any more definitive or true than others, the analyses conducted have certainly both shown long-known patterns more clearly and brought some new questions to the table. Data-led analysis is not a means to an end, but the beginning of a conversation on those patterns and problems.

This study has also made the case for returning to legacy data, to the vast datasets underused by historians and generated by the last 100 years of archaeological activity in Greece – but clearly part of the challenge is getting access to the data in the first place. It goes without saying that new archaeological investigation will continue, and new datasets will be generated, but there is still significant value in looking back: this will involve not just the Herculean task of publishing storerooms stuffed full of material, but also returning to old datasets with a tooth comb for cleaning, correcting old records and mapping old categories of information to new data standards. Trawling through old data is not glamorous work, nor does data management or the fine tuning of 'old stuff' attract the same level of scholarly kudos as launching the next big project. But, as demonstrated in this book, this grind is worth it for advancing our understanding of ancient history. By approaching legacy data in new and creative ways we might only have begun to uncover the patterns in the archaeology of the past century.

Big data might pose big challenges; but they also have even bigger potential.

Bibliography

Agelidis, S. 2017. 'The "Spatial Turn" in Ancient Greek Festival Research: Venues of the Athenian City Dionysia and the Great Panathenaia pompai', in L. Nevett (ed.) *Theoretical Approaches to the Archaeology of Ancient Greece: Manipulating Material Culture*: 230–45. Ann Arbor.

Akurgal, E. 1968. *The Birth of Greek Art: The Mediterranean and the Near East.* London.

—— 1983. *Alt-Smyrna*, Türk Tarih Kurumu yayınları. Basımevi, Ankara.

Alexandridou, A. 2011. *The Early Black-Figured Pottery of Attika in Context.* Leiden.

—— 2013. 'Archaic Pottery and Terracottas from the Sanctuary of Poseidon at Kalaureia'. *Opuscula* 6: 81–150.

Alexandridou, A., A. Alexandropoulou, M. Koutsoumpou, A. Mazarakis Ainian, D. Palaeothodoros, M. Panagou and P. Tsilogianni. 2017. 'Pottery and Clay Figurines From the Sanctuary of Kythnos', in A. Mazarakia Ainian (ed.) *Les sanctuaires Archaïques des Cyclades*: 135–92. Rennes.

Alfen, P. G. van. 2012. 'Problems in the Political Economy of Archaic Greek Coinage'. *Notae Numisticae* 7: 13–36.

Amyx, D. A. 1988. *Corinthian Vase-Painting of the Archaic Period.* Berkeley.

Amyx, D. A. and P. Lawrence. 1975. *Archaic Corinthian Pottery and the Anaploga Well* (Corinth 7:2). Princeton, NJ.

Anderson, B. 1983. *Imagined Communities: Reflections on the Origin and Spread of Nationalism.* London.

Anderson, G. 2018. *The Realness of Things Past: Ancient Greece and Ontological History.* Oxford.

Andreiomenou, A. K. 2007. *Τανάγρα: η ανασκαφή του νεκροταφείου (1976–1977, 1989)*. Athens.

—— 2015. *Το κεραμεικό εργαστήριο της Ακραιφίας: τα ανασκαφικά δεδομένα και τα αγγεία της κατηγορίας των Βοιωτικών κυλίκων μετά πτηνών.* Athens.

Angliker, E. M. 2017. 'Worshipping the Divinities at the Archaic Sanctuaries on the Cyclades', in A. Mazarakis Ainian (ed.) *Les sanctuaires Archaïques des Cyclades*: 29–53. Rennes.

Antonaccio, C. M. 2007. 'Colonization: Greece on the Move, 900–480', in H. A. Shapiro (ed.) *The Cambridge Companion to Archaic Greece*: 201–24. Cambridge.

Appadurai, A. 1986. 'Introduction: Commodities and the Politics of Value', in A. Appadurai (ed.) *The Social Life of Things: Commodities in Cultural Perspective*: 3–63. Cambridge.

Archibald, Z. H. 2013. 'Joining up the Dots: Making Economic Sense of Pottery Distributions in the Aegean and Beyond', in A. Tsingarida and D. Viviers (ed.) *Pottery Markets in the Ancient Greek World (8th – 1st centuries BC), Proceedings of the International Symposium held at the Université libre de Bruxelles, 19–21 June 2008*: 133–57. Brussels.

2016. 'Moving Upcountry: Ancient Travel from Coastal Ports to Inland Harbours', in K. Höghammar, B. Alroth and A. Lindhagen (ed.) *Ancient Ports: The Geography of Connections. Proceedings of an International Conference at the Department of Archaeology and Ancient History, Uppsala University, 23–25 September 2010*: 37–64. Uppsala.

2017. 'Does "Greek Archaeology" Matter?', in L. C. Nevett (ed.) *Theoretical Approaches to the Archaeology of Ancient Greece: Manipulating Material Culture*: 301–5. Ann Arbor.

Archibald, Z. H. and J. Davies. 2011. 'Introduction', in Z. Archibald, J. Davies and V. Gabrielsen (ed.) *The Economies of Hellenistic Societies, Third to First Centuries BC*: 1–18. Oxford.

Arnaud, P. 2005. *Les routes de la navigation antique: itinéraires en Méditerranée*. Paris.

Athanasiou, G. 2014. Πόρος, Τροιζηνία, Μέθανα με το βλέμμα των περιηγητών. Μια περιήγηση στον τόπο και στον χρόνο. Poros.

Attanasio, D. 2003. *Ancient White Marbles: Analysis and Identification by Paramagnetic Resonance Spectroscopy*. Rome.

Aurigny, H. 2020. 'Gathering in the Panhellenic Sanctuary at Delphi: An Archaeological Approach', in A. Collar and T. M. Kristensen (ed.) *Pilgrimage and Economy in the Ancient Mediterranean*: 93–115. Leiden.

Bagwell, K. and B. D. Bernheim. 1996. 'Veblen Effects in a Theory of Conspicuous Consumption'. *American Economic Review* 86: 349–73.

Balcer, J. 1984. *Sparda by the Bitter Sea. Imperial Interactions in Western Anatolia*. Chicago.

Balmuth, M. S. 1967. 'The Monetary Forerunners of Coinage in Phoenicia and Palestine', in A. Kindler (ed.) *Proceedings of the International Numismatic Convention, Jerusalem 1963: The Patterns of Development in Phoenicia and Palestine in Antiquity*: 25–32. Tel-Aviv.

Bammer, A. 1990. 'A Peripteros of the Geometric Period in the Artemision of Ephesus'. *Assyriological Studies* 40: 137–60.

1991. 'Les sanctuaires des VIIIe et VIIe siécles a l'Artemision d' Éphèse'. *Revue archéologique* 1: 63–84.

Barker, S. J. and B. Russell. 2012. 'Labour Figures for Roman Stone-Working: Pitfalls and Potential', in S. Camporeale, H. Dessales and A. Pizzo (ed.)

Archeologia della costruzione III. Les chantiers de construction de l'Italie et des provinces romaines: 83–94. Mérida.

Barnes, J. A. and F. Harary. 1983. 'Graph Theory in Network Analysis'. *Social Networks* 5: 235–44.

Barrandon, J.-N. and M. F. Guerra. 1998. 'Ion Beam Activation Analysis with a Cyclotron', in A. Oddy and M. Cowell (ed.) *Metallurgy in Numismatics* 4: 15–34. London.

Barrett, C. E. 2009. 'The Perceived Value of Minoan and Mycenaean Pottery in Egypt'. *Journal of Mediterranean Archaeology* 22: 211–34.

Baxter, M. J. 1994. *Exploratory Multivariate Analysis in Archaeology*. Edinburgh.

Bearzot, C. 1983. 'La guerra lelantina el il koinon degli Ioni d'Asia'. *Contributi dell'Istituto di storia antica* 9. 57–81.

Bell, T., A. Wilson and A. Wickham. 2013. 'Tracking the Samnites: Landscape and Communications Routes in the Sangro Valley, Italy'. *American Journal of Archaeology* 106: 169.

Bennet, J. 2021. 'Introduction', in J. Bennet (ed.) *Representations: Material and Immaterial Modes of Communication in the Bronze Age Aegean*: 1–10. Oxford.

Beresford, J. 2013. *The Ancient Sailing Season*. Leiden.

Berg, I. 2010. 'Re-capturing the Sea. The Past and Future of 'Island Archaeology' in Greece'. *The International Journal of Research into Island Cultures* 4: 16–26.

  2016. *Kalaureia 1894. A Cultural History of the First Swedish Excavation in Greece*. Stockholm.

Berger, A. H., M. E. H. Bloch, A. de Ruijter, I. C. Jarvie, J. O'Neill, I. Rossi, M. Sahlins, W. W. Stein and A. C. L. Zwaan. 1976. 'Structural and Eclectic Revisions of Marxist Strategy: A Cultural Materialist Critique'. *Current Anthropology* 17:

Bernheim, B. D. 1995. 'A Theory of Conformity'. *Journal of Political Economy* 102: 841–77.

Berry, C. J. 1994. *The Idea of Luxury: A Conceptual and Historical Investigation*. Cambridge.

Bevan, A. 2007. *Stone Vessels and Values in the Bronze Age Mediterranean*. Cambridge.

  2015. 'The Data Deluge'. *Antiquity* 89: 1473–84.

Bhabha, H. 1990. 'The Third Space', in J. Rutherford (ed.) *Identity: Community, Culture, Difference*: 207–21. London.

Bicho, N., J. Cascalheira and C. Gonçalves. 2017. 'Early Upper Paleolithic Colonization Across Europe: Time and Mode of the Gravettian Diffusion'. *PLOS ONE* 12: e0178506.

Bissa, E. 2009. *Governmental Intervention in Foreign Trade in Archaic and Classical Greece*. Leiden.

Bivar, A. D. H. 1971. 'Hoard of Ingot-Currency of the Median Period from Nūsh-i Jān, near Malayir'. *Iran* 9: 97–111.

Blackman, D., B. Rankov, K. Baika, H. Gerding and J. Pakkanen (ed.). 2013. *Shipsheds of the Ancient Mediterranean*. Cambridge.

Blaug, M. 1999. 'Misunderstanding Classical Economics: The Sraffian Interpretation of the Surplus Approach'. *History of Political Economy* 31: 214–36.

Blegen, C. W., H. Palmer and R. S. Young. 1964. *The North Cemetery* (Corinth 13). Princeton, NJ.

Blinkenberg, C. 1931. *Les petits objets, Lindos: fouilles et recherches 1902–1914*. Berlin.

Blok, J. 2017. *Citizenship in Classical Athens*. Cambridge.

Blondel, V. D., J. -L. Guillaume, R. Lambiotte and E. Lefebvre. 2008. 'Fast Unfolding of Communities in Large Networks'. *Journal of Statistical Mechanics: Theory and Experiment* 10: 10008.

Boardman, J. 1978. *Greek Sculpture. The Archaic Period*. London.

  1980. *The Greeks Overseas: Their Early Colonies and Trade*. London.

  2006. 'Sources and Models', in O. Palagia (ed.) *Greek Sculpture. Function, Materials, and Techniques in the Archaic and Classical Periods*: 1–31. Cambridge.

Bodard, G., H. Cayless, M. Depauw, L. Isaksen, K. F. Lawrence and S. Rahtz. 2017. 'Standards for Networking Ancient Person-Data: Digital Approaches to Problems in Prosopographical Space'. *Digital Classics Online* 3.2.

Bodard, G., T. Elliott, E. Mylonas, S. Stoyanova, C. Tupman and S. Vanderbilt. 2011. EpiDoc Guidelines.

Boffa, G. and B. Leone. 2017. 'Euboean Cults and Myths Outside Euboea: Poseidon and Briareos/Aigaion', in Z. Tankosić, F. Mavridis and M. Kosma (ed.) *An Island Between Two Worlds: The Archaeology of Euboea from Prehistoric to Byzantine Times*: 381–90. Athens.

Bonnier, A. 2014. *Coastal Hinterlands: Site Patterns, Microregions and Coast-Inland Interconnections by the Corinthian Gulf, c. 600-300 BC*. Oxford.

Boomert, A. and A. J. Bright. 2007. 'Island Archaeology: In Search of a New Horizon'. *Island Studies Journal* 2: 3–26.

Borken, A. and C. Rowan. 2014. 'Introduction. A Turkish Teapot, or Thinking Things Through', in A. Borken and C. Rowan (ed.) *Embodying Value? The Transformation of Objects In and From the Ancient World*: 1–10. Oxford.

Bourdieu, P. 1977. *Outline of a Theory of Practice*. New York.

Bourogiannis, G. 2017. 'Cypriot Evidence in Seventh-Century Rhodes: Discontinuity or Change?', in C. Morgan and X. Charalambidou (ed.) *Interpreting the Seventh Century BC. Tradition and Innovation*: 60-70. Oxford.

Bouzek, J. 1987. 'Some Recent Problems of the Study of Ionian Art'. *Listy filologické* 110: 68–70.

Bowman, A. and A. Wilson (ed.). 2009. *Quantifying the Roman Economy: Methods and Problems*. Oxford.

Brainerd, G. W. 1951. 'The Place of Chronological Ordering in Archaeological Analysis'. *American Antiquity* 18: 341–53.

Brann, E. T. H. 1962. *Late Geometric and Protoattic Pottery: Mid 8th to Late 7th Century B.C.* (Athenian Agora 8). Princeton, NJ.

Brashinskiĭ, I. B. 1984. *Metody issledovaniiā antichnoĭ torgovli*. Leningrad.

Braudel, F. 1949. *La Méditerranée et le monde méditerranéen à l'époque de Philippe II*. Paris.

Braun, K. 1996. Die Korinthische Keramik, in R. C. S. Felsch (ed.) *Kalapodi. Ergebnisse der Ausgrabungen im Heiligtum der Artemis und des Apollon von Hyampolis in der antiken Phokis*: 216–69. Mainz.

Bresson, A. 2008. *L'économie de la Grèce des cités*. Paris.

Broneer, O. 1930. *Terracotta Lamps* (Corinth 4.2). Princeton, NJ.

Broodbank, C. 2000. *An Island Archaeology of the Early Cyclades*. Cambridge.

2013. *The Making of the Middle Sea: A History of the Mediterranean From the Beginning to the Emergence of the Classical World*. Oxford.

Brughmans, T. 2010. 'Connecting the Dots: Towards Archaeological Network Analysis'. *Oxford Journal of Archaeology* 29: 277–303.

2012. 'Thinking Through Networks: A Review of Formal Network Methods in Archaeology'. *Journal of Archaeological Method and Theory* 20: 623–62.

2014. 'The Roots and Shoots of Archaeological Network Analysis: A Citation Analysis and Review of the Archaeological Use of Formal Network Methods'. *Archaeological Review from Cambridge* 29: 18–41.

Brughmans, T., A. Collar and F. S. Coward. 2016. *The Connected Past: Challenges to Network Studies in Archaeology and History*. Oxford.

Bruneau, P. and J. Ducat. 1983. *Guide de Délos*. Athens.

Burford, A. 1960. 'Heavy Transport in Classical Antiquity'. *The Economic History Review* 13: 1–18.

Calligas, P. G. 1988. 'Hero-Cult in Early Iron Age Greece', in R. Hägg, N. Marinatos and G. C. Nordquist (ed.) *Early Greek Cult Practice: Proceedings of the Fifth International Symposium at the Swedish Institute in Athens, 12– 13 May 1980*: 228–34. Stockholm.

Cambitoglou, A., J. K. Papadopoulos and O. T. Jones. 2001. *The Excavations of 1975, 1976 and 1978* (Torone 1). Athens.

Campbell, C. 1995. 'Conspicuous Confusion? A Critique of Veblen's Theory of Conspicuous Consumption'. *Sociological Theory* 13: 37–47.

Campbell, P. and G. Koutsouflakis. 2021. 'Aegean Navigation and the Shipwrecks of Fournoi: The Archipelago in Context', in S. Demesticha and L. Blue (ed.) *Under the Mediterranean I. Studies in Maritime Archaeology*: 278–98. Leiden.

Canuto, M. A. and J. Yaeger. 2000. *The Archaeology of Communities: A New World Perspective*. New York.

Cariolou, G. 1997. 'Kyrenia II: The Return from Cyprus to Greece of the Replica of a Hellenic Merchant Ship', in S. Swiny, R. Hohlfelder and H. W. Swiny (ed.)

Res Maritimae: Cyprus and the Eastern Mediterranean from Prehistory to Late Antiquity. Proceedings of the Second International Symposium 'Cities on the Sea', Nicosia, 18–22 October 1994: 83–97. Atlanta.

Carlson, J. D. 2012. 'Externality, Contact Periphery and Incorporation', in S. J. Babones and C. Chase-Dunn (ed.) *Routledge Handbook of World-Systems Analysis*: 96–7. New York.

Carneiro, R. L. 1967. 'On the Relationship Between Size of Population and Complexity of Social Organization'. *Southwestern Journal of Anthropology* 23: 234–43.

Carneiro, R. L. and S. F. Tobias. 1963. 'The Application of Scale Analysis to the Study of Cultural Evolution'. *Transactions of the New York Academy of Sciences* 26: 196–207.

Carpenter, R. 1960. *Greek Sculpture. A Critical Review*. Chicago.

Carr, C. and J. E. Neitzel. 1995. *Style, Society, and Person: Archaeological and Ethnological Perspectives*. New York; London.

Carradice, I. 1987. 'The "Regal" Coinage of the Persian Empire', in I. Carradice (ed.) *Coinage and Administration in the Athenian and Persian Empires*: 73–107. Oxford.

Carradice, I. and M. Price. 1988. *Coinage in the Greek World*. London.

Carson, R. A. G. 1975. *Asia Minor, 1935/1940. Coin Hoards* 1: 5.

Carter, G. F. and W. H. Carter. 1974. 'Chemical Compositions of Ten Septimius Severus Denarii'. *Numismatic Chronicle* 19: 67–73.

Carter, J. B. and L. J. Steinberg. 2010. 'Kouroi and Statistics'. *American Journal of Archaeology* 114: 103–28.

Caskey, L. D. 1924. 'The Proportions of the Apollo of Tenea'. *American Journal of Archaeology* 28: 358–67.

Caspari, O. B. 1915. 'The Ionian Confederacy'. *Journal of Hellenic Studies* 35: 173–88.

Casson, L. 1995. *Ships and Seamanship in the Ancient World*. Baltimore.

Catling, H. W. 1993. 'The Bronze Amphora and Burial Urn', in M. R. Popham, P. G. Calligas and L. H. Sackett (ed.) *Lefkandi II. The Protogeometric Building at Toumba*: 81–96. London.

Cherrier H. and J. Murray. 2002. 'Drifting Away from Excessive Consumption: A New Social Movement Based on Identity Construction'. *Advances in Consumer Research* 29: 245–7.

Clauset, A., M. E. J. Newman and C. Moore. 2004. 'Finding Community Structure in Very Large Networks'. *Physical Review* E70: 066111.

Coates, J. F. 1989. 'The Trieres, its Design and Construction', in H. Tzalas (ed.) *1st International Symposium on Ship Construction in Antiquity*: 83–90. Athens.

Coelho, P. R. P. and J. E. McClure. 1993. 'Toward an Economic Theory of Fashion'. *Economic Inquiry* 31: 595–608.

Cohen, A. P. 1985. *The Symbolic Construction of Community*. New York.
  2002. *Symbolic Construction of Community*. New York.

Coldstream, J. N. 1968. *Greek Geometric Pottery. A Survey of Ten Local Styles and Their Chronology*. London.

Collar, A., F. Coward, T. Brughmans and B. J. Mills. 2015. 'Networks in Archaeology: Phenomena, Abstraction, Representation'. *Journal of Archaeological Method and Theory* 22: 1–32.

Condamin, J. and M. Picon. 1964. 'Notes on Diffusion in Ancient Alloys'. *Archaeometry* 7: 98–105.

Connelly, J. 2011. 'Ritual Movement Through Greek Sacred Space: Towards an Archaeology of Performance', in A. Chaniotis (ed.) *Ritual Dynamics in the Ancient Mediterranean: Agency, Emotion, Gender, Reception*: 313–46. Stuttgart.

Constantakopoulou, C. 2007. *The Dance of the Islands: Insularity, Networks, the Athenian Empire, and the Aegean World*. Oxford.

Cook, J. M. 1961. 'The Problem of Classical Ionia'. *Proceedings of the Cambridge Philological Society* 187: 9–18.

 1962. *The Greeks in Ionia and the East*. London.

Cook, R. M. 1933–1934. 'Fikellura Pottery'. *The Annual of the British School at Athens* 34: 1–98.

 1958. 'Speculations on the Origins of Coinage'. *Historia: Zeitschrift für Alte Geschichte* 7: 257–62.

 1967. 'Origins of Greek Sculpture'. *Journal of Hellenic Studies* 87: 24–32.

 1979. 'Archaic Greek Trade: Three Conjectures'. *Journal of Hellenic Studies* 99: 152–4.

Cooper, A. and C. T. Green. 2015. 'Embracing the Complexities of 'Big Data' in Archaeology: the Case of the English Landscape and Identities Project'. *Journal of Archaeological Method and Theory* 23: 271–304.

Cope, L. H. 1972. 'The Metallurgical Analysis of Roman Imperial Silver and Aes Coinage', in E. T. Hall and D. M. Metcalf (ed.) *Methods of Chemical and Metallurgical Investigation of Ancient Coinage*: 3–47. London.

Corneo, G. and O. Jeanne. 1997. 'Conspicuous Consumption, Snobbism and Conformism'. *Journal of Public Economics* 66: 55–71.

Coulton, J. J. 1974. 'Lifting in Early Greek Architecture', *JHS* 94: 1–19.

 1975. 'Towards Understanding Greek Temple Design: General Considerations'. *Annual of the British School at Athens* 70: 59–95.

Courby, F. 1927. *La terrasse du Temple*. Paris.

Crawford, K. A. 2019. 'Visualising Ostia's Processional Landscape Through a Multi-Layered Computational Approach: Case Study of the Cult of the Magna Mater'. *Open Archaeology* 5: 444–67.

Crielaard, J. P. 2009. 'The Ionians in the Archaic Period. Shifting Identities in a Changing World', in T. Derks and N. Roymans (ed.) *Ethnic Constructs in Antiquity*: 37–84. Amsterdam.

Crisà, A., M. Gkikaki and C. Rowan. 2019. 'Introduction', in A. Crisà, M. Gkikaki and C. Rowan (ed.) *Tokens. Culture, Connections, Communities*: 1–10 (Special Publication 57). London.

Curtius, E. 1876. 'Der Seebund von Kalaureia'. *Hermes* 10 (385–92).

Dakaris, S., J. Vokotopoulou and A. P. Christidis. 2013. *Τα Χρηστήρια Ἐλάσματα της Δωδώνης των ἀνασκαφών Δ. Εὐαγγελίδη*. Athens.

Davies, J. K. 2009. 'The Historiography of Archaic Greece', in K. A. Raaflaub and H. Wees (ed.) *A Companion to Archaic Greece*: 3–21. Chichester.

Davis, J. L. 1982. 'Thoughts on Prehistoric and Archaic Delos', in *Temple University Aegean symposium 7, 1982: A Symposium Sponsored by the Department of Art History, Temple University, with the Theme 'Trade and Travel in the Cyclades During the Bronze Age,' Friday, March 5, 1982*: 23–33. Philadelphia.

Dawson, H. 2016. '"Brave New Worlds": Islands, Place-Making and Connectivity in the Bronze Age Mediterranean', in B. P. C. Molloy (ed.) *Of Odysseys and Oddities. Scales and Modes of Interaction between Prehistoric Aegean Societies and Their Neighbours*. Oxford.

2019. 'As Good As It Gets? "Optimal" Marginality in the Longue Durée of the Mediterranean Islands'. *Journal of Eastern Mediterranean Archaeology & Heritage Studies* 7: 451–65.

2021. 'Network Science and Island Archeology: Advancing the Debate'. *The Journal of Island and Coastal Archaeology* 16: 213–30.

Déderix, S. 2017. 'Communication Networks, Interactions, and Social Negotiation in Prepalatial South-Central Crete'. *American Journal of Archaeology* 121: 5–37.

DeMarrais, E. 2011. 'Figuring the Group'. *Cambridge Archaeological Journal* 21: 165–86.

2016. 'Making Pacts and Cooperative Acts: The Archaeology of Coalition and Consensus'. *World Archaeology* 48: 1–13.

Demetriou, D. 2011. 'What is an Emporion? A Reassessment'. *Historia: Zeitschrift für alte Geschichte* 60: 255–72.

2012. *Negotiating Identity in the Ancient Mediterranean: The Archaic and Classical Greek Multiethnic Emporia*. Cambridge.

Deonna, W. 1909. *Les Apollons Archaïques: étude sur le type masculin de la statuaire grecque au VIme siècle avant notre ère*. Geneva.

Devillers, M. 1988. *An Archaic and Classical Votive Deposit from a Mycenaean Tomb at Thorikos*. Ghent.

Dietz, S. and M. Stavropoulou-Gatsi. 2011. *Kalydon in Aitolia*. Athens.

Dimova, B. 2019. 'Archaeology in Macedonia and Thrace: Iron Age to Hellenistic, 2014–2019'. *Archaeological Reports* 65: 127–43.

Dinsmoor, W. B. 1947. 'The Hekatompedon on the Athenian Acropolis'. *American Journal of Archaeology* 51: 109–51.

Dobres, M. and J. E. Robb. 2000. *Agency in Archaeology: Paradigm or Platitude?* London.

Dommelen, P. van 2014. 'Moving On: Archaeological Perspectives on Mobility and Migration'. *World Archaeology* 46: 477–83.

Dommelen, P. van, F. Gerritsen and A. B. Knapp. 2005. 'Common Places. Archaeologies of Community and Landscape', in *Communities and Settlements from the Neolithic to the Early Medieval Period. Proceedings of the 6th Conference of Italian Archaeology held at the University of Groningen, Groningen Institute of Archaeology, the Netherlands*: 55–63. Oxford.

Donohue, A. A. 1988. *Xoana and the Origins of Greek Sculpture*. Atlanta.

Dornan, J. L. 2002. 'Agency and Archaeology: Past, Present, and Future Directions'. *Journal of Archaeological Method and Theory* 9: 303–29.

Dörpfeld, W. 1886. 'Athenatempel auf der Akropolis von Athen'. *Antike Denkmäler* 1: 1.

Drees, L. 1968. *Olympia: Gods, Artists and Athletes*. London.

Ducat, J. 1971. *Les kouroi du Ptoion: le sanctuaire d'Apollon Ptoieus a l'époque archaïque*. Paris.

Dugas, C. 1928. *Les vases de l'Héraion* (Delos 10). Paris.

Dugas, C., K. A. Rōmaios and C. Dugas. 1935. *Les vases orientalisants de style non mélien* (Delos 17). Paris.

Dunbabin, T. 1940. *Perachora: The Sanctuaries of Hera Akraia and Limenia, Excavations of the British School of Archaeology at Athens, 1930–1933*. Oxford.

Duplouy, A. 2002. 'L'aristocratie et la circulation des richesses'. *Apport de l'histoire économique à la définition des élites grecques*. *Revue belge de philologie et d'histoire* 80: 5–24.

   2005. 'Pouvoir ou prestige? Apports et limites de l'historiographie politique à la définition des élites grecques'. *Revue belge de philologie et d'histoire* 83: 5–23.

   2006. *La prestige des élites: recherches sur les modes de reconnaissance sociale en Grèce entre les Xe et Ve siècles avant J.-C.* Paris.

Dupont, P. 1983. 'Classification et détermination de provenance des céramiques grecques orientales Archaïques d'Istros. Rapport préliminaire'. *Dacia* 27: 19–46.

   1986. *Naturwissenschaftliche Bestimmung der archaischen Keramik Milets, in Milet 1899–1980'. Ergebnisse, Probleme und Perspektiven einer Ausgrabung*. Tübingen.

Dusenbery, E. 1998. *The Nekropoleis. Catalogues of Objects by Categories* (Samothrace 11). Princeton, NJ.

Eder, B. 2001. 'Continuity of Bronze Age Cult at Olympia? The Evidence of the Late Bronze Age and Early Iron Age Pottery', in R. Laffineur and R. Hägg (ed.) *Potnia: Deities and Religion in the Aegean Bronze Age. Proceedings of the Eighth International Aegean Conference*: 201–9. Liège.

Edwards, E. 1999. 'Photographs as Objects of Memory', in M. Kwint, C. Breward and J. Aynsley (ed.) *Material Memories*: 221–36. Oxford.

Edwards, K. A. 1933. *Coins, 1896–1929* (Corinth 6). Princeton, NJ.

Emberling, G. 1997. 'Ethnicity in Complex Societies: Archaeological Perspectives'. *Journal of Archaeological Research* 5: 295–344.

   1999. 'Review of: Ethnic Identity in Greek Antiquity by Jonathan M. Hall; The Archaeology of Ethnicity: Constructing Identities in the Past and Present by Siân Jones'. *American Journal of Archaeology* 103: 126–7.

Ersoy, Y. 1993. *Clazomenae: The Archaic Settlement*. Bryn Mawr, PE.

Evans, T., R. Rivers and C. Knappett. 2012. 'Interactions in Space for Archaeological Models'. *Advances in Complex Systems* 15 (01n02).

Featherstone, M. 2014. 'Luxury, Consumer Culture and Sumptuary Dynamics'. *Luxury: History, Culture, Consumption* 1: 47–70.

Feleppa, R. 1986. 'Emics, Etics and Social Objectivity'. *Current Anthropology* 27: 243–55.

Feuser, S. 2009. *Der Hafen von Alexandria Troas*. Bonn.

Fiechter, E. R., A. Furtwängler and H. Thiersch. 1906. *Aegina: das Heiligtum der Aphaia*. Munich.

Figueira, T. J. 1981. *Aigina: Society and Politics*. Salem.

Finley, M. I. 1956. *The World of Odysseus*. London.

   1971. 'Archaeology and History'. *Daedalus* 100: 168–86.

   1973. *The Ancient Economy*. London.

   1981. *Economy and Society in Ancient Greece*. London.

Fischer-Bossert, W. 2018. 'The Transfer of Large Sums of Money Within the Greek World Between the Invention of Coinage and the Time of Alexander', in B. Woytek (ed.) *Infrastructure and Distribution in Ancient Economies: The Flow of Money, Goods and Services*: 59–66. Vienna.

Fitzpatrick, S. M. 2004. *Voyages of Discovery: The Archaeology of Islands*. Westport.

Foley, A. 1988. *The Argolid 800–600 BC: An Archaeological Survey*. Gothenburg.

Forrest, W. G. 2000. 'The Pre-Polis Polis', in R. Brock and S. Hodkinson (ed.) *Alternatives to Athens: Varieties of Political Organisation and Community in Ancient Greece*: 280–92. Oxford.

Forsyth, D. 2021. 'The Linkage Between Innovation and Trade Routes: Examples from the Iron Age Cyclades', in D. Katsanopoulou (ed.) *Paros V. Paros Through the Ages. From Prehistoric Times to the 16th Century AD. Proceedings of the Fifth International Conference on the Archaeology of Paros and the Cyclades. Paroikia, Paros, 21–24 June 2019*: 509–20. Athens.

Foxhall, L. 2005. 'Village to City: Staples and Luxuries? Exchange Networks and Urbanization'. *Proceedings of the British Academy* 126: 233–48.

   2017. 'Theory and Method in Greek Archaeology. Some Opportunities and Challenges', in L.C. Nevett (ed.) *Theoretical Approaches to the Archaeology of Ancient Greece: Manipulating Material Culture*: 297–300. Ann Arbor.

Freeman, L. 2004. *The Development of Social Network Analysis*. Vancouver.

Freyer-Schauenburg, B. 1974. *Bildwerke der archaischen Zeit und des strengen Stils*. Bonn.

Frickenhaus, A. 1912. 'Die Hera von Tiryns', in *Tiryns. Die Ergebnisse der Ausgrabungen des Instituts*. Athens.

Furtwängler, A. 1982. 'Griechische Vieltypenprägung und Münzbeamte'. *Schweizerische numismatische Rundschau* 61: 5–29.

Furtwängler, A. E. and H. J. Kienast. 1989. *Der Nordbau im Heraion von Samos* (Samos 3). Bonn.

Gabrielsen, V. 2010. *Financing the Athenian Fleet: Public Taxation and Social Relations*. Baltimore.

  2015. 'Naval and Grain Networks and Associations in Fourth-Century Athens', in C. Taylor and K. Vlassopoulos (ed.) *Communities and Networks in the Ancient World*: 177–212. Oxford.

  2017. 'Financial, Human, Material and Economic Resources Required to Build and Operate Navies in the Classical Greek World', in P. de Souza, P. Arnaud and C. Buchet (ed.) *The Sea in History: The Ancient World*: 426–42. Suffolk and Rochester.

Gagarin, M. and P. J. Perlman. 2016. *The Laws of Ancient Crete, c. 650-400 BCE*. Oxford.

Gardiner, E. 1925. *Olympia: Its History and Remains*. Olympia.

Garlan, Y. 1983. 'Greek Amphorae and Trade', in P. Garnsey, K. Hopkins and C. R. Whittaker (ed.) *Trade in the Ancient Economy*: 27–35. London.

  1988. *Vin et amphoras de Thasos*. Paris.

Garnsey, P. 1988. *Famine and Food Supply in the Graeco-Roman World: Responses to Risk and Crisis*. Cambridge.

Garnsey, P. and I. Morris. 1989. 'Risk and the Polis: The Evolution of Institutionalised Responses to Food Supply Problems in the Ancient Greek State', in P. Halstead and J. O'Shea (ed.) *Bad Year Economics. Cultural Responses to Risk and Uncertainty*: 98–105. Cambridge.

Gattiglia, G. 2015. 'Think Big about Data: Archaeology and the Big Data Challenge'. *Archäologische Informationen* 38: 113–24.

Geertz, C. 1976. 'From the Native's Point of View: On the Nature of Anthropological Understanding', in K. Basso and H. Selby (ed.) *Meaning in Anthropology*: 221–37. Albuquerque.

Geniere, J. de la. 1991. 'Quelques observations sur les céramiques grecques présentes dans les nécropoles de Gela'. *Cronache de archeologia* 30: 167–71.

Germann, K., G. Gruben, H. Knoll, V. Valis and F. J. Winkler. 1988. 'Provenance Characteristics of Cycladic (Paros and Naxos) Marbles. A Multivariate Geological Approach', in M. Waelkens and N. Herz (ed.) *Classical Marble: Geochemistry, Technology, Trade*: 251–62. Dordrecht, Boston.

Ghali-Kahil, L. 1960. *La céramique grecque* (Thasos 7). Paris.

Giddens, A. 1984. *The Constitution of Society: Outline of the Theory of Structuration*. Berkeley.

Gill, D. W. J. 1991. 'Pots and Trade: Spacefillers or Objets D'Art?'. *Journal of Hellenic Studies* 111: 29–47.

Gitelman, L. and V. Jackson. 2013. 'Introduction', in *'Raw data' is an Oxymoron*: 1–14. Cambridge, MA.

Gitin, H. and A. Golani. 2001. 'The Tel Miqne-Ekron Silver Hoards: The Assyrian and Phoenician Connections', in M. Balmuth (ed.) *Hacksilber to Coinage: New Insights into the Monetary History of the Near East and Greece; A Collection of Eight Papers Presented at the 99th Annual Meeting of the Archaeological Institute of America, American Numismatic Society*: 27–48. New York.

Gitin, S. 1995. 'Tel Miqne-Ekron in the 7th cenutry B.C.E.: The Impact of Economic Innovation and Foreign Cultural Influences on a Neo-Assyrian Vassal City State', in S. Gitin (ed.) *Recent Excavations in Israel: A View to the West*: 61–71. Dubuque, Iowa.

Giudice, F. 1999. 'Il viaggio delle immagini dall Attica verse l'occidente', in F.-H. Massa-Pairault (ed.) *Le mythe grec dans l'Italic antique*: 267–327. Rome.

Godelier, M. 1999. *The Enigma of the Gift*. Cambridge.

Gosden, C. and Y. Marshall. 1999. 'The Cultural Biography of Objects'. *World Archaeology* 31: 169–78.

Grace, V. 1979. *Amphoras and the Ancient Wine Trade*. Princeton, NJ.

Grakov, B. N. 1935. 'Tara i khranenie sel'skokhoziaĭstvennykh produktov v klassicheskoĭ Gretsii VI–V vv. do n. è'. *IGAIMK* 108: 147–83.

Green, C. 2020. 'Challenges in the Analysis of Geospatial "Big Data"', in M. Gillings, P. Hacıgüzeller and G. Lock (ed.) *Archaeological Spatial Analysis. A Methodological Guide*: 430–43. London.

Greene, E. S., M. L. Lawall and M. Polzer. 2008. 'Inconspicuous Consumption: The Sixth-Century B.C.E. at Pabuç Burnu, Turkey'. *American Journal of Archaeology* 112: 685–711.

Greenwell, W. 1890. 'On a Find of Archaic Greek Coins, Principally of the Islands of the Aegean Sea'. *Numismatic Chronicle* 10.

Grewe, B.-S. and K. Hofmeester. 2016. 'Introduction: Luxury and Global History', in K. Hofmeester and B.-S. Grewe (ed.) *Luxury in Global Perspective: Objects and Practices, 1600–2000*: 1–26. New York.

Gruben, G. 2014. *Der polykratische Tempel im Heraion von Samos*. Wiesbaden.

Guarducci, M. 1967. *Epigrafia greca. Istituto poligrafico dello Stato*. Rome.

Guralnick, E. 1978. 'The Proportions of Kouroi'. *American Journal of Archaeology* 82: 461–72.

1981. 'Proportions of Korai'. *American Journal of Archaeology* 85: 269–80.

Haarer, P. 2000. *Obeloi and Iron in Archaic Greece*. Oxford.

Hadjidaki, E. 1996a. 'Excavation of a Classical Shipwreck at Alonnesos'. *Enalia Annual* IV: 37–45.

1996b. 'Underwater Excavations of a Late Fifth-Century Merchant Ship at Alonnesos, Greece: The 1991–1993 Seasons'. *Bulletin de correspondance hellénique* 120: 561–93.

Haggis, D. C. and C. M. Antonaccio. 2015. *Classical Archaeology in Context. Theory and Practice in Excavation in the Greek World*. Berlin.

Haggis, D. C., M. S. Mook, R. D. Fitzsimmons, C. M. Scarry, L. M. Snyder, M. I. Stefanakis and W. C. West III. 2007. 'Excavations at Azoria, 2003–2004. Pt. 1, the Archaic Civic Complex'. *Hesperia* 76: 243–321.

Haldon, J. 1993. *The State and the Tributary Mode of Production*. London.

Hall, J. M. 1997. *Ethnic Identity in Greek Antiquity*. Cambridge.

   2002. *Hellenicity: Between Ethnicity and Culture*. Chicago.

   2004. 'Culture, Cultures, and Acculturation', in R. Rollinger and C. Ulf (ed.) *Griechische Archaik: Interne Entwicklungen – Externe Impulse*: 35–50. Berlin.

   2007. *A History of the Archaic Greek World, ca. 1200–479 BCE*. Oxford.

   2009. 'Ethnicity and Cultural Exchange', in K.A. Raaflaub and H. Wees (ed.) *A Companion to Archaic Greece*: 604–17. Oxford.

Hall, T. D. 1987. 'Native Americans and Incorporation: Patterns and Problems'. *American Indian Culture and Research Journal* 11: 1–30.

   2006. '[Re]periphalization, [Re]incorporation, Frontiers and Non-State Societies', in B. K. Gillis and W. R. Thompson (ed.) *Globalization and Global History, Rethinking Globalizations*: 96–113. London.

   2012. 'Incorporation Into and Merger of World-Systems', in S. J. Babones and C. Chase-Dunn (ed.) *Routledge Handbook of World-Systems Analysis*: 47–55. New York.

Hall, T. D. and C. K. Chase-Dunn. 1997. *Rise and Demise: Comparing World Systems*. Colorado.

Hall, T. D., P. N. Kardulias and C. Chase-Dunn. 2011. 'World-Systems Analysis and Archaeology: Continuing the Dialogue'. *Journal of Archaeological Research* 19: 233–79.

Halstead, P. and G. Jones. 1989. 'Agrarian Ecology in the Greek Islands: Time Stress, Scale and Risk'. *Journal of Hellenic Studies* 109: 41–55.

Hanfmann, G. M. A. 1983. *Sardis from Prehistoric to Roman Times: Results of the Archaeological Exploration of Sardis 1958–1975*. Cambridge.

Hanneman, R. A. and M. Riddle. 2005. *Introduction to Social Network Methods*. Riverside.

Hansen, M. H. 2006. *The Shotgun Method. The Demography of the Ancient Greek City-State Culture*. Columbia.

Hansen, P. A. 1983. *Carmina Epigraphica Graeca. Saeculorum VIII-Va.Chr.n.* Berlin.

Harris, E. M. and D. M. Lewis. 2016. 'Introduction: Markets in Classical and Hellenistic Greece', in E. M. Harris, D. M. Lewis and M. Woolmer (ed.) *The Ancient Greek Economy: Markets, Households and City-States*: 1–37. New York, NY.

Harris, O. J. T. 2014. '(Re)assembling Communities'. *Journal of Archaeological Method and Theory* 21: 76–97.

Harrison, E. 1988. 'Sculpture in Stone', in J. Sweeney, T. Curry and Y. Tzedakis (ed.) *The Human Figure in Early Greek Art*: 50–4. Athens.

Hastorf, C. A. and M. W. Conkey (ed.). 1990. *The Uses of Style in Archaeology*. Cambridge.

Head, B. V. 1887. *Historia Numorum. A Manual of Greek Numismatics*. Oxford.
  1908. 'The Coins', in D.G. Hogarth (ed.) *Excavations at Ephesus: the Archaic Artemesia*: 74–93. London.

Healy, J. F. 1978. *Mining and Metallurgy in the Greek and Roman World*. London.

Held, W. and A. Ç. Gultekin. 2000. *Das Heiligtum der Athena in Milet, Milesische Forschungen* (Milesische Forschungen 2). Mainz am Rhein.

Hemans, F. P. 2015. 'The Archaic Temple of Poseidon: Problems of Design and Invention', in E. R. Gebhard and T. E. Gregory (ed.) *Bridge of the Untiring Sea*: 39–64. Princeton, NJ.

Herbert, S. 1977. *The Red-Figure Pottery*. Princeton, NJ.

Herda, A. 2006. 'Panionion-Melia, Mykalessos-Mykale, Pereus und Medusa: Überlegungen zur Besiedlungsgeschichte der Mykale in der frühen Eisenzeit'. *Istanbuler Mitteilungen* 56: 43–102.

Herz, N. 2010. 'The Classical Marble Quarries of Paros: Paros-1, Paros-2 and Paros-3', in D. U. Schilardi and D. Katsonopoulou (ed.) *Paria Lithos. Parian Quarries, Marble and Workshops of Sculpture. Proceedings of the First International Conference on the Archaeology of Paros and the Cyclades, Paros, 2-5 October 1997*: 27–34. Athens.

Hildebrandt, B. and C. Veit (ed.). 2009. *Der Wert der Dinge*. Munich.

Hind, J. 1995. 'Traders and Ports-of-Trade (Emporoi and emporia) in the Black Sea in Antiquity'. *Mar Nero* 2: 113–26.

Hochscheid, H. 2015. *Networks of Stone. Sculpture and Society in Archaic and Classical Athens*. Bern.

Hodder, I. 1982. *Symbols in Action: Ethnoarchaeological Studies of Material Culture*. Cambridge.
  1986. 'Digging for Symbols in Science and History: A Reply'. *Proceedings of the Prehistoric Society* 52: 352–56.
  2012. *Entangled: An Archaeology of the Relationships Between Humans and Things*. Malden, MA.

Hodson, F. R. 1969. 'Searching for Structure within Multivariate Archaeological Data'. *World Archaeology* 1: 90–105.

Hollinshead, M. B. 2015. *Shaping Ceremony: Monumental Steps in Greek Architecture*. Madison, Wisconsin.

Hollis, S. 2005. C'ontact, Incorporation, and the North American Southeast'. *Journal of World-Systems Research* 11: 95–130.

Holmberg, E. J. 1979. *Delphi and Olympia*. (ed.) Delphi and Olympia. Gothenburg.

Hoover, O. D. 2010. *Handbook of Coins of the Islands. Adriatic, Ionian, Thracian, Aegean, and Carpathian Seas (excluding Crete and Cyprus). Sixth to First Centuries BC*. London.

Horden, P. and N. Purcell. 2000. *The Corrupting Sea: A Study of Mediterranean History*. Oxford.

Houston, S. D., H. Escobedo and M. Child. 2003. 'The Moral Community: Maya Settlement Transformation at Piedras Negras, Guatemala', in M. L. Smith (ed.) *The Social Construction of Ancient Cities*: 212–53. Washington DC.

Howgego, C. 1990. 'Why Did Ancient States Strike Coins?', *Numismatic Chronicle* 150: 1–25.

  1995. *Ancient History from Coins*. London.

Huber, S., A. Jacquemin and D. Laroche. 2015. 'Sacrifices à Delphes 2014–2015'. *Bulletin de correspondance hellénique* 139–140: 775–84.

Huggett, J. 2012. 'Lost in Information? Ways of Knowing and Modes of Representation in e-Archaeology'. *World Archaeology* 44: 538–52.

Hughes, J. D. and J. V. Thirgood. 1982. 'Deforestation, Erosion, and Forest Management in Ancient Greece and Rome'. *Journal of Forest History*, 60–75.

Hurwit, J. M. 1999. *The Athenian Acropolis: History, Mythology, and Archaeology from the Neolithic to the Present*. Cambridge.

Iacono, F. 2016. 'From Networks to Society: Pottery Style and Hegemony in Bronze Age Southern Italy'. *Cambridge Archaeological Journal* 26: 121–40.

Ikeguchi, M. 2004. 'Settlement Patterns in Italy and Transport Costs in the Mediterranean'. *Kodai* 13: 239–49.

Irwin, G. 1992. *The Prehistoric Exploration and Colonisation of the Pacific*. Cambridge.

Isler, H. P. and T. E. Kalpaxis. 1978. *Das archaische Nordtor und seine Umgebung im Heraion von Samos* (Samos 3). Bonn.

James, S. A. 2018. *Hellenistic Pottery: The Fine Ware* (Corinth 7.7). Princeton, NJ.

Jantzen, U. 2004. *Die Wasserleitung des Eupalinos: die Funde* (Samos 20). Bonn.

Jeffery, L. H. 1961. *The Local Scripts of Archaic Greece: A Study of the Origin of the Greek Alphabet and its Development from the Eighth to the Fifth Centuries B.C.* Oxford.

Johnson, F. P. 1931. *Sculpture, 1896–1923* (Corinth 9.1). Princeton, NJ.

Jones, D. W. 2014. *Economic Theory and the Ancient Mediterranean*. Chichester.

Jones, S. 1997. *The Archaeology of Ethnicity: Constructing Identities in the Past and Present*. London.

Joy, J. 2002. 'Biography of a Medal: People and the Things They Value', in J. Schofield, W. G. Johnson and C. M. Beck (ed.) *Material Culture: The Archaeology of Twentieth-Century Conflict*: 132–42. London.

  2009. 'Reinvigorating the Object Biography: Reproducing the Drama of Object Lives'. *World Archaeology* 41: 540–56.

Judeich, W. 1933. 'Zur ionischen Wanderung'. *Rheinisches Museum für Philologie* 82: 307.

Kagan, J. H. 2006. 'Small Change and the Beginning of Coinage at Abdera', in P. G. Van Alfen (ed.) *Agoranomia: Studies in Money and Exchange Presented to John H. Kroll*: 49–60. New York.

Kakoaksis, T., A. Furtwängler and A. Schnapp. 1994. *Ελεύθερνα: τομέας ΙΙ: 2: Ένα ελληνιστικό σπίτι ("Σπίτι Α") στη θέση νησί*. Rethymno.

Kaplan, P. 2002. 'The Social Status of the Mercenary in Archaic Greece', in V. B. Gorman and E. W. Robinson (ed.) *Oikistes: Studies in Constitutions, Colonies, and Military Power in the Ancient World Offered in Honor of A. J. Graham*: 229–43. Leiden.

2003. 'Cross-Cultural Contacts Among Mercenary Communities in Saite and Persian Egypt'. *Mediterranean Historical Review* 18: 1–31.

Karakasi, K. 2003. *Archaic Korai*. Los Angeles.

Kardulias, P. N. and T. D. Hall. 2008. 'Archaeology and World-Systems Analysis'. *World Archaeology* 40: 572–83.

Katsanopoulou, D. (ed.). 2021. *Paros V. Paros Through the Ages. From Prehistoric Times to the 16th Century AD. Proceedings of the Fifth International Conference on the Archaeology of Paros and the Cyclades. Paroikia, Paros, 21–24 June 2019*. Athens.

Katzev, M. L. 1990. 'An Analysis of the Experimental Voyages of Kyrenia II'. *Tropis* 2: 245–56.

Keane, W. 2003. 'Semiotics and the Social Analysis of Material Things'. *Language and Communication* 23: 409–25.

Kelly, T. 1966. 'The Calaurian Amphictiony'. *American Journal of Archaeology* 29: 160–71.

Kerschner, M. 2017. 'East Greek Pottery Workshops in the Seventh Century BC: Tracing Regional Styles', in X. Charalambidou and C. Morgan (ed.) *Interpreting the Seventh Century BC. Tradition, Innovation and Meaning*: 100–13. Oxford.

Keyser, P. T. and D. D. Clark. 2001. 'Analyzing and Interpreting the Metallurgy of Early Electrum Coins', in M. S. Balmuth (ed.) *Hacksilber to Coinage: New Insights into the Monetary History of the Near East and Greece*: 105–26. New York.

Kim, H. S. 1994. *Greek Fractional Silver Coinage: A Reassessment of the Inception, Development, Prevalence, and Functions of Small Change During the Late Archaic and Early Classical Period*. PhD Thesis, University of Oxford.

2001. 'Archaic Coinage as Evidence for the Use of Money', in A. Meadows and K. Shipton (ed.) *Money and its Uses in the Ancient Greek World*: 7–22. Oxford.

2002. 'Small Change and the Moneyed Economy', in P. Cartledge, E. E. Cohen and L. Foxhall (ed.) *Money, Labour and Land. Approaches to the Economies of Ancient Greece*: 44–51. London.

Kim, H. S. and J. Kroll. 2008. 'A Hoard of Archaic Coin of Colophon and Unminted Silver'. *American Journal of Numismatics* 20: 53–103.

Kinch, K. F. 1914. *Vroulia*. Berlin.

Kintigh, K. 2006. 'The Promise and Challenge of Archaeological Data Integration'. *American Antiquity* 71: 567–78.

Kirchhoff, A. 1863. *Studien zur Geschichte des Griechischen Alphabets*. Gütersloh.

Kistler, E., B. Öhlinger, M. Mohr and M. Hoernes (ed.). 2015. *Sanctuaries and the Power of Consumption: Networking and the Formation of Elites in the Archaic Western Mediterranean World. Proceedings of the International Conference in Innsbruck, 20th–23rd March 2012*. Wiesbaden.

Kleiner, G., P. Hommel and W. Müller-Wiener. 1967. *Panionion und Melie*. Berlin.

Knapp, A. B. 2003. 'The Archaeology of Community on Bronze Age Cyprus: Politiko "Phorades" in Context'. *American Journal of Archaeology* 107: 559–80.

Knappett, C. 2011. *An Archaeology of Interaction: Network Perspectives on Material Culture and Society*. Oxford.

Knappett, C., T. Evans and R. Rivers. 2008. 'Modelling Maritime Interaction in the Aegean Bronze Age'. *Antiquity* 82: 1009–24.

Knoblauch, P. 1972. 'Die Hafenanlagen der Stadt Ägina'. *Archaiologikon Deltion* 27: 50–85.

Knodell, A. R. 2021. *Societies in Transition in Early Greece: An Archaeological History*. Oakland, CA.

Kokkorou-Alevras, G. 1995. 'Archaische Naxische Bildhauerei'. *Antike Plastik* 24: 37–138.

2010. 'The Use and Distribution of Parian Marble During the Archaic Period', in D. U. Schilardi and D. Katsonopoulou (ed.) *Paria Lithos. Parian Quarries, Marble and Workshops of Sculpture. Proceedings of the First International Conference on the Archaeology of Paros and the Cyclades, Paros, 2–5 October 1997*: 143–53. Athens.

Kokkorou-Alevras, G., E. Poupaki, A. Eustathopoulos and A. Chatzikonstantinou. 2014. *Corpus Αρχαίων Λατομείων. Λατομεία του ελλαδικού χώρου από τους προϊστορικούς έως τους μεσαιωνικούς χρόνους*. Athens.

Kolia, E. and A. Gadolou. 2007. Ναός γεωμετρικών χρόνων στην περιοχή της αρχαίας Ελίκης. *Αρχαιολογία και Τέχνες* 104: 71–73.

2011. 'Ναός γεωμετρικών χρόνων στα Νικολαΐικα Αχαΐας', in A. Mazarakis Ainian (ed.) *The 'Dark Ages' Revisited. Proceedings of an International Conference in Memory of William D. E. Coulson, Volos, 14–17 June 2007*: 147–65. Volos.

Kondoleon, N. M. 1963. *Archilochus und Paros*. Geneva.

Konstantinou, I. 1952. Ἔκθεσις ἐργασιῶν ἐν Ἐρετρίᾳ. *Praktika tis en Athinais Archaiologikis Etaireias*, 153–63.

1955. Ἀνασκαφὴ ἐν Ἐρετρίᾳ. *Praktika tis en Athinais Archaiologikis Etaireias*, 125–31.

Konuk, K. 2005. 'The Electrum Coinage of Samos is the Light of a Recent Hoard', in E. Schwertheim and E. Winter (ed.) *Neue Forschungen zu Ionien*: 44–53. Bonn.

2012. 'Asia Minor to the Ionian Revolt', in W. E. Metcalf (ed.) *The Oxford Handbook of Greek and Roman Coinage*: 43–60. Oxford.

Koporal, E. 2020. 'Breaking Free from Colonial and Intellectual Legacies in Ionian Archaeology: an Introduction to KLASP – Klazomenai Survey Project, in T. C. Wilkinson and A. Slawisch (ed.) *The Fieldwalker.org*.

Kopytoff, I. 1986. 'The Cultural Biography of Things: Commoditisation as Process', in A. Appadurai (ed.) *The Social Life of Things: Commodities in Cultural Perspective*: 64–91. Cambridge.

Kordellas, A. 1884. *Για την νεώτερη εκμετάλλευση Μαρμάρων στην Πάρο*. Athens.

Korres, C. J. and R. A. Tomlinson. 2002. 'Sphettia Hodos – Part of the Road to Kephale and Sounion', in H. R. Goette (ed.) '*Ancient Roads in Greece*: 43–59. Hamburg.

Korres, M. 1995. *From Pentelicon to the Parthenon. The Ancient Quarries and the Story of a Half-Worked Column Capital of the First Marble Parthenon*. Athens.

— 2010. 'The Underground Quarries of Paros', in D. Katsanopoulou and D. Schilardi (ed.) *Paria Lithos. Parian Quarries, Marble and Workshops of Sculpture. Proceedings of the First International Conference on the Archaeology of Paros and the Cyclades, Paros, 2–5 October 1997*: 61–82. Athens.

Kourou, N. 2003. 'Rhodes: The Phoenician Issue Revisited: Phoenicians at Vroulia?', in N. Stampolidis and V. Karageorghis (ed.) *Sea Routes: Interconnections in the Mediterranean 16th – 6th c. BC: Proceedings of the International Symposium Held at Rethymnon, Crete, September 29th – October 2nd 2002*: 249–62. Athens.

Kowalzig, B. 2005. 'Mapping out Communitas: Performances of Theoria in their Sacred and Political Context', in J. Elsner and I. Rutherford (ed.) *Pilgrimage in Graeco-Roman and Early Christian Antiquity: Seeing the Gods*: 41–72. Oxford.

— 2018. 'Cults, Cabotage and Connectivity: Experimenting with Religious and Economic Networks in the Greco-Roman Mediterranean', in J. Leidwanger and C. Knappett (ed.) *Maritime Networks in the Ancient Mediterranean World*: 93–131. Cambridge.

Kraay, C. M. 1964. 'Hoards, Small Change and the Origin of Coinage'. *Journal of Hellenic Studies* 84: 76–91.

— 1976. *Archaic and Classical Greek Coins*. London.

— 1984. 'Greek Coinage and War', in W. Heckel and R. Sullivan (ed.) *Ancient Coins of the Graeco-Roman World*: 3–18. Ontario.

Kreuzer, B. 1998. *Die attisch schwarzfigurige Keramik aus dem Heraion von Samos (Samos 22)*. Bonn.

Kristensen, T. M. 2018. 'Mobile Situations: *exedrae* as Stages of Gathering in Greek Sanctuaries'. *World Archaeology* 50: 86–99.

Kritzas, C. 2010. 'Παραρτημά: Φοινίκια γράμματα; Νεα αρχαϊκή επιγραφή απο την Ελτύνα', in G. Rethymiotakis and M. Englezou (ed.) *Το Γεωμετρικό νεκροταφείο της Ελτύνας, Παραρτημά*: 1–23. Heraklion.

Kroll, J. H. 1998. 'Silver in Solon's Laws', in R. Ashton and S. Hurter (ed.) *Studies in Greek Numismatics in Memory of Martin Jessop Price*: 225–32. London.

2008. 'The Monetrary Use of Weighed Bullion in Archaic Greece', in W. V. Harris (ed.) *The Monetary Systems of the Greeks and Romans*: 13–37. Oxford.

2012. 'The Monetary Background of Early Coinage', in W. E. Metcalf (ed.) *The Oxford Handbook of Greek and Roman Coinage*: 33–42. Oxford.

Kroll, J. H. and N. M. Waggoner. 1984. 'Dating the Earliest Coins of Athens, Corinth and Aegina'. *American Journal of Archaeology* 88: 325–40.

Kuklick, H. 1996. 'Islands in the Pacific: Darwinian Biogeography and British Anthropology'. *American Ethnologist* 23: 611–38.

Kunisch, N., T. Wiegand and N. Ehrhardt. 2016. *Die Attische Importkeramik, Milet. Ergebnisse der Ausgrabungen und Untersuchungen seit dem Jahr 1899* (Funde aus Milet 3). Berlin; Boston.

Kunze-Götte, E., J. Heiden and J. Burow. 2000. *Archaische Keramik aus Olympia* (Olympische Forschungen 28). Berlin.

Kurke, L. 1999. *Coins, Bodies, Games, and Gold: The Politics of Meaning in Archaic Greece*. Princeton, NJ.

Kyrieleis, H. 2006. *Anfänge und Frühzeit des Heiligtums von Olympia: Die Ausgrabungen am Pelopion 1987–1996*. Berlin.

Laimpi, K. 2016. Σίνδος: Το νεκροταφείο. Ανασκαφικές έρευνες 1980–1982 I: Η ανασκαφή των τάφων, τάφοι και ταφικά έθιμα, το σκελετικό υλικό II: Πήλινα, γυάλινα και φαγεντιανά αγγεία, πήλινοι λύχνοι, μεταλλικά αγγεία, πήλινα ειδώλια και πλαστικά αγγεία νομίσματα. Athens.

Langdon, M. 2015. 'Herders' Graffiti', in A. Matthaiou and N. Papazarkadas (ed.) *Αξων: Studies in Honor of Ronald S. Stroud*: 49–58. Athens.

Langridge-Noti, E. M. 2015. '"To Market, To Market": Pottery, the Individual, and Trade in Athens', in K. F. Daly and L. A. Riccardi (ed.) *Cities Called Athens. Studies Honoring John Camp II*: 165–95. Lewisburg.

Lavan, M. P. 2019. 'Epistemic Uncertainty, Subjective Probability and Ancient History'. *Journal of Interdisciplinary History*: 91–111.

Lawall, M. L. 2019. 'Transport Amphoras: Archaic and Classical, ca. 600–300 BC', in C. B. Rose and K. Lynch (ed.) *The West Sanctuary at Ilion 1: The Early Iron Age, Archaic and Classical Periods*: 496–543. Mainz.

Lawall, M. L. and Tzochev, C. 2020. 'New Research on Aegean & Pontic Transport Amphorae of the Ninth to First Century BC, 2010–2020'. *Archaeological Reports* 66. 117–44.

Lazzarini, L. 2004. 'Archaeometric Aspects of White and Coloured Marbles Used in Antiquity: The State of the Art'. *Periodico di Mineralogia* 73: 113–25.

Le Rider, G. 2001. *La naissance de la monnaie. Pratiques monétaires de l'Orient ancien*. Paris.

Leidwanger, J. 2013. 'Modeling Distance with Time in Ancient Mediterranean Seafaring: A GIS Application for the Interpretation of Maritime Connectivity'. *Journal of Archaeological Science* 40: 3302–8.

Leidwanger, J. and C. Knappett (ed.). 2018. *Maritime Networks in the Ancient Mediterranean World*. Cambridge.

Leone, B. 2012. 'A Trade Route between Euboea and the Northern Aegean'. *Mediterranean Archaeology* 25.

Lepsius, R. 2012. *Griechische Marmorstudien*. Los Angeles, CA.

Lewis, D. 2020. 'Labour Specialization in the Athenian Economy: Occupational Hazards', in E. Stewart, E. Harris and D. Lewis (ed.) *Skilled Labour and Professionalism in Ancient Greece and Rome*: 129-74. Cambridge.

Lockyear, K. 2013. 'Applying Bootstrapped Correspondence Analysis to Archaeological Data'. *Journal of Archaeological Science* 40: 4744-53.

Lohmann, H. 2005. 'Melia, das Panionion und der Kult des Poseidon Helikonios. Neue Forschungen zu Ionien', in E. Winter and E. Schwertheim (ed.) *Neue Forschungen zu Ionien: Fahri Işık zum 60*. 55-91. Bonn.

— 2007. 'Forschungen und Ausgrabungen in der Mykale 2001-2006'. *Istanbuler Mitteilungen* 57: 59-178.

Lohmann, H., G. Kalaitzoglou and G. Lüdorf (ed.). 2014. *Forschungen in der Mykale I, 2. Survey in der Mykale: Ergänzende Studien mit Beiträgen von H. Lohmann, J.- H. Hartung und G. Petzl*. Bonn.

Loy, M. 2019. 'Early-Modern Travellers in the Aegean: Routes and Networks'. *Annual of the British School at Athens* 114: 369-98.

— 2020a. 'Descent With Modification? Survey Methodologies and Scholarly Networks', in T. C. Wilkinson and A. Slawisch (ed.) *The Fieldwalker.org*.

— 2020b. 'The Islands of the Saronic Gulf: Connections and Cultural Histories'. *Archaeological Reports* 66: 161-72.

— 2021. 'The Export of Marble in the Sixth Century BC: Paros and its Networks', in D. Katsanopoulou (ed.) *Paros V. Paros Through the Ages. From Prehistoric Times to the 16th Century AD. Proceedings of the Fifth International Conference on the Archaeology of Paros and the Cyclades. Paroikia, Paros, 21-24 June 2019*: 181-96. Athens.

— Forthcoming. 'Travelling to the Temple of Poseidon at Sounion. Land Routes and Sea Routes', in E. Angliker and J. T. Jensen (ed.) *Traveling and Cult Practices in the Ancient Mediterranean*.

Loy, M. and A. Slawisch. 2021. 'Shedding Light on the Matter: Evaluating Changing Patterns of Object Dedication in Ionian Sanctuaries (7th/6th – 5th/4th centuries BC) with Lexicometrical Analysis'. *Journal of Greek Archaeology* 6: 166-99.

Lucy, S. 2005. 'Ethnic and Cultural Identities', in M. Díaz-Andreu García and S. Lucy (ed.) *The Archaeology of Identity: Approaches to Gender, Age, Status, Ethnicity and Religion*: 86-109. London.

Luraghi, N. 2010. 'The Local Scripts from Nature to Culture'. *Classical Antiquity* 29: 68-91.

Lynch, K. 2017. 'Reception, Intention, and Attic Vases', in L. Nevett (ed.) *Theory in Greek Archaeology*: 124-42. Michigan.

Ma, J. 2013. *Statues and Cities: Honorific Portraits and Civic Identity in the Hellenistic World*. Oxford.

Mac Sweeney, N. 2009. 'Beyond Ethnicity: The Overlooked Diversity of Group Identities'. *Journal of Mediterranean Archaeology* 22: 101–26.

2011. *Community Identity and Archaeology: Dynamic Communities at Aphrodisias and Beycesultan*. Ann Arbor.

2013. *Foundation Myths and Politics in Ancient Ionia*. Cambridge.

2017. 'Separating Fact from Fiction in the Ionian Migration'. *Hesperia* 86: 379–421.

MacDonald, B. R. 1986. 'The Diolkos'. *Journal of Hellenic Studies* 106: 191–5.

MacDougall, G. D. A. 1951. 'British and American Export: A Study Suggested by the Theory of Comparative Costs, Part I'. *Economic Journal* 61: 697–724.

Mackil, E. and P. Van Alfen. 2006. 'Cooperative Coinage', in P. Van Alfen (ed.) *Agoranomia: Studies in Money and Exchange Presented to John H. Kroll*. New York.

Malafouris, L. 2013. *How Things Shape the Mind. A Theory of Material Engagement*. Cambridge, MA.

Malkin, I. (ed.). 2001. *Ancient Perceptions of Greek Identity*. Cambridge, MA.

Mallwitz, A. 1972. *Olympia und seine Bauten*. Munich.

Mansvelt, J., M. Breheny and I. Hay. 2016. '"Life's Little Luxuries?" The Social and Spatial Construction of Luxury', in J. Armitage and J. Roberts (ed.) *Critical Luxury Studies: Art, Design, Media*: 88–107. Edinburgh.

Marinatos, N., R. Hägg and U. Sinn (ed.). 1993. 'Greek Sanctuaries as a Place of Refuge', in *Greek Sanctuaries: New Approaches*: 98–109. London.

Martin, T. R. 1995. 'Coins, Mints and the *Polis*', in M. H. Hansen (ed.) *Sources for the Ancient Greek City State*: 257–91. Copenhagen.

1996. 'Why Did the Greek *Polis* Originally Need Coins?' *Historia* 45: 257–83.

Martini, W. 1990. *Die archaische Plastik der Griechen*. Darmstadt.

Matthaiou, A. 2021. 'New Archaic Inscriptions. Attica, the Attic-Ionic Islands of the Cyclades, and the Doric Islands', in R. Parker and P. M. Steele (ed.) *The Early Greek Alphabets: Origin, Diffusion, Uses*: 249–66. Oxford.

Mazarakis Ainian, A. 1997. *From Rulers' Dwellings to Temples: Architecture, Religion and Society in Early Iron Age Greece*. Jonsered.

McCarter, P. K. 1975. *The Antiquity of the Greek Alphabet and the Early Phoenician Scripts*. Missoula.

McClain, T. D. and N. K. Rauh. 2011. 'The Brothels at Delos. The Evidence for Prostitution in the Maritime World', in A. Glazebrook and M. M. Henry (ed.) *Greek Prostitutes in the Ancient Mediterranean, 800 BCE–200 CE*. 147–71. Madison, WI.

McCoy, M. D. 2017. 'Geospatial Big Data and Archaeology: Prospects and Problems Too Great to Ignore'. *Journal of Archaeological Science* 84: 74–94.

McElreath, R. 2016. *Statistical Rethinking: A Bayesian Course with Examples in R and Stan*. Boca Raton, FL.

McInerney, J. 1999. *The Folds of Parnassos: Land and Ethnicity in Ancient Phokis*. Austin, TX.

McNairn, B. 1980. *The Method and Theory of V. Gordon Childe*. Edinburgh.

Medas, S. 2005. 'La navigazione di Posidonio dall' Iberia all' Italia e le rotte d' altura nel Mediterraneo occidentale in età Romana'. *Mayurqa* 30: 577–609.

Meeks, N. D. 2000. 'Scanning Electron Microscopy of the Refractory Remains and the Gold and from Sardis', in A. Ramage and P. Craddock (ed.) *King Croesus' Gold: Excavations at Sardis and the History of Gold Refining*: 99–156. London.

Meiggs, R. 1982. *Trees and Timber in the Ancient Mediterranean World*. New York.

Metcalf, D. M. and W. A. Oddy. 1980. *Metallurgy in Numismatics*. London.

Meyer, M. and N. Brüggemann. 2007. *Kore und Kouros: Weihegaben für die Götter*. Phoibos, Vienna.

Miller, D. 1985. *Artefacts as Categories: A Study of Ceramic Variability in Central India*. Cambridge.

Miller, S. G. 2004. *Ancient Greek Athletics*. New Haven, CT.

Mills, B. J. 2018. 'Navigating Mediterranean Archaeology's Maritime Networks', in J. Leidwanger and C. Knappett (ed.) *Maritime Networks in the Ancient Mediterranean World*: 238–56. Cambridge.

Mitchell, L. G. 2007. *Panhellenism and the Barbarian in Archaic and Classical Greece*. Swansea.

Mol, E. M. 2013. 'The Perception of Egypt in Networks of Being and Becoming: A Thing Theory Approach to Egyptianising Objects in Roman Domestic Contexts'. *Theoretical Roman Archaeology Journal*, 117–31.

Mommsen, H., D. Hertel and P. A. Mountjoy. 2001. 'Neutron Activation Analysis of the Pottery from Troy in the Berlin Schliemann Collection'. *Archäologischer Anzeiger* 2: 169–211.

Mommsen, H., M. Cowell, P. Fletcher and D. Hook. 2006. 'Neutron Activation Analysis of Pottery from Naukratis and Other Related Vessels', in U. Scholtzhauer and A. Villing (ed.) *Naukratis: Greek Diversity in Egypt*: 69–76. London.

Monachov, S. 1999. *Grecheskie amfory v Prichernomor'e: kompleksy keramicheskoĭ tary VII–II vv. do n.è.* Saratov.

2003. *Grecheskie amfory v Prichernomor'e: tipologiia amfor vedushchikh tsentrov-eksportëron tovarov v keramicheskoi tare*. Moscow.

Monachov, S. and E. Kuznetsova. 2017. 'Overseas Trade in the Black Sea Region from the Archaic to the Hellenistic Period', in V. Kozlovskaya (ed.) *The Northern Black Sea in Antiquity. Networks, Connectivity, and Cultural Interactions*: 55–99. Cambridge.

Moore, M. B. 1997. *Attic Red-Figured and White-Ground Pottery* (Athenian Agora 30). Princeton, NJ.

Morgan, C. 1990. *Athletes and Oracles: The Transformation of Olympia and Delphi in the Eighth Century BC*. Cambridge.

1999. 'The Archaeology of Ethnicity in the Colonial World of the Eighth to Sixth Centuries BC: Approaches and Prospects', in *Confini e frontiera nella Grecita d'occidente. Atti della 37o convegno internazionale di studi sulla Magna Grecia, Taranto 3-6 Ottobre 1997*: 85-145. Taranto.

2003. *Early Greek States Beyond the Polis*. London.

2009. 'Ethnic Expression on the Early Iron Age and Early Archaic Greek Mainland. Where Should We Be Looking?', in T. Derks and N. Roymans (ed.) *Ethnic Constructs in Antiquity*: 11-36. Amsterdam.

Morgan, C. and T. Whitelaw. 1991. 'Pots and Politics: Ceramic Evidence for the Rise of the Argive State'. *American Journal of Archaeology* 95: 79-108.

Mørkholm, O. 1982. 'Some Reflections on the Production and Use of Coinage in Ancient Greece'. *Historia* 31: 290-305.

Morris, I. 1986. 'Gift and Commodity in Archaic Greece'. *Man* 21: 1-17.

1987. *Burial and Ancient Society. The Rise of Greek City-State*. Cambridge.

2005. 'Archaeology, Standards of Living, and Greek Economy History', in J. G. Manning and I. Morris (ed.) *The Ancient Economy: Evidence and Models*: 91-126. Stanford.

Morton, J. 2001. *The Role of the Physical Environment in Ancient Greek Seafaring*. Leiden.

Mostowlansky, T. and A. Rota. 2020. 'Emic and Etic', in F. Stein, S. Lazar, M. Candea, H. Diemberger, J. Robbins, A. Sanchez and R. Stasch (ed.) *The Cambridge Encyclopedia of Anthropology*. Cambridge.

Mullen, A. 2013. *Southern Gaul and the Mediterranean*. Cambridge.

Müller, K. 1817. *Aegineticorum liber*. Berlin.

1820. *Die Dorier*. Breslau.

Murray, O. 1980. *Early Greece*. Brighton.

Murray, S. C. 2017. *The Collapse of the Mycenaean Economy: Trade, Imports, and Institutions, 1300-700 BCE*. Cambridge.

Mussche, H. 1998. *Thorikos: A Mining Town in Ancient Attika* (Fouilles de Thorikos 2). Ghent.

Mylona, D., M. Ntinou, P. Pakkanen, A. Penttinen, D. Serkeantson and T. Theodoropoulou. 2013. 'Integrating Archaeology and Science in a Greek Sanctuary. Issues of Practise and Interpretation in the Study of the Bioarchaeological Remains from the Sanctuary of Poseidon at Kalaureia', in S. Voutsaki and S. M. Valamoti (ed.) *Diet, Economy and Society in the Greek World. Towards a Better Integration of Archaeology and Science*: 187-203. Leuven.

Mylonopoulos, J. 2006. 'Von Helike nach Tainaron und von Kalaureia nach Samikon: Amphiktyonische Heiligtümer des Poseidon auf der Peloponnes', in K. Freitag, P. Funke and M. Haake (ed.) *Kult-Politik-Ethnos: Überregionale Heiligtümer im Spannungsfeld von Kult und Politik. Kolloquium, Münster, 23.-24. November 2001*: 121-55. Stuttgart.

Nagy, G. 1979. *The Best of the Achaeans. Concepts of the Hero in Archaic Greek Poetry*. London.
Naroll, R. 1956. 'A Preliminary Index of Social Development'. *American Anthropologist* 58: 687–715.
Neer, R. 2010. *The Emergence of the Classical Style in Greek Sculpture*. Chicago.
  2012. *Art and Archaeology of the Greek World: A New History, c. 2500–c.150 BCE*. London.
Nielsen, T. H. 2007. *Olympia and the Classical Hellenic City-State Culture*. Copenhagen.
Nixon, L. and S. Price. 1990. 'The Size and Resources of Greek Cities', in O. Murray and S. Price (ed.) *The Greek City*: 137–70. Oxford.
North, H. F. and R. Stilwell. 1932. *Introduction, Topography, Architecture* (Corinth 1.1). Cambridge, MA.
Ober, J. 1989. *Mass and Elite in Democratic Athens*. Princeton, NJ.
  2010. 'Wealthy Hellas'. *Transactions of the American Philological Association* 140: 241–86.
Orengo, H. A. and A. Livarda. 2016. 'The Seeds of Commerce: A Network Analysis-Based Approach to the Romano-British Transport System'. *Journal of Archaeological Science* 66: 21–35.
Osborne, R. 1985. *Demos: The Discovery of Classical Attika*. Cambridge.
  1987. *Classical Landscape with Figures: The Ancient Greek City and Countryside*. London.
  1991. 'Pride and Prejudice, Sense and Subsistence: Exchange and Society in the Greek City', in J. Rich and A. Wallace-Hadrill (ed.) *City and Country in the Ancient World*: 119–45. London.
  1994. 'Look on——Greek Style: Does the Sculpted Girl Speak to Women Too?', in I. Morris (ed.) *Classical Greece: Ancient Histories and Modern Archaeologies*: 81–96. Cambridge.
  1996a. *Greece in the Making, 1200–479 BC*. London.
  1996b. 'Pots, Trade and the Archaic Greek Economy'. *Antiquity* 70: 31–44.
  1998. 'Early Greek Colonisation? The Nature of Greek Settlement in the West', in N. F. H. van Wees (ed.) *Archaic Greece: New Approaches and New Evidence*: 251–69. London.
  2007. 'What Travelled with Greek pottery?'. *Mediterranean Historical Review* 22: 85–95.
  2021. 'The Politics of Flashing: From Wealth of Material to Discourse of Luxury in a World Full of Gods', in S. Hodkinson and C. Gallou (ed.) *Luxury and Wealth in Sparta and the Peloponnese*: 1–18. Swansea.
Osborne, R. and J. Tanner. 2007. *Art's Agency and Art History*. Oxford.
Østby, E. 2014. *Investigations in the Sanctuary of Athena Area 1990–94 and 2004* (Tegea 2). Athens.

Palagia, O. 2006. 'Classical Athens', in O. Palagia (ed.) *Greek Sculpture. Function, Materials, and Techniques in the Archaic and Classical Periods*: 119–62. Cambridge.

Papadopoulos, J. 2001. 'Review of Oscar Broneer, Mary C. (Mary Carol) Sturgeon, Timothy E. Gregory, Steven Lattimore, Isabelle K. (Isabelle Kelly) Raubitschek, Catherine Morgan, Joseph L. Rife, Birgitta Wohl, Isthmia: Excavations by the University of Chicago, Under the Auspices of the American School of Classical Studies at Athens'. *Bryn Mawr Classical Review* 2001.01.12.

2012. 'Money, Art, and the Construction of Value in the Ancient Mediterranean', in J. Papadopoulos and G. Urton (ed.) *The Construction of Value in the Ancient World*: 261–87. Los Angeles, CA.

Papadopoulos, J. and E. L. Smithson. 2017. *The Early Iron Age: The Cemeteries* (Athenian Agora 36). Princeton, NJ.

Papadopoulos, J. and G. Urton (ed.). 2012. *The Construction of Value in the Ancient World*. Los Angeles.

Papageorgiou, D. 2008. 'The Marine Environment and its Influence on Seafaring and Maritime Routes in the Prehistoric Aegean'. *European Journal of Archaeology* 11: 199–222.

Parikh, T. 2020. 'The Material of Polytheism in Archaic Greece: Understanding Greek Religion through Patterns of Dedicatory Practice and Thought, ca. 750–480 BCE'. PhD thesis, University of Cambridge.

Parker Pearson, M. 1999. *The Archaeology of Death and Burial*. Stroud.

Parker, V. 1997. *Untersuchungen zum Lelantischen Krieg und verwandten Problemen der frühgriechischen Geschichte*. Stuttgart.

Parthenos, H. Hollander, F. Morselli, F. Uiterwaal, F. Admiraal, T. Trippel and S. Di Giorgio. 2018. PARTHENOS Guidelines to FAIRify data management and make data reusable. *Zenodo*. https://doi.org/10.5281/zenodo.2668479.

Patterson, O. 1975. 'Context and Choice in Ethnic Allegiance. A Theoretical Framework and Caribbean Case Study', in N. Glazer and D. Moynihan (ed.) *Ethnicity: Theory and Experience*: 305–49. Cambridge.

Payne, H. (ed.). 1962. *Perachora, the Sanctuaries of Hera Akraia and Limenia; Excavations of the British School of Archaeology at Athens, 1930–1933 II. Pottery, Ivories, Scarabs, and Other Objects from the Votive Deposit of Hera Limenia*. Oxford.

Pedley, J. G. 1976. *Greek Sculpture of the Archaic Period. The Island Workshops*. Mainz.

Pemberton, E. G. and K. W. Slane. 1989. *The Sanctuary of Demeter and Kore: The Greek Pottery* (Corinth 18.1). Princeton, NJ.

Perlman, P. 2004. 'Writing On the Walls. The Architectural Context of Archaic Cretan Laws', in L. P. Day, M. S. Mook and J. D. Muhly (ed.) *Crete Beyond the Palaces: Proceedings of the Crete 2000 Conference*: 181–97. Philadelphia, PA.

Pesendorfer, W. 1995. 'Design Innovations and Fashion Cycles'. *American Economic Review* 85: 771–92.

Phillips, D. J. and D. Pritchard. 2003. *Sport and Festival in the Ancient Greek World*. Swansea.

Phillips, R. 2021. 'The Nature, Derivation and Use of Soft Power in the Ancient Cyclades'. PhD Thesis, Birkbeck College, University of London.

Picard, O. 1989. 'Innovations monétaires dans la Grèce du IVe siècle', *Comptes rendus des séances de l'Académie des inscriptions et belles-lettres* 133(3): 673–87.

Pierattini, A. 2019. 'Interpreting Rope channels: Lifting, Setting and the Birth of Greek Monumental Architecture'. *Annual of the British School at Athens* 114: 167–206.

Pike, K. 1954. *Language in Relation to a Unified Theory of the Structure of Human Behavior*. Glendale, CA.

Polanyi, K. 1968. 'The Semantics of Money-Uses', in G. Dalton (ed.) *Primitive, Archaic and Modern Economies: Essays of Karl Polanyi*: 175–203. Garden City.

Polignac, F. de. 1994. 'Mediation, Competition and Sovereignty: The Evolution of Rural Sanctuaries in Geometric Greece', in S. E. Alcock and R. Osborne (ed.) *Placing the Gods: Sanctuaries and Sacred Space in Ancient Greece*: 1–18. Oxford.

Pons, P. and M. Latapy. 2006. 'Computing Communities in Large Networks using Random Walks'. *Journal of Graph Algorithms and Applications* 10: 191–218.

Ponting, M. J. 2012. 'The Substance of Coinage: The Role of Scientific Analysis in Ancient Numismatics', in W. E. Metcalf (ed.) *The Oxford Handbook of Greek and Roman Coinage*: 12–30. Oxford.

Popham, M. R. 1993. 'The Sequence of Events and Conclusions', in M. R. Popham, P. G. Calligas and L. H. Sackett (ed.) *The Protogeometric Building at Toumba*: 97–101 (Lefkandi 2). London.

Popham, M. R., P. G. Calligas and L. H. Sackett. 1993. *The Protogeometric Building at Toumba* (Lefkandi 2). London.

Poulsen, F. 1973. *Delphi*. Washington DC.

Powell, M. A. 1990. 'Identification and Interpretation of Long Term Price Fluctuations in Babylonia: More on the History of Money in Mesopotamia'. *Altorientalische Forschungen* 17: 76–99.

Powlesland, D. and K. May. 2010. 'DigIT: archaeological summary report and experiments in digital recording in the field'. *Internet Archaeology* 27.

Pratt, C. E. 2021. *Oil, Wine, and the Cultural Economy of Ancient Greece: From the Bronze Age to the Archaic Era*. Cambridge and New York.

Preucel, R. W. 2006. *Archaeological Semiotics*. Malden, MA.

Price, M. J. 1968. 'Early Greek Bronze Coinage', in C. M. Kraay and G. K. Jenkins (ed.) *Essays in Greek Coinage Presented to Stanley Robinson*: 90–104. Oxford.

Price, M. J., C. N. L. Brooke, B. H. I. H. Stewart, J. G. Pollard and T. R. Volk. 1983. *Thoughts On the Beginning of Coinage*. Cambridge.

Prignitz, S. 2014. *Bauurkunden und Bauprogramm von Epidauros (400–350): Asklepiostempel, Tholos, Kultbild, Brunnenhaus*. Munich.

Psoma, S. E. 2006. 'Notes sur la terminologie monétaire en Grèce du Nord'. *Revue Numismatique* 162: 85–98.

2016. 'Choosing and Changing Monetary Standards in the Greek World during the Archaic and the Classical Periods', in E. M. Harris, D. M. Lewis and M. Woolmer (ed.) *The Ancient Greek Economy: Markets, Households and City-States*: 90–115. New York.

Rainbird, P. 2007. *The Archaeology of Islands*. Cambridge.

Ramage, A. and P. Craddock (ed.). 2000. *King Croesus' Gold: Excavations at Sardis and the History of Gold Refining*. London.

Rankov, B. 2013. 'Slipping and Launching', in D. Blackman, B. Rankov, K. Baika, H. Gerding and J. Pakkanen (ed.) *Shipsheds of the Ancient Mediterranean*: 102–23. Cambridge.

Raschke, W. J. 1988. 'Images of Victory: Some New Considerations of Athletic Monuments', in W. J. Raschke (ed.) *The Archaeology of the Olympics*: 38–54. Madison, WI.

Raubitschek, A. E. 1972. 'The Inscriptions', in H. Hoffmann (ed.) *Early Cretan Armorers*: 15–17. Mainz.

Rayet, O. 1880. 'Plaques votives en terre cuite trouvées a Corinthe'. *Gazette Archéologique* 6: 101–7.

Reger, G. 2016. 'Nodes of Sea and Sand. Ports, Human Geography and Networks of Trade', in K. Höghammar, B. Alroth and A. Lindhagen (ed.) *Ancient Ports. The Geography of Connections. Proceedings of an International Conference at the Department of Archaeology and Ancient History, Uppsala University, 23–25 September 2010*: 9–36. Uppsala.

Renfrew, C. 1986. 'Introduction: Peer Polity Interaction and Socio-Political Change', in C. Renfrew and J. F. Cherry (ed.) *Peer Polity Interaction and Socio-Political Change. New Directions in Archaeology*: 1–18. Cambridge.

Renfrew, C. and J. F. Cherry (ed.). 1986. *Peer Polity Interaction and Socio-Political Change. New Directions in Archaeology*. Cambridge.

Renfrew, C. and J. S. Peacey. 1968. 'Aegean Marble: A Petrological Study'. *Annual of the British School at Athens* 63: 45–66.

Rhodes, R. F. 1987. 'Rope Channels and Stone Quarrying in the Early Corinthia'. *American Journal of Archaeology* 91: 545–51.

Ricardo, D. 1817. *On the Principles of Political Economy and Taxation*. London.

Richter, G. M. A. 1934. 'The Proportions of the 'Apollo' in New York'. *Metropolitan Museum Studies* 5: 51–6.

1942. *Kouroi: A Study of the Development of the Greek Kouros from the Late Seventh to the Early Fifth Century B.C.* New York.

1968. *Korai: Archaic Greek Maidens. A Study of the Development of the Kore Type in Greek Sculpture*. London.

Ridgeway, B. 1990. 'Birds, "meniskoi", and Head Attributes in Archaic Greece'. *American Journal of Archaeology* 94: 583–612.

Riello, G. 2016. 'Luxury or Commodity? The Success of Indian Cotton Cloth in the First Global Age', in K. Hofmeester and B.-S. Grewe (ed.) *Luxury in Global Perspective: Objects and Practices, 1600–2000*: 138–68. New York.

Ringrose, T. J. 1992. 'Bootstrapping and Correspondence Analysis in Archaeology'. *Journal of Archaeological Science* 19: 615–29.

  2013. 'Bootstrap confidence regions for correspondence analysis'. *CRAN*. https://cran.r-project.org/web/packages/cabootcrs/cabootcrs.pdf.

Risser, M. K. 2001. *Corinthian Conventionalizing Pottery* (Corinth 7.5). Princeton, NJ.

Robins, G. 1994. *Proportion and Style in Ancient Egyptian Art*. Cambridge, MA.

Robinson, D. M. 1933. *Mosaics, Vases and Lamps of Olynthus Found in 1928 and 1931* (Excavations at Olynthos 5). Baltimore.

  1950. *Vases Found in 1934 and 1938* (Excavations at Olynthos 13). Baltimore.

Robinson, E. S. G. 1951a. 'The Coins from the Ephesian Artemision Reconsidered'. *Journal of Hellenic Studies* 71: 156–67.

Robinson, W. S. 1951b. 'A Method for Chronologically Ordering Archaeological Deposits'. *American Antiquity* 16: 293–301.

Roebuck, C. 1955a. 'The Early Ionian League'. *Classical Philology* 50: 26–40.

Roebuck, M. C. 1955b. 'Excavations at Corinth; 1954'. *Hesperia* 24: 147–57.

Rolley, C. 1994. *La sculpture grecque*. Paris.

Romeo, I. 2002. 'The Panhellenion and Ethnic Identity in Hadrianic Greece'. *Classical Philology* 97: 21–40.

Roskams, S. and M. Whyman. 2007. 'Categorising the Past: Lessons from the Archaeological Resource Assessment for Yorkshire'. *Internet Archaeology* 23.

Ruschenbusch, E. 1966. *Solonos Nomoi*. Wiesbaden.

Russell, B. 2013. *The Economics of the Roman Stone Trade*. Oxford.

  2017. 'Stone Quarrying in Greece: Ten Years of Research'. *Archaeological Reports* 63: 77–88.

Russell, B. and W. Wootton. 2015. 'Presenting and Interpreting the Process of Stone Carving: The Art of Making in Antiquity Project', in P. Pensabene and E. Gasparini (ed.) *Interdisciplinary Studies on Ancient Stone*: 851–60. Rome.

Sackett, L. H. 1992. *Knossos: From Greek City to Roman Colony: Excavations at the Unexplored Mansion II*. London.

Said, S. (ed.). 1990. *Ellenismos: quelques jalons pour une histoire de l'identité grecque*. Leiden.

Samuelson, P. 1953. 'Prices of Factors and Goods in General Equilibrium'. *Review of Economic Studies* 21: 1–20.

Santerre, H. G. 1959. *La terrasse des lions, le Létoon et le monument au granit*. (Delos 24). Paris.

Schilardi, D. 2010a. 'Observations on a Semi-Finished Marble *kouros* from Paros', in D. Katsanopoulou and D. Schilardi (ed.) *Paria Lithos. Parian Quarries, Marble and Workshops of Sculpture. Proceedings of the First International Conference on the Archaeology of Paros and the Cyclades, Paros, 2–5 October 1997*: 163–71. Athens.

2010b. 'Observations on the Quarries of Spilies, Lakkoi and Thapsana on Paros', in D. Katsanopoulou and D. Schilardi (ed.) *Paria Lithos. Parian Quarries, Marble and Workshops of Sculpture. Proceedings of the First International Conference on the Archaeology of Paros and the Cyclades, Paros, 2–5 October 1997*: 35–59. Athens.

Schneider, J. 1977. 'Was There a Pre-Capitalist World-System?'. *Peasant Studies* 6: 20–29.

Schneider, L. 1975. *Zur sozialen Bedeutung der archaischen Korenstatuen*. Hamburg.

Schortman, E. M. and P. A. Urban. 2011. *Networks of Power Political Relations in the Late Postclassic Naco Valley*. Boulder, CO.

Schrader, H., L. E. Langlotz and W. H. Schuchhardt. 1939. *Die archaischen Marmorbildwerke der Akropolis*. Frankfurt am Main.

Schumacher, R. W. M. 1993. 'Three Related Sanctuaries of Poseidon: Geraistos, Kalaureia, and Tainaron', in N. Marinatos and R. Hägg (ed.) *Greek Sanctuaries: New Approaches*: 51–69. London.

Scott, M. 2010. *Delphi and Olympia: The Spatial Politics of Panhellenism in the Archaic and Classical Periods*. Cambridge.

Seaford, R. 1994. *Reciprocity and Ritual: Homer and Tragedy in the Developing City-State*. Oxford.

2004. *Money and the Early Greek Mind: Homer, Philosophy, Tragedy*. Cambridge.

Seifried, R. M. and C. A. M. Gardner. 2019. 'Reconstructing Historical Journeys with Least-Cost Analysis: Colonel William Leake in the Mani Peninsula', Greece. *Journal of Archaeological Science: Reports* 24: 391–411.

Service, E. R. 1962. *Primitive Social Organization: An Evolutionary Perspective*. New York.

Sezgin, Y. 2012. *Arkaik dönem Ionia üretimi ticari amphoralar*. Istanbul.

Shanks, M. and C. Tilley. 1987. *Social Theory and Archaeology*. Cambridge.

Shaw, J. W. and M. C. Shaw. 2000. *The Greek Sanctuary* (Kommos 4). Princeton.

Shennan, S. 1989. *Archaeological Approaches to Cultural Identity*. London.

1999. 'Cost, Benefit and Value in the Organization of Early European Copper Production'. *Antiquity* 73: 352–63.

Shepherd, G. 2000. 'Greeks Bearing Gifts: Religious Relationships between Sicily and Greece in the Archaic Period', in C. J. Smith and J. Serrati (ed.) *Sicily from Aeneas to Augustus: New Approaches in Archaeology and History*: 55–70. Edinburgh.

Sherratt, S. E. 2000. 'Introduction to the Ashmolean Cycladic Collection', in *Catalogue of Cycladic Antiquities in the Ashmolean Museum*: 1–9. Oxford.

Sherratt, S. E. and A. Sherratt. 1993. 'The Growth of the Mediterranean Economy in the Early First Millennium BC'. *World Archaeology* 24: 361–78.

Shipley, G. 1987. *A History of Samos, 800–188 BC*. Oxford.

 1996. 'Calauria', in S. Hornblower and A. Spawforth (ed.) *Oxford Classical Dictionary*: 273. Oxford.

 2002. *Pseudo-Skylax's Periplous. The Circumnavigation of the Inhabited World. Text, Translation and Commentary*. Exeter.

Simmons, A. H. 2014. *Stone Age Sailors. Palaeolithic Seafaring in the Mediterranean*. Walnut Creek, CA.

Sinn, H.-W. 1980. 'A Rehabilitation of the Principle of Insufficient Reason'. *Quarterly Journal of Economics* 94: 493–506.

Slawisch, A. 2013. 'Absatzmarkt Ionien: zur Rolle attischer Keramik als Indikator für die Unterbrechung oder Verschiebung von Handelsnetzwerken in der Ägäis im 5. Jh. v. Chr', in A. Slawisch (ed.) *Handels- und Finanzgebaren in der Ägäis im 5. Jh. v. Chr. – Trade and Finance in the 5th C. BC Aegean World*: 185–206. Istanbul.

Slawisch, A. and T. C. Wilkinson. 2016. 'Introduction: Paracolonial Legacies in the Aegean'. Workshop, 16 December 2016. University of Cambridge.

Smith, R. R. R. 2007. 'Pindar, Athletes and the Early Greek Statue Habit', in C. Morgan and S. Hornblower (ed.) *Pindar's Poetry, Patrons and Festival: From Archaic Greece to the Roman Empire*: 83–139. Oxford.

Smithson, E. L. 1968. 'The Tomb of a Rich Athenian Lady, ca. 850 B.C'. *Hesperia* 37: 77–116.

Snodgrass, A. M. 1980. *Archaic Greece: The Age of Experiment*. London.

 1983. 'Heavy Freight in Archaic Greece', in P. Garnsey, K. Hopkins and C. R. Whittaker (ed.) *Trade in the Ancient Economy*: 16–26. London.

 1986. 'Interaction by Design: The Greek City State', in C. Renfrew and J. F. Cherry (ed.) *Peer Polity Interaction and Socio-Political Change. New Directions in Archaeology*: 47–58. Cambridge.

 1993. 'The Rise of the *Polis*: The Archaeological Evidence', in M. H. Hansen (ed.) *The Ancient Greek City State*: 30–40. Oxford.

 2007. 'What is Classical Archaeology?', in S. E. Alcock and R. Osborne (ed.) *Classical Archaeology*: 13–29. Oxford.

Sourvinou-Inwood, C. 1979. *Theseus as a Son and Stepson*. London.

Sparkes, B. and L. Talcott. 1970. *Black and Plain Pottery of the 6th, 5th, and 4th Centuries B.C.* (Athenian Agora 12.2). Princeton, NJ.

Spawforth, A. and S. Walker. 1985. 'The World of the Panhellenion I: Athens and Eleusis'. *Journal of Roman Studies* 75: 78–104.

Spier, J. 1990. 'Emblems in Archaic Greece'. *Bulletin of the Institute of Classical Studies of the University of London* 37: 107–29.

 1998. 'Notes on Early Electrum Coinage and a Die-Linked Issue from Lydia', in R. Ashton and S. Hurter (ed.) *Studies in Greek Numismatics in Memory of Martin Jessop Price*: 321–26. London.

Spivey, N. 1997. *Greek Art*. London.
  2013. *Greek Sculpture*. Cambridge.
Spriggs, M. 2008. 'Are Islands Islands? Some Thoughts on the History of Chalk and Cheese', in G. Clark, F. Leach and S. O'Connor (ed.) *Islands of Inquiry: Colonisation, Seafaring and the Archaeology of Maritime Landscapes*: 211–26. Canberra.
Steidl, C. 2020. 'Re-thinking Communities: Collective Identity and Social Experience in Iron-Age Western Anatolia'. *Journal of Social Archaeology* 20: 26–48.
Steiner, D. 2001. *Images in Mind. Statues in Archaic and Classical Greek Literature and Thought*. Princeton, NJ.
Steuben, H. 1980. *Kopf eines Kuros*. Darmstadt.
Stewart, A. F. 1986. 'When is a Kouros not an Apollo? The Tenea "Apollo" Revisited', in M. A. Del Chiario (ed.) *Corinthiaca. Studies in Honor of Darrell A. Amyx*: 54–80. Columbia.
  1990. *Greek Sculpture: An Exploration*. New Haven, CT.
Stillwell, A. N. 1948. *The Potters' Quarter* (Corinth 15.3). Princeton, NJ.
Stillwell, R. 1932. 'The Temple of Apollo', in H. N. Fowler and R. Stillwell (ed.) *Introduction, Topography, Architecture*: 115–34 (Corinth 1.1). Cambridge, MA.
Stillwell, R., R. L. Scranton and S. E. Freeman. 1941. *Architecture* (Corinth 1.2). Princeton, NJ.
Stos-Gale, Z. A. and C. Macdonald. 1991. The Sources of Metals and Trade in the Bronze Age, in N. H. Gale (ed.) *Bronze Age Trade in the Mediterranean*: 249–88. Göteborg.
Strauss Clay, J., I. Malkin and Y. Z. Tzifopoulos (ed.). 2017. *Panhellenes at Methone: Graphê in Late Geometric and ProtoArchaic Methone*. Berlin.
Strupler, N. and T. C. Wilkinson. 2017. 'Reproducibility in the Field: Transparency, Version Control and Collaboration on the Project Panormos Survey'. *Open Archaeology* 3: 279–304.
Stuart Jones, H. 1895. *Select Passages from Ancient Writers: Illustrative of the History of Greek Sculpture*. London.
Sturgeon, M. C. 2006. 'Archaic Athens and the Cyclades', in O. Palagia (ed.) *Greek Sculpture. Function, Materials, and Techniques in the Archaic and Classical Periods*: 32–76. Cambridge.
Su, G., A. Kuchinsky, J. H. Morris, D. J. States and F. Meng. 2010. 'GLay: Community Structure Analysis of Biological Networks'. *Bioinformatics* 26: 3135–37.
Tandy, D. W. 1997. *Warriors into Traders: The Power of the Market in Early Greece*. Berkeley.
Tausend, K. 1992. *Amphiktyonie und Symmachie*. Stuttgart.
Taylor, C. and K. Vlassopoulos. 2015. 'Introduction: An Agenda for the Study of Greek History', in C. Taylor and K. Vlassopoulos (ed.) *Communities and Networks in the Ancient Greek World*: 1–31. Oxford.

Taylor, T. and J. Whitley. 1985. 'Decoration, Description and Design'. *Archaeological Review from Cambridge* 4.

Themelis, P. 1981. "Ερέτρια". *To Ergon tes archaiologiskes etaireias* 1980: 26–28.

Theodoropoulou-Polychroniadis, Z. 2015. *Sounion Revisited: The Sanctuaries of Poseidon and Athena at Sounion in Attica*. Oxford.

Thompson, C. M. 2003. 'Sealed Silver in Iron Age Cisjordan and the "Invention" of Coinage'. *Oxford Journal of Archaeology* 22: 67–107.

Thompson, M., O. Mørkholm and C. M. Kraay. 1973. *An Inventory of Greek Coin Hoards*. New York.

Tölle-Kastenbein, R., R. Felsch and U. Jantzen. 1974. *Das Kastro Tigani: die Bauten und Funde griechischer, römischer und byzantinischer Zeit, Samos, Kommission bei Rudolf Habelt*. Bonn.

Trigg, A. B. 2001. 'Veblen, Bourdieu, and Conspicuous Consumption'. *Journal of Economic Issues* 35: 99–115.

Trigger, B. 1980. *Gordon Childe: Revolutions in Archaeology*. London.

Trinkl, E. 2013. 'Classical Black-Glazed Imports to Western Asia Minor', in A. Tsingardia and D. Viviers (ed.) *Pottery Markets in the Ancient Greek World*: 189–202. Brussels.

Tsatsopouolou-Kaloudi, P. 2015. *Το Ιερό του Απόλλωνα*. Komotini.

Tselekas, P. 1996. 'The Coinage of Acanthus'. PhD thesis, University of Oxford.

Tsiafaki, D. 2020. 'The Northern Aegean', in F. de Angelis (ed.) *A Companion to Greeks Across the Ancient World*: 409–30. Chichester.

Tsipopoulou, M. 2005. *Η Ανατολική Κρητή στην Πρωϊμή Εποχή του Σιδήρου*. Heraklion.

Tuchelt, K. 1970. *Die archaischen Skulpturen von Didyma: Beiträge zur frühgriechischen Plastik in Kleinasien*. Berlin.

Vaesen, K., M. Collard, R. Cosgrove and W. Roebroeks. 2016. 'Population Size Does Not Explain Past Changes in Cultural Complexity', in *Proceedings of the National Academy of Sciences of the United States of America*, 113: 2241–47.

Van de Moortel, A. and M. K. Langdon. 2017. 'Archaic Ship Graffiti from Southern Attica, Greece: Typology and Preliminary Contextual Analysis'. *International Journal of Nautical Archaeology* 46: 382–405.

Van Oyen, A. 2016. 'Historicising Material Agency: From Relations to Relational Constellations'. *Journal of Archaeological Method and Theory* 23: 354–78.

Veal, R. 2017. 'The Politics and Economics of Ancient Forests: Timber and Fuel as Levers of Greco-Roman Control', in P. Derron (ed.) *Economie et inégalité: ressources, échanges et pouvoir dans l'antiquité classique*: 317–67. Geneva.

Veblen, T. 1899. *The Theory of the Leisure Class: An Economic Study of Institutions*. London.

Verdelis, N. M. 1958. 'Die Ausgrabung des Diolkos während der Jahre 1957–1959'. *Mitteilungen des Deutschen Archäologischen Instituts, Athenische Abteilung* 73: 140–5.

1959. 'Ἀρχαιολογικὴ ἐφημερὶς-χρονικά: Σύντομος ἔκθεσις περὶ τῶν διεξαχθεισῶν κατὰ τὸ 1957 ἀνασκαφῶν ὑπὸ τῆς ἐφορείας ἀρχαιοτήτων Δ' Περιφερείας (Ἀργολιδοκορινθίας); Συνέχισις τῆς ἀνασκαφῆς τοῦ Διόλκου'. *Archaiologike Ephemeris* 1956: 1-3.

1966a. 'Ἀνασκαφή τοῦ Διόλκου. *Praktika tes en Athenais Archaiologikes Etaireias'* 1960: 136-43.

1966b. 'Ἀνασκαφή τοῦ Διόλκου. *Praktika tes en Athenais Archaiologikes Etaireias'* 1962: 48-50.

Villing, A. and H. Mommsen. 2017. 'Rhodes and Kos: East Dorian Pottery Production of the Archaic Period'. *Annual of the British School at Athens* 112: 99-154.

Vlachidis, A., C. Binding, K. May and D. Tudhope. 2010. 'Excavating Grey Literature: A Case Study on the Rich Indexing of Archaeological Documents via Natural Language Processing Techniques and Knowledge Based Resources'. *ASLIB Proceedings Journal* 62: 466-75.

Volioti, K. and A. Smith. 2019. 'Lesser Pots Go Places: The Attic "Brand" in Macedonia and Thrace', in E. Manakidou and A. Avramidou (ed.) *Classical Pottery of the Northern Aegean and its Periphery (480-323/300 BC)*: 175-87. Thessaloniki.

von Reden, S. 1995. *Exchange in Ancient Greece*. London.

1997. 'Law and Exchange: Coinage in the Greek Polis'. *Journal of Hellenic Studies* 117: 154-76.

2003. *Exchange in Ancient Greece*. London.

2010. *Money in Classical Antiquity*. Cambridge.

von Wilamowitz-Möllendorff, U. 1896. 'Die Amphiktionie von Kalaurea'. *Nachrichten von der Gesellschaft der Wissenschaften zu Göttingen*. 158-70.

1906. *Über die ionische Wanderung*. Berlin.

Voutiras, E. 2006. 'The Introduction of the Alphabet', in A.-F. Christidis (ed.) *A History of Ancient Greek. From the Beginnings to Late Antiquity*: 266-76. Cambridge.

Voutsaki, S. 1997. 'The Creation of Value and Prestige in the Aegean Late Bronze Age'. *Journal of European Archaeology* 5: 34-52.

Wachter, R. 2001. *Non-Attic Greek Vase Inscriptions*. Oxford.

2010. 'Inscriptions', in E. J. Bakker (ed.) *A Companion to the Ancient Greek Language*: 47-61. Chichester.

Waines, D. 2003. '"Luxury foods" in Medieval Islamic Societies'. *World Archaeology* 34: 571-80.

Walbank, F. 1969. *The Awful Revolution: The Decline of the Roman Empire in the West*. Liverpool.

Waldstein, C. 1902. *The Argive Heraeum*. Boston.

Wallace, R. W. 1987. 'The Origin of Electrum Coinage'. *American Journal of Archaeology* 91: 385-97.

Wallerstein, I. 1974. *The Modern World-System*. New York.

Wallinga, H. T. 1993. *Ships and Seapower before the Great Persian War. The Ancestry of the Ancient Trireme.* Leiden.

Wallrodt, J. 2016. 'Why Paperless: Technology and Changes in Archaeological Practice, 1996–2016', in E. W. Averett, J. M. Gordon and D. B. Counts (ed.) *Mobilizing the Past for a Digital Future*: 33–50. Grand Forks, MI.

Walter, H. 1968. *Frühe samische Gefässe: Chronologie und Landschaftsstile ostgriechischer Gefässe* (Samos 5). Bonn.

Walter, H. and K. Vierneisel. 1959. 'Heraion von Samos: die Funde der Kampagnen 1958 und 1959'. *Mitteilungen des Deutschen Archäologischen Instituts* 74: 10–34.

Walter-Karydi, E. 1973. *Samische Gefässe des 6. Jahrhunderts v. Chr. Landschaftsstile ostgriechischer Gefässe* (Samos 6.1). Bonn.

Walter-Karydi, E., W. Felten and R. Smetana-Scherrer. 1982. *Ostgriechische Keramik* (Alt-Ägina 2.1). Mainz/Rhein.

Wartenberg, U. and W. Fischer-Bossert. 2016. 'Early Electrum Coinage – Innovation or Continuity?', in *Paper Presented to Ex Ionia Scientia, 'Knowledge' in Archaic Greece*. Athens.

Wasserman, S. and K. Faust. 1994. *Social Network Analysis: Methods and Applications.* Cambridge.

Watson, J. 2011. 'Rethinking the Sanctuary of Aphaia', in D. Fearn (ed.) *Aegina: Contexts for Choral Lyric Poetry Myth, History, and Identity in the Fifth Century.* Oxford.

Wees, H. van. 1992. *Status Warriors: War, Violence and Society in Homer and History.* Amsterdam.

2002. 'Greed, Generosity and Gift-Exchange in Early Greece and the Western Pacific', in W. Jongman and M. Kleijwegt (ed.) *After the Past: Essays in Ancient History in Honour of H. W. Pleket*: 341–78. Leiden.

Wees, H. van and N. Fisher. 2015. 'Introduction. The Trouble with "Aristocracy"', in N. Fisher and H. Wees (ed.) *'Aristocracy' in Antiquity. Redefining Greek and Roman Elites*: 1–57. Swansea.

Weidauer, L. 1975. *Probleme der frühen Elektronprägung.* Fribourg.

Weinberg, S. S. 1943. *The Geometric and Orientalizing Pottery* (Corinth 7.1). Cambridge, MA.

Weissl, M. 2002. 'Grundzüge der Bau- und Schichtenfolge im Artemision von Ephesos'. *Jahreshefte des Österreichischen archäologischen Instituts in Wien* 71: 313–46.

2005. 'Zur Datierung des 'Foundation-Deposit' aus dem Artemision von Ephesos', in B. Brandt, V. Gassner and S. Ladstätter (ed.) *Synergia. Festschrift für Friedrich Krinzinger*: 363–70. Vienna.

Wells, B., A. Penttinen and F. Billot. 2003. 'Investigations in the Sanctuary of Poseidon on Kalaureia, 1997–2001'. *Opuscula Atheniensia* 28: 29–87.

Welter, F. G. 1938. *Aigina.* Berlin.

Werner, W. 1997. 'The Largest Ship Trackway in Ancient Times: The Diolkos of the Isthmus of Corinth, Greece, and Early Attempts to Build a Canal'. *The International Journal of Nautical Archaeology* 26: 98–119.

Whewell, W. 1831. 'Mathematical Exposition of Some of the Leading Doctrines in Mr Ricardo's Principles of Political Economy and Taxation'. *Transactions of the Cambridge Philosophical Society* 4: 155–98.

Whitewright, J. 2011. 'The Potential Performance of Ancient Mediterranean Sailing Rigs'. *International Journal of Nautical Archaeology* 40: 2–17.

Whitley, J. 1991. *Style and Society in Dark Age Greece. The Changing Face of a Pre-Literate Society 1100–700 BC*. Cambridge.

1997. 'Cretan Laws and Cretan Literacy'. *American Journal of Archaeology* 101: 635–61.

2002. 'Objects with Attitude: Biographical Facts and Fallacies in the Study of Late Bronze Age and Early Iron Age Warrior Graves'. *Cambridge Archaeological Journal* 12: 217–32.

2015a. 'Agnostic Aristocrats? The Curious Case of Archaic Crete', in N. Fisher and H. van Wees (ed.) *'Aristocracy' in Antiquity. Redefining Greek and Roman Elites.* Swansea.

2015b. 'Archaeology and State Theory: Subjects and Objects of Power. By Bruce Routledge, 2014. [Book Review]'. *The Archaeological Journal* 172: 499–500.

2017. 'The Material Entanglements of Writing Things Down', in L. C. Nevett (ed.) *Theoretical Approaches to the Archaeology of Ancient Greece*: 71–103. Ann Arbor, MI.

2018a. 'Introduction: Anthony Snodgrass and the Transformation of Classical Archaeology', in J. Whitley and L. Nevett (ed.) *An Age of Experiment: Classical Archaeology Transformed, 1976–2014*: 1–17. Cambridge.

2018b. 'Style and Personhood: The Case of the Amasis Painter'. *Cambridge Classics Journal* 64: 178–203.

2021a. 'Regions within Regions. Patterns of Epigraphic Habits within Archaic Crete', in R. Parker and P. M. Steele (ed.) *The Early Greek Alphabets: Origin, Diffusion, Uses.* 222–48. Oxford.

2021b. 'Why με? Personhood and Agency in the Earliest Greek Inscriptions (800–550 BC)', in P. J. Boyes, P. M. Steele and N. Elvira Astoreca (ed.) *The Social and Cultural Contexts of Historic Writing Practices.* Oxford.

In Press. 'The Case for Ethnological Antiquarianism: The Intellectual Life and Research Culture of the British School at Athens, 1900–1920', in B. Forsen, D. Shankland and G. Salmeri (ed.) *Approaches to Classical Lands; Proceedings of the Bristol Workshop.* Helsinki.

Whittaker, R. J. 1998. *Island Biogeography: Ecology, Evolution and Conservation.* Oxford.

Whittle, A. 2005. 'Lived Experience in the Neolithic of the Great Hungarian Plain', in D. W. Bailey, A. Whittle and V. Cummings (ed.) *Un-Settling the Neolithic*: 64–70. Oxford.

Wide, S. and L. Kjellberg. 1895. 'Ausgrabungen auf Kalaureia'. *Mitteilungen des Deutschen Archäologischen Instituts* 20: 267–362.

Wiegand, T. and H. Schrader. 1904. *Priene*. Berlin.

Wijngaarden, G. J. van. 1999. 'An Archaeological Approach to the Concept of Value: Mycenaean Pottery at Ugarit (Syria)'. *Archaeological Dialogues* 1: 2–23.

Wilkinson, T. C. 2014. *Tying the Threads of Eurasia: Trans-Regional Routes and Material Flows in Transcaucasia, Eastern Anatolia and Western Central Asia, c.3000–1500 BC*. Leiden.

Wilkinson, T. C. and A. Slawisch. (in press). 'Route Inertia and Route Dynamism: Myths, Materials and Landscapes', in L. Vandeput (ed.) *Pathways of Communication: Roads and Routes in Ancient Anatolia*. London.

Will, E. 1977. 'The Ancient Commercial Amphora'. *Archaeology* 30: 264–78.

Williams, D. J. R. 1991. 'The "pot-hoard" Pot from the Archaic Artemision at Ephesus'. *Bulletin of the Institute of Classical Studies* 38: 98–104.

Wilson, A. 2009. 'Approaches to Quantifying Roman Trade', in A. Bowman and A. Wilson (ed.) *Quantifying the Roman Economy: Methods and Problems*: 213–49. Oxford.

Woodard, R. D. 1997. *Greek Writing from Knossos to Homer: A Linguistic Interpretation of the Origin of the Greek Alphabet and the Continuity of Ancient Greek Literacy*. Oxford.

2010. 'Phoinikēia grammata: An Alphabet for the Greek language', in E. J. Bakker (ed.) *A Companion to the Ancient Greek Language*: 25–46. Chichester.

Woodford, S. 1986. *An Introduction to Greek Art*. London.

Yoffee, N. 2005. *Myths of the Archaic State: Evolution of the Earliest Cities, States and Civilizations*. Cambridge.

Zaphiropoulou, P. N. 2003. *La céramique mélienne* (Delos 41). Athens.

2017. 'Parian Ceramics of the Seventh Century BC in Cycladic Cemeteries and Sanctuaries', in C. Morgan and X. Charalambidou (ed.) *Interpreting the Seventh Century BC. Tradition and Innovation*: 150–9. Oxford.

Index

Abdera, 173
Abydos, 186
additional letters. *See* letter groups, additional letters
Aegina, 142, 153, 166, 167, 184, 185, 186, 212, 248, 252, 255, 270–2
 Aphaia, 118, 123, 124, 129, 255, 270, 271
 Kolonna, 118, 123, 124, 270, 271, 272
agency, 10, 71, 191, 202, 242, 284
Aigilia, 234
Akanthos, 172
Akraifia, 123, 129, 153, 164, 171, 185
Al Mina, 74
Alkman, 88
Alonnesos shipwreck, 67
Altertumswissenschaft, 3
American School of Classical Studies at Athens, 1
Amorgos, 69
amphiktyony, 252, 254, *See also* Kalaureian *amphiktyony*
amphora, 67, 74, 88, 89, 91, 124, 129, 177, 178, 179, 180, 181, 183, 248, 259, 266, 267, 268, 281
 Social Network Analysis (SNA), 177–84
Anafi, 236
Anagyrous, 210
anchorage. *See* harbour
Andros, 78, 153, 167, 171
Apollonia, 153, 171, 172
Apollonis Hyperteleatae, 217
Archaeology in Greece Online, 1, 5, 34, 147
Archaic Greece
 definition, geographic, 20–8
 definition, temporal, 18–19
Archilochus, 263
Argilos, 173
Argolid, 255
Arkades, 235
Arkhilochos, 88
aryballos, 95, 124, 129, 131, 132, 145, 146, 270
aspirates. *See* letter groups, aspirates

Athens, 77, 81, 83, 98, 112, 123, 124, 129, 135, 142, 167, 171, 172, 180, 209, 212, 248, 252, 255
Acropolis, 39, 46
 Hekatompedon, 83
 Old Parthenon, 83
 size of stone sculptures, 57–8
Agora, 32
Areopagus, 32
Kerameikos, 32
Penteli, 43, 46, 61
Attica, 136, 173, 176, 187, 234, 235, 241, 259
Axos, 235

Big Data, 5–10, 11, 16
 cleaning and mapping, 7–9, 20, 42, 90–1, 92–4, 194–5
 publication, 3–4, 90–1, 133, 194–5
 quality of data, 5–7
'Big Dig' archaeology, 1–4, 253
Black Sea, 27, 266
Boeotia, 46, 176
bootstrap, 118, 133
Brainerd-Robinson, 206, 208
Bresson, Alain, 134, 135, 144, 282
British School at Athens, 1, 31, 95, 147, 150
Bronze Age, 253, 271, 281
bullion, 163

cabooters, 117
cabotage, 136, 272, 273
Central Greece, 42, 77, 112, 117, 153, 153, 171, 173, 175, 176, 185, 209, 211, 213, 225, 264, 265
ceramics
 Attic, 94, 98, 103, 112, 117, 118, 123, 124, 136, 141, 142, 269, 270, 272
 consumption at funerary sites, 117, 123–4, 129–31
 consumption at sanctuary sites, 117, 118–31, 132, 248, 281
 consumption at urban sites, 117, 118–31, 248

Corinthian, 94, 103, 104, 112, 118, 123, 124, 131, 132, 136, 269, 270
Cycladic, 177
dating, 92
distribution by ware, 98–117
Ionian, 94, 108, 112, 117, 118, 123, 124, 136, 142, 270, 272
Local, 94, 112, 113, 117, 123, 124
places of production, 94
specialisation, 133, 260, 281
chaîne opératoire, 90, 146
Chalkis, 172
Chersonesos, 173
Chios, 81, 118, 124, 129, 132, 153, 170, 171, 186, 255, 257, 259, 266
Classical period, 69, 82, 83, 89, 135, 255, 258, 261, 288
coins
 as economic tools, 163
 as tokens, 160, 163
 billon, 151, 166
 bronze, 151, 166, 186
 dating, 150
 electrum, 150, 153, 163, 166, 186
 first coinage, 148, 153–64, 248
 gold, 151
 lead, 151, 166
 production process, 150–1
 silver, 151, 152, 165, 166, 173, 185
 spread of coinage, 153–60, 184
 value, 152
 weighing, 153, 163
commodity, 89–90, 142, 146, 183, 247, 255, 259, 266, 269, 270, 276
commodity and luxury, definition of. *See* luxury and commodity, definition of
community
 behavioural, 250, 251, 255, 277, 281
 decision-making, 164, 276
 distinctiveness within, 33, 37
 general framework, 14–18
 identity. *See* identity, collective
 island, 262, 264, 275, 286
 usefulness for network analysis, 16–18, 250, 284
comparative advantage, 134, 135
connectivity, 11, 15, 146, 265, 266
conspicuous consumption, 37, 88, 142
Corinth, 1–3, 66, 83, 112, 118, 123, 124, 129, 131, 132, 150, 153, 164, 167, 173, 175, 180, 184, 209, 211, 212, 231, 232, 241, 242, 248, 270
 Acrocorinth, 241

Corinthia, 136, 141, 160
Corinthian Gulf, 71, 72, 77, 136, 141, 270
corridor of movement, 74, 78, 136, 141, 142, 247, 255
craftspeople, 10, 70, 80, 89, 142, 242
Crete, 20, 34, 68, 91, 98, 112, 117, 136, 141, 153, 173, 209, 211, 212, 213, 214, 215, 217, 225, 234, 235, 236, 264, 265
Cyclades, 20, 71, 72, 74, 77, 91, 141, 142, 148, 153, 171, 176, 180, 184, 186, 187, 209, 212, 215, 225, 236, 249, 265, 272
Cyprus, 27, 32, 263

Delos, 1, 36, 42, 43, 77, 91, 98, 103, 112, 118, 124, 129, 131, 136, 141, 172, 178, 186, 209, 231, 236, 249, 255, 263, 264, 273
 size of stone sculptures, 57–8
Delphi, 1, 82, 83, 164, 231, 232, 233, 264, 273
 Siphnian Treasury, 82
Deutsches Archäologisches Institute, 1
Didyma, 234
Diodorus Siculus, 62
diolkos, 72
Dodecanese, 20, 74, 77, 91, 141
Dorian Hexapolis, 262

Early Iron Age, 18, 19, 31, 34, 83, 191, 195, 253, 273, 281, 288
École Française d'Athènes, 1
Economic networks, 80–5, 247–51, 280–3
 bulk transport, 83, 251, 277, 280
 distribution, 175–84
 embeddedness. *See* embedded economy
 facilitation, 160, 163, 175, 276, 280
 infrastructure, 70, 134, 143, 247, 271
 knowledge, 70, 134, 142, 143, 184–5, 187, 248, 277
 piggy-backing, 143, 183, 247, 248, 267, 277
 prestige goods, 251
 production, 184–7
 scale of production, 80–3
 targeting, 134
 transport overseas, 135–41, 247–8, 259, 269, 276, 281, *See also* marble, transport overseas
edge effect, 19
Egypt, 36, 62, 142
Eion, 153, 167
Eleusis, 32
Eleutherna, 235
elite. *See* peer
Eltynia, 235

embedded economy, 70, 80, 85, 133, 135, 143, 144, 233, 270, 274, 278, 282, 283
emic, 13, 260
Ephesos, 15, 148, 153, 167, 171, 186, 187, 234, 248, 256
  Artemision, 186
epichoric alphabet, 200, 249, 255, 264, 275
Epidauros, 82, 252, 255
  Temple of Asklepios, 82
Eretria, 34, 172
Erythrai, 234, 257
etic, 12, 206, 251
Euboea, 74, 77, 78, 141, 153, 173, 272–3

Finley, Moses, 144, 283
Fournoi, 74
funerary. *See* ceramics, consumption at funerary sites

games, pan-hellenic, 232
Gell, Alfred, 191
Gephi, 72, 166, 208
Gortyn, 235, 241, 243, 244
  Gortyn lawcode, 244

Hacksilber, 162, 175
Haliartos, 172, 185
Halikarnassos, 66, 262
harbour, 68, 70, 72, 74, 78, 232, 249, 270, 271, 276
Helike, 34
Hellenistic period, 82, 135, 252, 257, 261, 270
Hellespont, 266
Hermione, 252
Herodotus, 74, 256, 257, 258, 262, 266, 268
Hesiod, 66, 68, 88, 271
hoard, 148, 162, 163, 186, 187
Homer, 17, 271, 272
hydria, 124, 129

iconography, 192
identity
  and writing, 192–3, 224–44, 275
  collective, 189–90, 193, 233–7, 249, 258, 262, 263, 268, 275, *See also* Political networks
  local, 232, 244, 257, 263
  regional, 233
  study of, 189–92
Ikaria, 68, 74
Ikarion, 234
Inscriptiones Graecae, 194, 195
insularity, 265

Ionia, 20, 36, 74, 91, 103, 112, 117, 123, 129, 136, 141, 142, 148, 153, 162, 171, 173, 176, 178, 186, 187, 209, 212, 213, 214, 215, 225, 233, 234, 236, 241, 249, 266, 267, 268, 275
  Ionian League, 256–61
  Ionian Revolt, 258, 268
  North Ionia, 179, 209, 266
  South Ionia, 180, 211, 268
Ios, 69
iota. *See* letter groups, iota
island network. *See* community, island
Isocrates, 89
isthmus, 72, 255
Italy, 135, 141

Jeffery, Anne, 195, 202, 207, 222, 234, 236
  The Local Scripts of Archaic Greece, 195, 202

Kalapodi, 123, 129
Kalaureia, 129, 180, 252, 255
  Kalaureian *amphiktyony*, 252–6, 259, 260
Karystos, 153, 164, 171, 172
Keos, 186
Kimolos, 69
Kirchhoff, Adolf, 200–2, 207, 222, 225, 226, 228, 234, 236
  Studien zur Geschichte des griechischen Alphabets, 202
Klazomenai, 74, 112, 153, 164, 234, 256, 259, 266
Kleonai, 160
Knidos, 153, 164, 167, 171, 232, 262
Knossos, 91, 124, 129, 235
Kolophon, 148, 162, 234, 256
Kommos, 91, 103, 112, 118, 123
korai. *See* stone sculptures
Korkyra, 173, 212
Kos, 94, 153, 167, 186, 262
kouroi. *See* stone sculptures
krater, 124, 129, 131, 132, 259
kylix, 124, 129, 131
Kyrenia shipwreck, 69, 80
Kythera, 147
Kythnos, 68, 164

Larisa, 210, 231
Lebedos, 256
Lefkandi, 31–2
Lesbos, 74, 153, 166, 171, 173
Lete, 173
letter groups
  additional letters, 205, 209, 234, 235, 244

aspirates, 205, 209, 210, 234
iota, 205, 235, 244
long vowels, 205, 210, 234, 235, 236, 241, 244, 259
sibilants, 205, 235, 244, 259
Levant, 153
Libya, 27
limestone, 34
literacy, 193, 243
long vowels. *See* letter groups, long vowels
lumping and splitting, 8, 249, 250
luxury, 32, 37, 68, 89–90, 142, 146, 183, 266, 270
luxury and commodity, definitions of, 89–90
Lydia, 88, 153, 186, 248, 267

Macedonia, 173
Magna Graecia, 27, 58, 141
marble
  preference, 69
  preference of consumers, 81
  quarrying, 59–61, 80
  source, 43, 58, 69–70, 81, 264
  transport overland, 61, 80
  transport overseas, 40, 66–70, 80
market economy, 69, 134, 135, 143, 144, 248, 263, 267, 276, 277
Maroneia, 173
Massalia, 27
Melie, 234, 257
  Meliac War, 258
Melos, 69, 171, 186, 259
Mentor Shipwreck, 147
Mesopotamia, 153
Miletos, 74, 112, 118, 123, 124, 142, 153, 166, 167, 180, 186, 210, 234, 248, 256, 259, 263, 266
Miletos Archive, 91
multivariate statistics, 117
Mykale, 234, 257
Mykalessos, 153, 164, 171, 172, 185
Mykonos, 68
Myous, 234, 256, 257
Mytilene, 153, 164, 171, 173

Naukratis, 27
Nauplion, 252
Naxos, 43, 55, 61, 74, 81, 142, 171, 176, 209, 231, 236, 263
Neapolis, 173
nearest neighbour. *See* Proximal Point Analysis (PPA)
Network analysis
  computational, 12

distance and similarity, 207
general use in archaeology, 11–14
non-overlapping networks, 251, 267, 268, 282, 283
overlapping networks, 183, 263, 264, 278, 281
reverse network analysis, 274, 284
Social Network Analysis (SNA), 10, 11, 13, 166
Nikandre kore, 194, 249, 264
North Aegean, 20, 74, 91, 98, 103, 112, 131, 136, 141, 153, 167, 171, 172, 173, 175, 176, 210, 211, 213, 214, 259, 269–70, 272, 273
North Africa, 27

oinochoe, 124, 129, 131
Olympia, 1, 77, 103, 123, 129, 141, 210, 231, 232
Olynthos, 123, 129, 141
Orchomenos, 153, 164, 171, 172, 185, 252, 255
Oropos, 234

Pabuç Burnu shipwreck, 66
Paiania, 234
Panionian sanctuary. *See* Ionia, Panionian
Paros, 43, 55, 61, 66, 74, 81, 142, 171, 176, 178, 186, 231, 232, 236, 249, 263
  Marathi quarries, 61
Pausanias, 61
peer, 17, 143, 247, 263, 264, 268, 269, 273
  Peer Polity Interaction (PPI), 286
Peisistratus, 264
Peloponnese, 71, 103, 112, 117, 153, 184, 213, 214, 215, 225, 226, 231, 255, 264, 265
pentekonter, 66, 67
Perachora, 34, 123, 129, 131, 142, 231
Periplus. *See* Ps.-Scylax
Phleious, 160
Phokaia, 153, 164, 167, 170, 186, 248, 256
Phokis, 153, 171, 232
Phragou shipwreck, 67
pinax, 241, 243
Pindar, 262
Pliny, 58
polis, 14, 215, 250, 286
  rise of the *polis*, 286
Political networks, 247–51, 283–7
  affiliation, 242, 245–6, 248–9, 278, 282, 283
  alliance, 254, 257, 263
  back-projection, 261, 283
  competition, 248, 262, 263, 268, 269, 273, 277, 283, 284
  cultural knowledge, 251

Political networks (Cont.)
  knowledge, 233, 242
  militaristic, 251, 254, 256, 257, 258
Polykrates, 164, 264
Poros, 252, 255
Poteidaia, 172
Praisos, 235
Prasiai, 252, 255
Priene, 234, 256
Principal Component Analysis (PCA), 117
  ceramic shape, 124–9
  ceramic ware, 118–24
  general discussion, 117–18
Proximal Point Analysis (PPA), 71, 255
  Model Building, 72–3, 136
Ps.-Scylax, 68, 77
Ps.-Xenophon, 89
Ptoion, 40, 69
  size of stone sculptures, 46–57
pyxis, 124, 129, 131, 132, 270

regions, 39, 236, 242, 249, 250, 265, 282, 285
religious networks, 254, 256
Rheneia, 124, 264
Rhodes, 74, 91, 94, 98, 103, 124, 131, 141, 160, 180, 212, 215, 232, 259, 262, 263, 275
  Ialysos, 160, 164, 173, 212, 232, 262, 263, 275
  Kamiros, 164, 210, 262, 263, 275
  Lindos, 118, 123, 129, 131, 160, 255, 262, 263, 275
  Vroulia, 118
rich Athenian lady, 32–3
Richter, Gisela, 39, 40, 42, 141
risk, 69, 135
Roman period, 83, 257
roundship, 66
route fragments. *See* corridors of movement

Samos, 35, 66, 68, 74, 83, 98, 103, 112, 123, 124, 129, 132, 142, 153, 164, 167, 171, 173, 176, 180, 184, 209, 234, 257, 259, 268
Samothrace, 123, 129
sanctuary. *See also* ceramics, consumption at sanctuary sites
  pan-hellenic, 231, 249, 263, 273, 275, 276, 284
  Panionion, 257
Sappho, 88
Saronic Gulf, 20, 71, 72, 74, 77, 91, 98, 103, 112, 117, 136, 141, 209, 211, 212, 213, 215, 225, 226, 236, 247, 249, 254, 255, 256, 272
semi-luxuries, 88, 142

Seriphos, 171, 259
Setaia, 217, 235
seventh century, 143, 152, 194, 236, 249, 253, 257, 267, 285
  650–600 BC, 40–78, 98, 103, 112, 123, 124–9, 136, 148, 179, 183, 210–13, 224–6, 230, 231, 248, 266
  700–650 BC, 98, 103, 112, 118, 124, 136, 178, 209–10, 224–6, 229, 231, 236, 272, 280
ships
  capacity, 66–8
  routes, 68–9, 272, 282
  sailing conditions, 71, 254, 271
  sailing time, 69
sibilants. *See* letter groups, sibilants
Sicily, 27
Sikyon, 241
Sindos, 123, 129
Siphnos, 171, 184, 186
sixth century, 40–78, 152, 176, 186, 194, 236, 248, 249, 258, 267, 270
  550–500 BC, 46, 57, 98, 103, 112, 123–4, 129, 141, 153, 171–5, 176, 180, 183, 184, 185, 220, 224–6, 230, 234, 237, 250, 258, 263, 264, 266, 267, 268, 280, 281
  600–550 BC, 43, 57, 98, 103, 112, 123–4, 129, 141, 148, 153, 167–71, 180, 183, 185, 213–15, 224–6, 230, 241, 243, 248, 264, 286
skyphos, 95
Smyrna, 103, 112, 123, 129, 153, 167, 171, 209
Snodgrass, Anthony, 134
  heavy freight, 39–40, 65–6, 84, 86, 134
  Snodgrass School, 3
Social Network Analysis (SNA). *See* Network analysis, Social Network Analysis (SNA)
Sounion, 38, 81, 98, 118, 124, 129, 131
Sparta, 34, 232
Stadiasmus Maris Magni, 69, 77
Stagiros, 172
state, 14
stele, 238, 240
stone sculptures, 34, 142, 146, 259, 264
  artists, 81, 186
  production and consumption, 39, 59–66, 80–2
  sculptors, 80
  size, 43–58
Strabo, 77, 252, 256
style, 19–20, 162, 190, 191, 193, 262, 268
Swedish Institute at Athens, 252
symbols, 192

Syros, 68, 210

Tanagra, 123, 164
Tegea, 112, 129
temple construction, 82–3
Tenedos, 171
Teos, 171, 186, 256, 259
Thasos, 46, 58, 61, 69, 82, 103, 112, 124, 129, 136, 141, 269
Thebes, 172, 185, 209, 231
Thera, 171, 186, 212, 217, 236
Thorikos, 16, 98, 124, 234
Thrace, 173
Thucydides, 66, 89, 262, 264
Tinos, 78
Tiryns, 34
Torone, 118, 123, 129, 136, 141
Toumba. *See* Lefkandi
tyrant, 164

uncertainty, 207, *See also* bootstrap
urban. *See* ceramics, consumption at urban sites

value, 147
    cultural, 147
    economic, 146, 163
    wealth, 146
Vitruvius, 257

Wallerstein, Immanuel, 251
weight standard, 151, 163, 248, 260, 267, 275

Abderan, 175
Aeginitan, 165, 166, 167, 169, 170, 171, 173, 175, 176, 184, 185, 186, 187, 255
Attic, 165
Attic-Euboean, 166, 167, 171, 172, 173, 175, 176, 184, 187, 259, 264, 269
Chian, 165
Corinthian, 165, 167, 171
Euboean, 165
Ialysian, 165, 173
Lesbian, 165
Milesian, 165, 166, 167, 170, 171, 173, 175, 176, 187, 259, 262, 267
Persic, 165, 166, 173
Phokaian, 165, 167, 168, 170, 171, 173, 175, 176, 184, 187, 269
Samian, 165, 173, 184, 259
Social Network Analysis (SNA), 167–75, *See also amphora*, Social Network Analysis (SNA)
Thasian, 175
Thracian, 175
Western Greece, 42, 71, 72, 213, 214, 215, 225
writing
    alphabetic, 193
    dedicatory, 193, 194, 232, 240
    graffiti, 193, 240
    legal, 193, 240, 243, 244
    pinakes dipinti, 241

Zone, 98, 123, 124, 141